A MUSE FOR THE MASSES

A MUSE FOR THE MASSES

**Ritual and Music in an Age of Democratic Revolution
1770-1870**

Conrad L. Donakowski

The University of Chicago Press
Chicago and London

The University of Chicago Press,
Chicago 60637
The University of Chicago Press,
Ltd., London

Conrad L. Donakowski is
professor in the department of
humanities, Michigan State University.

Library of Congress Cataloging in Publication Data

Donakowski, Conrad L   1936–
    A muse for the masses.

    Bibliography: p.
    Includes index.
    1. Romanticism. 2. Music—History and criticism—
18th century. 3. Music—History and criticism—19th
century. 4. Enlightenment. 5. Popular culture.
6. Religion—History. I. Title.
ML196.D63   780'.903'4   77–6228
ISBN 0–226–15621–4

To my parents

Friends, the soil is poor;
We have to sow generously
To earn even a slender Harvest.

Novalis
Blütenstaub

Nor let this necessity of producing
immediate pleasure be considered as a degradation of the poet's
art. It is far otherwise. . . . It is a
homage paid to the native and
naked dignity of man, to the grand
elementary principle of pleasure,
by which he knows and feels, and
lives, and moves.

Wordsworth, Preface to
Lyrical Ballads (1802)

CONTENTS

ILLUSTRATIONS

PREFACE

The role of literature and art in the romantic revolution has been carefully examined by many intellectual and cultural historians. However, the cultural revolution that accompanied the political and industrial revolutions of the late eighteenth century also worked itself out in the mass media of those largely preliterate times. For the average citizen, public meetings, songs, festivals, and religious liturgies provided a theater for a new way of life. The role of music in these events seemed to require a new study to investigate how the idea and practice of music in the romantic era were integral to the awakening of a more complete and democratic view of human nature and society.

That study has evolved into a history of romanticism, focusing on the impulse that created religious and quasi-religious music from the time of the French Revolution until the later nineteenth century. This impulse played an important part in revolutionary and romantic music even in cultural situations where God and religion were rejected. The musical impulse could be translated into such related activities as revolutionary rhetoric, programs for progressive education, or designs for inspiring the communal energies of socialism. Thus did evangelistic techniques that had served Christianity and Judaism become propaganda for the new secular religion and its successors, ecclesiastical, civic, or commercial.

The changing forms of musical expression were rooted in the complex religious geography of Europe. Pietism was central to the German musical tradition; Catholicism to the music of Austria,

France, and Italy. The complicated relations between popular and establishment religions were equally important. The purpose of this work has been a fusion of several methods of historical investigation that study the relations among the arts, psychology, religion, and modern history.

For advice and criticism at once demanding and inspiring, I thank above all Professors Jacques Barzun and Denis Stevens of Columbia and Professor Arthur M. Wilson of Dartmouth, who read and annotated the original version of this book. My colleagues Judith Dundas and Dennis Burkh should be mentioned here for their helpful discussions and comments; so should Giovanni Colonella Burkh, an Italian who exemplifies the spirit of music. And my parents were always patient in their support of these seemingly arcane researches. For tireless help at every stage of the work and for everything that made the rest worthwhile, I thank my wife Judith.

INTRODUCTION

A Problem in Communication

The old way was dying while giving birth to the new. Two centuries ago, as in our own time, habits and ideas formerly kept separate and orderly were mixed and confused to the point where old certainties seemed erased without new ones being inscribed in their place. The supposition that society should be ruled by a superior class disintegrated. Meanwhile, the assumption that human nature should always be governed by intellect faltered, while new ideas of human nature seemed to stand the old ones on their heads. As a revolution in private thinking and public expression, this cultural revolution, romanticism, was as important as the contemporary political and industrial revolutions.

Many scholars of the modern era have studied the confrontation among political and economic movements between 1770 and 1870. Others have traced the subtle dialogue between reason and feelings. Still others explore popular culture or the communication of values through media other than print. Yet even those cultural historians who have convincingly examined other art forms within the framework of social and political development have usually neglected music, the most elusive of the arts. In particular, the connection between music and the rituals which were the most widespread mass media during the formative decades of modern civilization is relatively unexplored. The evolution of music and ritual in our own civilization awaits the same comprehensive open-mindedness that a sensitive anthropologist might bring to the diverse customs of an exotic tribe.

According to structuralist theories like those of Claude Lévi-Strauss, ritual can be thought of as an organically integral expression of myth and cult, which are archetypal modes of communication and education. If, as Lévi-Strauss thinks, myth and cult are eminently translatable, they have probably persisted into modern guise and are still forming us.

I

The most dramatic translation of western myth and cult in recent times took place between the late eighteenth and middle nineteenth centuries. In general, during the late eighteenth century western civilization began to reorient itself from the "higher" to the "lower" classes and faculties of man. Socially, this meant a change in reverence from the precepts of the classes to the instincts of the masses; philosophically, a reorientation from knowledge to experience; psychologically, a change in emphasis from reasoned assessment of an objective world toward spontaneous expression of the subjective; and sexually, a change from an Apollonian, masculine ideal toward the supposedly feminine, often resulting in an androgynous picture of the healthy personality. Cultural geography was changed from admiration of classicism, directed by Parisian philosophes, toward Gothicism,[1] meaning idealization of Germanic or other supposedly less sophisticated or more exotic cultures thought to have precisely those qualities formerly thought inferior. Historical ideals about the origins of civilization also changed. Rather than praise societies founded upon conscious social contract, both the right and the left began to idealize "organic," "primitive," or even medieval society as somehow more "natural" than modern civilization.

In sum, even as technology and science seemed about to bear the world away, the western humanities began to see man and the cosmos not as a concatenation of static laws and forces, but as an organism in dynamic evolution, full of discontinuous variety, spontaneity, and incongruity. In every season different; yet always itself and, therefore, always somehow the same.

Two hundred years ago the sciences of the mind and society which seek to understand human perception, attraction, and communication were still part of the humanities. Aesthetics, the science of sensitivity, had been recently founded and named after the Greek word for perception.[2] Meanwhile, the investigators of perception, attraction, education, and communication began to change their theories. As if to take account of the nascent mass culture, or as if to keep the triumphant mathematical-scientific mentality within bounds, ideas of what is good or beautiful and how we know it began a new cycle. Designs for reasoned contemplation and orderly calculation yielded to arguments for spontaneous outpouring of feelings.[3]

For most previous philosophies, geometry and mathematics had seemed the best way to explain a universe of changeless ideals, such as that found in Plato's *Republic* or Newton's *Principia*. Horace's classic phrase *ut pictura poesis*—which means not so much the literal "Make poetry like painting" but "make life like geometry"—had been taken almost as a command (see chapter 1). If the new generation could ever have agreed on a motto, it would have been *ut musica poesis*—not so much "make poetry like music" as "make life like music."

Originally among the ancient Greeks, the term music meant more than the production of pleasant sounds. *Mousiké*—music—embracing the whole imaginative life of humanity, was both an avenue to rational understanding of the underlying structure of the universe and a divine inspiration which the muses shared with humanity. Music in this sense was a manifestation of something magic and holy, ordinarily beyond human grasp. Since then, most things magic or holy have been explained away and the word music confined to its narrow meaning. Yet *Mousiké* flourished. To the romantics, music continued to mean more than pleasant sounds. It meant the presence of those magic things which were once religion; which are the Sublime.

Certain prophetic thinkers such as Diderot, Schiller, and Rousseau forecast that kinaesthetic artistic perception and expression, rather than mathematical calculation, would become the ideals of much modern humanistic culture, education, and social philosophy. Meanwhile, the old myths and rituals which had communicated western civilization were being pruned and, in some places, apparently killed. They were, however, ready to sprout again in new directions. Lagging one generation behind the leading thinkers, the mass media of public meetings, celebrations, and religious liturgies arrived in the neoclassical world just as the philosophers began to dismantle it. While the clearing away prior to renewal was underway amid the political revolutions of 1776 and 1789, the Industrial Revolution, Napoleonic world wars, and embryonic social reform, a new generation matured trying to find itself and its roots in a cultural landscape prepared for new life.

II

The new social and economic conditions dictated that culture could no longer remain the sport of an isolated elite. Therefore, among the most important public records of the Enlightenment and romantic cultural revolutions were the attempts to debate and teach the new ways of thinking to mass audiences.

This occurred in four ways: through civic cults, such as those of the French Revolution, which taught citizens to aspire to an earthly rather than a Heavenly City; through reformed ecclesiastical cults, whose goals were altered from the satisfaction of divine demands to the fulfillment of human needs; through utopian communities, which announced that their style of life was a model for future societies that would liberate humanity from old repressions while recovering old satisfactions; and through public aesthetic education, which sought to reconcile an aristocracy of talent with popular mass participation in politics, art, religion, and life generally. These attempts to blend elitism, populism, and all the other forces present in a nascent mass society began the modern debate over quantity versus quality in all aspects of a democratic public life.

The first chapter of this book is intellectual history dealing mainly with the philosophical and artistic background of the transition from the Enlightenment to Romanticism. The remainder of the work is cultural history which deals equally with ideas and their public manifestations.

The history of public civic, ecclesiastical, utopian, and artistic expressions of mass feeling shows that each had three phases:

The second through fourth chapters of part one, "Words," describe the first phase. This occurred in most lands during the late-eighteenth century when rationalists and nationalists were criticizing the old feudal and religious bases of communal celebrations. Enlightened despots and reformers worked to change old liturgies in order to popularize the Enlightenment. Secular and ecclesiastical authorities proposed the design and communication of a new culture which would teach rationalism, nationalism, or revolutionary fervor. When these reforms confronted the old communal festivals centered upon God or feudal status, the result was a mingling and cross-fertilization. The new cults, which were meant to teach the value of a free individual guided by his own educated reason within a nation-state dedicated to earthly fulfillment, were syncretized with the old, which were meant to teach obedience to Divine order and citizenship in a Heavenly City. Since the new rites absorbed much of the tools and personnel of the old, they readily adopted much of their content while trying to reach the same audience. In turn, the success of the new, secular styles oriented toward mass feeling—sometimes first tested as revolutionary or war propaganda—influenced deliberate attempts to reform the old supernatural religion.

Part two, "Music," concerns the romantic attempt to enlarge eighteenth-century beliefs concerning human educability and emancipation. Even when politically reactionary, the romantics were usually psychologically progressive. In response to the nascent mass society, they attempted to liberate, dignify, or maintain those kinds of people and ideas which had been excluded from the liberal drive for freedom. If the new social order was eventually to include the common people in liberty, fraternity, and equality, a new philosophy would have to enfranchise "common" impulses, the feelings, and the irrational in a comprehensive picture of human nature.

One sign of this new outlook was its revised opinion of the imaginative side of life, especially the musical impulse. The musician, denigrated as almost subrational by some Enlightenment writers, became the archetypal man of talent and subconscious wisdom. Music was thought to be the last holy thing. Church musicians, servants of the Old Regime, appear in romantic novels as socially therapeutic heroes. Music, formerly thought to be the least among the arts, became the favorite metaphor of social and psychological restoration and experimentation. From Poland to California, from Sicily to Scandinavia, the romantic goal was reintegration of the western psyche and culture under leadership of artistic insight.

In particular, praise for the musical above all other faculties was virtually the only idea that the Romantics could agree on. Because they were, on the whole, as ready to find truth under the dome of Saint Peter's, the vault of the starry sky, or the poles of a tepee in the Great American Desert, they were as full of contradiction as of variety. In order to show how so many seemingly contrary ideologies and practices continued and mirrored one another, I consider myth and ritual as a structural anthropologist might consider them. They are the eminently translatable language of a cultural system so embracing that it must be called religion. Further, the cults will be considered not only as they were intended, but also as they were perceived (see Appendix 1).

Historians working solely from documentary sources have difficulties caused by not knowing the nuance or meaning of a ritual to its participants. These difficulties have not been solved by dividing culture into oral and printed. In order to escape such restricting definitions of documents, I attend not only to the plans of theorists and reports of literati, but also to the unwritten and often unspoken craftlike traditions of performers and participants.[4] During their careers most used the same techniques and ideas to serve many regimes.

Many studies are heavily biased toward the more dramatic types of movements that alarm civil and religious authorities or clash openly with them. Modern scholars are, after all, reared in a tradition whose major myths and rituals were last overhauled during the Age of Democratic Revolutions. No wonder that many studies assume—as is so often the case in western systems of thought since the beginning of the Christian era—that whatever is, is wrong; that "change" is good. Such studies assume that the authorities are maintaining the system and the rebels are trying to change it.

Perhaps the rebels are conservative or perhaps both the authorities and the rebels are speaking the same language and differing only in details. By relying upon the attitudes of the more ordinary citizens or upon those who remain settled in their traditional beliefs, as much as upon flamboyant or well-spoken rebels, I seek to avoid dealing only with the spectacular mass movements of the time. Concentration upon such exceptions can mislead one into thinking that one deals with fundamental change rather than with an evolutionary permutation of a continuing mentality.

Part three, "Formulas," emphasizes the ossification of Romantic attitudes during the third quarter of the nineteenth century. By 1870 there was a reaction against the dream of reconciliation between the "higher" and the "lower" classes or faculties of humanity. The liberal revolutions hardened into *Realpolitik* and the industrial revolution became self-congratulating materialism. Civic celebrations hardened into xenophobic nationalism; the refurbishing of ecclesiastical rites retreated into repetition of set formulas; the utopians joined the bourgeoisie or were absorbed into "scientific" socialism; and popular aesthetic education became the cult of art.

Nevertheless, the romantic ideal that artistic leadership exercised through communal celebration would further humanistic education, freedom of expression, and social harmony has continued among us in the kinaesthetic, musical metaphors of the free-association psychologies and existential philosophies. In these, one orders experience not mathematically but rhapsodically; one declares not *ut pictura poesis*, but *ut musica poesis*: Make life not geometry but music.

WORDS

The Artist as Propagandist, Music as Decoration

1

I have among men of parts and business . . . seldom heard any one commended or esteemed for having an excellency in music.

John Locke
Some Thoughts Concerning Education

Sculpture and painting are very justly called liberal arts; a lively and strong imagination, together with a just observation being absolutely necessary to excel in either, which, in my opinion, is by no means the case with music, though called a liberal art. . . . The former are connected with history and poetry; the latter, with nothing that I know of, but bad company.

Lord Chesterfield,
Letters, Sentences, and Maxims

CHILDREN OF THE ENLIGHTENMENT

Music According to Eighteenth-Century Social Psychology

1

The revolution in consciousness which accompanied the industrial and political revolutions of the late eighteenth century began among a European elite who set out to reform the world. Instead, they transformed themselves. The most striking thing about this elite was their critical spirit. Whereas the leaders of other civilizations educated themselves and their society to revere ancestral precepts, the western elite taught irreverence. Granted that these philosophes admired classical antiquity and were not alienated revolutionaries; they were seeking to distinguish themselves within the establishment.[1] Yet they hoped to teach subsequent generations how to leave behind ancestral superstitions and progress to a higher and better civilization. The philosophes were hopeful that through the application of reason and diligence to human problems, the youngest generation could avoid the errors of its parents. In fact the youngest often believed they *were* "the ancients," morally wiser than preceding generations because of a generation's longer experience. Such faith did the Enlightenment have in the power of the critical intelligence liberated from tradition and revelation that any subsequent reform in almost any field must thank them for daring to know and daring to do.

However, as in most such Oedipal tales, liberators slew old monsters only to be overcome in turn by their own creations. Although the philosophes overturned the old hierarchical system sanctioned by tradition and revelation, they substituted a new system of the psyche and society.[2] For Christian tradition they substituted secular learning; for divine revelation, the independent investigations of reason; for authority, criticism; in a word, in place of the supernatural, the natural. As applied to the human mind and its creations, their theory was often beautifully simple. The human mind was usually deemed a rational and orderly part of rational and orderly universe run according to the laws of Newtonian physics and Lockean psychology. Human creation should proceed similarly. It should be rational, orderly, well-organized, and harmonious with the mathematical precepts which Newton had shown underlay the cosmos.

The glory and destruction of the Enlightenment was that it showed following generations how to apply critical standards to reason itself. Having established the habit of questioning old certainties and replacing them with new ideas, the liberals of the Enlightenment had to live with the consequences of their lessons. Having painted the adult smile of Voltaire over the docile medieval gape of their offspring, our cultural parents made rebellion normal.

Some historians argue that the more it changes, the more it's the same. For example, some say the French, American, and other political revolutions merely completed the monarchical work of unifying a nation. So too in mental revolutions of individual and communal consciousness? Yes and no. Yes, in many ways the continuing rebellion of individual and communal sensibility against artificial restrictions completed the Enlightenment's rebellion against unreasonable restrictions upon human freedom. But no. The drive for freedom did not envision canonization of the subconscious, the irrational, and the Gothic which soon joined the normal culture of a purportedly sober and bourgeois civilization.[3] The original liberals believed in reason over passion. Their Enlightenment ended when reason distributed the tools to criticize itself.

Although this cultural revolution worked itself out publicly in the mass media of those times, it was forecast within the minds and work of several eighteenth-century thinkers. Among these were Denis Diderot and Friedrich Schiller. Both saw that Rousseau was right. Reason is what makes us human, but we are driven by our feelings. The ensuing debates over the relationship between reason and feelings have continued to the present day. In modern mass culture there is no question that one must move the heart before the head. Therefore, the training of the whole person, including the feelings—aesthetic education Schiller called it—is fundamental to education.

I

As ancient Athens was the school of Hellas, Paris was the school of reasonable men in the eighteenth century. Voltaire points out in *Candide* that there were French doctors everywhere from Constantinople to Philadelphia diagnosing and prescribing for the moral ills of mankind. (Americans will recall that to communicate enlightened values to a democratic populace, Thomas Jefferson prescribed neoclassical buildings whose style Parisian aestheticians had pronounced the proper architectural medium for teaching rational ethics in a republic.)

The cultural revolution was becoming a public issue in Paris in 1753 during a quarrel over the social function of music. When some popular singers of Italian opera began to excite the classes dedicated to rational discussion of society and man's place therein, it was said that new and dangerous political values were flowing from excessively sensual music. Sophisticated Parisians took sides, not so much in a quarrel over musical style, as a war over life style. In order to understand why this Bouffons' Quarrel may have been the first shot of a psychological revolution, we must understand the philosophes' psychological and social language.

Speaking logically, music was for them the ultimate immorality. Most thinking people in the eighteenth century would have agreed that art, which is to say the best that man can do, is like a mirror,[4] reflecting the true order of nature. Art should, therefore, imitate an objective reality outside the artist and communicate this reality to an observer. Painting, then quite realistic, seemed the most immediate and truest mirror of nature. Painting was also a static (as opposed to a performing) art and was therefore fittingly admired by those who fostered belief in the static Newtonian world machine or the purposeful precision of a deistic God. Since any transcendence was usually explained in mathematical terms, painting seemed an ennobled application of geometry. The philosophes, who loved to call themselves geometers of man and society, advised politicians and artists alike *ut pictura poesis*. One might freely translate their construction of that line from Horace not as "Make poetry like painting," but "Make life like geometry."

Music could not do that, for, if one starts from such premises and begins to sort out the idols of the mind, one will have to put

William Hogarth's *Masked Ball and Opera* (1723) describes the neoclassical suspicion of music. Literary works are sold as waste paper, and the door to the academy is ignored. Meanwhile, crowds are diverted by "irrational" entertainments. The opera goers are so infatuated by their spectacle that they imitate the characters seen on the stage.

music in last place among the arts. Of direct imitation of external
nature, such as found then in painting, music has almost none, save
for trumpet calls, thunder on drums, birdlike fluting, and other questionable programmatic bits. Of expression of the internal state of
the artist, music clearly has more. Music can interpret a situation
or imitate one's emotional reaction to a situation.[5] Optimists that
they were, the philosophers hoped that musicians would someday
learn how better to exploit the directly imitative possibilities of
their art. Until they did, however, music would have to keep the
last place. In the meantime, music could realize its imitative potential only when allied with words, whose conscious message it should
enhance, but never overwhelm.[6]

The philosophes believed that French culture had already produced a well-ordered blend of the arts to reflect and instruct a well-
ordered society in a well-ordered cosmos. Such were the tragedies
of Corneille and Racine, which conformed to Aristotle's canons of
tragedy in which the literary affect, the plot, was dominant, and the
music, if any, was subordinate. In French tragedy the philosophes
noted a proper metaphor of the psyche and society. Music was employed because its passion served morality.[7]

A few discords marred this harmonious cosmos. One was the
philosophes' logical admission that the Gregorian chant of the despised Middle Ages exemplified their theory of music as heightened
declamation. In plainchant the music seemed to clothe the words
without smothering them in counterpoint or purely musical excur-
sions—or so it seemed to the philosophes. They excused this success
of the Gothic Middle Ages by claiming that the plainchant was a
remnant of classical Greek and Roman music. The most feared antirationalistic aesthetic threat was the public's mania for that ostenta-
tious musical spectacle, Italian opera.

Today most semieducated North Americans still combine the aesthetics of Ben Franklin's century with a puritanical suspicion of
gorgeous spectacle and think that opera is a play decorated—or corrupted—with too much music. Opera may seem undemocratic today
because of its associations with boiled shirts and catering to the taste
of ignorant but well-heeled patrons. And in truth opera has always
been an aristocratic world full of gods and heroes designed to the
specifications of the class which patronized it. But the most important message of the operatic medium was that it broke the "natural
laws" to which the arbiters of that time appealed. Yes, the plots

were quite fixed, but then so is the agenda for a tribal dance. There is something about opera and its cousins—reaching all the way from the ancient Dionysian rites to modern rock festivals—which makes them a threat to rationalism.

The classicists recognized this when they demanded "what is this continual noise that *accompanies* the action on stage? Is it not but an appeal to the senses?"[8] Yes, for in opera people can give themselves over to sensibility; in a play nobody ever quite stops thinking.[9] Perhaps the modern literarily inclined reader ought to take his investigatory trip into the nature of opera by way of the mind of that opera fan, James Joyce, in whose works the stream of verbal music that "accompanies" the action turns out to *be* the action.

As one scholar puts it, opera loosed what *philosophie* restrained. "Imagine a nation of enthusiasts and zealots living in a constant state of exaltation. These people, although sharing our principles and passion, would be much superior to us in subtlety, finesse, and delicate sensibilities. With more highly developed sensory organs than ours, such a community would sing rather than speak, and music would be their natural language."[10] In this vein critics began to have second thoughts about the rationalistic dictum that opera is an abnormal state. The systematic soliloquizing of drama through music[11] now began to seem normal. And so did Shakespeare's mad songs, soliloquys, and other transgressions of the Aristotelian rubrics about unity. Soon critics were saying that a businesslike civilization needs to celebrate, to reach ecstasy more than to increase efficiency. The success of opera among those who might logically have despised it, its very violation of "natural laws," may be one reason for its success as a spectacle. By providing a place where the *merveilleux* is normal, opera provided a complement for the rationalizing tendency of the age.[12] By implication not only the actors but everyone who witnessed the spectacle escaped into the heroic. In a word, opera goers were opera heroes in potential, flying on the wings of imagination while pedants smothered the grand passions for not obeying the Aristotelian unities.[13] The philosophers liked opera enough to let it stand as music although it disrupted their theories. But they were bothered by the tendency of proper French opera to remain fixed in grand pageantry while the other arts progressed. Could not some scientific basis be found to bring progress to the French operatic stage in particular, to music, and to the emotional life of man in general?

A collaborator of the philosophes, the eminent French composer Jean-Philippe Rameau tried to make study of music scientific—read geometric—so that it too might progress. His discussions of music became the basis for the articles on it in the *Encyclopédie* and have remained the basis of musical discussion even among those who, like Berlioz, Wagner, Nietzsche, and the Utopian socialists, believed that the philosophes misled the analysis of music, the psyche, and society. But when Rameau the practicing musician left his métier and claimed that music was the highest form of geometry, the geometricians d'Alembert, Diderot, Rousseau, and the other Encyclopedists sensibly disagreed. But by disallowing the claim that music is geometry, they helped to ensconce music as the symbol of everything not geometric.[14]

The geometers admonished the musician that the ear, not geometry, is the final judge of music. There are scientific aspects to music, but for its practical study and appreciation these aspects are negligible. This distinction suffused the Encyclopedists'—especially Rousseau's—articles on music, which relied upon Rameau's musical theories but stopped his pretensions at *philosophie*. On the surface this was a rebuke for Rameau. But in the long run the philosophes' common sense attitude toward music criticism helped to liberate the psychic and social forces which would complement as well as undermine rationalism. By separating music from geometry, the Encyclopedists also separated all that music and musicians stood for in the psyche and society.

In truth, the Encyclopedists were not intentionally revolutionary. They were propagating reforms based squarely upon the six tenets of classical French music criticism which was descended from Plato via medieval and Renaissance philosophy. First, music is enhanced declamation; second, music paints interior sentiments rather than external situations. Opera should not be judged as a branch of literature but as a conglomerate form of art; in opera the marvelous is the normal; in order to have strong passion for music to interpret, authors must continually introduce emotional conflict; the strongest emotion to deal with musically is passionate love, which is therefore the most important in opera.[15] In sum, one has a world where the abnormal is normal; where passion will not remain subordinate to reason.

Such were the theories. The public discussion of the impending cultural revolution began as we saw, with the Bouffons' Quarrel in

1753, when the philosophes who were publishing the *Encyclopédie* began to debate in aesthetic terms the social and psychological questions which continue to agitate western culture, and hence world culture.

The quarrel arose between the status quo and the new, as well as between reason and feelings. While the Encyclopedists were arguing that French composers should build upon Rameau's innovations which in turn built upon Lully's effective use of music integrated with drama, an Italian troupe arrived in Paris to perform *opera buffa*. They soon had the cultural capital of the world at loggerheads. The Encyclopedists sallied from the Queen's Corner (they sat near her box in the opera house) to defend the new Italianate recitative-plus-aria style. The recitative gave literature and the plot its due; the aria allowed music interpretative freedom from the tyranny of the word. Meanwhile, Rousseau published his *Letter on French Music* (*Lettre sur la musique française*), in which he argued that the French language was so unmusical that no good opera could be built upon it. This was like telling someone today that his culture can produce no good material for the cinema. Rousseau's attack evoked over twenty-five opposing works from the King's Corner, who were defenders of the dominant French culture and its rationalism. It seemed to the conservatives that the Italian style allowed music to run riot beyond the natural ordering of passion to a reasoned end which ought to be governed by a tight plot. The constant reference to and working up of sexual passion was sensual and so banal, indeed, that such entertainment, while possibly to be tolerated, was not to be idealized as the mirror of a properly ordered society. Most hurtful was the blow to French and classical pride accustomed to swaying the educated world. The partisans of changeless standards won back some of their ground in part because Rousseau's own opera *The Village Soothsayer* (*Le devin du village*, 1753), was based upon classical declamation and French folklore as well as some Italianate music. Even so, the implication of successful operas on a local—as opposed to an heroic—subject was that each culture has a style appropriate to itself.[16] Were there standards valid for all mankind?

Although Rousseau's life and work afford the most complete discussion of this question, the most succinct one was in an appropriately posthumous masterpiece of the master philosopher of the *Encyclopédie*, the masterwork of the Enlightenment. In Denis Diderot's dialogue *Rameau's Nephew* (*Le neveu de Rameau*, 1761), the new

generation could hardly care less about making music or life acceptable as geometry. In one more generation geometry would go on the
defensive in the aesthetic world.

No, Diderot's philosopher keeps saying to Rameau's Nephew. No,
the freedom which the liberal Enlightenment had in mind is not
sensual whim, nihilism, and anarchy. But the philosopher's adversary
will not let him deny the dangers of humanism. In the conversation
between Diderot and Rameau's shiftless nephew, the stoic philosopher keeps making the careful distinctions proper to a high-minded
man who believes that through education individuals and their society might in the long run make progress toward the rational ordering of human life. Diderot's attempt to calculate the greatest good
of the greatest number sends his opponent into a contrary aspect of
psychological and social calculation. The Nephew argues that such
a utilitarian calculus of pleasure and pain would indicate that humanity operates more from the brute determinism of animal sensuality
than from conscious choice. For, he asserts, who does not prefer
immediate gratification of his libido to its subordination for some
social good? He intimates that for a genius more dangerous, antisocial thoughts are better because they are more exhilarating. They
are more fun.

Hence good and evil are manifestations of interior human appe-
tites rather than reflections of some immutable rational order outside
man. It follows, as it would for Nietzsche a century later, that life is
but a game. Therefore the idlers playing chess daily in the Café de
la Régence can be better men than a reforming philosopher. The
philosopher is not amazed, for he has scheduled himself an hour to
communicate with just such anarchical freaks. Surely, he reaffirms,
good moral goals measure the good of an action. No, returns the
anarchist. Emotional intensity measures the worth of an action.
Therefore, good and evil are inside the mind of the doer.

The discussion turns to music by way of a dispute over what sort
of education is most useful morally. The philosopher argues the
classical position. Music and the other performing arts are a nice
adjunct to the education of a philosopher's offspring. But they are
of little utility, save that singing lessons might improve the orator's
declamation and dancing lessons might improve one's posture. Not
so for the Nephew. For him music is the heart of education, which
is the process of learning how to externalize one's feelings and instincts. Hence there is no question of standards, means, or ends
outside oneself to imitate. To "throw a good fit" is as praiseworthy

as to persuade the commonwealth to some good policy. Ironically, the rebel asserts that all good teachers must be old men, for it is impossible to learn or to teach with authority because everything is relative to each individual. Therefore, experience is the only teacher. You see, he says, young professionals may know the grammar and paradigms of a subject, but only an experienced head can handle the "idioms," which are the most important part of the language of life.[17]

The philosopher replies that embedded in the natural order are rules of discourse; so are there rules of art and of society. Moral intent and emotional demeanor should be related as ends and means.[18] He reiterates the Stoic commandment that virtue gives pleasure. The sensualist turns the argument around to read: pleasure is virtue. In every civilization, time, and place, he says, people find it useful to praise the appearance of virtue and find it beautiful. But everywhere men have local definitions of what is beautiful or virtuous. And so it is only the pleasing appearance of morality that counts. Since the philosopher agrees that the world is a machine, the urging of one's senses to experience pleasure must be granted as determining for man what instinct does for the animals. Since it is not the essentialist definition, but the existential attraction that determines the beauty and hence the morality of an action, whatever is most pleasurable has to be judged most moral. If finesse is what one admires, then immorality can be admirable. Indeed the most immoral action might be the most admirable, demanding as it does the most spontaneous and thoroughgoing rebellion against the artificial restraints of society.

The Nephew declares that great creative geniuses such as he, whether they have produced anything admired by anyone else or not, are artists greater than any political reformer. Since the philosopher's theories do not always fit the facts, they are worse—and therefore perhaps better!—lies than a madman's fantasies. When the philosopher realizes that his opponent has placed the connoisseur above the moralist and the artist above the philosopher by declaring that one should not mean, but be; one should not analyze, but do, the philosopher is exasperated. He declares that Rameau's Nephew understands good music far better than good morals.[19]

Then the sensualist delivers his ultimate argument. He begins to sing. Rather, he *pretends* to sing, giving himself great subjective pleasure. Of course the philosopher observes, notes, and admires how well the nephew pantomimes the various performers, their instruments, and their arias. The music has induced a complete dropping out from conscious control! Diderot calls it enthusiasm. As once among the followers of the god of music, Orpheus, in ancient Greece, now again absorption in music induces madness and alienation.[20] Diderot observes that the Nephew, and by implication any civilization which discards wisdom and seeks instant gratification, progresses from rational discourse or declamation through music into a drunken stupor.

The immoralist then concludes: man is a creature of chance, not reason; genius is its own self-appointed and privileged law; since man knows for certain only his own fantasies, man can be what he wills; not the noble, but the banal is important. This parasite concludes with a lament over the fickleness of his ex-wife, whom he married in order to sell for others to use. He then breaks off to be *on time* for the Italian opera and parts with a cliché *hoping that civilization will endure to support him.*

What of this liberation of the sentiments? Is it the ultimate creativity and freedom or is it the ultimate immorality and enslavement to sensual determinism?

II

What had been speculation in Diderot's generation became history in the next. More than in the political and industrial revolutions, those classes and faculties of man formerly thought contemptible became normal. For example, the German began to displace the French as the "normal" European culture. The Germans did this by serving European mythology the way women have served European and dark men have served American literature.[21]

Formerly the Germans were thought to be "the womanly race," more sensual and less rational than the French, thought to dwell in dark forests rather than lighted boulevards, to believe in all manner of quaint superstitions which they expressed in outlandishly baroque artifices, and to be maladroit at literature, politics, and such "higher" functions of civilization. Who doubts that the "Bulgarians" in *Candide* were the "Vulgarians" across the Rhine? But the Germans were deemed good at the "lower" functions—like procreation and folksong. Then during Revolutionary and Napoleonic times, the French-inspired ideas of liberty, fraternity, and equality helped to cause the replacement of French precepts with native, German models. In this context arose one of the most ambivalent aspects of the romantic rebellion.

Here again, characteristics once despised were now admired without questioning their existence. The romantics revolutionized the Enlightenment's world picture not by changing it but by changing their perception of it. Madame de Staël's *On Germany* (*De l'Allemagne*, 1810), for example, taught French and English readers to keep thinking that Germany was a "fantastic country where men dance and sing like the birds."[22] In America, the romantic abolitionists were about to argue similarly for black liberty. Negroes were also the "womanly race," music-loving, instinctively artistic, passive, and home-loving—exotically inferior and superior at once.[23] Women themselves, ever since Sappho and the Great Earth Mother, have celebrated and been celebrated as a triumph of instinct over abstraction. Modern feminism has been encouraged as well as discouraged by this quest for something androgynous to complete a culture thought too masculine and Apollonian. Therefore, despite rationalists like Simone de Beauvoir, praise of the feminine, black "soul," and "the people" are all inextricably rooted in the ancient stereotypes which they seem to oppose.

To generalize, the Enlightenment was curious to investigate, analyze, and publicize the unknown. Soon however, investigation of the life and arts of every land made the aristocratically inclined philosophers lean toward a more democratic aesthetic. Explorers and researchers pointed out that universal laws seemed less important than unique local conditions in producing ideas of good, truth, and beauty. Standards seemed to flow less from definition than from practice, less from the pronouncements of the erudite than from the experience of the multitude. But, alas for the philosophes, the multitude seemed incorrigibly mired in medieval darkness. They seemed mired in tradition.

Now tradition is but another name for the sum of preexisting, unique, local cultural conditions. It is no accident that Edmund Burke, who wrote the century's most subjective philosophy of beauty, also wrote its best-known praise of tradition.[24]

Because Christian tradition and German culture had been thought irrational and vulgar, they were a powerful antiestablishment syndrome for the new generation to affect. They were all the more powerful because they criticized criticism and tested empiricism. As in *Rameau's Nephew*, the unifying symbol of all the things undervalued by rationalists was to be music. The model man of the new generation, Goethe's Faust, would attack his alienated despair and begin his psychic reintegration upon hearing a medieval Easter carol. Similarly, the Storm and Stress movement (*Sturm und Drang*) prepared the opinion makers of Germany to believe in themselves by praising the Gothic, including the musical mind.

To use constructively those ideas which the philosophes suspected to be destructive was the goal of the Storm and Stress generation. Its faults and successes are epitomized in the life and work of Friedrich Schiller, today claimed for both Enlightenment and for romanticism. On his way to a science of freedom in which aristocratic reason and common sensuality might be allies rather than enemies, he passed through pietistic religiosity, radical Storm and Stress, and individualistic rationalism, to communitarian romanticism. He concluded that there is no a priori psychic hierarchy within an individual anymore than there should be in society. Rather, each human faculty, person, and group has a unique contribution to make. To achieve psychic and social integrity Schiller recommended "aesthetic education" whose catalyst would be development of the kinaesthetic, musical sense. Schiller's favorite metaphor for sensual or aesthetic education was music drama in which he thought sensual impulses and rational deliberation could be balanced and united.

Schiller's theories and dramas were a bridge which connected the old romanticism of the baroque to classicism and hence to romanticism. The remnants of Schiller's personal subculture, his imaginative childhood, persisted into his maturity.

The child Schiller was a pietist. Like many other great souls formed in religious households from his time to Hermann Hesse's, he oscillated in his most impressionable years between emotional repression and copious expression. On the surface bourgeois respectability was all important. Within the heart, imagination ruled. Pietistic "songs for the religious home" molded Schiller's sensibility at his mother's knee and informed it later in Weimar. This city was poor in professional performances but rich in *Hausmusik*, which was, like pietism, an emotional outlet for the German middle class. Two other influences, baroque opera and Shakespeare's Elizabethan total work of art, were also important in the childhood education of this model romantic dramatist.[25]

As a boy, Schiller was entranced by the opera in Stuttgart at the court of Duke Karl Eugen of Württemberg. He first went because the duke ordered military officers like Schiller's father to come and

bring their families in order to assure a full house. The duke's theater
and its equipment were among the best in the world. The grandiose
baroque works mounted there sometimes required hundreds of extras
to help one of Europe's best companies unite poetry, music, dance,
and pageantry in a play where the dominant affect was music.[26] The
child was very impressed and never ceased to relish music. Even
when under house arrest for his Sturm und Drang play, *The Robbers*
(*Die Räuber*, Mannheim, 1781), he went to hear music in the Sturm
und Drang style played by the famous Mannheim orchestra.[27]

In 1783 the youthful Schiller revised his childhood fascination in
favor of the borrowed French neoclassicism common among the
educated throughout western civilization. Neoclassical canons of
taste condemned opera as an impure mélange of sensuality, violence,
and spectacle comparable to Gothic architecture or ridiculous baroque exotica. Opera represented either the return of the barbarous
irrationality of past ages or the advent of excessive realism. Schiller
decided, as did many Germans from the classicist Gottsched and the
pietist Matthias Claudius to Goethe and Nietzsche that such "un-
natural and superficial" Italianate spectacles were less like Greek
tragedy and more like an auto-da-fé.[28]

Yet, since the German public was more musically than literarily
inclined, a celebration of German culture would have to take advantage of this idiosyncrasy while integrating it with the more liberal
and verbal western civilization. But musical culture in Germany as
everywhere was so dominated by Italians that native artists seemed
to have no chance. Schiller was delighted when Gluck, a composer
of Austrian background, showed Paris how to produce a less stilted,
more imaginative style of opera which integrated the various arts
and their claims on the human psyche.

And so, when Schiller matured, he changed his mind again and
celebrated Gluck's operas for dissolving the boundaries between music, poetry, and the stage. Union of the arts as an example for
psychic or social wholeness became a topic that Schiller often celebrated in poems and thoughts on Grecian mythology. In 1796
Gluck's opera on a Greek theme, *Iphigenia in Tauris*, inspired
Schiller to write to Goethe concerning the birth of tragedy out of
the spirit of music.[29]

"I have always had a certain confidence in the opera," he said,
"that in it, as in the choruses of the old Bacchic festivals, the tragedy
can unravel in a noble form. In the opera one is really released
from all slavish copying of nature, and only in this way under the

name of indulgence, can it achieve theatrical ideal. The opera arises from the power of music, and through a free and harmonious charming of the senses the spirit (is elevated) to a beautiful conception; pathos is also given free rein because the music accompanies it and the marvelous, which is tolerated here, must necessarily be made subordinate to the plot."[30]

Bacchic, i.e., Dionysian, festivals and Athenian tragedies sprung from them may have been a most thorough exposition of the human condition, but they were incomplete—more so in Schiller's day than now—and their music was lost irretrievably. They were opera without music. What Schiller desired of opera and found in Gluck's was the experience of a total artwork, such as he believed the festival of Dionysios had once provided. Though the tragedies from the Greek theater were incomplete, Schiller found available some complete *Gesamtkunstwerke*—total environments we might call them— by a romantic mind from a nearer time.[31]

The romantic idealization of Shakespeare, which Schiller shared, was analogous to the romantic idea of antiquity, a chance to extend while rebelling against the Enlightenment. As the first scientific archaeologists like Winckelmann went to the Mediterranean in order to explore the sources of reason and ordered thinking but eventually found that these were one with the irrational side of ancient culture, so too did the romantics explore the Christian era. It soon appeared that the supposedly turbid Middle Ages were inextricably linked with the lucid humanism of the Renaissance and modern times.

Shakespeare became a model for romantics struggling to learn how best to give public expression to the total human psyche. In retrospect this seems logical because Shakespeare's generation had been in a position similar to Schiller's and the romantics'. In the late sixteenth as in the late eighteenth century the assumptions of centuries were undermined. The old rituals, liturgies,[32] and *opera*—at least the *opus dei* in the bare ruined monastic choirs "where late the sweet birds sang"—were dying or had been abolished. What, then, should be the place of the night side of life—art and religion, for example—in the new, down-to-business, less aristocratic society?

Shakespeare's answer we learn from his discourses on the social and psychological role of art in his late comedies and mature tragedies, such as *Antony and Cleopatra*.[33] In this play, Shakespeare had Octavius Caesar, who might well have been a Puritan member of the London City Council which kept Shakespeare's distraction out of the city's center, break up a song to Bacchus and argue words close to "Early to bed, early to rise. . . ." In a world ruled by such a calculating, cold fish, who will supply the psychic demands formerly met by popish pageantry and the medieval festivals? Courtly Antony failed to keep alive a romantic ethos, but Shakespeare succeeded, for "Elizabethan drama was an integration of all the arts, not only literature, but also poetry, music, and dance."[34] Shakespeare's practice fit his theory so well that the way in which he integrated the arts became a romantic ideal—one that approaches what authors in the twentieth century would like to do with "stream of consciousness" or the art of the film editor, who can insert scenes outside the limitations of space and time. Schiller, like his Elizabethan model, employed music seldom as a diversion or for its own sake, but often as a means of dramatic economy, such as trumpet calls, other programmatic bits, and the rites of various groups and communities performed on stage. Music often set the scene and was then commented upon; often it affected the casting by requiring a character to sing or dance (as Schiller could not).[35]

Schiller's inspiration was analogous to that of his French contemporaries Lesueur, Grétry, Méhul, Dalayrac, and other composers who derived some of their musical ideals from Gluck. These composers of "rescue operas" and *fêtes* made to satisfy audiences during the French Revolution might have written effective music in collaboration with Schiller. For they shared "the elevation, the attempts at the sublime, and even the occasional elements of bombast"[36] in Schiller's and Shakespeare's poetic language.

Furthermore, Schiller's philosophical and dramatic writing also connected Renaissance, that is, classical, theories about how the human microcosm mirrors the universe's macrocosm with romantic speculation about how the individual organism shapes and is shaped by every facet of its environment.[37] Thus again evolutionary organicism married *l'esprit géométrique*. But Schiller remained a thinker of the eighteenth century, because he continued to distrust music, which is "perceived through the senses, not through the intellect"[38] and has a closer affinity with the senses than true aesthetic feeling allows. He believed that one must master one's sensual life and progress to good taste before attaining good morals.

Nevertheless, he asserted that whereas "the plastic arts . . . depict the *external* man, . . . the poet (which term includes the maker of sounds) . . . takes the *inner* man as his object . . . . The path of the ear is the most direct and closest to our hearts."[39] Whereas the Enlightenment had thought music was, at best, morally indifferent, Schiller began to think like a romantic.

His theory of individual and social morality anticipated the evolutionary maxim "ontogeny recapitulates phylogeny." The ancient Greeks had been natural, that is, sensual; the culture of Schiller's enlightened time was approaching the aesthetic stage; the reasonable and moral stage was yet to come. The individual man was said to repeat these stages. In support of his views on the aesthetic education of man, Schiller quoted Rousseau's "If reason makes the man, sentiment guides him."[40] He found music ethical: "Every beautiful harmony of form, tone, and light which delights the aesthetic sense satisfies at the same time the moral sense; every consistency with which lines follow each other in time is a natural symbol of the inner harmony of the spirit with itself and the customary coherence of action with feeling, and in the beautiful harmony of a painting or piece of music there is the even more beautiful harmony of an ethically disposed soul."[41] Therefore, *ut musica poesis*, "live like music" is as valid as "live like geometry."

Schiller's *On the Aesthetic Education of Man in a Series of Letters* (*Über die ästhetische Erziehung des Menschen in einer Reihe von Briefen*, 1793–94) argued for removal of artificial boundaries between aspects of human activity. Repeatedly he spoke of dissolving the boundaries among the arts, and considered form-versus-content controversies "merely an entertaining game."[42] "The more general the mood and the less limited the tendency which is given to our feelings through a given art genre, the more noble is the art and the product. One sees this in works from the different arts and in different works from the same art. . . . Perfect style in any art . . . is capable of removing the characteristic limitations of that art without removing its specific excellences."[43]

Music, as Schiller would say in his essay *On Naive and Sentimental Poetry* (*Über naive und sentimentalische Dichtung*, 1795), here "refers . . . to all those effects which poetry is able to bring forth without dominating the power of imagination through a definite object,"[44] as the pictorial, and indeed all, arts save music had done hitherto. Schiller's opinion about which music actually employed "the art's proper nature" again shows us an author's retaining an eighteenth-century theme while modulating to a nineteenth-century key.[45] His youthful remarks on opera had been almost *contre la musique*. He was hostile to music which was not useful. He changed to a promusical aesthetic during those years, the 1790s, which saw perhaps the most rapid social change of any decade in history. It was clear that there would be more apparent political freedom in Europe. But would there be more cultural freedom? Or would everything be leveled to the taste of the middle-brow middle class? The least bother for the greatest number?

Like Beethoven, Schumann, Berlioz, Liszt, Wagner, Nietzsche, and every other critic since, Schiller wondered whether purveyors of light entertainment for mass consumption might drive all other styles from the mass media, which were then the concert hall and the choir loft. Hence, we should not be surprised that Schiller did not care for "modern, agreeable music . . . aimed only toward sensuality and . . . the dominating taste which wants only to be agreeably tickled, not affected, not powerfully stirred, nor exalted." Still, Schiller also remained wary of new 'serious' music which used "new resources for practiced ears only."[46]

He preferred simple music, meaning philosophically simple—having no parts, that is: unified, like the *affect* which informed baroque music. Perhaps such were the impressions Schiller remembered from those operas he saw as a boy. He did not care for Haydn's *Creation* or other works, like Mozart's operas, where styles were mixed.[47] Simple also connoted both folklike and classic: "The peoples of antiquity achieved such an astonishing effect with their music because it was *simple*. Its single chords pressed to the heart and stirred it."[48] Schiller liked to hear music that was either based on a simple melody or was written in a monumentally simple style: as a poet he was reluctant to have his texts smothered in vocal coloratura, piano figurations, or settings which contained "too much music."

Lessing, Wieland, Herder, and Goethe agreed with Schiller. All were in accord with European cultural tendencies signalized in Rousseau's philosophy. "All . . . demonstrated their ideal of song in their creative efforts and expressed themselves in no uncertain terms in their aesthetic writings. . . . They strove for simplicity and poignancy of the folk-song and not for the ambitious art song with its demand for professional singers and accompanists."[49] As had the Enlightenment's reformers, they demanded "settings of their lyrics"—strophic musical forms, which would not distort the lyrics so much as through-composed music.[50]

Among art music, Schiller preferred Palestrina's solemn declamation as a model union of text and tone, because "in music solemnity is produced through slow, uniform, strong tones; the strength awakens and braces the spirit, the slowness lengthens the satisfaction, and the uniformity of the rhythm lets impatience perceive no end to it. Solemnity supports the impression of greatness and exaltation, and is used with great success in religious services and mysteries."[51]

Schiller knew and respected Anton Friedrich Thibault, a collector
of German folksongs, who was later markedly to influence musicology through his book in praise of classic polyphony, *On the Purity
of Music (Über die Reinheit der Tonkunst)*.[52] Schiller's literary
friends Herder and Goethe[53] also may have encouraged him in this
interest, which anticipated Romantic interest in the rich aesthetic
possibilities of Catholicism. Another influence may have been the
vogue of choral music,[54] which had been seldom performed in his
youth. Schiller wanted to see this communal music keep an elevated
style of text and music[55] and steer away from what we in the twentieth century hear in glee-club sentimentalism or corporation fight
songs. Though Schiller called Protestant congregational singing
"ugly" in *The Robbers* (II, iii), he praised Catholic church music
as "from heaven" in *Mary Stuart* (I, vi).

Schiller's works approach ritual, because they, like opera, are
"works of a highly conscious type of art . . . deliberately anti-
naturalistic in style, concerned with heroic themes and attempting to
interpret the common fate of mankind."[56] If one makes everyman or
Christ the hero, that definition also fits religious, especially Christian,
liturgy. For a Romanticist like Schiller, God is not separate from
creation. Therefore, he who is most in tune with unfolding creation
has the most grace. The most creative are saved.

Hence Schiller, like the Storm and Stress rebels of our own day,
was busy upon themes which have always concerned religions. But
since the old rites of passage and community were moribund, he was
trying to create a new language to speak old truths. In the face of
disintegration, he sought reintegration.

III

The new language of life and art assured that the scientific geometrical spirit would take account of musical humanism. By daring
to know or doubt all things, the Enlightenment created modernity,
its offspring, its double and its enemy.

Romanticism is what we have named those ingredients of modernity which the Enlightenment suspected. Romanticism is ultimately
named after Rome, which means here not law and engineering, but
Romance—a cast of mind where emotional expression counts for
much. Emotiveness is something that the popular mind has often

associated with Romance and Mediterranean peoples, most of all Italians, not the least on account of their reputed love for music, especially singing. Indeed, Charlemagne was but the first of a procession of northern leaders who imported Italian singing teachers. Yet many northerners have been suspicious of Romantic mannerisms, including the tendency to give important matters an extensive musical treatment. Like Calvin and Erasmus before them, the northern humanists of the eighteenth century called the elaborate music of the era "stufft full of popish trash and trinkets," which indicates that they must have recognized something particularly Roman Catholic in its spirit, which they equated with the hereditary sensualism of the Mediterranean region.[57] The new pagans confronted the realization that much of the original pagan wisdom came to them scraped up and passed down by that infamous thing, the Roman Church. So the western mind began a journey like that of the heroine in Hawthorne's *Marble Faun* or like the pious North Americans who used to be so shocked at the free manners and operatic music of eastern and southern Europeans.

Although few enlightened thinkers were willing to grant that so playful a "trinket" as, for example, Italianate masses or opera could contain of themselves anything morally instructive, composers did speak in music of the dignity of man. By appealing frankly to the emotions of the laymen, as well as to the intellect of the experts,[58] eighteenth-century musicians were revitalizing a humanizing tendency in western myth and ritual. They were composing in the popularizing tradition of the medieval mystery and morality plays, out of which had come drama like Shakespeare's, alive to every human possibility.[59]

Ordinary listeners could understand this "concert style," with its clear melodic line and homophonic, dancelike accompaniment, more easily than the labyrinths which composers used to construct upon the rules of counterpoint. Once the melody-plus-accompaniment style had made music seem less mysterious, amateur choir directors usually could not resist trying their hands. Their self-composed masses might not be up to concert-hall standards, but this made the music all the more a communal offering. It could also make the professionals ashamed (as Liszt would be embarrassed by the "trash" which accompanied the Oberammergau passion play). Puritans of church and civic music were shocked at the virtuosity displayed in some of these masses, good and bad, just as they have been chagrined since to learn how much coloratura singing is in the Gregorian *Liber usualis*.

Classical music was, therefore, originally in part a folk style which said "Sursum corda" to the drama and procession-loving Catholics of Europe. Being a situation where music dominated, this "Lift up your hearts" may have been—with opera—among the first dominions of Romanticism in the culture of Europe.

In those places where literature was closely censored, humanism usually was more evident in music. "In this case as in others, the Church with its political sagacity knew how to assimilate the most heterogeneous elements, at the same time defending and assuring its fundamental existence, and incidentally preventing any sharp interruption in the flow of intellectual and artistic currents."[60] "The Roman Catholic Church in these countries gave expression to national tendencies by surrounding its services with the glamour and sensuality of dramatic effect. In other words, it is the prerogative of the composer . . . to make his offering to God in his own kind."[61] What Huizinga's mentor Romano Guardini has called the playfulness of the liturgy[62] appealed more to the Italians—and Joseph II's Viennese—than did doctrinal definitions, whether by pope or illuminati. Here they made music in praise of God because it was fun to sing and hear. Italians and Austrians had long taken their church services cheerfully and saw little reason to disapprove of good singing, "however solemn the moment or flamboyant the performance."[63] Even monasteries had orchestras in Hapsburg lands until Joseph II secularized the convents, banned orchestras in churches, and let their libraries and players scatter.[64] Along with the intended moral improvement of the people, this ban occasioned a gap in Haydn's religious composition and the end of most of Mozart's church composition just as his adult life began. Haydn, Mozart, and Beethoven breathed this folk spirit. And their masses were scandalously gay.

The spirit stood in the same relation to the Counterreformation rigidities of the Roman Church following the Council of Trent as the vernacularist spirit of the Gothic styles had stood in relation to the church of Innocent III. Eighteenth-century music was also the direct continuation of a romanticism through a classical era.[65] It linked the baroque to the romantic. Baroque music had subordinated the poet to the musician before and transformed human sentiment into music. Though the *da capo* aria broke the ecclesiastical rubrics about altering the order of the text, it should be judged as a musical, not a literary structure. Contrary to ecclesiastical or rationalistic strictures, baroque music contained no "senseless repetition of words," because composers were not setting words to music. They were turning them into music. It was not so much that the musicians, including Bach and Handel, were inspired by the poet as that they compelled him to accommodate their musical imagination.

Composers from Haydn and Mozart through Beethoven, Rossini, Berlioz, Verdi, Bruckner, and Dvorak remained individuals when writing for the church. By freely interpreting the Latin text, they tested even a sensitive listener's appreciation of it. By so doing, the best composers were prophets of the possible tensions and reconciliations between Christianity and humanism. And so, in southern and central Europe where the people could not read or the Enlightenment was kept out of books, music was the Enlightenment. The composers of the Enlightenment served it well by liberating music from artificial restrictions. By proving that music has its own logic, its own "pure reason," the composers we call classical declared and established the independence of music.[66] The very complexity of music invited its choice as a tool for extending the exploration of human nature.

The communication of the romantic cultural revolution to the entire civilization often occurred through a transvaluation of the old religious myth into secular terms. One such transformation began during the French Revolution, which substituted the nation state for the City of God in the mind of modern man.

SINGING THE CITY OF MAN

Music as Expression of Mass Feeling in the
French Revolution

2

The essence of 1791 was that politics became religion, Michelet once said.[1] Not since the Thirty Years War had Europeans taken their creeds so seriously. Equality was as sacred as transubstantiation; Marat's funeral as pompous as papal coronation.

Michelet was right. And what happened in France, the normal country of the world's ruling civilization, communicated a sense of revolutionary change that the modern world takes for granted. True, the contemporary industrial revolution was equally important. But the *idea* of revolution consummated at the acknowledged center of the civilization was somehow a conversion more impressive, complete, and final.

For average citizens of those still largely preliterate days, public meetings, songs, and festivals were the mass media which communicated the new religion, as they had sustained the old. Yet what changed during the revolutionary decade was more than a product for mass advertising. The new celebrations featuring mass involvement were meant to be less a theater featuring a new style of art than the theater for a new style of life.[2]

The new religion had precursors. The eschatological content of the revolutionary message owed much to the endless Judeo-Christian debate over what form the idealized mythical future might take. Like the secularized carnivals and Mardis Gras in Latin countries, celebrations of the Revolution kept a flavor related to manifestations of popular religion in Catholic countries. The form of the message also owed much to the behavioralist psychology of the leading eighteenth-century thinkers. Following John Locke they believed that human nature is malleable and that virtues can be inculcated by associating them with pleasant sensations. This doctrine was reinforced through its relation to the classic debate over the balance between reason and emotion, which had become part of Christian liturgical theory. Revolutionary theorists also argued from historical examples of how the Hebrews, Greeks, Romans, and Christians had used attractive music to inculcate ideas or duties. However, classical ideals soon encountered the exigencies of mass emotion. Before long the balance of reason and emotion ceased to be upheld as the guiding light of a free people. Instead, the systematic manipulation of mass feelings became one of the most expedient methods of social engineering.[3] Then as now, social engineering finds subtlety useless. So the revolutionary propaganda was not made to induce rational contemplation of alternatives but to excite, anger, and polarize. The French Revolution therefore defined in practice a massive attempt to change the way people think and organize by changing the way they feel.

If manipulation of mass feeling is the goal of a cult during a rapidly changing situation, music had certain advantages over other media such as painting, sculpture, or literature. By using existing tunes and arrangements, music can be turned out quickly. It can reach semiliterate or illiterate masses and can be spread by memory. Traditional airs were available to carry new texts—which explains why only about five percent of revolutionary songs were set to new music. Music can be attached to other events and institutions such as meetings, the theater, military or civic ceremony, and above all to didactic school syllabuses. The hope in each instance was that the pupil or participant might go home humming a tune which carried revolutionary attitudes into his and his family's every day life.

Throughout its course the Revolution demanded art and music less contemplative and passive than that demanded of the same composers by the self-assured hierarchy of the Old Regime. The new rites for citizens of the New Regime were meant to express a religion of action not contemplation. "Now God was not so much invoked or implored as called upon to witness the mighty actions of the day. Far from expressing any sense of humility, or of man's littleness and dependence, the new rites struck a note of defiance and grandeur, or pride in the Revolution and confidence in the new republican order."[4] These *fêtes*—even Robespierre's humorless moralizing—also differed from the old, hierarchial habits in that an official cult once again resembled a spontaneous gathering, "like

Swiss peasants lighting bonfires on peaks and breaking into song."[5] Since the people, not privileged Levites, were to be the principals of the new covenant, its liturgies were more for them to take part in or witness, never merely to get the prescribed forms over and done with the most grace and least boredom. Because the people were still largely illiterate, songs and music were an indispensable part of oral propaganda. Every phase of the Revolution had and valued its songs. To meet people, share their music, or sing with them was one of the most cherished opportunities afforded by the mood of national rejoicing.[6]

Yet the great historians' interpretations of religion in the French Revolution seem to leave something out. Aulard has such a political viewpoint that he sees any cult as a mere expedient of national defense.[7] Mathiez, following Durkheim's sociological method, concentrates on the forms given to the new liturgies. This method fits the self-image of many established religions in the late eighteenth century when "reasonable" official practice was supposed to be separate from "sentimental" private piety. However, like Aulard, Mathiez tends to overlook the syncretism which took place with Catholicism. More recently, Peter Gay has emphasized how faded the medieval Catholic world picture had become.[8] And most Catholic historians have until recently been disgusted with any hint that the church somehow contributed fervor to or copied the Revolution.

So when speaking of religion the historians have tended to concentrate on startling innovations such as the Cult of Reason or the great festivals such as that of the Supreme Being in June of ninety-four. These celebrations were artificial creations of the directing revolutionary powers and as such have less to do with the spontaneous evolution of popular styles of religious practice evolved from Catholicism than do some others. When dechristianization got under way in 1793–94, it was under the direction of the bourgeoisie, who tended to see imagery in terms of their classical education. Not so in the countryside or among the true sans-culottes, who still perceived imagery in terms of their socialization more through the church than through schools.[9] Although the oral, verbal aspect of civic rites great and small was essentially political, the religious sentiments of the ordinary people changed their attachments from the old to the new laws only little by little if at all. The processions, images, chanted litanies, and fervor of the mostly female crowds came less for philosophy and more to venerate the latest revolutionary saints who demonstrated God's miraculous providence for his people. Soboul believes that it is impossible to gather the evidence

which could show how much the revolutionary cults continued the
traditional religion. How much was the dechristianizing trend and
policy a new anti-Christian religion, a regeneration of traditional
fervor, or an intermediate step on the way to unbelief? Each of these
hypotheses is true to a degree. However, some evidence of the balance between continuity and discontinuity may be adduced from the
musical syncretism practiced by the personnel who executed all the
liturgies used in France between 1787 and 1814. Their careers show
how Catholic piety left its mark on the revolutionary cults and, conversely, how the Revolution in turn left its mark on the practices of
restored Catholicism.

Just as the political history of the French Revolution had three
phases, so did its religious history. Like the constitutional monarchy,
the rites and music of the first two years, 1789–91, adjusted rather
than displaced those of the Old Regime. The official festivals, meant
to teach rational thinking and build national loyalties, retained
Christian and monarchical imagery. Spontaneous popular fervor was
also clearly syncretic between Catholicism and the Revolution. The
second two years of the Revolution show ideas and imagery rather
equally balanced between Christianity and neopaganism. By late
1793 the revolutionaries were consciously working for dechristianization, although they were unable fully to discard the Christian
metaphors embedded in the sacrament, assuring that the moment of
salvation is always available.

I

In eighteenth-century France there had been proposals for a national, simple, and didactic Christian cult, but the course of the
Revolution forced the issue. Among the cahiers presented to the
Estates General in 1789 were a few requests that the Catholic liturgy
be adjusted to help the uneducated and revivify the Christian faith.
Some more sophisticated addresses urged that a national cult would
reunite Protestants with orthodoxy and that the medieval Latin of
the liturgy was a more barbarous language than French.[10]

While France waited for the Estates General to convene for the
first time in a century and three-quarters, Christian and patriarchal
images persisted in political songs and celebrations. A *Hymn in*

A folk painting of the first Bastille Day, *La fête de la fédération*, depicts Talleyrand, Bishop of Autun, celebrating Mass at the altar of *la Patrie* on the Champ de Mars. The habits and personnel of the Catholic cult helped to shape the revolutionary festivals. In turn, revolutionary styles would influence the restored Catholic cult. (Musée Carnavalet, Paris.)

Honor of the Resurrection of the Estates General (misspelled in
the original as *Etates Généraux*), which circulated early in 1789,
implied that something miraculous was about to happen. Much of
its imagery, which anticipated a new golden age, deliberately secularized Christian eschatology, which had formed its cult around the
story of man's rebirth through a second Adam who conquered the
curse of death caused by the first Adam. Logically the new resurrection song used the music and most of the words from the best-known
French Easter carol, *Ye Sons and Daughters*,

> Long live the fateful morn
> When all is as if reborn
> The Kingdom is restored!
> Alleluia.[11]

Then the refrain of three alleluias.

The form of *O filii et filiae* was admirably suited to mass singing,
because everyone could join in the alleluia refrains while a precentor
carried forward the verses. From Dionysios' Thrace to the Champ de
Mars to Yasgur's Farm, popular cults have often favored the re-
sponsorial form in which a song leader can link the mass emotion
to the official doctrine while the people respond with amens and
alleluias.[12] In May the exuberance of 1789 bred a *New "O filii" of
the Estates General*. Its almost Bacchic, eschatological stanzas, such
as

> The vine that we thought dead
> A new crop of grapes has bred
> Oh what a miracle![13]

promised a new life, a resurrection.

Most of the songs used during the first phase of the Revolution
were folk tunes or hymns already known. These were used not only
because of their popularity but also because music was usually
deemed subordinate to verbal propaganda by eighteenth-century aestheticians. On the infrequent occasions when a musician was commissioned to create a hymn to the new order, publishers included
a reference to a known alternate tune which fit the meter of the
text.[14]

Although the divine-right theory of monarchy was not in vogue
among the eighteenth-century philosophers, the patriarchal symbolism of Christianity—indeed it is the symbolism of the Hebraic, the
Hellenic, and the Germanic streams in western culture—still flour-

ished among the uneducated. During the first two years of the Revolution, filial respect still identified the image of the king with that of God, the compassionate father. So in this hymn:

> A long time spent in the throes
> Of such misery and woes;
> In our poor little rooms
> We were near to our tombs.
> Then LOUIS our father royal
> Did vanquish the foes of all
> He summoned in our travail
> The Estates General.[15]

If King Louis XVI was likened to the Christian God, his minister, the Swiss Protestant banker Jacques Necker, was likened to a Saint Michael the Archangel who would cast out the forces of darkness.

> Great Necker will no doubt
> Put hell to route
> For he crushes with his foot
> All discord and envy.
> Ah! He has an arm of iron
> To smash all calumny.[16]

Or perhaps Necker was a Christ, the annointed savior sent by the Father:

> 'Mid the trouble and fury,
> The result of a minister-oppressor,
> *Necker* appeared as a Savior.
>   Alleluia.[17]

Among the several new stanzas to be sung to the tune of *O filii* was one verse translated from the original Latin.[18] It rebuked doubting Thomases.

> How blest are they who have not seen,
> And yet whose faith has constant been,
> For they eternal life shall win.
>   Alleluia.

The "eternal life," however, was at least by implication more earthly than heavenly. Thus the revolutionary hymn retained Christian eschatology but shifted the golden age from faith in paradise to faith in the City of Man.

After the storming of the Bastille and the dismissal of Necker, the religious symbolism used in revolutionary songs shifted from filial respect for the Christian king to a patriotism with more pagan classical images:

> This august Assembly
> Of heroes and immortals
> Groans, and desolate,
> Erects altars to patriotism.[19]

By August, when the church's lands were put up for sale, the new verses sung to old religious songs often satirized the clergy though dogmas were left unassailed.

> The Pope is a turkey,
> The Cardinal's a knave,
> And the Archbishop a scoundrel.
>   Alleluia.[20]

Songs like *The Veil Lifted* (*Le voile levé*), a fifty-six verse catalogue of ecclesiastical abuses, satirized the thievery of luxury-loving prelates and useless monks. Parish curés, however, were often portrayed as oppressed patriots.[21] Even as in Chaucer's parson, they were closest to the people; after all, had not their votes been the crucial ones when the Estates General became the National Assembly?

Meanwhile, on a more formal level, the fall of the Bastille had been celebrated by an orthodox *Te Deum* sung in Notre Dame, singing in the streets, and dancing in the fields.[21] The following year included a few sermons by patriot-priests who said, "It is the aristocracy who crucified Christ" and therefore the sacrifices made at the Bastille were like Christ's.[22] This implies that the patriots were Christian martyrs and therefore saints in heaven. The year wore on with numerous Blessings of Banners for the National Guard, including one when a military band is said to have played in Notre Dame for the first time.[23] In these ceremonies, solemn oaths among the guardsmen and to the nation joined the religious sanctions[24] as they would have in any Christian nation.

Then, one year after the fall of the Bastille, the rising curve of the cult of the nation and the declining curve of the Catholic cult intersected.

On the eve of the first Bastille Day, a Gallican-Gothic oratorio mingled with secular patriotism to form a "religious drama drawn from Holy Scripture and entitled *The Fall of the Bastille*"! Scraps of biblical text were strung together to compose a topical political drama with interchanges in obvious parody of the litanies and antiphonal psalmody chanted in the Latin liturgy. This passage commented on the dismissal of Necker:

CITIZEN: Shall not the land tremble for this, and every one mourn that dwelleth therein?
THE PEOPLE: Why?
CITIZEN: Our protector is taken away.

A citizen announced the exile of a "minister in whom they trust."

THE PEOPLE: Woe unto us!
THE WOMEN: O Lord, have mercy upon us and upon our children.
ALL: Help us O Lord.[25]

After several such exchanges, military marches, fanfares, and orchestral cannon fire, the chorus capped the service with a passage from the book of Judith: "Woe be unto the nation that riseth up against my people; for the Lord almighty will take revenge on them. In the day of judgement he will visit them."[26] This rite was but the first of many unusual dramas to be played in Notre Dame during the Revolution.[27]

The next day (the first Bastille Day), *la fête de la Fédération*, was a celebration of the Catholic and monarchical liturgy modified to suit the needs of a political revolution in *la grande nation*. Three hundred priests—including the Bishop of Autun, Talleyrand—said Mass. Each wore a tricolor cincture. Two hundred musicians played, and the king, the queen, the Assembly, and representatives from all ranks and localities of France were in their appointed places to celebrate the marriage of all factions in France.[28] As it turned out, however, this festival marked not the beginning but the end of deliberate cooperation between the Catholic and the revolutionary cults.

After *la fête de la Fédération*, which had been a vast Catholic mass, the next important revolutionary celebration displaced the Catholic cult. Voltaire, who had been denied a Catholic burial, was made a saint of the new order[29] when his ashes were borne to the Panthéon on 11 July 1791. Along the way, the cortege paused to hear selections by a military band, which was being employed for the first time to accompany the churchly medium, a chorus. The music was by Gossec, who took the words from Voltaire's own opera libretto *Samson*, whose story—biblical though it was—was soon deemed a subversive subject outside France.

People, awake, break your chains,
Reclaim your original greatness,
Just as, one day, God from on high
Will recall the dead to the light
From the dust of the earth
And will reanimate the universe![30]

The Christian churches—and their opponents—have often been surprised to see how the radically millenarian message of the Bible crops up in unanticipated places.[31]

A year later, biblical and monarchical symbolism were absent from the fête which celebrated the third anniversary of the fall of the Bastille. There was only austere, martial music and no special stands for the royal family or other distinctions of rank. Only the nation encamped—the king and private alike—on the Champ de Mars under the tricolor.[32] In another year, the Revolution, having executed the king, would persecute the old while building a new religion. Meanwhile, a bishop withdrew from the Catholic Church and spoke to the Convention about Holy Equality; a Calvinist minister declared that "Henceforth I shall have no other gospel than the republican constitution;" and the *Marseillaise* sang of "sacred love of the motherland."[33]

Most delegates to the Estates had assumed that the Christian cult was the clergy's business. So the Second Estate, which in 1790 had become the juring clergy (those who swore allegiance), loyal to the Revolution when the Estates General became the National Assembly, debated how to improve the Gallican cult. By the time the juring bishops came around to decreeing substantive changes in the Gallican liturgy, the Revolution was bent on replacing, not reforming, Christianity. Meanwhile, these constitutional clergy, French classicists in their own right, remained sons of Bossuet and hesitated to go the way of the Protestants with their tendency to divide the well-ordered and unified church into sects. Loyal Gallicans to the end, these successors of Richelieu would never interfere with the consolidation of the French national state whose creation had taken the thousand years from Clovis to Louis XIV. No, they said, we must not fragment the nation we have just completed by opening the door to liturgies in every patois. They therefore rejected a vernacular sacramentary.[34]

As the Revolution sped on, progressives departed the upper ranks of even the constitutional clergy in most dioceses. Vernacular Catholic rites of any kind were performed in only a few parishes and one cannot be sure that Mass was ever said in French during the Revolution.[35] The refractory, nonjuring, clergy of course declared that in such times it was sufficient for the priest to understand the Latin rites and the people to attend. Napoleon's Concordat settled the question in 1801 by restoring the liturgical *status quo ante*. After the Revolution, an émigré mentality dominated the French Catholic Church. There remained no concession to the vernacular except in paraliturgical devotions and oratorios or hymns during, but technically not part of, liturgical rites. So the energies which elsewhere went into the reform of existing cults were used in France to create the new civic cult of the First Republic.

In 1792 the *Marseillaise* announced that the "day of glory has happened," with all the overtones of the last judgment that such a phrase still aroused. Like the anthems chosen for other nations founded in revolutions—the United States and Italy, for example— the *Marseillaise* asks extraordinary singing of ordinary people. These anthems run over an octave—*The Star Spangled Banner* runs an impossible twelfth—thus demanding of amateur vocal resources what had been a professional's range. The text does not call for help from any authority but tells the people to form their own battalions and spring to arms spontaneously. Contrast the dotted rhythms and topical texts of those songs with the Burkean hymn and music used in *God Save the King*.

Even better known than the *Marseillaise* at the time was *Ça ira*— "Things are going to be all right." Surely no other nation has ever been so restless about getting on with the future and its new consciousness.

II

When considering whether republics would not necessarily have a drab public life because they would have no marvelous cult to inspire the citizens, Jean-Jacques Rousseau had argued that republics could outdo monarchies by turning the spectators into the spectacle. Everyone would recognize and love himself in his fellow man, so that all would be one.[36] Other republicans also thought that humanistic festivals would teach man to "love thy neighbor as thyself." The revolutionary publicist Anacharsis Clootz said that fathers should take their sons to the festivals of the year II and say, "Come my

child and see your nation, France. Every person as one, of one soul
and one heart."[37] Revolutionaries liked to speak of whole villages
"adorned like brides on their wedding day" to celebrate the new
covenant of solidarity and love. Christianity was now spoken of as
the legalistic Old Covenant yielding to the New Law of Love.

During the anti-Christian phase of the Revolution, the playwrights
of its festivals looked to ancient Greece and Rome for models. Before the Revolution philosophers had argued that in antiquity there
had been an organic relationship among the arts, politics, and the
quality of public life. It seemed that in classical times the arts were
not practiced merely to buy a god's favor or amuse human leisure.
They were said to have been practiced, as in Plato's *Republic*, to
assist education in ethics; to inculcate virtues.[38] The arts were therefore to be considered a branch of moral philosophy. Montesquieu's
On the Spirit of the Laws[39] had recalled the Greek belief that controlled cultivation of an harmonious, musical, mentality was essential to the state. Voltaire had written that the culture of the arts
renders souls more honest and pure.[40] Rousseau's *Reflections on the
Government of Poland and Its Reformation*[41] had advised the Poles
to institute national festivals, "such as the ancients had held." Diderot
had said that the duty of the artist was to celebrate the good, to
make us love virtue and hate vice, and to create not heavenly Christian, but earthly pagan immortality by eternalizing great and noble
actions, honoring virtue, and stigmatizing vice.[42] All the writers of
the Enlightenment would have agreed with Montesquieu, who totally rejected the idea that music *by itself* was able to inspire virtue.[43] Yet, as in the encounter between the Philosopher and the
Nephew in Diderot's mind, a cultural revolution forecast a social
revolution. This change was reflected in the revolutionaries' increased
respect for imagination and music, which they recognized as more
effective keys to mass action than scientific reasoning. And, of course,
mass action had become a fact of life.

About a year before the outbreak of the Revolution a progressive
French priest had produced one of the first international bestsellers
of modern times. The semifictional tract in social psychology, J.-J.
Barthélemy's *The Travels of Anacharsis the Younger, in Greece
about the Middle of the Fourth Century before the Common Era*.
The two chapters on music evaluated critically the contemporary
French scene. The book was at once a capsule review of the Bouffons' Quarrel and a program for social action. While ostensibly
discussing the classical conceptions of the role and nature of music,

Barthélemy's personae revealed themselves as Gluckists arguing against the Piccinists, who would have turned the musical imagination loose unrestrained by the logical necessity for a dramatic unity of the text to govern the whole affect. The vocal frippery of Italian opera was thought to reflect a society seeking psychological escape rather than moral edification. "This sweet softness, those seductive sounds captivate the masses and, lacking any definite meaning, are always interpreted in terms of currently prevailing emotions."[44] Where moral law has been abandoned, only the consumption of pleasure remains.

This aesthetic classicism anticipated the musical ultraconservatism of all official revolutionary pronouncements on matters musical. Throughout the revolutionary decade, plans for a purified and practical nationalistic education for the people appealed to the Abbé Barthélemy's precepts.[45] Many plans for a liturgy of people's democracy referred both to the prophet of all revolutionary music, the foreigner Gluck, and his French preacher Barthélemy. As confident as orthodox Marxists or true believers in the Woodstock Nation that the "selfish frivolity reflected in formerly respected music" would wither away, the revolutionaries claimed that a new consciousness would be catalyzed by the people's hearing music with a strong beat, based on popular tunes, and simple enough so that the whole community could be swept up when hearing it for the first time.

And so, during the post-Christian phase of the Revolution, hymns and songs were planned to form virtues in the citizens. As under Plato's *Republic*, the Catholic reformation following Trent, Calvin's Genevan syndics, or Mao's China, they were to be approved by legal authority.[46] They were not to be art for art's sake but art for revolution's sake. In 1791 the legislators voted into the first French constitution a provision for national festivals, major artistic events to unify public opinion on basic national issues.[47] When the radical Jacobins gained power, they were even more certain that the art of persuasion depends upon the ability to arouse people emotionally.[48] France was to become a laboratory for social change through application of a pleasure-pain calculus. As Danton put it, "exhaltation is what makes the building of republics possible."[49] The Revolution now purported to view the arts not as "mere ornaments on the social structure," but "a part of its foundations."[50]

During the national emergency the Jacobins tried to enforce the type of communized patriotism which "made the democracy of Athens unparalleled in the most brilliant period of her own or any

recorded human history."[51] Faith in the socially regenerative qualities of enthusiasm directed through music soared. "Send me a thousand men and one copy of the *Marseillaise*, and victory shall be my
reply," wrote one general to the Convention. The official *Révolu-
tions de Paris* declared that "With the tune *Ça ira* one leads the
people to the end of the world, right through the combined armies
of Europe." Theater performances were inevitably preceded and
often spontaneously interrupted by community singing which appropriately reminded one English visitor of Congregational psalmody.[52]

Like the philosophes and the enlightened ecclesiastical liturgists
elsewhere,[53] Robespierre, who had the most theological temperament
among the revolutionaries, wanted a didactic liturgy "Good men
instead of good company; [a society where] the arts are an adorn-
ment of the liberty that ennobles them."[54] Though the revolutionaries
cared for moral instruction, not tribal experiences, they still thought
that the masses needed an impressive cult.

The beginning was almost easy, for, as we have noticed, revolutionary fêtes and ethical Christianity were compatible well into the
1790s. Jansenists, who were numerous in Catholic countries, favored
a pristine, purely ethical Christianity and could be expected to get
along well with the neo-Stoics among the revolutionaries—indeed
they were often the same men. In 1794 Cardinal Buonarroti might
have been mistaken for Robespierre when the former said of Jesus
Christ, "Philosopher-founder of Christianity, the day of fulfillment
of your wishes is not far removed. Your doctrine, disfigured by
tyrants, is ours. The time has now come when, following your pre-
diction, science and nature will join all men into a single flock.
Brothers and friends, let us give thanks to the Eternal. The Revolution, new proof of his existence, is his work."[55] As late as Christmas
1797, the future pope Pius VII was declaring, "The democratic
form of government adopted among us, dear brethren, is not in opposition to the maxims I have set before you; it is not contrary to
the Gospel. . . . Be good Christians and you will be excellent demo-
crats."[56] Pagan Stoicism and Christian charity seemed more compatible in the new Jerusalem than in the old.

Soon Christianity in France became a persecuted religion. A
Grande Bible compiled and published by Thomas Rousseau in 1792
was full of patriotic and secular songs.[57] By late 1793 a *Hymn for
the Inauguration of a Temple of Liberty* with music by Lesueur and
text by François de Neufchâteau had thought not merely to displace
but to exorcise the Catholic cult.

O Liberty, blessed Liberty!
Goddess of an enlightened people!
Reign today in this enclosure,
By you is this temple purified!
Liberty! before you, Reason banishes deception;
Error flees, fanaticism is laid low,
Our gospel is nature,
And our cult is virtue.
To love Country and Brother
To serve the sovereign People,
These are the sacred badges,
And the faith of a Republican.
Of an imaginary Hell
He does not fear the empty flame;
From a lying Heaven
He does not expect false treasures;
Heaven is found in peace of soul,
Hell is in remorse.[58]

After those two stanzas exorcising the old beliefs, a third instructs
in the Republican catechism:

Uphold against vile slaves
The Republic and her children.
Our cause is just, they are brave.
Make them return triumphant.
When they punish
The impotent rage of tyrants,
Let us keep watch for them
And may France, when they return
Offer them a family united
By nature and by love.[59]

Republican sentiments were not the only ones expressed in the
thousands of songs and instrumental pieces used to propagandize
during the Revolution. Demonstrations and songs calling for freedom
and equality provoked counterdemonstrations calling for the old law
and order.[60] At first the royalists missed the point, which was to win
the illiterate masses.[61] Witty parodies and ironical satires of dour
revolutionary figures entirely lacked the righteous tone so evident on
the patriot side. By ninety-three, no one made jokes. The monarchist
counterrebels in the Vendée had songs which were at once martial
and modal and occasionally seemed to be versions of Gregorian
chant, especially when sung unaccompanied.[62] One writer claimed
that it was the magic powers of music which caused that province's

attachment to "a religion that otherwise offers nothing that is not disgusting."[63] Occasionally, when revolutionary excess diminished revolutionary fraternity, the royalist *People's Reveille* sometimes won the war of songs against the Jacobin *Marseillaise*—a Thermidorean reaction in music.[64] During the violent phases of the Revolution, musicians enjoyed relative peace if they seemed willing to use their talent to promote the doctrines of the new covenant.[65]

The poet Marie-Joseph Chénier,[66] who headed the committee on public festivals until theologians like Robespierre assumed direct control, believed that the way to replace Catholicism in the affections of the people was through public education by way of a new cult that should be intelligible—read didactic—and impressive. The republicans wanted both to equal the antique Roman pomp and to outdo the religious aura of the old ecclesiastical festivals.

Chénier pleaded for a "universal religion with neither sects nor mysteries, in which the human family burns its incense only at the altar of *la Patrie*, common mother and divinity."[67] His assistant, the classicist painter Jacques-Louis David, who was in charge of mounting many of the more successful revolutionary fêtes, labored to communicate republican ideas of beauty and truth to the masses.[68]

Though many republicans shared the common failing of propagandists, who often think that artists should be happy merely to serve an ideology for nothing,[69] the Convention thought enough of music as a propaganda weapon to pay well for both official and nonliturgical songs. Patriotic music and singers were exported to assist the Revolution in neighboring countries.[70] Along with an elementary school system, the Ecole Polytechnique, and the metric system, the Convention founded the National Institute of Music, soon to be renamed the National Conservatory.[71]

The musicians of the institute were technically the musical section of the National Guard. As such, they issued a military manual for music. The Committee of Public Safety, which—with its laws of the maximum, etc.—was outwardly more socialistic than the original bourgeois revolutionaries, encouraged musicians to eliminate the publisher, who was a middleman between the musician and his public. The Magasin, which was a music-publishing association of composers, published twelve issues of *Music for the Use of National Festivals*. Beginning in April 1794, these issues were a compendium of ritual and music for every festival and grade of solemnity in the republican calendar, from the simple weekend *decadi* in a village to the splendor of the Festival of the Supreme Being on the Champ de

Mars in the capital.[72] Considering the ecclesiastical background of the makers of the Magasin, perhaps it was less like an army manual and more like the Ordo which had structured the day-to-day, hour-to-hour, Catholic ritual.

In May of 1794 the same group of musicians proposed another monthly with simpler music for country folk or the armed forces. More a parochial than a cathedral liturgy, each issue of the *Periodical of Civic Songs and Ballads* contained three or four unison selections with figured bass. Up to 18,000 copies of single pages were printed of this official book for the national holidays. Songs included *Verses against Luxury* by Piis with music by Solié, and *To the Saltpeter Festival* (saltpeter is needed for making gunpowder), words by Pilet, music by Catel.[73]

As the socialist historian Mathiez would later say, the republicans hoped that this lay religion would "lift the yoke of theocracy from the neck of the people." At the Festival of Liberty in Notre Dame, the priestess who represented the first word of the revolutionary trinity, *liberté*, intoned the first line from one of M.-J. Chénier's poems: "Come, holy Liberty, inhabit this temple."[74] This ritual invocation might have reminded people of the then well-known Gregorian hymn *Veni creator spiritus*, which was usually sung to commence solemn Catholic festivals. There is evidence that, from the English Channel all the way to Poland and Hungary, revolutionary leaders believed that their moralistic and non-Christian messages would be more agreeable if they were clothed with music and dramatic pageantry like the cults which the people were used to.[75]

Like contemporary "enlightened" rites in Germany, or twentieth-century ones in the Catholic Church, everything was "made plain and simple by order."[76] Political events began to dominate artistic ones; censors decided there were to be no more "graces" or "manners," which might recall entertainments created for the leisure of aristocrats. Musical art therefore abandoned prettiness in favor of declamatory enthusiasm, which manifested itself in simple chorale-like melody lines, vocal masses, and ignorance of or disdain for contrapuntal and rhythmic subtleties.[77] These might have made the music more interesting for connoisseurs but would have obscured its texts for the average listeners. Moreover, many of the performers were nonprofessionals. So musical directions and devices had to be easy to perform. Consonance and one note per syllable were the rule.

There was a similar revolution in instrumentation. Musicians found quasi-scriptural justification for replacing strings with winds because the classical Greeks, Romans, and ancient Hebrews had used brass and reed instruments. Composers' music for the Revolution was less meditative and more martial than their church music had been, not necessarily because they were eager to fight for *la patrie* but because they had to reach huge crowds gathered out-of-doors. Too, there was no longer any suggestion of music's being a pleasant background to a mystical or elegant routine. When used, music was for instant effect. Musicians combined the Christian theology of music—where their art was sacred but nonetheless subordinate to the text—and their favorite Gluckist or pictorial style with the blunt folk and military styles appropriate to a nation at war. While war, neoclassicism, and mass audience dictated wind instruments, advancing technology was giving composers better and more varied ones to write for. Hence another reason for replacing the mild, "indoor" strings with "outdoor" brasses in the rites of the sovereign people, "who should be contained within no building except the vault of heaven."[78] In music as in politics, revolutionary innovations were not sports but signs of the times. Massive music to express mass feelings was becoming normal.

To spread the new Good News the people were called upon to participate *en masse* in its liturgies. The Cult of the Supreme Being, into which the Civic Cult evolved under Robespierre, was a compromise among strict republican atheism, deism, and the old cult of a supernatural God and immortal soul. Among the yearly high points of popular Catholicism had been Pentecost—birthday of the church in early summer, when the descending Holy Spirit impelled the apostles to evangelize the world—and the Fête Dieu or Corpus Christi at the end of June. The latter day's procession of the Body of Christ was particularly elaborate. With candles, incense, banners, vestments, and costumes a contingent from every status and organization of Catholic society accompanied the priests bearing the Sacred Host in the ostensorium beneath a canopy through the streets to an outdoor altar of benediction. All sang Thomas Aquinas' well-known processional hymn *Pange lingua gloriosi* on the theme of the invisible God's miraculous works for man—the bread of the Eucharist transubstantiated into the flesh of Christ. Fireworks and other midsummer festivities might continue through the night. It was reasonable to place a spectacular outdoor republican festival at that time of year.

Robespierre wanted all Paris to join in singing Théodore Désourgues' *Hymn to the Supreme Being* at the Festival of the Supreme Being on 20 Prairial III (8 June 1794). So professors of music, each accompanied by a young singer, were sent to all the districts of Paris to teach the populace the hymn and Gossec's melody. Professional musicians were organized to sing parts in harmony to accompany a hymn to the invisible God's benevolent works:

Father of the Universe, Supreme Intelligence,
Benefactor ignored by blind mortals
You revealed yourself to the gratitude
Which alone raised altars to you.

Your temple is on the mountain, in the heavens, on the waves
You have no past you have no future;
And living not in time, you fill the entire universe
Which cannot contain you.[79]

Each of the forty-eight districts sent ten men, mothers, youths, girls, and little boys to form the 2,400-voice choir which sang the verses of Marie-Joseph Chénier's *Hymn to the Eternal*. The multitude on the Champ de Mars joined in the refrain, accompanied by cannon, which were echoed by others across the Seine. Similar techniques were used on other occasions to achieve congregational participation through a musical *levée en masse*, a seemingly spontaneous rising of citizens to join the forces of the republic.

The fall of Robespierre in Thermidor of the year III (July 1794) did not end the attempt to create a new Platonic republic by manipulating the popular imagination. In the early days of the Directory, which followed the Thermidorean reaction, Chénier warned of "incompetent legislators who treat human beings as abstractions." He argued "that the ability to lead men is nothing else than the ability to direct their sensibilities, that the basis of all human institutions is morality, public and private, and that the fine arts are essentially moral because they make the individual devoted to them better and happier. If this is true for all the arts," he exclaimed, "how much more evident is it in the case of music," which vanquished the heart of Alexander and was even cultivated by the rustic Spartans.[80] The Directory, which succeeded the Robespierrean Republic of Virtue, also tried to unify a bitterly divided public through music. Orders concerning which songs might or might not be sung in theaters occasioned much blowing of noses, shuffling, or ironic applause whenever the official policy did not suit the sentiments of the audience. Eventually the theater audiences settled down to a respectful silence— that is, boredom—during the formalities before the approved plays or operas. The Directory also wanted to continue the republican festivals, only in ways that would make them practical throughout the provinces. François de Neufchâteau as a member of the executive of the Directory and then as minister of the interior set about creating a collection of songs and music abbreviated or arranged for use in smaller communities. A new school curriculum was written around republican maxims, poetry, eulogies, and songs. Official songs were recorded on cylinders for mechanical organs in order to achieve uniform reproduction even in remote villages.[81]

The planting of liberty trees and the crowning of statues of Liberty (rather than statues of the Virgin Mary) were revolutionary rites which spread throughout Europe. The patriotic mood mingled with deistic theodicy at such events is one of those things which the Revolution and Napoleonic wars made part of every Europeanized nation's life. Grétry wrote a song for solo voice and wind sextet for such a planting in 1799 to commemorate a military victory. The text was by Mahérault.

Unite your hearts and your arms,
Children, citizens, magistrates,
Let us plant the sacred tree,
The honor of our shore!
May your emblem, O Liberty,
Be the signal of gaiety;
Sadness, on this day, is but for slavery.
Games and songs do homage
To the success of the French![82]

In the revolutionary calendar the *décadi*, a tenth day, was provided for rest following nine days of work. Like tree planting, the festivals for the *décadi* were suited to provincial recreation. For 10 prairial an VII (10 May 1799), Cherubini wrote a hymn with accompaniment by a wind band to a pastoral text by Mahérault.

Adorned with flowers and greenery,
Young summer calls us to the fields,
Of the meadows which the scythe renews
To Heaven let us consecrate the first fruits!
Our altars are their pyramids,
Their simple perfume our incense.
Plenty, with joyful rhyme,
Sings upon their moist peaks
Daughter of Nature, O Mother of virtue,
Bond of hearts, blessed gratitude,
Come, upon ingratitude and pride laid low
Found the laws and their sweet power![83]

To recover the Millennial Eden, the Revolution may have had "no need of chemists," runs the saying, but it did need gunpowder. It may not have needed contrapuntists, but it did need a *Marseillaise*. The revolutionaries were no exception to the rule among ideologists who insist that they must control artists, who are thus acknowledged to be the world's true legislators. The revolutionaries therefore desired propaganda for their system and no frivolity like the chemist Lavoisier's weighing the air or musicians who fiddled while Rome burned.[84]

Seen from the altar, that is by the radical Jacobin theologians, the liturgies proposed for the French Revolution were to be strictly didactic; their art and music only a decorative coating for moralistic propaganda.[85] Thus the Revolution could aggravate the inquisitorial attitude that makes the greatness of a work of art depend on the extent to which the mind of its maker was molded by doctrine.[86]

Seen from the music stand, however, such tedious righteousness had a saving virtue. The revolutionary doctrine of equality dignified the musician by changing him from a servant—hired and judged by a superior patron—into a professional who served a public vocation. During and after the Revolution, musicians penetrated even the First Estate. Military band leaders, who had always been sergeants, were now officers.[87]

Thus, although the revolutionary celebrations continued to enforce political submission, they also helped to create a demand for artistic liberation. Although music remained subordinate to the text—the "program," in both senses, of the French Revolution—the revolutionary leaders did not restrict musicians artistically as much as did contemporary ecclesiastical reformers, who still thought artists ought only to serve a superior caste. To sketch the careers of a few musicians and to recall the rationale for music which they brought to the Revolution will help to understand the cults which now superseded Christianity in France and the world at large.

Most of the musicians who helped to teach patriotism had been thoroughly trained in Catholicism. The two dogmas may have been contrary but their psychologies could be similar. Never, ran the official theories of both cults, is music alone with no other duty except to fill the ear with sound and declare relationships that words cannot paraphrase or explicate. The evangelistic techniques—propaganda—that had evolved in the service of Christianity were enlarged and continued in the service of the new secular religion and its successors, whether ecclesiastical, civic, or commercial.

III

The first question many people ask about a piece of music, especially one which has no understandable text, is "What does it mean?" They are asking for a "program." This is the question which Diderot and the Encyclopedists had asked of absolute music and the opera. The question had been long debated by philosophers and theologians not only since the Renaissance and Reformation, not only since Augustine in the patristic age, not only since Plato's *Republic*, but as far back as the tension between Dionysios the musician and Apollo the lawyer. Was it morally healthy to let oneself go into revery upon hearing music? Or was music-for-its-own-sake the ultimate immorality in a well-ordered system of personal and social consciousness?[88]

Before the Revolution, when the churches still had a monopoly on public education, ecclesiastical liturgies had provided such a program for the masses' experience of music. (Opera did the same for the "classes.") For instance, cathedrals and what went on in and around them were meant to be a complete symbolical language, a multimedial "Bible in stone." A snatch of *O filii et filiae* instantly recalled the Resurrection; a phrase from the *Veni creator* recreated Pentecost in the mind of the listener.[89] Though the medieval symbolical language was dying, eighteenth-century church musicians, like the Jesuits[90] of their day, were in fact modernists trying to breathe life into an atrophying institution.

Program music has always been an option for any composer,[91] but program music was required of church musicians, whose job it is to set ecclesiastical texts to music which would interpret them for a mass audience. The revolutionaries used this skill; out of the banalities of the Civic Cult came a monumental style which exalted man and his city. Lesueur, Gossec, and the other revolutionary musicians were Beethoven's prophets: not his causes, but among his precursors just the same. For they strove to make the sublime popular and the popular sublime.

The revolutionary musicians also modernized the Gallican liturgical tradition and thus accomplished the modernization that the juring clergy avoided. In the Middle Ages there had been essentially two kinds of Mass north of the Alps. The Roman Mass was executed entirely by clerics. The Gallican Mass had a freer form and permitted congregational participation, especially in the Ordinary. When Rome ended lay participation in the twelfth century, she retained liturgical dramas to explain the rites to the laity.[92] Liturgical drama was integral to the Gallican liturgy.

Such connections between ritual and drama led social philosophers from Rousseau to Dilthey to Huizinga to theorize that all art had developed from communal ritual:[93] music, dance, poetry, and nature were initially part of one tribal environment. Later, stylized actors and other specialists were introduced; this deepened artistic interpretation but made the ritual more a performance than a communal creation. Greek tragedy, medieval shepherds piping in the midnight Mass with a Nativity play, Jesuit pageantry, and Lutheran Passion music had all sprung from communal cults; oratorio and opera were said to be extensions or renewals of the same experiences. But in the meantime, Calvin's Geneva and the Council of Trent, both puritanical,[94] had severed this easygoing connection between rites and arts by submitting to a Zwinglian, authoritarian aesthetic.

At the time of the French Revolution, both philosophes and Catholics had their jesuits, who were eager to use art, and jansenists, who were eager to avoid its distractions. For their part, the artists and musicians who were to serve the Revolution were ready with ideas congenial to a transvaluation of the old myths into more democratic terms. In the late eighteenth century, a French church musician, Jean-François Lesueur (1760–1837), deliberately combined the Gallican tradition of popular liturgical drama with Gluck's musical devices and the aesthetic theory of the philosophes. Lesueur and his colleagues served the Catholic, the constitutional, the republican, the Napoleonic, and the restored Catholic cults. Most important was their creation of a style for mass secular celebrations.

Lesueur had been educated by following the usual choirboy's curriculum of singing the Office between instruction in music and Latin at the Choir School of Saint Wolfram's Academy in Abbeville.[95] The great Saint Wolfram's church, even after Nazi bombs, is still a fantastic conglomerate of styles from severe Norman to lavish late Gothic. It must have been a fine stimulus to the boy's imagination. After studying the writings of Rousseau and Gluck, Lesueur concluded that composers must be left free to interpret the text rather than merely support it. Public music would be best "if composers wrote their own words."[96] Yet, like his model, Gluck, he also wrote that music which has a story to tell must portray the drama and not indulge in musical display for its own sake.[97] When Lesueur employed Gluck's "imitation," he called it "pictorial music." We call it "program music."

This marriage of liturgical drama and "pictorial," Gluckist musical style done according to Rousseau's theories, was successful enough to make an ultramontane musicologist, Felix Clément, later praise Lesueur for "restoring the liturgical drama of the thirteenth century." Though his musical means were not those of the Gregorian chant that Clément preferred, he granted that "Lesueur always put portrayal of the liturgy ahead of art for art's sake."[98]

From 1782 to 1783 Lesueur was organist at the cathedral of Mans, in whose diocese lay the priory of Solesmes. (A generation later the restored monks there would campaign against allowing contemporary music like Lesueur's in churches because they believed it was liturgical Gallicanism.) After obtaining successively improved posts through open competition, in 1785 Lesueur became director of music at the cathedral of Notre Dame de Paris, where he remained until 1787.[99] The sacred concerts which he gave there during Holy Week, when the theaters were closed, were so popular that haughty folk called them "beggars' operas."[100]

At Notre Dame, Lesueur was preoccupied with introducing popular religious songs into the development of his compositions, so that everyone could understand the message of the prescribed Latin text.[101] Never satisfied to give only the music stipulated in the liturgy, he wished his music to bring the text fully into existence without dominating it.[102] Rather than vocal tours de force, composers should create songs which follow the natural rise and fall of declamation "found in both ancient Greek and Gregorian music."[103] Like many other composers trying to reach a mass audience, Lesueur eschewed the "science of counterpoint," used simple means rather than elaborate ones, and preferred an impressive beginning to a complex development. He asserted that music to reach the common man could hope for only a poor reception unless it had words, by which he meant either a sung text or an accompanying program.[104]

In fact, it is Lesueur's teachings about "faithfully portraying the text" which make him important for the history of public music. As his pupil Hector Berlioz said, "Everything Lesueur did flowed from a body of doctrine which was at once musical, philosophic, and religious. Though these theories were unique with him, all contemporaries acclaimed their worth."[105] Since he was in tune with both the church and the Enlightenment, Lesueur believed that the true end of art is to teach and gradually to improve the human soul.[106] "In teaching, sympathy is the great method," and this, he thought, "is what music can achieve." Like Liszt, Lesueur would have called himself not a doctor of music, but a doctor of philosophy.

At the urging of his students, in 1787 he published his theories in his *Exposé d'une musique*—plans for four important festivals of the liturgical year. These plans, "unified, imitative, and specific to each solemnity," were distributed to the congregation to assist their participation. There was one stating the general principles upon which one builds the music fitted to Christmas; others gave guidelines for music for Easter, for Pentecost, and for the Assumption (15 August). Although he was still a servant of the Old Regime, he made it clear at the outset that he believed in no hierarchies among the arts. The arts, he said, "are a republic, where all lead by turns."[107] Lesueur went on to tell his pupils, "who will be composing for our temples," how to put "into their work as much poetry, painting, and expression as possible." The gist of his pamphlets is the same as that of Rousseau's article "Imitation" in the *Dictionary of Music*. Imitation in music means to elicit the same emotional response that the artist had while beholding the event itself. Of course, both Rousseau and Lesueur are enthusiasts for music. In a few sentences they do come close to saying that music, nonverbal and nonvisual though it is, can be exact enough to give the dimensions of specific events. However, one ceases to doubt their common sense when they offer illustrations—for example, how a well-placed silence in music can suggest a vivid sensation—which reassure one that they mean emotion and not automation: one's reaction to an event, not the event itself.

Lesueur's development of texts and music according to the poetic logic he called imitation had sound precedents in the evolution of the liturgy. Antiphonal songs and acclamations combined with cantorial improvisation and dialogued tropes had formed the Latin rite according to the needs and talents of each century. Localized reinterpretations are again common today, following the Second Vatican Council. However, between the Council of Trent and Vatican II, liturgical texts remained fixed while music continued to evolve. This Tridentine tradition, combined with neoclassical aesthetic doctrine and the inveterate Platonizing of seminary education, would always militate against acceptance of new musical departures. To explain himself Lesueur offered several parallels. Painters of biblical scenes often included figures not mentioned in scripture; preachers interpreted texts figuratively rather than literally; and the liturgy itself used scriptural passages in different contexts.[108] In spite of—or because of—these explanations, the authorities remained suspicious of the young innovator.

The mere existence of a church musician's published theoretical writing is evidence of a new artistic vocation. Previously musicians were sometimes illiterate and often thought incapable of reasoning. Conscious of what some titled cleric might say about an organ-pounder's keeping his place, Lesueur forestalled any surprise at a mere musician's writing books by dropping a few quotations from Cicero—a model practice for anyone aspiring to *philosophie*.[109] When Lesueur employed modal tonalities, as he frequently did, he called them classical Greek rather than medieval, as any self-respecting eighteenth-century intellectual would have done.

Like his music, Lesueur's literary style combined *philosophie* and *sensibilité*, the latter a French equivalent of Sturm und Drang, in apostrophes like "O Sensitivity, sacred fire kindled from the light of genius," or "O thou, gentle humanity, like a faithful lover, ever at the side of true genius."[110] He also combined Enlightenment classicism with romantic folklorism when he speculated that the ancient Greeks must have used music of the various sections of Greece to express various emotions, "just as we would employ German music to express strong passions, Italian music to render light and joyful sentiment, or Spanish music to portray noble or religious sentiments."[111]

Throughout his career Lesueur had applied these "principles of pictorial music" not only to paraliturgical pageants and concerts when the theaters were closed, but also to the Catholic liturgy itself in the Gallican tradition. He rearranged the required Latin text "to emphasize its poetic meaning." As he proposed in his *Exposé*, he used an idée fixe from popular religious songs "to give unity to the music of an entire service."[112] This motivic expansion led Karl Nef to call Lesueur "Beethoven's John the Baptist."

Lesueur knew that certain themes from Gregorian chant and popular hymns came with built-in associations. When describing his treatment of the Easter Mass, he explained how the music of the Gloria employed music from the Introit's *Resurrexit*, a few moments before.[113] After a prelude, "the choir of the blessed, restored to their bodily vigor, form the Redeemer's cortege and raise the hymn 'Gloria.' " In the same way, Lesueur's music for the Credo on Easter recalled the music of the Sequence, which had preceded the Credo and ended with a phrase put in the mouth of Mary Magdalene, "Surrexit Christus spes mea . . ." ("He is risen, Christ, my hope"), to which a chorus representing the disciples replied "Scimus Christum surrexisse a mortuis vere . . ." ("Christ, we know, is truly risen from the dead") to the same music.[114] Before each profession in the Credo, Lesueur recalled the Surrexit from the Sequence's final verse, "to portray an entire people responding that nothing is unbelievable since the Resurrection." To dramatize the events of the Resurrection, he added an offertory motet based on the simple and popular Gregorian Regina Coeli and full of "tumbling alleluias appropriate to a people abandoning itself to transports of joy."[115]

Music for mass or group participation, Lesueur believed, should be as clear as the didactic paintings and moralistic plays advocated by the philosophes. Like most philosophers and liturgical reformers of his day, he insisted on observing the dramatic unities. Just as Schiller, the Encyclopedists, and the Gluckists insisted that music and text be mimetically parallel in opera, Lesueur thought to revitalize these ancient principles in the Catholic liturgy. His program included a revamping education to eliminate the separation of musical and academic studies.[116]

Lesueur's career as a liturgical musician spanned the change from small, professional *scholae* of men and boys, whose whole career was absorbed in the daily round of church music, to massive music built on vast orchestras and large, volunteer, mixed choruses of citizens. These amateurs needed clearer musical and programmatic directions than the professionals had required.[117] So he gave explicit directions to assure that his interpretation of the text would be clear during the performance. For example, he headed the score of the Gloria in one Christmas Mass with a note that the composer intended "the simple joy proper to the angels as they announced the news of heaven's favors showered upon mankind." Later he inserted an encouragement to perform the work so as "to inspire everyone with religious emotion."[118] Such notes may seem superfluous, even humorous, but on the job in the choir stalls such suggestions often get the work done.

They must have done so for Lesueur, because most critics made remarks like "the listener feels the presence of the Almighty in this imposing but succinct song."[119] The critics praised his skill in achieving an effect in the echoing vaults of a great cathedral. In order to avoid rapid changes in harmony, which would blur the text, he usually used only one chord per measure. This was a technique he admired in the "majestic" Italian school of Palestrina,[120] who also used motifs from Gregorian chant. His fellow artists supported his experiments. Marie Antoinette, who may have been interested in a musician who could build royal entertainment out of folklore, promised him her chapelmastership. But his employers, the monks of the cathedral chapter, did not share her enthusiasm for him. They disliked him.

Since Lesueur was in charge of the whole musical menage at Notre Dame, he had to arrange for their eating and sleeping and for the choirboys' education, and so on.[121] Soon he was in debt. The monks of the chapter said his music cost too much; he said they never paid him his salary and expenses. Lesueur was absent-minded, fatigued, and not litigious enough to recover his due from such august personages as cathedral rectors so long as the Old Regime lasted. The cathedral chapter did pay in 1791, obeying a judgment of the National Assembly.[122]

Jealous of his success and giving heed to anonymous pamphlets against him, the monks of the chapter were receptive to the advice of "certain pious persons," who were scandalized by the orchestra and soloists in the sanctuary. They fired him when he asked for a year's leave to travel and perform in England. Other musicians refused to accept the position when they learned how Lesueur had been treated. Eventually he received a standard letter of reference which said that he had done everything he should, and done it without reproach.[123]

In the meantime, Marie-Joseph Chénier, who was to be Lesueur's commander during the fêtes of the Revolution, had offered praise *Au musicien Le Sueur* and confusion to his enemies:

> Whence spring thy vexations, child of harmony?
> What? Soldiers of slander, your enemies,
> Have set contemptible snakes to hissing against you!
> Artists without genius are treacherous, insidious.
> Happy at others' misfortunes, every success tortures them.
> They become enemies from the time when they must admire.
> What worse enemy, great gods, than a humiliated rival![124]

Chénier continued by comparing Leseuer to a half-dozen greats, Rousseau and Milton among them, who had lived in poverty while lesser men were lionized. Chénier concluded by assuring Lesueur that his songs were as pleasing to the King of Kings as David's, who had led the Hebrews against the original Philistines.

Despite Lesueur's kudos from an official republican poet-to-be, during the Revolution his enemies tried to embarrass him by nick-naming him Abbé, on account of his tonsure and former connection with the chapter of Notre Dame.[125] During the terror he was arrested "because he had made music for Jesus Christ." Although Lesueur was not so enthusiastic a republican as some other musicians, his announced goal had long been to have the people share in the artist's creation. Moreover, his musical party, the Gluckists, were in politi-cal favor; so he survived and found a place as deputy inspector of instruction in the Garde nationale. Once his friends had pulled him into public life, he continued as a music maker to the Revolution. We have noted his composition for the *Hymn for the Inauguration of a Temple of Liberty* of '93.[126]

In that same year, at the peak of the First Republic, Lesueur produced his hit horror opera, *The Cavern*, with a plot and tech-nique reminiscent of Schiller's *The Robbers*. A noble outlaw, a self-sacrificing aristocrat, a beautiful woman in captivity, disguises, love across class lines, and a spectacularly climactic brawl on stage, all set amid rough, untamed nature, created a microcosm of the actual storm and stress being enacted on the streets of Paris. The outnum-bered good men do, of course, just manage to wipe out the bad, save the beautiful woman, and the piece concludes with a churchlike chorus in praise of virtue.[127]

Lesueur's *Songs of the Triumphs of the French Revolution*, on an ode by Voltaire's friend LaHarpe, was heard in October, 1794, when the French were beating back the reactionary invaders. In 1798 Le-sueur's *Song for the Anniversary of January 21st* was performed in the church of St. Sulpice, then called the Temple of Victory. This piece was set to Lebrun's "text in the style of classical Greece," which celebrated the fifth anniversary of the new Athenians'—or Romans'—beheading their last monarch. After his *Dithyrambic Song* had helped celebrate a peace treaty in the same year, the Directory officially thanked Lesueur for his "distinguished career in the ser-vice of the Republic" and "for the glory he had helped to bring France."[128]

For the seventh birthday of the Republic in 1799, Lesueur pre-pared what a scholar of revolutionary fêtes, Julien Tiersot, has called the best of the fête music. The year before, Méhul had used three orchestras to construct a tonal monument. Lesueur now used four, each of which was to have its unique role while fitting into the whole

—democratically. Today we still hear this piece's musical descendant, the Berlioz Requiem, which also spread an ensemble of chorus and orchestra with four adjoining brass bands stereophonically beneath the dome of the same building, the Invalides, which was the Temple of Mars during the Revolution. According to a critic writing in the political journal, *Le Moniteur*, Lesueur was able to achieve a "religious and very moving effect."[129]

After the Concordat, whereby Napoleon wished to turn the reestablished Catholic cult to political use, he founded an Imperial Chapel (the term includes all music for a court, secular as well as sacred), under the direction of Paisiello, of whom Napoleon remarked, "His operas do not take my mind off important things." Lesueur was soon appointed codirector, in charge of putting revolutionary fervor into the renewed ecclesiastical cult. Napoleon emphasized the military side of everything while hiding behind religious and republican trappings, as Tacitus says the early Roman emperors had done.[130] He personally selected an architectural plan which looked "sufficiently ancient and pagan" for the Temple of Glory[131] to house his military liturgy. Then he attempted to win over artists by commissioning the Legion of Honor to include the "best of French art, music, and poetry in the annual celebration of his three great battles, Ulm, Austerlitz, and Jena.

In the emperor's service Lesueur coordinated the music of the imperial coronation and continued to compose according to the whole-making theories he had used to combine literature, music, and the dramatic arts in Notre Dame and the Temple of Mars.[132] Believing that his music was the work of a public teacher of morality and therefore worthy of public support, he appealed for government aid in mounting the elaborate Gothic opera *The Bards*.[133] This work was based upon the supposed antique epic *Ossian*, whose characters and themes were being employed throughout European art and literature to argue the virtue of primitive, "natural" peoples and culture. Soon Lesueur became the emperor's favorite musician, and he survived Napoleon's fall. Under Louis XVIII he shared the chapelmastership with the king's favorite, Cherubini, who had not served Napoleon. Charles X retained him as chapelmaster but mistrusted him as a Bonapartist.[134]

Before Lesueur died, the reactionary regime of Charles X was displaced by the bourgeois monarchy of Louis-Philippe in the revolution of 1830. Lesueur hoped that his artistic reputation would outlive succeeding political regimes. He evidently found it expedient to cover himself with the Napoleonic legend by writing as though his compositions for the coronation of Charles X were in fact for that of Napoleon twenty years earlier. True to his prerevolutionary philosophy of music, Lesueur wrote of himself as no mere lackey fulfilling an order, but as the people's artistic interpreter and a teacher above sectarianism. His "processional oratorio" contained music "for the coronation of any prince in Christendom, no matter what his communion."[135] In fact, Lesueur gave a choice of three oratorios. The first emphasized the military, the second the religious, and the third the patriarchal aspect of a coronation. There was appropriate music for the entry of every grade of dignitary, whether ecclesiastical, military, or civil; it was an Ecce Sacerdos Magnus (the hymn then specified in the Roman rite for the reception of a bishop) for secular shepherds. Lesueur also choreographed where and how the dignitaries already arrived in the chancel should stand to greet the next higher ranks as these arrived. He was practicing what he had preached in the *Exposé* of 1787 and continuing the Gallican tradition of popular drama to explain Roman pomp.

While the generation which made the Revolution still lived, Lesueur was the most popular and influential French church composer. Perhaps he reminded people of those glorious decades of conquest and revolution. Though his ideas were not completely original, he was more successful than most innovators in founding a school to practice his theories. Lesueur's most famous student, Hector Berlioz, thought that Lesueur's musical means were well adapted to antique and Hebrew themes but that his religion was stronger than his music.[136] Berlioz romantically praised Lesueur's oratorios *Debora, Rachel, Noémi,* and *Ruth et Booz,* "whose naive simplicity and restrained force differentiate them from contemporary music much as the Bible differs from modern poetry."[137]

On the other hand, pious critics continued to find Lesueur's music stronger than his religion. They were careful to condemn anyone who had served the wicked City of Man during the Revolution: of the oratorios that Berlioz praised and of Lesueur's treatment of the gospel Passions, they said, "One finds there every passion except that of Jesus Christ."[138]

Lesueur bequeathed his blend of Gallican liturgical drama, revolutionary fête, Napoleonic grandeur, and extant church styles to more pupils than Gounod and Berlioz. When the teacher died in

1837, another pupil, Ambroise Thomas, composed the music for the dedication of Lesueur's monument at Abbeville. The ceremony concluded with a festival of folk music.[139]

Another erstwhile choirmaster, who had been educated in choir schools, served the revolutionary fêtes, and later made public music for Napoleon and the restored Bourbons, was Joseph Gossec (1734–1829). Like his comrades Grétry, Méhul, and Lesueur, Gossec followed Gluck. As the musician most enthusiastically republican, he was made chief of the musical section of the Garde Nationale, forerunner of the Conservatoire. His biographers[140] claim that he founded the style which led to Berlioz and Wagner; some of his works are still played. At the time, his best-known composition was a prerevolutionary O Salutaris, cast in his preferred form of monody with choruses. Such ecclesiastical antiphony was easily recast to set revolutionary fêtes and returned to its original use after the Revolution. Of course, these musical *gardes* did not neglect to offer written descriptions of their musical intent and hinted that all composers ought to do so.

Méhul, too, persisted in the musicianly habit of using the same compositions in different liturgies. While director of *concerts spirituels* for a Parisian church in 1788, he mounted a Te Deum for massed choruses and double orchestra. Two years later he added a military band and produced the same music to celebrate The Festival of the Federation.[141] He also composed a vast Requiem. He returned some of this music to its original ecclesiastical use after the Revolution.

In sum, the musicians who had cultivated liturgical music during the last years of the Old Regime made peace with the new order over a century-and-a-half ahead of their would-be spiritual lords, the ecclesiastical hierarchy. The musicians also created a national style of art which blended high and popular culture. Their sons in art were the generation of 1830, Berlioz's; their grandsons, that of 1870, Saint-Saëns's.[142] By trying to combine the music and the aesthetic theory of the eighteenth century with the principles of 1789, they made art for the masses momentarily respectable. Whatever spontaneity the civic cult had was due to their music, which needed only a changed text in order to seem up-to-date.

Musicians were more successful than writers or workers in the static visual arts in avoiding an ideological label which would prevent their working under more than one political regime.[143] This fact may have influenced the romanticists of the next generation to think of music as the model unifying human activity.

To be freed from having to flatter clerics and nobles and become part of universal public education seemed the artist's and musician's franchise. Despite the banal music which was used to clothe much of the official rhetoric, the ultimate effect of the Revolution on musicians was beneficial. In the Greek polis music had once been gentlemanly and civic, but music's theme was now to be "brotherhood of *all* men."[144] This was a concept foreign to Periclean Athens but appropriate to music, which is not limited by political boundaries. When musicians exchanged their livery or surplice for the uniform of the Garde nationale, bureaucratic red tape might still throttle the muse, but enlarging the musician's mission to include all men helped to create the modern cult of the artist as prophet and creator. Loss of a patron's pension was compensated by the hope of being one's own man. Ultimately, artists remained the true revolutionaries, for, although the desire behind propaganda is to achieve at all costs some immediate end, the desire behind a work of art is to be faithful to a total perception of reality.

IV

On the deepest level, therefore, the revolutionary cult helped to create the idea of the artist as a hero who, relying solely on his own ability, rejects the established system to create his own better one. And so moralistic classicism was a forerunner of the romantic and existentialist vision of the Promethean rebel as an ideal human type who does not submit to an imperfect world. Because every political system is in some way repressive, it was inevitable that the pure revolutionary zeal of the angry man young at heart became attributable ultimately only to the nonpolitical artist. The genius of the Revolution went underground and emerged in, for one, Beethoven, a paradigm of the enragé in the cause of freedom.[145]

After the Revolution, composers were eager to set texts which they could interpret for the people. The humanism of Beethoven's *Ninth* and the patriotism of Berlioz's *Symphonie funèbre* remind us of revolutionary fêtes. The peasant dances in Schubert's Masses, the solemn declamation of restored Palestrinian works, and the recita-

tives—whether strascinando or secco—in authenticated Gregorian
chant were, like the fêtes, musical attempts to reconcile reasoned
text and appealing tone while reconciling the human community.
New compositions combined the politically inspired mass-music of
the Revolution with the musical methods of Beethoven and the symphonic school to form a monumental style. Even archaists like Joseph d'Ortigue and Felix Clément had to admit that this strong style
suited public celebrations. What they objected to more than its
bombastic tendencies were its revolutionary and humanistic conno-
tations.[146]

The chapelmasters who returned to their original profession after
the French Revolution were preoccupied with problems like Schiller's when they hoped to reconcile the Enlightenment's moralism
and the remaining religious traditions. Many hoped that the churches
would do what they had done before: Christianize the pagan festivals. These musicians often assumed an original identity of all the
arts in liturgical drama; this led them to form or accept theories like
Schiller's about creating a new total work of art. Public celebrations
with music, whether civic or religious, tended to take the place of
drama for its own sake. (Hence, the nineteenth century became "the
golden age of dance and song,"[147] two arts which had been the backbone of primitive liturgies and are always employed in religious
rites in stylized form.) Many nineteenth-century composers were
preoccupied with the recurring problem of liturgical music: given
the public purpose of art and the Platonic views of theologians—
whether revolutionary or reactionary—about the primacy of the text,
how does one integrate text and tone to make a whole?[148]

When syncretism with pagan cults had been unconscious, it was
slow but inevitable. In a historically self-conscious age, syncretism
would have to be deliberate. Whereas romantic historicism went
questing after several styles, which the researchers hoped were
still valid communication, the churches eventually selected only a
"uniquely Christian" art. This, they hoped, would insulate them
from an unfriendly world. Along the way, they were suspicious that
musicians who had served the pagan Revolution might be thinking
Lucifer's motto *non serviam*. In truth, once a musician had been
taken seriously, he could never go back to being "Your Grace's
humble servant" and like it. "The classical conception of man, as
servant of a static civilization governed by church and state authority, yielded to the romantic conception of the dynamic free individual, working in brotherhood with his fellows towards full self-

realization in a perfect society created by himself."[149] The choirmasters who now returned to their prerevolutionary posts believed that they had as much right to interpret the liturgy musically as clerics had to preach in it.

Yet for the artist the revolutionary era created as many problems as it solved. "If the Revolution in ideas meant the natural goodness of man, the Revolution in fact meant the supremacy of an ill-educated middle class."[150] Though the musician now had fewer ecclesiastical or aristocratic patrons, neither did he seem to fit bourgeois values. In one instance a high-minded, devoted, and financially successful musician was not considered as good a match for an English widow as her gonorrhea-ridden husband had been. *He* had been a successful brewer.[151] In short, no sooner had the artist found himself liberated from a noble or prelatic master than he found himself again in bondage, this time to bourgeois taste. Hence the discomfiture of serious musicians with both the archaists within the ossifying churches and the hacks in their own profession, who pandered to crowds interested only in the tenor's high C.[152] Thinking himself a prophet, the romantic artist set out to save the masses from themselves while preserving their folk culture. The nascent mass culture, he thought, would not be served by merely relying on manufactured "folk" expressions, for if anything, these would have more sameness than hackwork from the academy. It was Athene that he wanted, "high culture with its infinity of aspects, its luxuries, its large comprehension."[153] Art, in the romantic view, was never the average, whether of agora or academy.

In the romantic view, the artist is the aesthetic educator of the people. He rises from the people, or at any rate loves them, and uses their folk expressions as his raw material. This aesthetic education had two sides. One side was maintenance of and instruction in viable artistic traditions; the other was new creation. To a musician building a new work to express the feelings of humanity gathered in a public festival, monumental styles will seem more attractive than the bald statement of some local song or hymn, although these might provide the raw material for his expression in depth.

Beethoven's life and work were the epitome of this new thinking. His biographers thought that he was the composer who succeeded best in combining high art with something the average man could understand. Some said he was, therefore, the "best painter in music."[154] Others pointed out that, by restoring the motivic unity which had given such magnificent continuity to the liturgical polyphony of the fifteenth and sixteenth centuries,"[155] he accomplished what Lesueur intended. We know from Beethoven's writings that, if he had a creed, it was that his music was no mere meaningless addition to reality, but an effort to "make explicit, through the medium of his art, the state of consciousness evoked by his profoundest experiences."[156] Yet in his work the words of the text become secondary in order to make possible the full realization of its thought in music.

The *Missa Solemnis* transcended the Catholic liturgy while depending upon Christian ideals and musical traditions for its inspiration. The Ninth Symphony transcended the propagandistic chauvinism of the Revolutionary fêtes while depending upon the ideals of liberty, fraternity, and mass-oriented equality for its style. In other hands, the Christian and humanistic legacies were often sordidly manipulated. Napoleon prostituted revolutionary fervor to feed his personal glory; the restoration alliance of throne and altar tried to stifle revolutions by prostituting Christian beliefs to serve repressive political regimes. From the romantic viewpoint, a great artist might employ the many honorable ideals which had sprung from civilization without degrading them. The personal ideals of the romantics' favorite rebel, creator and hero, Beethoven, are not simple to define. That he was a humanist of the eighteenth century who proclaimed his Promethean independence in his life and music is common knowledge. That he believed music to be an exact though unliteral manifestation of the truth is also evident. That he became a humble man believing in the redemptive value of suffering is equally clear from his writings and music.

Beethoven's heterodoxy might be compared to that of the one Catholic writer he seems to have admired, Johann Michael Sailer.[157] The first romantic Catholic theologian, Sailer admired Beethoven's music and had written a book, *The Union of Religion and Art*. Central Europe in the wake of the Napoleonic wars felt itself in great turmoil. Sailer was attempting to combine traditional Catholic doctrine, the humanism of the Enlightenment, and the upsurge of popular religious movements responding to the stream of the Napoleonic years. Both Beethoven and Sailer probably achieved a more balanced understanding of Christianity in general and Catholicism in particular than was communicated either through the arid civil religion taught by the rationalistic clergy of the Josephin establishment or the perfervid piety preached by the Ligourian ultramontane revivalists. "Beethoven was a man who was brought up formally as a Catholic Christian and never formally renounced his Church membership, but only came at the end of his life, through misfortune and illness, to understand the close connection between the religious sentiments and often unformulated convictions of a lifetime and the fundamental teachings of the Church to which he had been for the most part indifferent or hostile.[158]

The music of Beethoven's two great choral monuments, the *Ninth* and the *Missa Solemnis,* is not a statement of this or that proposition but an expression of the state of soul that can be aroused by those beliefs—the one text humanistic, the other religious.[159] For Beethoven there was no difference. His biographers say that, ideally, the audience should join in singing the last movement of the *Ninth,* that the Gloria of his *Missa Solemnis* is an acclamation by the whole congregation,[160] and that the Finale of the *Ninth* should be a shout, not a meticulous dissection of high A.[161] Beethoven wanted to appeal to the multitude, "for he felt the need to communicate his ideas to the masses and to make music a factor in the cultural life of humanity."[162] He wrote that his primary intention in writing the *Missa Solemnis* was to express religious sentiment and impart it to the hearers.[163] His treatment was too individual and too humanistic to be contained within any sectarian liturgy, but it is superior to the safe, inexpressive music with which the church intended to replace such work and to the frivolous music by which the church does replace it.

Ecclesiastical rejection of a Beethovenian vocation for music presaged resigned contemplation of an antiworldly goal and rejection of faith in human possibility. Though Beethoven's first Mass had shown a naïve acceptance of ecclesiastical dogma, the second, the *Solemnis,* showed a more critical interpretation. The first fitted the rubrics, the second did not.[164] To perform or appreciate the latter demands a wider outlook than mere adherence to the tenets of a certain sect or church.[165] "In Beethoven's fugues and Masses the most diverse hearers have found symbols of their own innermost conviction not knowing or caring whether the composer was Catholic, Protestant, or agnostic. Music in short remains exact but unliteral."[166] Or as Joseph d'Ortigue, a pious but understanding critic, was to put it, "Those who see only a musician in Beethoven are badly mistaken: the musician is pedestal for the poet, and I might add for the philosopher."[167] Nevertheless, liturgists and theologians began to say of all artists what one of their number said of Beethoven: "There is nothing religious about him. In vain would one seek an attitude of

prayer in his two Masses."[168] A more plausible criticism would have
been Wagner's statement that one must consider Beethoven's work
in historical perspective and realize that the composer was naïvely
trying to reform society.[169]

Beethoven was the greatest writer of music for humanistic liturgies. Berlioz, Liszt, Mendelssohn, Mahler, and the whole romantic
galaxy freed themselves from old liturgical forms only in order to
create new ones expressing reformed mystical or social ideals.[170]
Appropriately, a popular subject in these musical monuments to the
City of Man was the Faust legend, though the urge to blend Hellenistic with Christian humanism often brought forth a Faust redeemed in a religious coda. Mahler's Eighth Symphony, for example,
would combine humanism and religion by taking a theme from the
Veni Creator as musical raw material for the final scene about
Faust.[171] In short, we find that the romanticists produced their best
work within the rubrics of neither traditional religious rites nor the
stage. But they were at work on liturgies and drama.

Among those who carried forward the Revolution in music, Hector Berlioz (1803–69) "was a successful Lesueur, as Lesueur was
an unsuccessful Berlioz."[172] Both said they were Gluckists, but Lesueur carried Gluck's proposals to their logical conclusion, thus
making some of his music unintelligible without the program. Berlioz
often wrote his own texts but refrained from making music the
servant of the book and followed Gluck's common-sense compromise
between the two arts. Berlioz's works are primarily musical experiences.

Teacher Lesueur and pupil Berlioz both disliked the piano, which
had been an introspective, salon instrument descended from the
clavichord. Both were often musically—and verbally—blunt, as were
the revolutionary fêtes. This, they said, was because they were more
at home in church or concert hall, where belief and music spoke,
than in salon or opera, where vocal pyrotechnics dominated. Berlioz
continued Lesueur's practice of giving detailed musical directions to
assure concerted action among his battalions of performers; both
used "antique" modes to affect styles outside those normal in western
music.[173] Both avoided counterpoint for its own sake, because they
thought it an academic show unsuited to church or other music intended for a mass audience. Though Berlioz disclaimed his teacher's
admiration for "the majestic Italian school," he was a musical cousin
of Palestrina in spite of his contempt for the archaism which would
make Palestrina the mold for church composers. For Berlioz was

closer to Palestrina's than to Haydn's harmonic methods, modulating
as he did by means of common tones rather than by diminished
sevenths, as did the German school. His zeal to construct musical
phrases which would clarify and dramatize the thought behind a
text also corresponded to Palestrina's intention to strip away vocal
display so that he could enhance the Catholic liturgy according to
the demands of the Counter Reformation.

But whereas Lesueur, a first-generation revolutionary, had trusted
popular judgment implicitly, Berlioz learned to have little faith in
the bourgeoisie, their king, or the nascent mass audience.[174] Like his
teacher and so many other artists and musicians, Berlioz was not
wholly committed to either of the two Frances.

> Neither in his friendships, writings, or musical subjects did Berlioz
> ally himself with Right or Left. He loathed politics. . . . His style,
> like his subjects, transcends the political and social divisions of
> France.
>
> To particularize: he was reared on the Catholic liturgy and
> southern folksongs and therefore wrote a great deal of sacred
> music whose melodic idiom reflects both these sources. Indeed, he
> included religious and pastoral themes and scenes in almost all
> his works. This was enough to make an anti-clerical government,
> such as that of the Third Republic, consider him a man of the
> Right and boycott him as such. He received no favors from the
> Second Empire, yet he had not gone into exile with the Republi-
> cans: he had remained a musician. Meanwhile the Right, thinking
> of Berlioz's lifelong willingness to compose "music for the masses,"
> to celebrate the July Revolution or the Napoleonic ideal, were
> bound to class him with the men of the Left. Besides, the origi-
> nality and antiacademicism visible in all he wrote did not recom-
> mend him to the would-be upholders of conventional order.
>
> The clinching argument was Berlioz's part in the Romantic
> movement. . . . All joined in repudiating a style they found too
> exuberant, vivid, and dramatic.[175]

Richard Wagner would wrestle with the problem of creating his own
festivals of the supreme being; he also knew how to find his competition's weaknesses. Either out of a zeal for truth or for the chance
to condescend, Wagner said of Berlioz:

> No one can deny him the power to compose works that are wholly
> popular: I say "popular" in the best sense of the word. When I
> hear the symphony that he wrote for the commemoration of the
> victims of the July Revolution, I felt most vividly that every urchin

in a blue blouse and a red cap would understand it—a kind of
understanding which for my part I should call "national" rather
than popular.[176]

Like his *Symphonie funèbre et triomphale* and his favorite work,
the Requiem, Berlioz's Te Deum showed its revolutionary background. Since he was afraid that the archbishop of Paris would forbid the performance of so grandiose a work in a church, Berlioz
wrote his brother-in-law, Marc Suat, to make sure that he publicized
it as religious art, not a concert.[177] The archbishop's fears were correct: at the same time as the Catholic Church was immuring itself
to escape the Revolution, musicians were assuring that their revolutionary tradition did not end in a cul de sac but continued to
develop.[178] Art and its makers are notoriously hard to control, it
seems to rulers. So pious critics had to remind composers not to
follow Berlioz's bad example: they should stay away from "materi-
alist—dramatic—passionate—worldly" music![179] In truth, artists, ultimately men of talent only, are subtle revolutionaries.

Another extension of the revolutionary musical influence was planning for rites which would combine traditional Christianity with
revolutionary humanism. In 1834 Franz Liszt published a manifesto
On the Future of Church Music. His theme was that the church had
lost touch with civilization. Instead of Christianizing and using the
best of modern culture to attract its leaders and their followers, the
church either issues anathemas or accepts cheap imitations which
show no ability to do anything constructive.

Liszt's plan reads as though it expanded the one which Lesueur
had published in 1787: combine liturgy, drama, and music in a
church style which would enlarge the minds of the congregation
while it drew them into the church. Kings and gods have fallen, he
said, their places claimed by the people sovereign under God. Since
God and the people will now be the source of music, let us not lose
confidence—Liszt and his friends were disgusted with the Bourgeois
King's financial indifference to the arts—but recognize our mission
to teach all men to know the best. "Humanistic music is what we
need. This new music should be mystical, forceful, and readily intelligible. It should unite theater and church in one great synthesis
which is at once dramatic and holy, solemn and plain, joyful and
serious, passionate and restrained, stormy and restful, clear and
mystical."[180] Liszt used the *Marseillaise* as an example of the type

of music he hoped would replace the pompous and silly show tunes heard in most churches. His friend Berlioz had just orchestrated the *Marseillaise*, calling not for tenors or basses but for every living thing to join in the chorus.[181]

Liszt proposed to campaign for the best art in churches, so that artists would be attracted to serve the church and thereby educate the public. Churches and governments should sponsor music festivals, give musical instruction in their schools, and restore dignity to the honored chapelmasterships, which formerly had supported musicians in the service of the church. The public should be encouraged to form philharmonic societies like those in England and Germany. There ought to be public lyric theaters and concerts, chairs of applied music and musicology at universities, definitive editions of musical masterworks, and leaders for the whole enterprise formed in a school less hidebound than the Conservatoire had become. But, alas, Louis Philippe's clique was interested only in assuring itself a profitable place, and the church was disendowed and afraid.[182] Archaism and banality, Liszt thought, are the symbols of the church's alienation from today's people, art, and life.

Liszt was introduced to the Catholic visionary Lamennais by the devout music critic Joseph d'Ortigue. They visited together at La Chênaie in 1834, during the time when Guéranger was reactivating the Benedictines of Solesmes and the Saint-Simonians were on their apostolic journeys. Liszt, though he was a self-made Grand Seigneur, always had had more sympathy with revolutionary and democratic movements—he liked "Abbé" Joseph Mainzer's pop festivals—than did Berlioz, whose career had been disturbed by revolutions and who had been vilified by the crowd-pleaser Mainzer. Liszt, whose social philosophy had been Saint-Simonian, became a Mennaisian. The year of his conversion was the year of his manifesto on religious music as the basis of mass culture.[183] It was also the year he foreswore recitals for the first time in order to quit being the virtuoso "merry Andrew of the drawing room." From Lamennais he was pleased to hear that music's function is "to divine human sentiment wherever it may occur," and that the regeneration of art is regeneration of society.[184] In 1835 Liszt dedicated an instrumental De profundis to his friend saying, "The theme preserves the plainsong that you like so much."[185]

Liszt and Lamennais were philosophically complementary. In Lamennais's eyes, Liszt was the heroic ideal of the artist; for Liszt, Lamennais was the high priest of imagination who looked for social

regeneration in the regeneration of the arts through their collaboration with the Christian religion.[186] Both men had an ambivalent
attitude toward modern culture, but Liszt's ambivalence between
romanticism and ultramontanism came consecutively rather than
contemporaneously.

Thirty years after the introduction, Liszt would say, "From the
time I met Lamennais I was inspired to give up mere virtuosity for
education, charity, and Wagnerism" (which in church music meant
archaism).[187] But Liszt's aesthetics remained more progressive, more
Mennaisian, than his religious music. This is evident from a comparison between two critiques of Raphael's painting *Saint Cecilia* (see
page 257), one written by Liszt, the other by a thoroughgoing ultramontane Catholic, Paul Charreire. Their analyses contrast the romantic and the strict classical definition of an artist.

Liszt's critique, written in 1852 when the romantic youth had
long matured, still exalted the inspired musician Cecilia and hinted
that the preachers, saints Augustine and Paul, envy her success.
Saint John, "the disciple whom the Lord loved," stands watching,
"chastened and purified." Only the symbol of sensuality, Mary Magdalene, seems to dare to be frankly edified by the music's tonal
richness.[188] Magdalene invites the spectator to join her.

Charreire, writing on the same picture ten years later, thought it
was Saint Cecilia, not the Fathers, who was doing the listening.
Though their mouths are closed, Charreire thought that Saint Paul
was revealing true dogma and Saint John was telling her the Golden
Rule. Charreire declared that true music eschews all identification
with sensual passion, "and consecrates itself without reserve, chaste
priestess of the ideal." Music is called a priestess, but she is servant
not exemplar.[189] She may steady the neoplatonic ladder for man but
does not climb it first.

One might compare the puritan distaste of many critics—ecclesiastical and otherwise—for the monumental, romantic, or revolutionary style to those old-fashioned guidebooks which said that Bernini was "a fine artist but he is too exuberant, too restless, strives
for originality too much, and strains to catch our attention."[190] As
far as such critics were concerned, the romantics' capital sin was
to bring the French Revolution, where the people or their surrogate,
the artist, and not just privileged clerics, were the actors, into the
church. The churches, like the classicists, wanted only humble "handmaidens of theology." Artists thought that liberty, fraternity, and
equality meant freedom to fulfill their design. Musicians failed to

create a new ecclesiastical art which would combine high standards with broad appeal not because they were theatrical or aloof. They failed because in fact the clergy preferred light opera—the top-forty music of its day—to either "passionate, individualistic" Beethoven or "passionless, impersonal" Palestrina.

On the secular side, the revolution in music continued in several ways which were part of a tendency to believe in the artist as an incorruptible hero. There were two obvious results: patriotic celebrations with their mass-singing of nationalistic songs, and the ever-larger marching bands which grace holiday liturgies such as athletic games and parades. An almost infinite number of subtle influences as old as Plato were reinforced by the Revolution: the continuing artistic and popular quest for theatrical happenings which combine all the arts as symbols of a reintegrated psyche and society; the belief that social revolution will be accomplished under a radical change of artistic styles which will be more popular and therefore more democratic; the belief that somehow the new styles of song and dance are getting back to "nature"; that new model human communities must have their own style or artistic language; that public aesthetic education is necessary and desirable in a democracy; that certain past styles are models which ought to be revived; and that God and the people are one.

Before turning to the public cults of the nineteenth century, let us return to the eighteenth to examine the more conservative societies of the European continent and see the same revolutionary forces at work. In the Germanies, Austria, Spain, and Italy we shall see a less radical transvaluation of old religions into new secular mythologies than in France. Yet the attempt to reform and recover a classical, purified Christianity and communicate it to the masses was a cultural revolution as important as the one in France.

GOD IN MAN'S NEW IMAGE

Religious Rites as Mass Media During the Enlightenment

3

Everywhere among the most forceful and frequent advertisements of the privileges and presuppositions guarding the old hierarchical society were rituals once venerated because of dogma or tradition. Merely to touch, let alone to abolish, these ancient liturgies was to communicate a revolutionary idea of the universe and man's place in it.

Because the events of the eighteenth century were a single revolutionary movement, the impulse to reform the Christian and Jewish cults was like the one that urged the French revolutionaries to liquidate the Middle Ages. However different in various countries and situations, a revolution was everywhere aimed against forms of special privilege and closed systems that seemed no longer to serve any useful purpose. Immanuel Kant epitomized the critical humanism at work even within the established churches when he said of religious rites, "Since there is nothing man can give God, there is no particular duty we owe to God."[1] Therefore, the goal of a cult must be found on earth, in the education and edification of man. Because ritual is not an essential of religion but an accident, the best rites will be formed not by tradition or divine mandate, but by reasoned investigation.[2]

The dramaturgists of the French Revolution achieved a new myth and cult of earthly fulfillment by teaching citizens to know, love, and serve their nation-state. Outside France during its Revolution and Empire, conditions were often quite different. In the Hapsburg Empire, Poland, Spain, Italy, Scandinavia, the Catholic Germanies, among the Catholics in Protestant North America, and among Jews, it was still unthinkable to abolish the traditional cult in favor of a rationalistic and nationalistic civic religion.

Among these peoples the intellectual and cultural life remained more closely united to formal Christianity and Judaism. Hence reform of religious practice is the history of the Enlightenment as it penetrated the minds of the common folk. In the Catholic Germanies of the late eighteenth century the contest between the old supernatural and the new natural view of things was especially lively because it was fairly equal. Elsewhere the contest was not equal.[3] The Catholic Germanies are, therefore, a surveyor's benchmark ideologically midway between revolutionary France and medieval—or rather Counterreformation—Spain and Italy.

The first attempts to communicate a modernized religion among Jews and Catholics outside France were deliberately rationalistic and nationalistic. In fact, orthodox theologians turned out to be far more rationalistic than contemporary secular philosophers. Similarly, the theologians were more nationalistic than the philosophers; for, as Christianity ceased to support feudalism, it hastened to assist the inculcation of nationalism.

I

When in the 1700s the clergy saw natural replacing revealed religion, they fought back. Yet, since the clergy were literate—and perhaps also educated—men of the eighteenth century, the methods which they used to combat the growing skepticism of their age were usually those of the new philosophy itself: religion should be made clear, rational, and nonmystical.[4] In this spirit the clergy of every western religion criticized rituals which were formerly privileged by being thought holy in themselves. The clergy within were not alone, for old liturgical habits were being undermined from without in a hundred ways. Governmental decrees, secularized education, the revolutionary and Napoleonic wars which interrupted traditions and brought didactic civic rituals to people formerly content with worship as community recreation, the industrial revolution which broke the old daily and seasonal routines that underlay the liturgical year, and myriad other exchanges of secular for ecclesiastical influence ended, at last, the Middle Ages.

The older and more venerable the liturgical habits of a church, the more radical were the reforms proposed in favor of simpler, national, and didactic rites. The most radical proposals for liturgical reform came from enlightened Catholics, because they found so much to criticize within the elaborate structure of rites whereby their church meant to interpret and sanctify every human act. Moreover, the Roman rite, being the very bones of the Middle Ages, was "irrational." It was a conglomerate tradition established in the pontificate of Gregory I during the dark ages after Christianity had subverted the Hellenistic culture admired by humanists. By then the medieval pope had long replaced the Roman emperor as head of the official cult; only now the cult was intolerant. The Roman rite had continued its haphazard cultural imperialism until the Council of Trent, when the aimless syncretism of the Middle Ages was petrified in canon law, the Justinian code of ultramontane Catholicism.[5]

So, in every Catholic land, writers now condemned the Gregorian liturgical books "which bear the name of a pope and teach ultramontanism to the younger clergy."[6] Enlightened priests argued that the Common of the Saints[7] taught superstition, "for there is no proof that most of those names published by the Curia did anything worth admiring; indeed, monastic saints, even the authentic ones, are useless examples for modern men."[8]

The argument over the value of religious traditions and celebrations was sharpest over music and all it stood for. Like the philosophes, enlightened Christians believed that music and all art when used in public celebrations ought to assist the teaching of proper morals and the training of good citizens. Since music contained scant moral nourishment in itself, its function should be to season moralistic and civic preaching in order to make it more palatable. Music and art which took a congregation's mind off these objectives must be subordinated or eliminated.

By applying to the various Opera Dei the same criteria which the encyclopedists applied to the secular art form opera, ecclesiastical critics found melismatic, Latinate music reprehensible. Whether it was in the fashionable Italian style or in ancient Gregorian chant, it was useless! What ethical culture did it impart? "Let this expensive and domineering musical contraption yield to more reverent prayers and songs which the people can understand. Let us have no more aphrodisial sopranos or touchy castrati. Rather, give us respectable people to enrich our worship and improve the hearts and souls of our people."[9] Those are the words of a moderate, Franz Xaver

Turin, who became an editor of the most-used and copied German Catholic prayer and hymn book during the Aufklärung, the *Mainz Hymnal* (*Mainzer Gesangbuch*). He believed both in a vernacular, didactic Catholic liturgy and in papal primacy. Although he would later curse the "atheistical French" for singing the *Marseillaise* in German churches, he was a German influenced by French thought.

Although Catholic theologians wanted to enrich their liturgy with lessons in brotherhood and tolerance, Catholic theories about human liberty, fraternity, and equality were hampered by a clerical and hierarchical liturgical tradition whose elaborate music and pomp seemed to reinforce a retrograde division of the Christian community into clerical professionals and lay outsiders. It seemed that if Catholicism were ever to regain a pristine community of love, its rites and music should follow the Protestant lead and harken back to primitive Christianity. Protestant theologians seemed better able to rationalize their liturgical tradition without contradicting it. "Preaching the Word," witnessing to personal religious experience, and explaining natural theology suited the anticlerical, nationalistic, and democratic trends of the eighteenth century even more than they had suited the Reformers of the sixteenth. Theologians of both centuries idealized the same golden age, Biblical Christianity. If Protestant apostles of enlightenment now warned that the church of Jesus had "no mission to produce art critics, because the more artistic music becomes, the fewer it reaches,"[10] Catholics agreed. Less elaborate music would give the Word a better chance to reach everyone. As with the neo-pagans outside the churches, so too within them a rededication to a useful and beloved antiquity seemed inseparable from modernity. Many Christians welcomed this trend because it seemed to promise a return to the golden age of Christianity before Caesar's heir, Constantine, had subverted the church to a department of state.

Reformers in any tradition often declare that they will repristinate while renewing. This is a classicism. Another is admiration for styles which emphasize simplicity, purity, and order. Enlightened reformers combined admiration for evangelical simplicity, Aristotelian dramatic unities, and Cartesian clarity. Thus they united Christian with pagan classicisms. In order to recover the simplicity of Christianity's classical period, theologians in all European religions rewrote their liturgies according to the unities of classical drama as described by Aristotle and interpreted by seventeenth- and eighteenth-century aestheticians. According to their dicta, good taste in anything from urban planning to cooking demands a clearly evident unifying theme

The Old South Meeting House, Boston, exemplifies the affinity between the architectural styles of Protestantism and those of the Enlightenment. The simple design and decor is intended to facilitate the hearing and consideration of the Word, rather than mystical ceremonies and worship. (Courtesy of Old South Associates, Boston.)

with variations to suit the peculiar moment. Such ideas, analogous to the Aristotelian dramatic unities of time, place, and action, were applied by liturgical theorists speaking about unities of text, action, and place.

Unity of text required that each service have a moralistic theme with variations. Unity of action meant that only one thing was to go on at a time. Unity of place meant that the architecture should focus one's attention on the unified action. The theorists proposed to alter Christian practice according to these deliberately neoclassical anti-Gothic precepts.

"In order to win the emotions for the intellect," as Kant put it, the liturgical editors first proceeded to replace rambling traditional services with rites built around a single didactic theme, unity of text. The published experiments usually began with an introductory essay tying the proposed reforms to the systematic theology of the day.[11] The authors reasoned that Christians must abandon the "pagan and Hebrew" notion of God as an eastern potentate, and must adopt instead the Christian image of a father, whose family we are, and whose rite, the Eucharist, symbolizes a meal of the family of man, not the supine awe of subjects for a "king of kings."[12] Next, the writers found their model for democratic rites in the simple congregational singing of the primitive Christian church. They then set about dismantling the existing "imperial" rites by editing hymnals and service books so that tunes and texts both taught and obeyed rational rules, the better to inculcate rational morality.

There was a practical reason for turning continental church music into simple community singing. The contemporary secularization of church property, together with the advent of more civil and fewer ecclesiastical schools, meant that many religious institutions would no longer have the resources to support elaborate musical establishments. Hence, zeal for a democratic and didactic liturgy augmented an unwillingness or an inability to train and support musicians who could perform music which required professional talents like the ability to decipher thorough-bass at sight. Beginning in the late eighteenth century, one written-out accompaniment sufficed for all verses, and tune books eschewed any hint of an instrumental interlude between verses. Note-values were equalized throughout the hymn. In short, there was no longer any attempt musically to interpret the sentiment behind the words; the tune became a vehicle to carry the text, and no more.[13]

Meanwhile, musicians ceased to rely upon the ecclesiastical choir schools[14] for training and employment because there were now more interested secular patrons of art—both noble and bourgeois. A chapelmaster might now never set foot in his prince's choir loft. In turn, when the enlightened princes began to make education a state concern, they usually dropped the choir schools, whose exclusively Latin and musical curriculum seemed to serve only the clergy, who were the civil ruler's competitors. Consequently, both the demand for and supply of professional church musicians declined relative to the demand for secular music.

The chorale tunes which were to be the musical backbone of a congregationally sung worship were rationalized with regular measures, evenly scanned lines, and didactic texts. Since the oldest chorales had preceded measured music, they lacked those attributes which neo-classicists now said made a hymn: four eight-measure phrases setting rhymed couplets. The classicists therefore stretched archaic patterns of speech to fit modern grammatical paradigms, cut or padded tunes to fit regular meters, and replaced imagery with logic. One *Aufklärer* was sure that common men would be confused by the image of more than one sun in "He [God] will touch the suns with fire." He dared to support his contention with quotations from Herder, who never would have tampered with the old chorales.[15] To assure that no one would drift into meditation or daydreaming, reformers modernized the tunes by translating the semibreves and minims into eighths and sixteenths. So while the liturgiologists were casting dance and opera-inspired music from their temples, they made the chorales obey the rhythmic conventions of the new music they banned.[16]

When in 1791 the Duke of Württemberg introduced in his domains a "corrected" hymnal for Protestants, they complained that it would "make them Catholics" because it had some hymns by Catholic authors. Christmas carolers found that if they used the new books, their tips were small indeed.[17] Catholics worried over the protestantizing danger of the "corrected" hymnals given them. A Lutheran minister, writing in the *Liturgisches Journal* for 1806, treated the question of how one ought to introduce enlightened hymnals and prayerbooks among one's congregation by recommending that preachers proceed "according to the intelligence of their congregations."[18] But above all, he said, the clergy must do their duty by requiring the spread of enlightenment and morality.

"Faith comes by hearing," Saint Paul had said. Would not too much singing and music-making tire out the congregation for the all-important sermon? Listening to music would only obscure the service's unity, for the average person would only "waste whatever time he spent listening to music in daydreaming." Music was an unnecessary ornament in serious business. For example, in order to avoid "too much singing, which becomes superstitious incantation," Evangelical churches discarded those vestiges of Gregorian chant with Latin texts which Luther had retained. A few Evangelical liturgists would have retained the chant with German texts in the most solemn Lutheran ceremony, the *Abendmahl* (Lord's Supper). As in Luther's time, most Evangelical reformers took the simplifying and Germanizing route. They changed the sung dialogue between minister and people from Gregorian chant to phrases from German chorales.[19]

However, simplifying and biblicizing was not always democratic, as we shall see. From the throne and stagelike pulpits which dominate the east end of churches built during the late eighteenth century, the clergy dominated Protestant services more completely than it has before or since.[20]

Protestants might find such rationalization merely an extension of their tradition. Within the Roman Catholic Church such reforms were radical, for the Catholic Church officially recognized scant popular participation in its liturgy. Indeed, holding its rites in Latin meant that strictly speaking it had no "hearing of the Word." Vernacular readings and sermons, though sometimes delivered within, were technically outside the Mass. Still, local synods began to adopt the dicta of eighteenth-century theologians and decreed that *logos*, which they translated narrowly as "preaching," must take precedence over the *ethos*, "tradition," "as it did in the cult of the Apostles."[21]

The liturgists now looked for vernacular hymns wherewith to sing the new liturgy. Those Catholic hymns which had precedents in the Latin rite were retranslated with a twist which moved them from the Hebrew to the Greek side of Christian theology. Those outside the canonical rites were metamorphosed into lessons in social ethics.

The hymns with precedents in the Roman rite were those directly connected with the Mass and Eucharist or the sacramental system. Few new eucharistic hymns dared to treat the Mass in Zwinglian fashion as a memorial rather than a reenactment. Consequently, Catholic reformers' proposals resembled those offered recently after

Vatican II: they dropped redundant prayers which obscured the unity of the Mass and shortened long texts. The proposed outlines of the Mass also retained its three traditional parts—offertory, consecration, and communion. Johann Baptist Hirscher was supposed to be a "radical," yet in his *Missae in genuinam notionem formula composita,* published in the 1780s, he expressed orthodox thinking on the Eucharist: "Everything in a well-planned Mass should be arranged to make the eucharistic idea dominant."[22]

Hymns which followed the yearly liturgical cycle remained close to its supernatural dogmas. Christmas carols were often adjusted to point moral lessons drawn from the youth of Jesus, but he was still referred to as the God-man. Passiontide hymns spoke less of cosmic atonement and more of lessons to be learned from Christ's suffering; however, this is as Jesuit as it is Protestant. Easter hymns remained jubilation, close to the spirit of the Latin liturgy.[23]

Nevertheless, a didactic purpose could find its way even into the highly controlled texts of the Mass. For example, the more Greek than Hebrew bent of Enlightenment theology is apparent in a translation (here retranslated into English) of the Prayers at the Foot of the Altar, which began Mass.

> Lord, may now Thy omnipresence uplift our prayers.
> Joyfully shall we sing of Your Kindness.
> Your truths alone be in our thoughts.[24]

The Latin text used in the Mass read

> Deus tu conversus vivificabis nos,
> Et plebs tua laetabitur in te.
> Ostende nobis Domine misericordiam tuam,
> Et salutare tuum da nobis.[25]

Note how *misericordiam et salutare*—mercy and redemption—was translated as "truths"!

In the Catholic hymns less closely bound up with the official liturgy, the didactic trend was not variant but dominant. Any local pastor could easily fit a rhymed sermon to some familiar tune and have it sung at a paraliturgical service. Here the congregation would be less likely to resist a change than in the words of the official liturgy, which in turn was of a piece with the elaborate music built around the Latin. Moreover, "subjective," paraliturgical devotions and hymns had been more popular during the preceding baroque-pietist period than "objective" hymns about God, salvation, and the like. Catholics were therefore used to paraliturgical hymns narrating personal religious experiences. Thanks to this tendency, the Enlightenment successfully merged its didactic purpose with popular custom.

Among new hymns outside the Mass and sacraments, those to the Blessed Virgin venerated her less as a mystical and spiritual mother and more as an example of Christian morality and bourgeois devotion to duty. From the hymnal *Daughter of Zion* (*Tochter Sion*), which exemplified the waxing Enlightenment style in other of its hymns, here is an example of the waning baroque-pietist style of Marian hymn, a miracle narrative and lyrical laud:

> Ye winds and gentle breezes,
> Come and spread your wings—
> Carry the mother of our Lord
> Into Zachary's house.
> Ye hills and dales, everywhere,
> Be adorned in fine array
> To honor her today with sprays of flowers.[26]

A Marian stanza from Werkmeister's *Constance Hymnal* (*Konstanzer Gesangbuch*) of 1812,[27] edited while the bishop there was Napoleon's appointee, exemplifies a more "enlightened" style:

> Let us sing and praise the virtues,
> The glories of Mary.
> With her grace, let us strive
> For honor and reward in heaven.
> May her life encourage us to follow her
> Joyfully on the path of virtue.

If Mary seemed more of a stoic, lesser saints followed her example. Pious legends and pleas for intercession had been the principal types of hymns to the saints. Such hymns do not appeal to those theologians who debunk legends and teach reliance on human effort. A call to duty or a recital of worthy accomplishments often joined rhapsodizing about heavenly bliss.[28] Here is one which could be sung of any saint:

> We praise in holy hymns and songs
> The saints who, fighting for the truth,
> Untiring, when duty called,
> In endless strife, triumphantly marched forward,
> Victorious, in bloody sacrifice.[29]

Hymns which combined personal religious experience with an
ethics lesson included Werkmeister's *Jesus, Our Example*, which had
few precedents in Hebrew or Christian rites: It was a tolerance
hymn, a *Candide* for the pious.

> A Christian's joy and duty it is
> To always, and without conceit,
> Show love for one's neighbor
> Whoever he may be
> A Moslem, Jew or Heathen
> He is a man like me,
> And often better still than many a Christian.[30]

He also included a civic hymn to exhort respect for oaths taken
before the law and a hymn to instill willingness to serve.

> While others lament,
> May I never ask: What will it profit me?
> Before I lend a helping hand.
> O God, in Your image,
> Grant me gentle kindness
> And fervent charity.[31]

The same hymnal had a hymn on one's duty to animals—very practical in those days—and two warnings against superstition. The first
went, in part:

> Too much credence Neighbor Martin gives
> To sorcery and witchcraft and such things;
> He paints three crosses on the wall
> To banish evil spirits thus, he thinks.
> Who would not laugh at that?[32]

The second antisuperstition hymn was more general. Its fifth stanza
spoke of apparitions:

> No one, once Death has taken him away,
> Has been allowed to reappear on earth.
> Scripture and reason tell us: No![33]

The editor hoped that students would help to spread his ideas by
making and distributing copies of hymns by him and other authors
with the same ideals. Their hopes for a Christian Enlightenment are
summed up in a change proposed for the Litany of the Saints, which
is part of the liturgy for the Resurrection (then Holy Saturday morning) and some other solemn days of the church year. The Latin in-

vocation "That you may bring low the enemies of holy Church" should become "That you may give us the grace to love our enemies."[34]

By disposing of accretions to Christianity since its first, underground centuries, the Enlightenment wished to make the ethical message of the gospel stand out in its pristine simplicity and unity. Once the way back to the original integrity of Christianity was cleared, the reformers hoped to apply its principles in everyday life.

Complementary to their quest for unity and simplicity, the reformers sought to enliven their rites with variety. "To make Christianity relevant in all situations for all types of people" meant to avoid "dulling repetition of mechanical devotions which are the essence of priestcraft, for morality and religion cannot be taught *ex opere operato*" (automatically, whenever the sacramental formula is spoken).[35]

Catholic classicists worked to end the "aimless repetition" in the Roman missal, wherein a few Masses from the Common of the Saints sufficed for most days not Sundays or major festivals. The prayers and readings from the Common spoke in general terms about "loving justice and hating iniquity" or declared that "the souls of the just are in the hands of God." The reformers wished that such "vague repetition" would yield to more pointed Propers with lessons on specific ethical and philosophical themes. Among the festivals which apostles of Enlightenment would have added to a German Catholic missal were some which contemporary French liturgists like Robespierre were making major festivals in their civic cults.[36] Among these were celebrations to honor the state, peace, and education, or to explain ideas from natural religion, such as "the Unity of God" and "the Rational Order of the Universe."[37] The inflexible canon of the Roman Mass was to be loosened in favor of daily changes to point moral lessons. In every Mass, the climax of popular participation would be a principal hymn written specifically for the occasion and sung in place of the Preface and its response, the Sanctus.

New hymns with lessons for everyday situations were to replace the old poetical or generalized songs which had been bound to the yearly liturgical cycle. One new hymn encouraged workmen to do their best so that specie would remain in their home city or country. Another warned mothers that uneducated lads grow up to be vagrants.[38]

Strange to say, these dourly practical songs were immediately related to the lyrical side of Christianity. Though one might look for their ancestors in the florid songs of the Jesuits or other propaganda during the Counterreformation, a first cousin was the "home and hearth" hymnody of bourgeois pietism.

Roman Catholic pietism was and is usually manifested in para-liturgical devotions like pilgrimages or the veneration of a favorite saint where theological correctness yields to heartfelt sentiment. In the baroque and rococo eras one could still meet courtly knights on a personal quest for the Lord:

> In heat and cold,
> In field and countryside,
> In silent woods
> My bugle sounds.
> With effort and pain
> I hunt the deer—
> I, your faithful servant,
> O Diana![39]

After several chivalrous verses (and references to Diana), each with an echo chorus, our courtier reached his goal—the infant Jesus and his mother! A more prosaic call to pilgrimage came from the late eighteenth century:

> Make ready to pray,
> Ye pious hosts of pilgrims.
> We are in great need
> And not devoid of danger.[40]

To insure that Christianity be useful in all situations, some apostles of enlightenment went beyond moral advice. A Catholic prayerbook of 1791 added "advice for the practical life," which included recommendations about what to do in a storm or fire and precautions to help preserve one's health or alleviate pains and toothaches—if right living did not forestall them.[41]

Thus pietistic personal religion and rationalistic demands for instructional religious rites touched. Such homely piety was, of course, not a comfortable ally of the rationalistic theology. Pietism found the rhetorical *trivium* of the Enlightenment less attractive than the deliberate lyricism which the romanticists would use in their attempts at mass education through religious rites. For all—*Aufklärer*, pietist, and romantic—music and the imaginative side of life was what Luther had said it was, a kind of school of virtue (*eine Art Tugend-schule*), but each gave that definition his own peculiar twist. To popularize the Enlightenment and keep Christianity alive, the eighteenth-century theologians sometimes combined the pietistic first person singular and anthropomorphism with Newtonesque, academic, and Latinized German in metaphors like:

My Jesus knows how to
Add and multiply,
Even where
There are but noughts.[42]

It was an uncomfortable marriage.

"Unity of text" organized Christian rites around a moralistic theme; "variety of text" applied the moralizing to concrete situations. But it was "unity of action" which occasioned the most conflict over using the liturgy to popularize the Enlightenment. "Unity of action" intended to teach brotherhood by uniting all present in the communal rather than the sacerdotal performance of sacred rites. Such a new priesthood of all believers was a direct challenge to clerical privileges.

In order to create a festival of Christian love, reformers demanded Christian rites without social or educational distinctions. Meanwhile, in order to dignify national culture, princes commanded that services be in words that everyone could understand. Protestants simplified and modernized the texts and music of their services; Catholics switched from Latin to the vernacular. Their common motto could well have been the words from Paul, I Corinthians 14, which a Bavarian priest used on the title page of his *German Catholic Ritual* in 1813: "I would rather speak five intelligible words to the congregation, so as to instruct others, than ten thousand in a foreign tongue." The change of languages had profound musical and psychological consequences.

The official music of the Roman Catholic Church, printed in the missal, was Gregorian chant, which is in part a folk art suitable for community singing. But the difficulties of adapting what seemed a vehicle for the Latin language to congregational singing in other languages were as apparent to modernizers in the eighteenth century as they are in the twentieth.[43]

Historical or biographical books and articles about the leaders of the Roman Catholic Church in Germany during the late eighteenth and early nineteenth centuries, usually state that "in his province, [diocese, or parish] he introduced congregational singing of German hymns to parallel or replace sacerdotal performance of the same action."[44] Many liturgists would have eliminated all music except

congregational chorales, which would be "more intelligible to uneducated peasants, workers, and nuns than elaborate, operatic Masses
in the Italian style." This was a bolder step than merely singing new
hymns at paraliturgical services or during liturgical services like the
Mass.

The new Mass and prayer books included various forms for the
German Mass. Usually the congregation was to sing a hymn translating the idea of the original Latin text. In the more cautious versions, the priest would intone the Gloria or invocations and continue
quietly in Latin while the people sang a hymn or response in German. The Latin texts of those Hours of the Office ordinarily done
publicly in parishes (Sunday Vespers and Compline) were replaced
by related or unrelated German songs. Not until Bismarck's *Kulturkampf* did it again become fashionable among educated German
Catholics to be liturgical Guelfs—preferring the Roman language
and style.[45]

Some of the German Catholic hierarchy attempted to impose vernacular rites. Like their ecclesiological descendants at the First and
Second Vatican Councils, they were Ghibelline—believing that local
committees of bishops should be responsible for constructing rites
suited to the time and place. Local bishops were to propose and
carry out liturgical changes within their dioceses; national committees of bishops were then to blend the local rites into a national
one.[46] Those enlightened liturgical reformers who were not bishops
were usually cathedral canons, seminary professors, or other diocesan
officials, all of whom could be as independent as their bishop if they
had his protection.

If the goal of the apostles of enlightenment was to restore the
practice of the early Christian church, their tactics were "gradually
to replace the mechanical devotion inherent in old forms with the
confident use of one's intellect." This they proposed to do by teaching the new style of worship to children and by capturing local lay
leaders for the new ideas. Despite this peaceful intention, there was
public violence in some places over the new vernacular service books.
Quarrels over the new books mirrored political and cultural changes
from the 1780s to the 1830s, continued during the ultramontane
domination of the Catholic Church, and persisted until today.

One such quarrel between traditionalists and progressives occurred
in rural Eichsfeld, which lay in the middle of Germany on the border of Electoral Saxony. During the old regime Eichsfeld had been

ruled spiritually and temporally by the archbishop of Mainz, who in 1787 required Catholics in his lands to adopt Turin's *Mainz Hymnal*. Before this could occur, the wars against the revolutionary French had begun. To preach Enlightenment now seemed a concession to the enemy's way of thinking. So most peasants in this Catholic land lying at the confluence of Evangelical, Catholic, and Reformed Germany continued to use the Roman rite until they were conquered by Napoleon.

In 1807 Eichsfeld became part of the Harzdepartment of the kingdom of Westphalia, whose enlightened, French-approved officials favored the new forms of worship. King Jerome Bonaparte's religious commissar was a priest named Wuerschmidt, who orthodox commentators caution us was "proud of being a Freemason and Illuminist."[47] He expunged the apparently illogical invocation "Mother of the Creator" from the Litany of the Blessed Virgin and instituted a few other minor changes in the rites. But he started a community-wide controversy in 1811, when he recommended that the Westphalian Catholic Church discard the Gregorian Latin service books in favor of the *Catholic Hymn and Prayer Book for Catholic Churches and Schools in the Harzdepartment*, which was an edition of the *Mainz Hymnal* printed for Eichsfeld. The commissar believed that this service book would create a modern Christian community. He rhapsodized over how wonderful it will be when "the whole congregation with one mind and heart prays and sings the 'Have Mercy on Us.' The whole church supported by the full organ, with all eyes on the altar and their hearts uplifted, will recapitulate all that their priest has taught them. Will not this be better instruction that merely teaching the people to mouth the *Kyrie* in Greek and the rest of the Mass in another foreign tongue?"[48]

After the king's assessor took a survey in June 1812 to see whether Latin was still being used in the diocese, Würschmidt reported that, wherever priests had explained the new hymnal to the congregation, it had been accepted. A year later, he boasted to Bishop von Wendt of nearby Kassel that Eichsfeld was catching up with Mainz and other metropolises by discarding service books which were full of intolerance, concerned more with sin and the saints than with God, and in a language now unknown even among the educated.

The French then placed Eichsfeld in the diocese of Regensburg in Bavaria. Although the new bishop refused to make "an inquisitorial visitation" to the rural parishes to see whether the prescribed changes were being accomplished, he did advise pastors not to shrink from calling the police if some "crackpots in the congregation" insisted on singing the old Latin hymns to disrupt the new vernacular services.[49] In the year of Waterloo, the bishop reiterated that the time in which we live demands full attention to popular participation in the liturgy. "To make religious concepts tangible through religious songs and actions," he said, is the goal of our reforms, for "so long as there is a difference between the teachings of our church and what our people believe, we may not rest." The test of a true pastor would be whether he implemented the decree of 1787 about a German liturgy, for the people seemed willing to accept the new book until reactionary priests told them not to.[50]

Educated people usually favored the new hymnals because they believed that the books would diminish superstition and teach tolerance. Those favoring the old service books in Latin argued that the new books actually destroyed the unity of the congregation because the elderly—who could not read—were reduced to standing and watching while the young joined in a "protestant" service. The elderly argued that they had been participating actively in the Latin High Mass, whose music all knew.[51] Some older parishioners signified their distaste for the new "oversimplified, broken-German hymnal" by offering stipends only for Low Masses, where there was no music.[52]

Sometimes the police actually were called in to remove some diehard who insisted upon bellowing Latin while everyone else was singing German. In Rüdesheim near Mainz, gradual popular enlightenment met trouble after Napoleon's appointees were expelled. Some congregations which had willingly switched to German before the French invasion now hated vernacular rites. Troops and rioters killed forty people when one parish protested against their own German civil and ecclesiastical government's requiring them "to sing at Mass in the German language as the French invader had done."[53]

To placate these objectors, their bishop included twenty-six old songs in a new edition of the hymnal in 1815 and asked the new Prussian—i.e., post-Napoleonic—military governor's help. The governor referred the case to King Frederick William III. The king, who was still promising his subjects a constitution, ordered his governor to side with the educated but to begin by introducing the new services only in the schools. Commissar Father Wuerschmidt was disappointed, for, he said, his district was now the only one not using a modern service-book. The Prussian governor thought the populace evenly divided among those for, those against, and those indifferent to the new books.[54]

By the time Napoleon had been gone ten years, most Continental rulers, both secular and ecclesiastical, were putting more trust in the Holy Alliance and the rights and rituals of legitimacy than in constitutions and popular enlightenment. The Vicar Apostolic of Paderborn, in whose jurisdiction Eichsfeld now lay, noted that the new hymnal had never been totally accepted and thought that perhaps this was better than allowing it freely to "infect clergy and youth with liberalism." Soon he was pleased to restore Latin at the Asperges and at all orations.[55] After the troubles of 1848, several among the Eichsfeld clergy avowed that the new hymnal had never been accepted in the villages. In 1866, when Germany was consolidated around Protestant Prussia, Catholics looked across the Alps. A Latin hymnal was made the official one in many German bishoprics, and a year later the *Caecilienverein* (Cecilia Society), dedicated both to improving church music and to rooting out anything anti-Roman from the Catholic liturgy, was founded in Bavarian Regensburg.

Although these reforms begun in the eighteenth century sometimes divided rather than united, their goal was "unity of action," whereby the people and priest would unite "not just spiritually but in voice and heart." Thereby, a feeling of unity and brotherhood would be created among all at the service and among all men. As we have seen, such proposals are most controversial within the Roman Catholic Church, where unity of action meant a departure from established sacerdotal ritual.[56]

To support unity of action, the reformers insisted upon "unity of place." As had the classicists of the Renaissance, the neoclassicists believed that architecture ought to conform to simple proportions. To assure that church buildings would contain nothing to distract from the communal ritual and to enable everyone to see, hear, and sing together, vast Gothic halls with elaborate decoration should no longer be built. To install but one altar in a church would emphasize community worship over the sacerdotalism of many priests saying private Masses at many altars. In order to convince their flocks of the need for these changes, the reformers adduced the precedent of the early Christians and, to win over conservatives, the central position of the high altar at Saint Peter's in Rome.[57] In 1785 Joseph II decreed that all future churches in his Empire were to be built in this fashion. He also required the removal of vigil lights, shrines, pictures, statues, and all unnecessary devotional paraphernalia. Stained glass windows might be removed; lights to see by were to be added, medieval gloom to be dispelled.

A Bavarian priest of the turn of the century called for brightly decorated churches and for grass-green vestments rather than somber black.[58] Black vestments were used most often at weekday requiem Masses said in behalf of the soul of a particular deceased for whom a stipend had been paid. Green vestments imply more than the color of nature. They are the color used on the Sundays after Pentecost, when the church prays for all mankind. To prefer "green" to "black" Masses would be a priest's way of preferring all humanity to a patron who paid stipends.

II

Paradoxically, the intended recovery of the classic simplicity of pre-Constantinian Christianity became an alliance with the new Constantines who were modernizing and centralizing the secular state. Christian rationalists often acquired the freedom to counsel a return to primitive Christianity by preaching support of the embryonic nationalism of the so-called enlightened despots. These rulers wanted religion to foster vernacular culture and the loyalty of equal citizens in a rationally organized state. Rationalized liturgies were an essential part of the mass media being used to teach nationalistic politics to the masses just emerging from feudalism.

In 1783 the believing but enlightened archbishop of Vienna looked about his ornate cathedral during a sermon and asked, "How can we have religion amid these caricatures?" Today, beneath another Viennese church, the plain tomb of the archbishop's sovereign, the enlightened Emperor Joseph II, stands opposite the baroque sarcophagus of his pious mother, Empress Maria Theresa. To this day, the son's tomb continues to ask the mother's the archbishop's question.[59]

Joseph, who thought Mozart's music had too many notes,[60] abolished elaborate music in the churches of his empire.[61] Everything was to be plain, orderly, and sung to German chorale tunes. For the emperor thought that the Catholic liturgy should teach morality and serve his *raison d'état* by forming loyal (that is, Germanized) citizens for his polyglot empire.

Though religious rites had been part of public education before for Aquinas, Augustine, Augustus, and Aeschylus, the public education of the eighteenth century was a more immediate heir to the Erastian doctrine of *cujus regio, ejus religio*,[62] which anticipated the rise of national states. Civil rulers were interested in secular, not eternal salvation; as long as the new liturgical *agendas*—as these proposals were called—spoke well of the prince, were in the vernacular, economical, and simple enough for all the subjects to participate in, the government usually left the tactics to local pastors.

Many prelates in Joseph's Holy Roman Empire were of like mind. In 1786 during a synod at Pistoia in Tuscany, several Italian bishops endorsed doctrines of "Febronius," who was coadjutor bishop of Trier. Justinus Febronius von Hontheim's *De statu ecclesiae* had urged that councils of bishops unite with civil rulers and limit papal pretentions to run the entire life of the church.[63] The synod advised liturgical reforms like those being established in Austria.[64] The reforms excited mixed feelings in Italy. Tourists there noticed that Milan's streets were unwontedly clean and the beggars gone. However, not all people were charmed by these advantages, for there were fewer processions to enjoy, holidays were nearly abolished, musicians unemployed, and the clergy terrified that they soon would be.[65]

Things went more smoothly in the three relatively liberal principalities of Württemberg, Baden, and Bavaria. They had a fairly mixed religious population and were more in touch with the critical spirit of the times than was Austria, which faced more toward eastern and southern Europe. The rulers of the southwest German states were, for example, still offering constitutions when Metternich was hunting down constitutionalists.

The chief spokesmen in southwestern Germany for a Kantian and Josephin (after Emperor Joseph II of Austria) liturgiology were three priests, Werkmeister, Wessenberg, and Winter. Benedict Maria Leonhard Werkmeister (1745–1823), who spent his mature years in Württemberg, wanted a simpler, more democratic liturgy. He wrote that the superstitious reverence which Catholics felt toward their rites came from "having philosophized over nothing so little as over the liturgy."[66] Catholics, he said, should dispose of accretions to their faith in order to regain an appreciation of its essentials.[67] He was a nationalist who argued that Germans could never be spiritually healthy until they stopped absorbing ultramontanism from their liturgical books and quit groveling before the Italian Curia.[68]

The Catholic Church should be governed democratically by parish elders and ecumenical world councils. "But first," he said, "our liturgy must be rid of the tasteless Romanism which lacks simplicity, purity, and order."[69]

While Werkmeister was court librarian in Württemberg, he read and distributed works by French and English freethinkers. As court preacher to the duke, he taught that the church should be a moral policeman that builds loyalty to the state. As author of several pamphlets and hymnals published after 1784, he tried to popularize his cismontane and moralizing theology among ordinary Catholics.[70] He favored the didactic over the aesthetic side of the liturgy enough to propose that congregations sing their entire High Mass to a single meter and tune. This, he thought, would become normal, for there would no longer be enough skilled performers to carry out the prescribed Latin music after the monasteries and convents were dissolved.[71] Werkmeister's patron was the duke of Württemberg, who in 1786 felt oppressed by the atmosphere at Mass and ordered a German explanation to accompany all rites in his chapel henceforth. Werkmeister said Mass in German except for the canon. The prince bishop of Speyer, ordinary of the place, balked. He ordered that such innovations be limited to the ducal chapel and in October of that year forced Werkmeister to resign as court preacher. The next duke yielded and restored the Mass totally in Latin.[72]

The second of the three priests, Ignaz Heinrich von Wessenberg of Baden (1774–1860), was probably the best-known Catholic *Aufklärer*. He wanted to introduce vernacular songs and prayers into the Catholic liturgy to assert German independence of Latin culture and to make the services more understandable for the common folk. In his twenties he became vicar general of Constance, whose bishop was later prince-primate of Napoleon's Confederation of the Rhine.[73] Wessenberg's great learning and small experience made him seem a martinet when he fostered a "demedievalizing" of German society analogous to the dechristianizing going on in the "more advanced" French society. Ecclesiastical bureaucrats and academics like him had little sympathy for folkways, so they expunged them and replaced festal worship with straightforward Celebrations of Brotherly Love and Neighborly Care. At many village churches where his translations and editions of services were introduced, the common folk, whom he intended to liberate, violently resisted what they called "Protestant worship." Of a hymn which had been "improved" from "Death is dead, life Lives" to "Death flees, now Life is victorious," one commonsensical layman said that "If death is dead, we're rid of him. But if he's only gone away, he might come back."[74]

By 1806, when the war of Liberation against the French began, most southwestern Germans had been instructed in the virtues of hymnals improved under the influence of French rationalism and of the commissars who had accompanied Napoleon's armies. The people were ashamed to appear at public functions without their new books. Then the fight against Napoleon and French ways fed opposition to the new hymnals and by 1813 rural Germany was singing from the old ones again. Some people hoped that the conservative Russian emperor, Alexander of the "Third Rome," would restore the Catholic religion of the "First Rome."[75]

Many of Wessenberg's educated contemporaries thought that he was a German patriot and scholar of things German. Though he became bishop of Constance in 1817,[76] he ended his career appropriately as an administrator in the government of Baden because Rome soon dissolved the diocese of Constance[77]—perhaps because of Wessenberg's incumbency. At any rate, the Curia never ratified the decisions of other chapters which elected him their bishop.

Until he died in 1860, Wessenberg remained ambivalently sympathetic to both critical rationalism and folkloric romanticism. He hoped to educate the common people to their German heritage through the liturgy, yet he despised any custom which appeared grounded in the Middle Ages. Enlightened Catholics pleased him by accepting his ideas, but he thought that the common people, rather than being liberated from superstition, were growing only more stupid. He worked for a didactic liturgy, yet he praised mysticism and the pietistic tradition. He hated private religious exercises, but occasionally penned hymn lines like "Oh kindle me with Thee!" He praised Schiller and Goethe and ranked Rousseau (with Voltaire) among the best men of his time.[78]

The same ambivalence appeared in the Bavarian spokesman for a Josephin liturgiology, Vitus Anton Winter (1751–1814), who was a more decided romantic. He insisted that the quality of art one employs reflects the worth of one's message. Consequently, he believed in using art and music as integral parts of the liturgy, rather than solely to decorate ethical instruction. In this he learned both from apostles of enlightenment like Werkmeister and from romanticists like Johann Michael Sailer.[79] Winter published a comprehensive philosophy of religious rites in more than a dozen works specifically on the liturgy.

He urged that the Catholic Church first undo the harm which the Roman Rite had done. The church ought to begin teaching brotherhood and tolerance by removing from its liturgy all cursing of enemies and deprecating references to other religions. If simpler ritual practices were introduced, closer to Protestantism, they, too, would help bind up old wounds.[80] Sounding much like his heirs in the *aggiornamento* of the twentieth century, Winter wrote that the Catholic liturgy could attain its "sole purpose, which is the exterior expression of interior belief," by reform on biblical principles using the first Christian centuries as a model of how to put these principles into practice.[81] Since society ought to express its common beliefs, socially organized ritual is a necessity, wherein the educated will lead the others. However, not the experts but the mass of men should understand the meaning that the rites intend to convey. Hence music should never be over the heads of the congregation.[82]

Yet Winter was not a "radical" reformer like Wessenberg, who might have been satisfied with one tune for a whole Mass. Winter hoped that the best composers, artists, and musicians would be invited to create rites which were at once popular and lofty.[83] Reformers should employ sufficient variety in the music they prescribed, so that the tunes would interpret the text, not merely unify the congregation in the act of singing. Thus, the liturgy would have power—and he quoted Kant's words—"to win our sensual nature for the intellect."[84]

In his attempt to reconcile rational criticism with medieval tradition, Winter took his motto from the first theologian to attempt a reconciliation between Hellenistic philosophy and Hebraic poetry, Saint Paul, who said, "In Christ there is neither Jew, nor Greek, there is neither bond nor free, there is neither male nor female: for ye are all one in Christ Jesus."[85] Therefore, Winter wrote, drinking from the same cup and eating the same bread in the Lord's Supper should symbolize the bond between man and man which extends to all the living and the dead. To unite citizen to citizen in a spirit of community should create civil peace. To sanctify secular relationships should make business more honest and reduce crime.[86] All people would see that despotism, slavery, and luxury in the face of poverty contradict the spirit of love. Proper symbols would make them think of the good they can do; the result would be that everyone would gladly do his social duty. Winter's ethical goal to be achieved by aesthetic means recalls Kant's definition of the purpose of religious rites. Both were enlightened humanists, modern Stoics who linked aesthetic pleasure and ethical duty. The same blend of rationalism and nationalism was evident even in the ecclesiastical states. In 1786 the three ecclesiastical electors who governed much of the Rhineland, together with the archbishop of Salzburg, issued their Punctuation of Ems, which demanded religious autonomy from Rome. The document spoke out against Italianate ritual practices such as processions, the many sodalities and confraternities which fragmented the community, exorcisms, blessings, and the mumbling of the rosary during Mass.[87] These bishops' remedies for liturgical ultramontanism were like the emperor's: to begin with, Germans should abandon the Roman rite and unite in singing a unison-chorale, German setting of the Catholic liturgy.

Similarly, in Spain, the southern part of Italy, and Sicily, where the Spanish Bourbons ruled, enlightened thinkers desired rationalistic and nationalistic reforms in the church. First, the reformers said, it should return to the simplicity of the gospels; second, it should help rather than hinder the development of a modern nation state. The crux of their argument was a desire "to replace a religion based mostly on mechanical exterior devotion with one which sought moral perfection."[88] Spanish critics pointed out that the church had forgotten its humble origins and covered itself instead with gold and jewels. As elsewhere, the protest mingled biblical righteousness with neoclassical canons of taste. "The very essence of religion is overturned when it is so enmeshed in ostentation, in the merely external things. . . . Such trivia can hardly please God, for one recalls that in planning the temple at Jerusalem, He called only for pleasing architecture: good proportions and grandeur."[89] When the Holy Office of the Inquisition punished such critics with a term in some monastery, they often emerged to satirize their "penance" with tales of how good the food, wine, and music was in the cloisters.[90]

As far as the enlightened King Charles III and his ministers were concerned, the immense crowds from all social classes which paraded the streets on Corpus Christi and other holidays seemed drawn only by curiosity, vanity, sloth, and a vagrant tendency which draws men to mere movement and agitation. Poor Spain, parading as though she were still a crusading knight conquering the world, when in reality her dreams were only Don Quixote's windmills!

Enlightened Spanish bishops sought to end religious excuses for such revelry and to ban other "unwholesome practices." Some of the latter included processions of flagellants, wherein young men showed animal courage before their señoritas, and processions with stuffed eagles, which were made to "dance for Jesus in the Eucharist." The ancient *autos sacramentales*, which sometimes had accompanied these processions, were also suppressed.[91] Economists joined theologians and aestheticians to attack the Spanish custom of bejeweling statues of the saints, who were then addressed in passionate hymns. And, as for relics, they were worse than superstitions. Later word had it that no monks wept over the monasteries full of relics destroyed by Napoleon's invaders. Relics were easy to manufacture.

To most Spaniards, however, the Enlightenment's proposals seemed a drastic plot to replace Catholicism with a purely interior Christianity, which would abolish the church's mediation between God and man. The crusading mentality still enshrined in the Inquisition allowed no tampering with the Mass and sacraments, such as occurred in Germany, though the coalition between the Spanish Enlightenment, Jansenism, and nationalism did destroy the Jesuits. Although most of the Spanish clergy could hardly have cared less for the Enlightenment, they were suspicious of musicians, plays, and playwrights. At any rate, the conservative Spanish clergy were as willing to sweep Calderón's richly musical *autos* on religious themes from the church steps and cathedral squares as Charles III was willing to insist upon nothing but translations from the French classical school for his royal theaters.[92] And so the puritanical impulse of a clergy still partly Jansenist and still imbued with the military austerity of crusaders reinforced the rationalism, statism, and iconoclasm of the court.

The trend toward a freer religion rested only momentarily in the Enlightenment's call to renew religion according to natural law interpreted by reason. That trend was the seed of the Romantic doctrine that the "objective" assent of the head must be balanced by the "subjective" desire of the heart. Furthermore, among the Romance—indeed among many—countries outside France, the armies of Napoleon that enforced certain aspects of the Enlightenment caused a reaction against it. Witness, for example, the fantastic creations that Goya made to enlighten his nation and warn it against Napoleon's dictatorship. They are thoroughly romantic examples of the imagination from a land of romance par excellence, Spain. Under such circumstances, religious policy was easy to change. Like the Soviets in World War II, the government asserted that national self-respect and religious orthodoxy, including the ancient liturgy, were one in the Peninsular War, which was Napoleon's Stalingrad.

Across the Atlantic in the year of the Ems Punctuation, many Roman Catholics wanted to bring their church up to date and show their loyalty to a suspicious Protestant nation by adopting a republican style of government and worship. The first Catholic bishop in the United States, John Carroll of Baltimore, thought it "preposterous that a small district around Mount Libanus should have a liturgy in its own tongue, while the immense extent of countries containing Great Britain, Ireland, North America, the West Indies, etc., are obliged to perform divine service in an unknown tongue."[93] His colleague, Bishop John England of Charleston, South Carolina, wrote a translation of the missal, which Rome condemned in 1822. Rome also condemned the constitution which Bishop England had issued for his diocese in 1820 to emulate the Protestant practice of giving the laity a voice in church government.[94] Though translation of the missal was forbidden to lands or people considered already Roman, Catholic missionaries usually translated the nonsacerdotal passages of the liturgy into whatever language their proselytes could understand, and then set these texts to native music. Hence there are eighteenth-century hymnals and missals in several American Indian dialects.[95]

On the eastern border of western Christendom, the Polish provinces under Prussia used a partially vernacular liturgy something like the German High Mass.[96] A similar combination of Latin and (non-English) vernacular was normal among Slavic-American Catholics through mid-twentieth century.[97]

III

The history of Jewish rites during this period is a précis of the whole story. So long as the Jews believed that their lot was to be compulsory exiles within European society, they had maintained their religion and its ritual in the cantorial style of the Levant. When in the eighteenth century more Jews began to enter European society as equals, many became convinced that Hebraism was no longer justified. They now preferred a religion that looked and sounded European.[98] Some became enlightened Christians; others retained only the humanitarian and ethical parts of Judaism in order to conform to the bent of European thought, which was more Greek than Hebrew during the Enlightenment.

Enlightened Jews outdid their Christian counterparts in contempt for what seemed to them "ugly medievalism." The culture of the 1800 years between dispersion and emancipation seemed a dark age indeed, when persecution and superstition had suppressed Jewish talent. Like their Christian counterparts, who harkened back to the "classical" period of Christianity—the Apostolic and patristic eras—enlightened Jews exalted the "classical" period of Hebrew tradition —the pre-Christian.

On the other hand, conservative Jews believed that their medieval culture was "uniquely Jewish"—something not to be denied but worn proudly, even defiantly. They began research into the Jewish literature, poetry, and liturgy of the Middle Ages.[99] This split between rationalists and traditionalists was most evident in eastern Europe, where the most Jews lived and where they had been the most isolated. Conservatives complained of Gentile intrusions into their sacred ceremonies, while liberals complained of meaningless superstitions. The conservatives were usually led by rabbis, who were more isolated from Gentile culture than were laymen. The latter were more conscious of Jewish isolation and often hoped to end it.

Some congregations tried to combine "recognizably Jewish" music with European harmonic structures. The results were usually slight, because the Jewish musicians, who knew little harmony, relied upon the approval of Gentile musicians, who hardly appreciated the cantorial tradition. Even *chazzanim* (cantors) were convinced that all nonmajor modes sounded "sad." By about 1800 in western Europe, most synagogue services were read, not sung; the rabbi spoke in the vernacular, not in Hebrew. Vernacular hymns in major or minor tonality, accompanied by organs, began to replace the modal Hebrew chants of the cantor. But even when synagogues employed a Gentile to lead a mixed choir in music based on chorale tunes, most congregations retained a *chazzan*.[100]

During the remaking of Germany under Napoleon and the French, a rich merchant of Cologne, Israel Jacobson, undertook to reform Judaism in western Germany. With the help of the reigning monarch, Jerome of Westphalia (Napoleon's brother), in 1810 Jacobson published at Kassel a hymnal containing Hebrew translations of Protestant texts set to such melodies as *O Sacred Head*. The printed music read, like Hebrew, from the right to the left. Meanwhile, some synagogues abandoned the traditional reading of the Torah, introduced instead a Protestant style liturgy, and installed bells. Thus, one result of emancipation was a reaction against the old ghetto tradition in favor of mingling Hebraic and European styles.

One musician who mingled tunes from Stamitz symphonies and Paisiello operas with chants from the synagogue was the father of Jacques Offenbach, born Isaac Ebert[101] in the ghetto of Offenbach. In 1811 his operetta *The Carpenter in His Workshop* was performed at the christening festivities of Napoleon's son, the King of Rome. After the War of Liberation, Offenbach moved to Cologne, where he was listed as "guitar, flute, violin and voice teacher, and *chazzan.*" His compositions for the Jewish liturgy reflected not only the trend to the vernacular, but also the vogue of choral music. His setting of the 118th psalm was arranged for a four-part men's choir with tenor solo and a chorus for mixed choir entitled *The Festive Rites Are Completed.* In 1839 he published a *General Prayer Book* in German and Hebrew as a companion to his previously published translation of the *Hagadah.* Several of his melodies occur in the operas of his son.[102]

In the way of all flesh, once emancipated, some Jews grew nostalgic. Heinrich Heine, who was the younger Offenbach's contemporary and who often satirized German romanticism's nostalgia, showed himself a romanticist in his remarks on the faith of his fathers. "Rabbi von Bacharach" recalled the Passover Seder as

a strange mixture of legends of their forefathers, wondrous tales of Egypt, questions of theology, prayers, and festival songs. . . . Mournfully merry, seriously gay, and mysteriously secret as some dark old legend, is the character of this nocturnal festival. The traditional singing intonation with which the Hagadah is read by the father and now and again echoed in chorus by the hearers at one time thrills the inmost soul with a shudder, anon calms it as if it were a mother's lullaby, and anon startles it so suddenly into waking that even those Jews who have long fallen away from the faith of their fathers and run after strange joys and honors, are moved to their very hearts, when by chance the old, well-known tones of the Passover songs ring in their ears.[103]

Heine's nostalgia was typical of reformed and Europeanized Jews the world over. Romantic Jewish zealots tried to recover the spirit of the first Israel.[104] But as with, say, the Gothic revival, what happened was not the rebirth of the old style but the birth of a dream of what things might have been.

IV

In these proposals born of the Enlightenment one can see the theologian at work fashioning God in man's new image. Influenced by the humanitarian ideals of the Enlightenment, theologians eschewed texts about the fear of God and told Christians not to think of themselves as servants bound to a traditional order but as full and equal heirs. Even when the reformers' taste was sophisticated, they advocated reducing music and art to its simplest, in order to teach brotherhood and tolerance through didactic texts made attractive in the simplest and most immediate way. The mere action of uniting to sing intelligible texts and simple music, which expressed the lowest common denominator of taste and emotion, was to be a symbol of human equality and fraternity.

> It is hoped . . . that the reader can now see these events of the eighteenth century as a single movement, revolutionary in character, for which the word "democratic" is appropriate and enlightening; a movement which, however different in different countries, was everywhere aimed against closed elites, self-electing power groups, hereditary castes, and forms of special advantage or discrimination that no longer served any useful purpose. These were summed-up in such terms as feudalism, aristocracy, and privilege, against which the idea of common citizenship in a more centralized state, or of common membership in a free political nation, was offered as a more satisfactory basis for the human community.[105]

Rites holy in themselves—*ex opere operato*—had been to religion what noble birth was to the feudal class structure. They conferred nobility regardless of individual worth. By abolishing reverence for such traditional forms, the reformers prepared for the romanticists' Faustian individual assertion. As had the philosophes and the apostles of enlightenment, so would the romanticists value a work according to how well it served man's education and edification, rather than according to which sect had authored it. Hence, new liturgical agendas continued to circulate. When rationalistic influences upon religious thought declined, the number of new hymnals and liturgical agendas continued to grow, for a new generation was busy recovering "authentic" versions of hymns which its fathers had discarded.

The two thought currents overlapped. For example, that same *Mainz Hymnal* which the bishop of Mainz had ordered to replace the Gregorian chant service books in 1787 did not become uniform in its home diocese until 1837. By then, a new generation educated on it had grown up. When the hymnal was first published, some German Protestants were still singing Latin Gregorian chant. When at last it was accepted popularly, scholars were at work restoring the "lost Gregorian chant"[106] which it had replaced.

All reformers during the age of democratic revolution wanted music to unite congregations in a feeling of common humanity. The difference in style between the rationalists and the romanticists sprang from different needs. The rationalists had first to prune away dead wood. In their haste to prune back to the viable roots and branches of religion, they removed everything which they did not understand or could not turn to a didactic purpose. The romanticists would favor the aesthetic argument that man does not live by the word alone. Most important for religion and for life in the wider sense, the investigators of religion began to realize that the Word is not the same as the words. They were not the first to see that aesthetic quality in every mode of human expression is an integral part of moral worth; the Enlightenment knew that. But the new generation realized that even seemingly grotesque superstitions can have human value and civilizing functions. Western man then began to explore the exotic recesses of the soul and of the world not to find some tool for toppling domestic idols but to find proof that unity, variety, and a well-organized life contain stranger things than are dreamed of in our philosophy.

MUSIC

The Artist as Hero, Music as Communication

2

Father Bernard Vaughan's sermon
first. Christ or Pilate? Christ, but
don't keep us all night over it.
Music they wanted.

James Joyce
Ulysses

Music stands too high for any
understanding to reach, and an
all-mastering efficacy goes forth
from it, of which, however, no
man is able to give an account.
Religious worship cannot therefore
do without music. It is one of the
foremost means to work upon
men with effect of *marvel*.

Goethe
Conversations with Eckermann

MEMORIES OF A PIOUS CHILDHOOD

Traditional Religion as Counterculture among the European Intelligentsia

4

Yes, all those allurements that the Enlightenment was so deliciously suspicious and enamored of psychologically might be summed up in the idea of music; all of those things that it was suspicious of socially could be summed up in religion. This religion was not so much the comparatively reasonable beliefs of the enghteenth-century clergy, but the traditional piety which these educated men were trying to eradicate—superstitions which uneducated women remote from metropolises taught to their children, thereby perpetuating primitive habits. Yet these ghostly tales and practices were their own sort of Enlightenment, the search for the Sublime.

The essence of popular religion was often thought to be the seemingly spontaneous outpouring of the feelings. And this outpouring does stand in the same relation to the deistic moral universe as music stood to the classical aesthetic universe, because neither music nor the manifestations of popular religion could be fitted into a cosmos where reason must always be seen to govern passion. Yet, for the truly irreverent skeptical man, this association could only make the idea of religion, like the idea of music, more fascinating in an age trying to find an original way to sin.

There is, however, a deeper connection between Christian theology and the feelings widespread in an era of revolutions. During any time of swift, radical, and irrevocable change, Christian conversion affords a ready vessel for crossing social or psychological floodwaters. For the making of a new man with a new consciousness under a new law, which was the original Christian social and psychological paradigm, had continued to permeate western sensibility with feelings of impermanence. As it was in the beginning; so it was at the fall of the City of Man, Rome; so at the Reformation; so it remained in the age of democratic revolution, and may ever be wherever the west has influence: the restless eschatalogical, messianic tendency remains potent even when dormant. In fact, the revolution of consciousness which accompanies cyclical rites of passage in many civilizations became in the west a series of unique signposts along the one-way route of linear history. The very cycle of the seasons was made into an allegory of the *uncyclical* cosmogony of the universe. The original Christian preachers had told their subjects to have a "change of mind" (*metanoia* in Greek, *conversio* in Latin). Until the revolutions of 1640 transferred the word to secular politics, "revolution" in the English language meant personal conversion.[1] In sum, Judeo-Christian indoctrination in the hope that present suffering shall lead to salvation in a mythical future has been so interiorized that westerners —including the churches—often do not recognize how easily our happy-ending oriented culture slips into a frame of reference once Christian.[2]

This frame of reference can be manifested in many subtle interlocking ways both private and public. The fact that popular religion, or any other movement, makes personal experiences all-important does not mean that it will be unstructured or consist of isolated individuals. On the contrary, there is often a heavy emphasis upon ritual in emotionally charged religion. Shakers, Quakers, Swedenborgians, Pentecostals of every type, Jewish cabalists, or votaries of certain Catholic saints, and virtually all manner of utopian or millenarian sects that one might think of, often rejuvenate the ritual or dramatic elements of a religious environment which seems to have become too coldly intellectual to console the alienated people of its time or place. Even avowedly antiritualistic sects, such as the Quakers, deliberately seek to form a milieu that will help internal and personal promptings of the spirit to be manifested externally. Frequently what new popular religions offer is a *method*, as in Methodism, for *ordering* one's life once and for all. Hence the new sects often demand a stern ascetic morality with strict taboos against—or at least strict channels for—sensual pleasure. The saved are a well-regulated elect, monks in the world, though not of its careless habits. Nay, more, the saved are out of this world. Life itself becomes a mimetic ritual in which one shows forth accurately and spontaneously the promptings of the spirit.[3]

Let us now compare the psychological paradigm of life led according to the spontaneous prompting of a religion of the heart with the Enlightenment's world view. The Enlightenment was consciously suspicious of any life or art which did not proceed according to an intelligent plan. Yet the Enlightenment was also developing a fascination with lives and styles which seemed to express a spontaneous outpouring of emotion. Witness the "noble savage;" Diderot's *Rameau's Nephew*; or that dream world of a new consciousness based upon musical kinesthesia rather than logical development, the Italian opera, over which more stones were thrown or engraved than were thrown or printed over rock music in the nineteen-sixties. Pietistic religious communities offered a living example of some aspects of life that the intelligentsia dared to put only on the stage or in books. When Rousseau[4] declared that a pious community like Geneva needed no playhouses, he was implying that houses of prayer were themselves houses of play.

I

No matter what the established cult is, the religious practices of the common folk seem to remain more pietist than the official practices. Pietism has a narrow meaning referring to the movement founded by Jacob Spener in the seventeenth century. But the impulse toward a religion of "inner enlightenment" is much wider than one sect. Including Methodism in England, revivalism in America, and multifarious private devotions among Catholics, the traditional religiosity of pietism may have hindered the Enlightenment, but the individualism and moralism of pietism sometimes was itself a species of liberalism. Hence pietism could foster as well as hinder the Enlightenment. Both movements admired what seemed the simplicity of early Christianity. The homely moralizing of pietist "hymns for home and hearth" and "church festival songs"[5] paralleled the purely ethical religion preached by the philosophes. Like the French—and other—revolutions, pietism offered a comprehensive liturgy to replace or complement the official liturgies of the established churches. Out of the home and hearth songs some pietists built liturgies virtually as comprehensive as the office of the Roman church. There were hymnals for every occasion and vocation; songs for every personal experience: for students, for accompanying a wife's daily chores, and for every lower-middle-class occupation and group. Ordinary folk were finding printed hymnals and songs which dignified their feelings in hymns and songs written by and for themselves,[6] much in the same way that artists and composers in the eighteenth century began to feel free to realize their own vision independent of a noble or ecclesiastical patron.

More than a sentimental religion, which swept the late-eighteenth-century churches, pietism described the entire life style of those classes struggling for respectability. Functionally, *pious* meant two things: one best described etymologically, the other psychologically. *Pius* in Latin meant loyal and described the petits bourgeois, who valued the appearance of stability, sobriety, hard work, and houses smelling of soap and water and furniture polish—as did the mother of Hermann Hesse's *Steppenwolf*. Pietists were the very definition of bourgeois conservatism. To freethinking aristocrats, they seemed repressed.

Yet a psychological definition could make pietists seem radical. For their loyalty was not to a reasoned external system but to an interior feeling. Every one of them hoped to experience what Paul Goodman or Jacques Ellul might call a New Reformation. Each pietist at some time in his life—and perhaps often—expected to experience the grace of God working through an "inner light." This was the common man's application of the "Protestant principle" and was also the common man's Enlightenment. And it went by the same name. Its subjects believed that righteousness was individual and based upon a feeling. By so believing they were learning not to repress but to express themselves.

The four marks of such a countercult were the same in modern times as they had been in ancient Greece among the Dionysians. Passionate intensity rather than theological objectivity measured the validity of a religious experience. The subject is an underground man, either in the sense of being an outsider in fact of the lower classes or wishing to identify with the lowly, even with the contemptible. The subject achieves identity with the beloved through a radical conversion or revolution of consciousness whereby he dies to the old order of consciousness and is born to a new one.[7] Finally, such cults tend to be woman-centered in two ways. First they appeal to women, whose role has usually been to seek private or personal rather than public satisfaction. Like the poetess Sappho, piety declares that it is not what one conquers that matters but how and whom one loves. Such love might center upon a man like Christ or Orpheus, but

Title page of *The Youth's Magic Horn*, part 2 (1808), a collection of medieval folk lyrics. Like the new romantic poetry, such as the *Lyrical Ballads* of Wordsworth and Coleridge, these historical collections implied that the songs, stories, and medieval fantasies which the Enlightenment dismissed as superstition were not childish but childlike. Similarly, folk or primitive cultures were deemed to be of permanent value, not to be outgrown and discarded.

always stresses personal love and feelings, a stereotypically feminine virtue, over orthodox correctness, a stereotypically masculine virtue.

Second, popular piety sometimes tends to replace the image of a just father with that of a loving mother.[8] Catholics had their paraliturgical devotions where emotional sermons in the vernacular were technically and sometimes doctrinally outside the bounds of doctrine concerning the church as mediator. Personal petitions were read; first-person singular pronouns addressed Jesus in the second person singular, and Mary, the Blessed Virgin, the Mother of God seemed more worshiped than venerated. This familiar grammar overcame one of the differences between Catholics and Protestants. (French Protestants were sometimes called "tutoyeurs," because they used the singular familiar forms of the pronouns to address God while the Catholic liturgy preferred the first and second person plural.) Familiar singulars reigned in the paraliturgical devotions where flamboyant pictures, songs, sermons, and even testimony of private miracles, visions, and revelations elevated personal feelings above institutional mediation.

Theologically the pietistic attitude toward the imaginative or musical side of life had an affinity with that of the purportedly didactic Enlightenment. The Encyclopedists always insisted that the imaginative support the moralistic, lyrical effusions for their own sake were disorderly and hence immoral.[9]

Likewise the pietists, though their religion was emotionally charged, insisted that this emotion follow the plot laid down in scripture. As the philosophes were verbalists, so were the pietists literalists who thought that an uncontrolled imagination might be the work of the devil and rarely emphasized music or art in their services. Rather than the thoroughly musical interpretation with which baroque musicians were wont to dramatize the sacred text, pietists usually said they preferred congregational hymns at the beginning and end of the scriptural reading and rarely used more than a simple chant when they sang the gospel itself.[10] In their strictures they included the lyricism of a Sebastian Bach, even when he built his music on pietist religious feelings and songs.[11] The Word—which theologians restricted to "words"—always remained primary.

This dialectic between the Word and music was a religious analogue to the same controversy among secular philosophers, who argued the reason-versus-emotion question in terms of the words-versus-music question in opera. Neoclassical secular culture, therefore, had its analogues in baroque religious culture. Bach's cantatas, for example, were a drama of systematic soliloquy through music which portrayed the drama of Christian conversion.[12] Similarly the Spanish *autos* of Calderón and the Jesuit pageants translated the Counterreformation into popular language. Like all masterpieces of the lyrical tradition, the baroque religious music drama externalized an inward struggle. Such liturgies were the religious or popular equivalent of the Italian opera discussed by the encyclopedists. Yet again, just as the Enlightenment's critique, irreverent of all preconceived systems, could leave man naked with his instincts to seek pleasure or avoid pain, pietism might make truth a matter of individual feeling.

Of course, pietism was not directly compatible with its urbane contemporary, the Enlightenment. When religious rationalists rhymed syllogisms about nonanthropomorphic monotheism, ordinary men preferred a lyric urging all God's children to get along. Pietism—including Methodism in England and private devotions in the Catholic Church—was not fashionable among the sophisticated. It was "too baroque."[13] Sophisticates usually preferred the naturalistic and deistic theology which accompanied the dissemination of scientific thought and revulsion against the doctrinal strife during the wars of religion. But pietism was to come into fashion again as the lyrical, personal side of religious romanticism.[14]

Meanwhile, pietists wrote hymns replete with moral advice and with the flow from some unique, personal religious experience, which would have seemed illicit if addressed to anyone other than God. Older mystics like John of the Cross and Theresa of Avila would have understood the "holy lust" and familiar pronouns of a verse written in the land of John of Leiden:

I run to Thee
With bated breath,
With sighing and with longing,
With tears I seek Thee,
Fondest treasure all within.
Then Thy perfume awakes in me,
Lord Jesus, eternal loving.[15]

II

That lyric was from Germany. There was something special about German culture in the eighteenth century that made its Enlightenment have different feelings about Christianity, including individualistic piety and the communitarian Middle Ages. The Aufklärung was in part a rebellion against the subtle imposition of the foreign standards of French classicism, something like the resentment which accompanies militant nationalism in former colonies today as they move to emulate the European nationalism which conquered them. If the French philosophes were skeptics, German apostles of the enlightenment might be believers.[16] Once again, the stereotype of the past and its religion did not change. It was reevaluated.

Just as biologists went exploring for the missing link with our preconscious ancestors, philosophers sought to recollect the ebbing fervor and awesome images which had animated the preanalytical subconscious. Criticism may have shown that the sacred old books and mysteries with which the imagination clothed our precedents were at best art and at worst intoxicating delusions. But did looking at drunken old Noah bare really foster the greatest good of the greatest number? Even though educated Europeans may have thought that religion had outlived whatever utility it may have had, a sense of wonder clung to the barely remembered times which had fashioned medieval Christendom.

And so high culture set out to learn how to use childlike piety in a scientific age. Since then civilization plucks every uncultivated herb it can find to see whether each exotic culture does not offer a potion that adult civilized man has forgotten.

Inside the near border of western Europe then lay the Germanies, a much more old-fashioned place than England or France, still relatively full of castles with knights, princesses, uncertain communications, and probably witches. For their part, the Germans were just discovering themselves by declaring that what once seemed a backward superstitious *Volk* in fact embodied just what the world needed. For the rest of Europe, Germany became a model romantic cultural landscape.

There was a prototypical poet both of pietism and of German romanticism, Friedrich Gottlieb Klopstock (1724–1803).[17] He collaborated with Gluck,[18] the German reformer of the Parisian stage, and interested himself in northern folk epics, which he thought were the fountainhead of Germanic culture.[19] Since he and his immediate followers believed communal worship, not moralizing, to be the primary object of religion, his lyrics were prayers. They were also music. They attempted a symbiosis between music and language—as well as between pietism and the Enlightenment—as in "the first naturally rough compositions . . . the holy songs."[20] Therefore, they were modeled not on the "Alexandrine lockstep" but on the psalms and the lyric strophes of Greek drama, both of which had been intimately connected with music.[21] Imitation of Klopstock's style was to become a mark of romantic as distinguished from rationalistic poets.

If Klopstock was German romanticism's founding poet, Johann Georg Hamann (1730–88), was its founding philosopher. As the Catholic musical restoration in France would, so did the chorale restoration in Germany begin philosophically with a Rousseau. If the apostles of enlightenment preferred French and Latin mottos, Hamann preferred Hebrew—especially cabalist—epigrams, which he sprinkled throughout his work in their original language. Those Greek and Latin quotations which he did employ alongside the Hebrew were used to argue that poetry is the common mother tongue of all humanity and to contradict haughty dicta like Horace's *Odi Profanum Vulgus et Arceo* favored among French-speaking intellectuals.[22] The Prussian Rousseau, Hamann, taught that individual and communal life is a continuum. It seemed to him that the Enlightenment and Kant were wrong to speak of reason apart from tradition, belief, and experience; wrong to separate matter and form, sense and understanding. The French Rousseau had had no single disciple to make his work respectable. Hence, some readers have ever since been confused into mistaking an untidy life for a disordered mind. Hamann was luckier.

His teachings were subsumed by his pupil, Johann Gottfried von Herder (1744–1803), who passed them to Goethe. For Herder, man is organically part of nature and can leap Kantian dualism by reconstructing a cultural environment which does not split reason and emotion. For Herder, myth and ritual were aboriginal humanism, a total language compassing the total environment. One is not surprised to note that Herder's life work revolved around recovering the letter and spirit of works made in the "state of nature": *Voices of Peoples in their Songs* (1788), *On the Spirit of Hebraic Poetry* (1782), *Ideas toward a Philosophy of History* (1784–91), *On the Origin of Language* (1772). In all of these he showed sympathetic insight into the feelings and popular songs of Greenlanders, Spaniards, Indians, and Scots.[23] This advance guard of the second War of Liberation (Luther's being the first) put humanity above German nationality; this coiner of "evolution" in Germany was no fatalist. He despised despotism more, the more subtle it was.[24] Part of Herder's campaign for liberation of the German spirit was restoration of folksongs and other work not made in imitation of foreign models. One of his favorite lyrics was also the pietist's favorite hymn, *The Moon Has Risen (Der Mond ist aufgegangen)* by Matthias Claudius.[25] It was also the favorite of Herder's south-German Catholic counterpart, Johann Michael Sailer. Herder praised its "simple naive language of the people" and agreed with its author, who said, "It is better to make the intellect believe than to make belief intellectual."[26]

Such statements were in part merely complaints against rationalism. They also proclaimed a love of many things formerly thought contemptible. In this instance, the urge to explore and liberate discovered the Christian past.

At the center of the exchanges of ideas and agendas among rationalists, pietists, and incipient romantics—all unhindered by copyrights—was a pre-Reformation sect, the Moravian Brethren. Since they were descendants of the Hussites, they were Utraquists, whose doctrine of the cup for the laity had foreshadowed Protestantism. The Moravians were one of the few utopian sects whose communitarian life had survived the establishment's campaign against the left wing of the Reformation. Moreover, their communitarian life linked a near medieval, though not celibate, monasticism, via Protestant sectarianism, to nineteenth-century socialism and educational reform. They were not missionary Christians so much as a social laboratory or pilot plant with wide influence.

In the eighteenth century the Moravian community found a refuge at Herrnhut on the estates of Count Zinzendorf in Electoral Saxony. For this well-born pietist, there was "no Christianity without community. Salvation was not a calculus of guilt, pain, sin, and distress but a joyful apprehension of a loving father, persistently yet gently leading his child into a new life of happy companionship with himself."[27]

> Under the influence of Zinzendorf the religion of the Moravians came to develop certain definite characteristics. It stressed religious feeling (*Gefühl*) and experience over and above dogma and doctrinal uniqueness. It was Christocentric and adhered to a belief in salvation based upon joyful and loving apprehension of Christ whose sufferings upon the Cross had atoned for man's sins. It regarded religion as a social experience in which the faithful were bound together in a community of brotherly love but at the same time separated from the rest of mankind, who did not adhere to their beliefs, and who, therefore, were not to be numbered among God's chosen people.[28]

Unlike some radically Protestant sects, the Moravians welcomed art and music as a valuable catalyst for building their community. Under the count's patronage, the Moravian cult developed into an elaborate musical liturgy, in which it was virtually impossible to separate religious experience and emotion from any aspect of secular life. A schedule of tunes was worked out in mid-eighteenth century and later printed in the German Moravian Liturgy Books of 1791. It provided special chorales for each occasion in the life and worship of the community.[29] For example, a trombone quartet would memorialize the death of a member of the community with the chorale *O Sacred Head*. The Moravian rituals eventually included hundreds of songs to accompany the most formal and the most routine actions, done with all manner of communal singing, litanies, and chanting. Almost invariably, an institutional act was climaxed by a "love feast." "This celebration, derived from the Agapé of the ancient apostolic tradition, consisted of hymn-singing or the chanting of a liturgy, in the course of which a simple meal of coffee and bread or rolls was consumed."[30]

The renewal of Moravian communal life expressed in music had a profound influence on contemporary religious, educational, and social reformers.[31] Although no major composers or performers learned their art from Moravian teachers either in Herrnhut, Saxony, or Bethlehem, Pennsylvania, the Moravian Brethren linked baroque —or even gothic—emotionalism to mass feeling through religion.[32] At the end of the Enlightenment, the Moravians were a living example of an attempt to combine mass feeling with high art.

The Moravian liturgy first became a secular influence in Germany by way of the adaptation made by Johann Bernard Basedow (1723– 90) for his "institute for education," Philanthropin, at Dessau. In his *Proposal to Educational Philanthropists, with a Plan for a Primer of Human Nature* of 1767, Basedow hoped to apply educational theories like Rousseau's and Pestalozzi's about using the heart as well as the head to educate the young.[33] The book was based on *Emile* and the Moravian liturgy. Basedow hoped to make his students so adept musically that they would sound "like a choir of great composers." Judging from the number of liturgical reformers indebted to Basedow's version of the Moravian liturgy, he must have appeared successful in his plan to "develop the intelligence of pupils by bringing them into contact with the reality of good music, not mere words about it."[34]

Basedow published a number of hymnals intended to be sung textbooks on ethics and aesthetics. The first was his *Private Hymnal*

(*Privatgesangbuch*) of 1767 "for the social and peaceful upbringing of Christians of whatever belief." In 1781 he published a *General Christian Hymnal for All Churches and Sects.* Three years later there appeared his most popular hymnal, *Songbook of a Philadelphic Society for Christians and Their Philosophical Compatriots, Germany in the Reign of Joseph II.*[35] Enlightened statesmen like Joseph II's Chancellor Kaunitz approved of these hymnals, wherein they thought the didactic replaced the lyric tone. The hymnals document a junction among high culture, populism, philosophy, and Christian piety. Furthermore, they help to establish the lineage between Enlightenment and romanticism.

The Moravians' communal religious music also impressed John Wesley (1703–91), the founder of Methodism, who sailed to Georgia in the company of some Moravians and their sponsor, Count Zinzendorf. Wesley's admiration for their musico-liturgical year mollified his previous low-church prejudice against liturgical music in general and "man-made"—i.e., nonscriptural—songs in particular.[36] Wesley copied the Moravians' organization by "choirs," which he renamed "bands," after an earlier Moravian designation.[37]

In England, as elsewhere, fervent hymns were the musical sign of the pietist style. They are the Sublime for the people. Hogarth's people sing hymns; novelists make wretched characters sing hymns with words and music by John Wesley and his brother Charles, to loosen high-church formalism[38] and to express ideas that such characters would not have been able to express otherwise. The old metrical psalter had spoken of God, salvation, and the world in a general, impersonal—liturgical—way. Now, when the Wesleys and Whitefield drew Hogarth's people to their meetings, which were supposed to be an outreach of the Church of England, they used lines with a personal appeal:

His blood can make the foulest clean
His blood availed for me.[39]

On the didactic side, pietism was subtly radical. We have seen musicians during the French Revolution learning to be their own men; the whole lower middle class was learning the same thing. The influence of pietism upon them was two-edged. On the one hand, a quietistic acceptance of a difficult world might create docile subjects for political and economic exploitation. Or, on the other, pietism could strengthen individualism. Someone who trusted the inner light to put him in contact with the Ultimate of the next world would likely trust it in the face of the exalted in this world. Crying in private might be submissive; crying in public is subversive.

Methodism, for example, meant political radicalism to the Establishment, if not to Thomas Paine. Methodist revivalism was marked by cooperation for common social objectives: education, temperance, abolition, international peace, the missions; and it gave final prominence to the lay element within Protestantism.[40] "Methodist clergy in England tried to be officially neutral on political questions. The effects of Methodism, however, were by no means conservative. Men taught to read in Methodist Sunday Schools, or to speak up in Wesleyan meetings, often figured as leaders in radical clubs. . . . [Methodism] offered a kind of competing program to that of the French Revolution as a force calling the established order into question."[41] It was not only Wesley's doctrine but his method of spreading it that gave to Methodism its revolutionary characteristic.[42] Political radicals in England picked up the ideals and techniques of the Methodist meetings. Prime Minister Pitt was terrified of meetings which sang democratic hymns and read from Paine instead of limiting themselves to singing Charles Wesley and reading from the Bible.[43]

A summary of the old *Zeitgeist* and forecast of the new is found in the writings of Immanuel Kant. His closing pages on *Religion within the Limits of Reason Alone* balanced logos and ethos (here translatable as "reason" and "custom"). He would have the Christian begin with moral righteousness, but links it inseparably to the inner light and to communal celebrations.[44] His chapter on the schemata of the imagination contains the outline of a theory that could be developed far beyond the limits of objective discourse. The point of his argument seems to be that, if religion is not purely objective, its symbols must be different from those of objective language.[45]

When the Storm and Stress generation looked at early Christianity, what struck them was not how plain and simple everything had been, but the predominance of metaphor as perhaps the only way to express the inexpressible, short of silence. The wild metaphors used in the New Testament or "by bishops like Chrysostom in his sermons make those in creeds seem very tame."[46] The rationalists, in their search for human community, had stressed the propositions of natural religion; the new trend stressed the common genealogy of religious practices and searched history for a more accurate idea of

that genealogy. Some were interested in eastern Christianity, where
early records were more copious than in the west and where art,
cult, and life still seemed one total environment. However, it was
the Middle Ages and their gothic extensions, like Shakespeare,[47]
that were most often to fascinate the romantics.

III

Although medievalism was later associated with the conservative side
of romanticism, it began like the admiration for the supposed primitive, childlike simplicity of the pietists. It was a rebellion.

Many researchers believed that in the medieval and similar eras
art had sprung immediately from the people, rather than from an
aristocracy. Therefore, manuscripts of medieval poetry and music
were searched for examples of uninhibited folk expression, now
valued more than the products of cosmopolitan sophistication. Abbé
Vogler, chapelmaster at Mannheim and one of the romantic generation's teachers, collected songs in Greenland;[48] the brothers Grimm
went into the European countryside; and Napoleonic officers notated
the songs of Egyptian *fellahin*.[49] All such research into living oral
traditions was linked in a kind of cultural populism with the new
creation of poets such as Wordsworth and Coleridge, who announced
in the Preface to their *Lyrical Ballads*, that they would deliberately
draw "the matter of their art from every class and condition of
men."[50]

Other romanticists insisted that the offshoots of medieval liturgy
were equally worthwhile. Herder spoke of oratorio, sprung from the
dramatization of the gospel, as an act wherein music and poetry
united to express the thoughts of a group,[51] which, "adding the expressiveness of Italian vocal music to Christian myth," fulfilled the
same function—a unified interpreter of society's values—as tragedy
had for the Greeks. Herder's followers thought that artists should
continue to do what Luther, and eventually Bach, had done with
German folk tunes, and what every great poet and composer does
in his own way: sublimate the popular raw material, or record one's
unique vision, and return it to the people as a means of their education or edification. The reputedly risqué son of *The Armed Man*
(*L'homme armé*) may have been overdone as a polyphonic *cantus
firmus*; Bach's preludes were too long for some in his congregation;
Goudimel's psalms too jumpy; and the Viennese composers too

folksy and too sophisticated at once. Yet none of these creations were something exclusively for "nice" people, who tend to confuse cleverness with virtue. They were for anyone who had ears to hear, regardless of status. For composers, performers, and audiences, they were open to talent.

While retaining and expanding the first definition of liturgy— public service—the romanticists also expanded the Enlightenment's estimate of the musicians who served these cults and celebrations. During the eighteenth century, the social position of musicians had sunk to the lowest.[52] Now musicians were no longer expected merely to decorate the words of a moralist. Artists were to be the chief public moral teachers because their instruction transcended creeds.

The fact that hyperorthodox critics would reproach Christian romanticists for being "followers of Pascal" gives a clue to the romantic sense of mission. Pascal had wrestled with the problem of finding a place for religious belief between rationalism and superstition. He had concluded that mankind must wager on the existence of God, and that each man must work out his own salvation. Pascal's individualism was analogous to the Faust myth, in which so many romanticists recognized their own destiny. "Faust's life is the life of everyman. In the romantic view, the lesson of Faust has to be relearned individually through experience. . . ."[53] [Such a] view of life is basically Christian, for it combines the infinite worth of the individual soul in its power and weakness, the search for union with the infinite, and the gospel of work for one's fellow man."[54] The new generation was convinced that it is impossible to reduce the Christian, or any, gospel to creeds, *summae*, or ethical maxims—even the most enlightened ones. Righteousness in the midst of humanity, they believed, could never be separated from the awe felt for an Ultimate beyond man. Practical moralists accused such "mystics" of lacking interest in the timely issues of the day. Conversely, the so-called mystics wondered what the "practical" men were driving at and questioned the idea of moral progress. For the "mystics," the cult which came closest to being un-moral was narrow evangelism for one's opinion, which all too easily becomes dogma.[55]

Among ecclesiastical cults, the German romantics found Luther's philosophy[56] of music a congenial *via media* between Catholic declarations that music could be identical with the cult—which admission was always qualified by calling music the *ancilla liturgiae*, the "humble handmaiden of the liturgy"—and the blunt, Calvinist view of liturgical music as strictly utilitarian. Earthy Luther had taught that, "After theology I assign to music the highest and most prominent

place of distinction and honor. Music reigns in days of peace. . . .
I have little use for those who, like fanatics, despise music. Whole-
some popular music for the people and difficult music sung by choirs
willing to take the time to rehearse it both belong in the Church."[57]
According to a Lutheran liturgical theorist of the nineteenth century,
Georg Rietschl, Luther meant that art need not enter the church as
"humble handmaiden." If an expression is valid artistically, its vocation is true.[58] The choir stands in relation to music as the preacher
does to oratory. Both interpret the gospel.

In their pamphlets, the German romanticists described better liturgical music as a return to Luther's tradition of giving good things to
the people. Klopstock, Hamann, Herder, Schiller, Goethe, Reichardt,
Arndt, Mendelssohn, and others insisted that the religious music and
poetry handed down from the Reformation and before were organic
continua, not to be "improved" by bringing the grammar and images
of the texts up to date or by "rationalizing" the free rhythms of the
tunes into regular measures.[59] Those early ethnomusicologists believed that the old chorales had absorbed—or better, sublimated—
contemporary secular tunes. The chorales were, therefore, models
for the modern church. Their words and music seemed the inseparable mirror image of each other.[60] Later improvements, intended
to teach community and enlightenment, seemed to destroy the noblest things the people knew, leaving only banal Gebrauchsmusik
in their place.

Appreciation of Luther's chorales grew apace until they were featured at celebrations of the three-hundredth anniversary of the Reformation in 1817 even in Catholic Vienna. Many of the works used
were by Catholic composers—for there were no Protestants in Vienna. Many of the festive pieces were built around some sixteenth-
century chorale and gave play to a musical priesthood of all believers:
choir, orchestra, and audience or congregation.[61]

Within the Evangelical Church, the urge for authenticity aided
attempts to restore the Gregorian sung dialogue which Luther had
retained in his liturgical agendas.[62] Here again the restorers intended
to reconcile old and new, clerical and popular, didactic and symbolic, artful and homely styles.[63] They purported to "overcome the
passivity of the congregation engendered by a century of worship
based upon preaching and monotonous hymns."[64]

Several writers dealt specifically with the question of how to combine a religious heritage with modern life. Friedrich Wilhelm Joseph
von Schelling's (1775–1854) doctrine of nature as "das werdende

Ich" ("evolving consciousness") gave a cogent development to the doctrine of cosmic, organic evolution "in the spirit of Herder." In 1791 Schelling was suspected of translating the *Marseillaise*, but he soon became and remained an academic philosopher always promising the magnum opus which would unriddle the universe. For a more popular influence one must turn to a man born into popular religion, Friedrich Schleiermacher (1768–1834).[65]

Schleiermacher grew up in a Moravian household at Herrnhut and passed from the pietism of his youth, through the Enlightenment, to romanticism. While romantic aesthetic theory was substituting *ut musica poesis* for the Renaissance's and Enlightenment's *ut pictura poesis*, Schleiermacher was substituting his acoustic, evolutionary theology for the formal, scholastic kind. That is, he preferred dynamic, kinesthetic to static, geometrical metaphors. His image of the church was that of an organic community of believers with a corporate experience of God and a corporate role in the process of redemption.[66] Of the individual, Schleiermacher said, "Your feeling is piety in so far as it is the result of the operation of God in you by means of the operation of the world upon you."[67] Religion is the sum of all higher feelings. "It alone removes man from one-sidedness and narrowness."[68] "More than any other at his time [he] elaborated a philosophy of national education intended to infuse a common spirit into the people by transmitting to the succeeding generations the values and spirit that had become part of the national heritage."[69] In ethics and aesthetics, and therefore in liturgiology, he found uniformity repugnant. The true superiority of Christianity lies precisely, according to Schleiermacher, in its lack of exclusiveness. "As nothing is more irreligious than to demand general uniformity in mankind," he writes, "so nothing is more un-Christian than to seek uniformity in religion."[70]

In 1804 he insisted that reformers leave alone the free rhythms and folk poetry in German hymnody. Didactic hymns only robbed the people of their artistic treasure while leaving nothing in exchange.

In the midst of German disenchantment with Napoleon's new Imperium, earthy chorales seemed the "finest expression of the finest German act"—the Reformation, another war against a Latinate despotism. Various other restorers of German chorales used various arguments. Some, mostly artists, poets, and musicians, talked the romantic, populist jargon: artful reinterpretations of religion could liberate the people from their old idols and lead them into the promised land of a democratic community. Others, mostly blooded politicians, were pessimists even before some students overdid a celebration of the first war of Liberation at the Wartburg Castle in 1817. The patriotism which the French had grown from the bottom up, the fearful German princes wished to instill only from the top down.[71] Some Germans tried to reconcile the two mentalities. They were living Lamennais's problems a generation early.

While Schleiermacher was at work on a theology of religion as aesthetic experience, other romanticists were collecting and collating the chorales he treasured. *The Youth's Magic Horn* (*Des Knaben Wunderhorn*) by Achim von Arnim and Clemens Brentano was the most famous collection of antique German songs, including religious lyrics, published before and during the war to drive out Napoleon. From the German victory over Napoleon at Jena in 1806 until the Prussian king subverted the cult for legitimism in the twenties (as we shall see) and drove creative minds out of formal religion, there was a ferment in the Evangelical Church over which liturgical forms would unite Germans, preserve their traditions, educate them aesthetically, and steer a middle course between rationalism and obscurantism. A chronological bibliography[72] would show that more and more religio-patriotic liturgical agendas were published while the Germans worked harder and harder to expel Napoleon.

Some liturgical manifestos published during the Befreiungskrieg were strictly patriotic. Max von Schenckendorf, who dreamt of restoring the medieval German Empire, dedicated his hymn-writing talents to the Prussian general staff.[73] Theodor Koerner, a member of the *Lyra und Schwert* (Lyre and Sword), published a hymnal with the same name which idealized falling patriotically on the battlefield—as he soon did, while carrying a guitar Schiller had given his father.[74]

Other agendas remained closer to Schleiermacher's non-Erastian theology. In these, artistry was to supersede didacticism just as self-revelation superseded moralizing in Schleiermacherian sermons.[75] Some observations about "Church Vocal Music" in the *Liturgisches Journal* for 1807[76] tried to combine Enlightened with romantic liturgiology: authors should use only "provable" material in their hymns; express it in diction with a universal, not local, appeal; and create images to express the concept and not vice versa. These neoclassical dicta were tempered with romantic injunctions always to use "good music" to set the text and an assertion that "community prayer, not instruction, is the highest purpose of a hymn." The same volume carried an article "Church and Theater," which sounded like Liszt's *Manifesto* a generation later: the church should avoid the theatrical but not shrink from making its services as artistic as the offerings in concert hall or opera house.[77]

Also during these anti-imperial years, Anton Friedrich Thibault was assembling a *German Unity Hymnal* to replace the dozens of local hymnals used in the various sovereignties of Germany. Though this friend of Schiller's was a Huguenot who believed that Palestrina was the model liturgical composer, he thought he had a mission to "restore to Germans one of their outstanding cultural accomplishments."[78]

Such populist intentions were soon put to work in the Prussian civil service. We recall that Prussia, now a kingdom equal in rank to Austria and enlarged with a piece of the wealthy Rhineland, was the real winner of the Napoleonic wars. Whatever this much-enlarged Prussia did was bound to influence the rest of northern Germany. After the Congress of Vienna, Frederick William III and his advisers continued to exploit the Evangelical cult. In 1816 he established a choir to display the riches of the choral repertoire at the Berlin Cathedral and returned the services there to Luther's agenda. The choir was directed by Goethe's friend and Mendelssohn's teacher, Carl Friedrich Zelter. In the following year, as if to contradict the liberal students celebrating at the Wartburg, the king exercised his prerogative, *cujus regio, ejus religio*, to force a union of the Evangelical and Reformed churches in all the far-flung Prussian domains. Within a decade Hesse, Nassau, Anhalt, and the Rhenish Palatinate —areas where there were many German Reformed—also forced a Protestant unification. These unions were well-received by liberal nationalists until the twenties, when they were recognized as tools of the alliance between throne and altar against constitutionalism.[79]

By 1821 most monarchs were stifling constitutionalism; Frederick William III did what Luther wisely had not done.[80] He ended debate over which liturgical forms were to mirror the community by imposing uniform Prussian liturgical rubrics. "Uniformity" was the word Schleiermacher hated most.[81] Thereafter, he, Schopenhauer, and many other romanticists considered the attempt to restore the authentic chorales "attention to belief at the expense of intellect and emotion." Others lamented what seemed an attempt by the hierarchy to reassert control over local congregations.[82] Henceforth, pietist-rooted romantic theologians tended to leave established religion to the statists.

Some musicians were happy to see these liturgical reforms, even if they were Prussian-style, which meant that choral platoons were formed in the royal army to provide model choirs for the new, unified church.[83] The king announced that he did this to help build a unity in his army and kingdom equal to that he so admired in the soldiers of the Russian czar. Yet, an imperial caesar, whether a Napoleon or a czar, remained an uncongenial model for most romanticists. From Tübingen the Catholic theologian and noted author of *Symbolik*, Moehler, scoffed that the Hohenzollern had too much of a soldier's view of religion—the king was only looking for another division wherewith to fight the pope.[84] (Catholics were suspicious of Prussian hegemony in "their" Rhineland.) Schleiermacher was disgusted that bureaucrats should still presume to order what he thought was the prerogative of every congregation. In 1830 he would say dryly of church-state relations: "Where the Evangelical Church is wholly separate from the State no one wishes it to be otherwise, but where a closer tie exists between the two there is a division of opinion within the Church."[85]

If the king was going to play the Protestant pope, why not have the real thing? Some Protestants, like Friedrich and Dorothea Schlegel, became crypto or even practicing Catholics. Many musicians and other artists too admired the Catholic Church because it seemed to offer more opportunity for musical talent than did the Evangelical and Reformed Church, with its tedious sermons and dragging hymns led by a "cock and hen" choir.[86] Though much of the Evangelical and Reformed service was now set to music, it remained one essentially of preaching and hymn singing.

Some Evangelicals attempted to restore the sung dialogue in Gregorian chant which Luther had retained in his liturgical agendas.[87] Here again the reformers intended to reconcile old and new, clerical and popular, didactic and symbolic, artful and homely styles.[88] They purported to "overcome the passivity of the congregation engendered by a century of worship based upon preaching and monotonous hymns."[89] Actually, there was to be a double exchange during this continuing enthusiasm for experiences at once popular and elevated. While Protestants were again publishing Latin services with German tropes in the middle of the *Kyrie* and German Propers set to Gregorian melodies,[90] Catholics were manifesting protestant tendencies in Pentecostal movements.[91] Such campaigns for the restoration of Gregorian chant with German texts evidently continued throughout the *Vormärz*—the period between the Congress of Vienna in 1815 and the revolutions of March 1848. A periodical, *Die liturgischen Blätter* (*Liturgical Bulletin*)[92] was published at Mecklenberg in the forties.

When cultural nationalism was conscripted for the Prussian war effort, medievalism had proved attractive because it seemed of the people. Freiherr vom Stein thought that the Catholic Church had preserved the Germanic culture of the Middle Ages more faithfully because of Rome's unchanged dogmatic and liturgical structure. He thought that the Protestants had produced the best hymns, but Catholics had been most steady in preserving tradition, so he preferred liturgical forms which approached the Catholic Church's. He praised Chateaubriand's *Le génie du christianisme*, whose round of Masses, offices, and processions, offered a model for preaching and religious festivals which he thought might enliven German patriotism.[93] The rubrics which Frederick William III imposed upon his unified Evangelical and Reformed Church in 1816 restored the Gregorian chant Luther had used. Other German states soon followed the king's example.[94]

Lutheran music historians like Johann Häuser thought of Luther's chorales the way Catholic contemporaries thought of Gregorian chant.[95] Music, they thought, originated in heightened speech. But as devout Protestants they were bound to argue that during the Middle Ages Christian music had declined from its early success, when it was in the hands of all believers. Medieval music symbolized the division of Christianity into clerical and lay castes, beginning when Pope Gregory I had made what had been a communal art into a clerical mystery. Although purely professional, esoteric, music made great advances henceforth, congregational singing was thought unnecessary by the medieval church. Only the Reformation again exalted the people.[96]

Häuser wrote that Luther's chorales were the noblest examples of music, the noblest art. Through the unison chorales, the *Volk* make one great artwork, which is a better expression of mass feeling than the intricacies of classic polyphony or of trying to harmonize around the tune.[97] Professional music in the church he thought an expression of that Voltairean error, individualism.[98] (Similarly some French romanticists became ultramontane partly because they thought the Roman church more democratic, because of its unbroken tradition, than the parade of selfish families playing musical chairs around the French throne.)

For many liberal Germans, as well as for conservatives like Häuser, the Prussian king should be obeyed because the principle *cujus regio, ejus religio* gave him the power to decide a practical matter of public order. Since the king was thought to be the heir of Luther as

well as of Teutonism, this made him for "Protestant freedom" and
against ultramontane pretensions to exploit Germany from the outside—a charge the Hapsburgs could never quite shake off. He was
also thought to be as near to a pope as anything Protestants could
stand: that is, a paternal figure above sectarianism; the monarch
was even said to be democratic in the sense of embodying a long-
standing concensus of his people. His vocation was then to foster a
common market religiously and culturally, just as he fostered a German economic common market, the Zollverein. Hence the justification of a common spiritual coinage and measures. Häuser argued
that loyalty to ritual forms decreed by the king should be a German's
way to demonstrate loyalty to the natural social order decreed by
God.

The established churches also remained one of the major possible
sources for patronage of artistic accomplishment. Lately, Häuser
complained, music in the Evangelical and Reformed Church was
declining, though secular music in Germany was flourishing.[99] Popular music education seemed to be raising the average level of taste,
but the churches were not participating in the upthrust. Now, in the
1830s it was again up to musicians to build a bridge between the
masses and the Sublime.[100] While doing this, composers must avoid
the extreme of theatricality, which makes nonmusicians wish to go
to the other extreme of banning music from the church altogether.[101]
Secular music is in a golden age, but before sacred music can catch
up, it must pick up the thread of organic development where it was
cut by insensitive, egotistical tampering. Therefore, authentic rendi-
tions of the treasure already at hand must precede new composition.[102] And in the new age, congregational singing must be the basis
even for the rites of Jews and Catholics.[103]

Other Lutheran liturgists and musicologists were more moderate.
Ludwig Schoeberlein, who was the foremost Lutheran liturgist of
the early nineteenth century as Carl von Winterfeld was their foremost musicologist,[104] taught that the Evangelical church must return
to Luther's common sense by steering between two types of clericalism: preachiness and ritualism, both of which leave the congregation
passive and produce an amoral church. A congregation meets to
express their common beliefs and concerns not to hear sermons or
concerts. Art music by professionals is necessary, but communal
singing of our treasured chorales must be the backbone of the service.[105] Schoeberlein was less broad-minded than the apostles of
enlightenment, who did not limit the community to Christians. But
within the community of worshipers, he favored "democratic" forms,

such as mixed (not strictly male) choirs to perform the treasures of choral literature. The church should honor art, unlike the Calvinists.[106] Neither the Prussian king's male chorus nor boys' choirs could do this, for by excluding women both were pseudo-clerical. Services should contain antiphony between the choir and people, rather than be dominated by a clerical caste, as was Catholic worship, where people behave as though at a concert and boys' choirs gave the impression that choral music is for children.

On the other hand, many of the Protestant romanticists prized the effect of the Catholic liturgy because they thought that it successfully integrated art, music, architecture, and "dance." Of all the arts used, music seemed to be the most active. These Protestants valued an artistic vocation as religious in itself, not as a "handmaiden of the liturgy," which it was in orthodox Catholic theology, whether it be of the curial or the progressive variety.[107]

Meanwhile, religion had become the laughingstock of liberal young Germans after the government overresponded to the demonstrations at the Wartburg in 1817.[108] Intelligent men had to choose between religious tradition, which was fast becoming a branch of the government's propaganda office, and modern ideas. Henceforth, arguments in liturgical and musical journals became less a plea for a blend of new ideas with artistic traditions and more either a screen for archaism or a protest against it.

From the Prussian king's point of view, the unification of religious rites in his domains intended what Joseph II's liturgical reforms were to have done in the Hapsburg territories: enhance the building of a nation-state out of his feudal domains. From the historian's point of view, the restraints on free inquiry employed by the Restoration have a bad odor. Perhaps the musicians and artists who served the Restoration of throne and altar share the blame for its repressiveness. Their dilemma resembles that of the political Liberals who, by 1848, were also cornered into serving absolutism or having nothing.

IV

In Scandinavia, the liberal spirit rationalized "improvement" of an indigenous, free-rhythm hymnody in favor of didactic hymns in regular meters a generation later than in Germany.[109] From the beginning of the nineteenth century, congregations there were taught to sing rhymed sermons on the duty of self-improvement, choirs were abolished, and professional musicians departed the churches. One of the results was that tempos dragged so that at least one church synod at length set minimum tempi.[110]

As in other modernizations of religion, one profound effect of the end of local liturgies was to assist the end of feudalism. For example, the uniformity of the imported *Haeffner Choralbuch* of 1814 was unpopular, but it did help to end the residual manoralism which had been sustained by maintaining local variants of the Lutheran rites in every parish.[111] The ultimate acceptance of the new style is not surprising, for the Swedes during these same years accepted an imported king, the French General Bernadotte, who also set about ending feudal localism and enhancing the unitary state.

Looking back through the age of the First Vatican Council one tends to see the antidemocratic aspects of the liturgical restorations and contrast them with the liberalism normal in mid-twentieth century. But, as in Germany, the movement to restore polyrhythmic chorales in Scandinavia began as a populism as ambivalent toward modern civilization as was Kierkegaard.

This ambivalence is demonstrated in the life of a Danish hymn writer, Nikolai Frederik Severin Grundtvig (1783–1872), who grew up a heretic and died a bishop. After ordination he became enamoured of Schelling's philosophy. By 1808 he was publishing collections of Norse and Eddic folk poetry and at work on his own epic, *The Decline of the Heroic Life in the North*.[112] As a pastor he was at work trying to carve out a place for religion among rationalism, Lutheran dogmatism, and fundamentalist pietism. His assertion that Christianity is not a frozen set of commentaries, but a growing, "living" organism offended the established church. The "folk schools" he inaugurated to offer training in practical subjects were imitated throughout Scandinavia; so were the rural cooperatives he organized as an eminently practical—and successful—contribution to community life. But Grundtvig's enthusiasm and evolutionary theology alienated rationalists, fundamentalists, and dogmatists. In 1825 he was fined, suspended, and not reinstated until 1832. In the meantime, he studied Anglo-Saxon and wrote poetry of his own. As a liturgiologist, Grundtvig sought a "joyful Christianity," which he thought would come in large part from a "singing church." He wrote more than fourteen hundred religious lyrics.[113] His son continued the work of collecting Norse and Danish poetry.

Ironically, the liturgical revival within the northern European Protestant churches on the continent had less effect upon those members who stayed than upon those who emigrated to America.[114] In Europe, urbanization, industrialization, and a generally richer cultural environment inevitably made religion only one among many aspects of a society's cultural life. In the New World, religious meetings and rituals were one of the few ways that those beyond the Atlantic fall line could share their humanity. Revivalism and formal religion thus did serve in America—itself always deemed at least a halfway return to the state of nature—the purpose they were supposed to have served in the prehistoric state of nature. They were an opportunity for heightened speech amid a prosaic routine where biological nature was still looked upon more as a captor than as a liberator. Small wonder that psychological nature wanted so often to be burned over. Poetry (the Bible), singing together, kinesthesia en masse, riding to the meeting at dawn, and camping-out together if the meeting was too far, were a touch of the Sublime amid a very prosaic life.

Max Weber believed that western civilization has disenchanted everything, except perhaps music.[115] The educated of European civilization became acutely aware of this in the eighteenth century and sought to recover the innocence they imagined themselves to have just outgrown. Unfortunately, to try to be innocent is a contradiction in terms. The harder one tries, the less possibility there is of succeeding, for the effort itself is a component of the deficiency.[116] In that quandary European culture was forced to reexamine its myths, such as the fall from grace, and the relationship between reason and passion.[117]

The quest for an enchanted world of lost childlike innocence has traveled many roads, including the path from sentimental species of traditional Christianity, like pietism, down to our own times. Romantic paths to the Sublime included also the quasi-folk culture of simple tales like *Undine*, the high-church revival of medievalism and art-for-the-masses. The same paths converge again in our own time. They serve, for example, D. H. Lawrence's works and Herbert Marcuse's *Eros and Civilization*. Throughout, innocence must be reached, as Blake put it, through "an improvement in sensuous delight," until the whole body becomes an erogenous zone. More generally speaking, innocence, so far considered, is the ability to feel.[118] Was simple, childlike faith the natural music of uncorrupted souls? Could religion, music, or history answer that question?

The quest for innocence is of a piece with the cultural revolution which flowered in Europe during the eighteenth century and eventually tended to reverse western civilization's idea of the "higher" and "lower" faculties and classes of man. This reversal had many dimensions. Among them were a psychological reorientation from the objective world outside one to the subjective world of imagination and feelings within; a social reorientation from idealizing the privileged classes to idealizing the lower classes; a geographical reorientation not only from classical culture lately borne by the French to culture led by relative outsiders of the eighteenth century, the Germans; a sexual reorientation from a masculine ideal to an androgynous one; from the adult to the child; from the civilized sophisticate to the noble savage; and so on. All of these changes mark a fresh emphasis on certain themes continuous in the western cultural tradition and inseparable from the industrial and political revolutions of the same years. Together they bracket the romantic search for democratic culture, in which self-esteemed "reasonable men" must come to terms with the unreasonableness of mass feeling, often expressed in popular religion. The next step would be to attempt the recovery and creation of a civilization believed to be uncorruptedly natural.

A MUSICAL RETURN TO THE STATE
OF NATURE

The Restoration of Plain Chant

5

Who would say that his philosophy is not "natural"? Like scriptural quotations "natural" means all things to all men. Following the trend of the eighteenth and nineteenth centuries, to the former "natural" meant "rational and intelligible"; to the latter, it meant things-as-they-grow. Newtonian physics was the ultimate science for one century; evolutionary biology for the other.

In harmony with that historical tendency, the romantic generations believed that the individual and the community are less the products of conscious choice or contract than the offspring of an organic evolution. Considered organically, the acorn is no less important than the oak, the child no less than the man, the primitive no less than the sophisticated, the Gothic no less than the classic, and the medieval no less than the modern. Each is unique and worthwhile in itself. Each is natural.

Both the eighteenth and nineteenth centuries also had hierarchies in the arts. As we have seen, lyricism in general and music in particular stood toward the bottom of the scale in the eighteenth century. At the turn of the century, music was moving from last to first place in the aesthetic hierarchy. The reasoning behind this change also favored a new-found respect for cultures other than the modern European. Whereas the Enlightenment idealized classical antiquity and had begun to investigate other cultures, the romantics went a step further. They tended to promote the discussion of exotic times and places from a device for criticizing contemporary life to a search for any civilization deserving emulation. This tendency has had many effects. One is the idealization of the primitive, childlike, and spontaneous qualities, which westerners sometimes see in other cultures. Another is the search for nonartificial and inward products of western culture to counter what seems to be the technological and aggressive mainstream.

One important example of the reevaluation of the western cultural inheritance was the romanticization of the Middle Ages, which were now thought to be a European epoch closer to the "state of nature." This romantic tendency, found in the young Marx as well as in the liberal Lamennais, the tory Chateaubriand, and the reactionary de Maistre, inspired the beginning of historicism, including musicology, which considers the arts as expressions of the cultural soils and seasons that produced them. Application of this organic theory of society and creativity influenced thinkers throughout the artistic and political spectrum. Much of their work, which debated the origins of language and culture, was carried on in terms of the attempted recovery of early music.

I

According to the aesthetics which accompanied the organic theory of the psyche and society, civilization had begun and flourished in communal celebrations where music, drama, dance, and poetry were one. The spirit of those primitive gatherings was often supposed to be an ecstatic catharsis of inhibitions and a sublimation of instinctual drives. Communication among people close to the state of nature was said to be multimedial, not differentiated into the patterns of language, steps of the dance, or melodic and rhythmic modes of music. The romantics believed that some of the same emotional release was necessary and good for every civilization and every human being[1]—especially for modern western man.

While proceeding to new creation in this spirit, the romantics usually thought it necessary simultaneously to reestablish contact with living or viable traditions where emotion or imagination had flourished. That part of the human past which most fascinated them was that which lay psychicly anterior to calculation and historically prior to civilization and its discontents.[2] There the function of the arts was to give a healing outlet for secret emotions, to speak the unspeakable. Under these circumstances all the arts, including music, sculpture, and architecture, were supposed to have been linked by their expressing the same feeling in diverse media.[3] Such a romantic fascination with primitivism, folkways, and stream of consciousness unity is now taken for granted. Who today would assert that it is only through a chronicle of kings and conquests, rather than through songs and stories whereby we see people as they really are?[4]

In applying such theories, many anthropologists and social historians have called the release of emotion in ritualized celebrations and games playful.[5] The definition of play resembles the classical definition of a liberal art, something done for itself and not to earn something else. It is the opposite of work. In medieval Christianity such sacred play surrounded the sacraments, which *are* the divine, not a comment upon it. In the romantic view, art too is strongly playful, and artists are childlike. The purpose of art is first to look like life.[6] Didacticism or moralizing is only incidental. Art is to be, rather than to mean. Ever since romantic times it has remained quite reasonable to be "against interpretation." This opposition to dissecting an institution or creation unites the religiously orthodox like Romano Guardini, the religiously neutral like Wilhelm Dilthey or Johan Huizinga, the heterodox like Sigmund Freud, and many modern ethnomusicologists,[7] psychologists, and anthropologists who find such play useful. Dilthey called it man's consummate artwork. Romantic aestheticians valued religious liturgies in part because they seemed playful, ingenuous, childlike, natural, primitive, or "eastern." Wordsworth's *Ode on Intimations of Immortality from Recollections of Early Childhood*, Chateaubriand's *Atala* and *René*, Goethe's *Elective Affinities (Die Wahlverwandtschaften)*, Mark Twain's *Huckleberry Finn*, and Manzoni's *The Betrothal* are the merest beginning of a list of works which affirm the worth of simple, childlike, primitive, or natural impulses.

And of all human talents, the one which seemed most "natural," always manifests itself early, everywhere, and usually seems quite independent of efforts to instill it, is musical genius. A mind trying to leap from the merry-go-round of sufficient reason might conclude that the very uselessness of music, its playfulness, is what makes it most useful. For such a mind, if it were religiously inclined, music might be viewed neo-Platonically. It would be what Pythagoras said it was, part of a supernatural action which can delight the gods and make man one with them. (A Lockean behavioralist could support

this belief by arguing like Rameau's Nephew: music occurs when
the free play of natural impulses is allowed.)

Many romantics believed that medieval civilization was a high
culture which still had the primitive view of public religious ceremonies as a sacred play blending sight, sound, and motion.[8] To
reconcile their fascination with the holy and the Enlightenment's
fascination with skepticism, they enunciated organized religion's ultimate task. Suppose, as Kant had said, there is nothing man can give
God. Too, nontheists certainly can have acceptable morals. More,
suppose that Isaiah's visions and Guéranger's history are only wish-
ful thinking so far as most people can tell: the theist must now
justify himself with aesthetic, playful, arguments such as: "The important thing is not who comes or doesn't come, but that the artists
have a place to present their vision."[9] And so the reverence that
hopes to conserve past religion comes to support the belief that artistic imagination is the key to future religion and therefore to future
civilization.

Speaking of the playfulness of the liturgy, Romano Guardini, a
pupil of the romantics and a teacher of Johan Huizinga, compared
its apparent purposelessness with didactic syllabuses like Ignatius of
Loyola's *Spiritual Exercises*: "The difference resembles that which
exists between a gymnasium, in which every detail of the apparatus
and every exercise aims at a calculated effect, and the open woods
and fields. In the first, everything is consciously directed towards
discipline and development, in the second life is lived with Nature,
and internal growth takes place in her."[10]

The researchers were wrong when they believed that Gregorian
chant was a vestige of primitive rites, but they began the researches
which seek out the who, where, what, and when about all music.
Those who believed that a communal art work began civilization
were not quite right either, but there was in fact community participation in music among so-called primitive cultures. Furthermore,
music and religion may have been in fact the first specializations,
that is, the first steps toward civilization.[11]

II

In those places where medieval ritual and music survived through
the eighteenth into the nineteenth centuries, their use was like the

Caspar David Friedrich, *The Cross and the Cathedral in the Mountains* (ca. 1811). The assertion of a correspondence between nature and Christian visual symbols paralleled speculation that medieval music might also be the expression of an uncorrupted communion with the elemental forces of life. (Kunstmuseum Düsseldorf.)

churches they served, often more a habit than a conviction. Still, there was no lack of eminent writers and musicians who hoped to restore the medieval cult to its former integrity. Like so many things, the restoration of Gregorian chant was suggested by Jean-Jacques Rousseau, whose *Dictionnaire de Musique* disseminated some of the first scholarly information on primitive, folk, and oriental music. His delineation of these three types foreshadowed the organization of comparative musicology.[12]

As a philosopher of the eighteenth century, Rousseau believed that the surviving chant was a "noble relic of classical Greek music. Despite its desecration at the hands of barbarians, it still retained much of its ancient beauty."[13] In another place Rousseau praised chant without submitting it to such antimedieval canons: "To prefer modern music over the chant in churches means not that one has no piety but that one has no taste."[14] Plain chant, he said, was certainly preferable to the syrupy, theatrical rubbish usually heard in churches. The operatic style heard there was usually a mere display of vocal technique, whereas the chant clothed the text it set and thus expressed it better for the listeners. Rousseau also preferred that chant influence modern music rather than vice versa. There can be no doubt that musical encyclopedists and scholars of the chant for several generations afterwards copied Rousseau's thoughts, even when they did not know or acknowledge their debt.

Nine years after Rousseau's dictionary, Fürstabt Martin II Gerbert von St. Blasien, who is sometimes called the founder of the Catholic musical restoration, published the then-known manuscripts of treatises by *Scriptores ecclesiasticae de musica sacra a prima ecclesiae aetate usque ad praesens tempus.*[15] Though Gerbert evinced an interest in the general history of religious practices,[16] his thesis was a musicological apologia for Catholicism. Music, he said, had progressed until Palestrina's time—the time of the Reformation—but had declined since then. Gerbert thought that modern music was too proud to be submissive to the text. So, ignoring stumbling blocks like Gregorian coloratura alleluias, he urged that the church restore services in Gregorian chant exclusively and thereby discard all secular influences in her music. Since Gerbert, too, was a mind of the eighteenth century, he tempered his medievalism with rationalism and nationalism. He taught that Latin hymns are of no use to a peasant, who should sing in his native tongue for edification and for piety's sake as he did in the old germanic liturgy. Certain other theorists drew Gerbert's theories to the logical conclusion that valid music must always employ all the cultural materials at hand. Among those theorists were the first musicologists.[17] Burney, Hawkins, Forkel, and Fétis among others knowingly followed Rousseau when they praised Plain Chant for its simplicity and folklike qualities.

The next generation of musicologists matured after the French Revolution and knew that the people would have to be recognized in all matters, cultural as well as political. Several educational reformers labored to make art music, which had been an aristocratic perquisite, available to everyone. Alexandre Choron (1772–1834) applied similar theories to the situation in France during the Empire and Restoration. In his pamphlet *Considerations on the Necessity of Reestablishing the Chant of the Church of Rome in All Churches of the French Empire*,[19] he pleaded with Napoleon's ministers to restore the church's musical establishment if they wanted the people to attend its services. He faced a bureaucracy accustomed to think of the church as, at best, useful for controlling the lower classes.

It would take a prophet to revivify the old religion in such an age. At least two such arose. One, Chateaubriand, convinced many educated people to consider religion beyond the limits of pure reason. His *Genius of Christianity* (*Le génie du christianisme*) retreated behind one of the impregnable barricades of Catholicism—its aesthetic richness. Religion as a system whereby life is lived as a total aesthetic —Lockeans read "sensory"—environment became in his conservative hands revolutionary-in-spite-of-itself against the seeming one-dimensionality of bourgeois materialism. The other prophet was the firebrand Lamennais.[20] Like Thomas Merton and Teilhard de Chardin more recently, Lamennais and Chateaubriand impressed an unlikely public with the aesthetic riches and evolutionary energy of Catholicism but have remained suspected heretics within official ecclesiastical circles. It is curious how all such romantic apologists seem more vehemently anathematized than the Voltairean skeptics. But then, why not? The philosophes and the theologians were frequently quarreling about details of the same model, *static* natural law. The romantic apologists and critics were trying to cope with a new *dynamic* conception of the cosmos which was only implied in the work of the eighteenth century. The philosophical Old Regime was at heart Newtonian and believed that life should approach the static condition of Euclidean geometry. The new regime is kinesthetic and believes that life should approach the evolutionary condition of music.

III

The dialectic between those two cultures is illustrated by the attempt to relate medieval liturgical traditions to modern times. The first generation of French Catholics who could not remember the Old Regime had one liberal prophet in aesthetic as well as political and social matters, Félicité de Lamennais (1782–1854). Mazzini called him the Martin Luther of the nineteenth century;[21] Berlioz expressed Europe's admiration in, "A demon of a man! I tremble with admiration;"[22] the pope damned him; and Liszt dedicated to him the piece "Lyons" in his *Traveler's Album* with the motto of that city's rebellious silk workers (who cheered the Saint-Simonians): "Live working, die fighting" ("Vivre en travaillant/Mourir en combattant").[23]

Lamennais's aesthetics, like the rest of his philosophy, were not original with him but were assimilated from a milieu which included Burke's *On the Sublime*, Schelling, Victor Cousin, Coleridge, and Hegel, making him the more typical. Moreover, Lamennais delighted in the friendship of the great musicians who were his contemporaries. He was "mad about music."[24]

Like his contemporaries, the utopian socialists, Lamennais dreamed of a community of love. The utopians were bound to fail. For they had to make up their vision in full view of prospective proselytes. Lamennais had the advantage of publicizing a creed whose origins were still effectively beyond history for most people in 1830.

Turning to Lamennais's writing on religious rites and their music, we find him undergoing a typical romantic development. The horrors of the revolutionary era, which he was old enough to remember, made young Félicité declare that he could never belong to the philosophes, whom he held responsible for the violence. He thought their acid had been too strong; having loosened the corrosion, it began to dissolve the vessel of civilization without having a new one ready. When Lamennais chose Pascal over Descartes, he was like Coleridge, Scott, and Wordsworth across the Channel, who also feared to trust fallible reasoning. Faced with the fact that one's assumptions are always beyond rationality, they postulated their own version of democracy: the normal experience of all men is a surer guide to truth than limited, individual experience. "Indeed, there are truths which one does not prove, that one cannot prove logically. They are, however, not only true but are the certainties whereby one establishes the certitude of all else."[25] Since what determines the course of one's reasoning is beyond reasoning, "art is prior to science" because "before perceiving any abstract idea, man perceives it under the conditions of its creaturely existence, united with a phenomenon."[26]

After thus philosophizing that the Good and True is first apprehended as the Beautiful, Lamennais speculated on the historical origin of art. This, he said, lay in the need for men "to come together in order to accomplish civic or religious actions."[27] In other words, art was originally a communal expression, "liturgical" in the etymological sense. Lamennais seemed to understand the perennial problem of liturgical musicians (text versus music) and made the usual concession to the usual mentality of the philosophes and the theologians by writing that "the proper function of singing or of the musical component in speech is to unite unseparably the abstraction with the sentiment properly associated with it. This sentiment is the product of the psychological and physiological aspects of the voice expressed in its intonation, accent, and rhythm. Music viewed in this way is the expression of one's total intellectual and social life."[28] After those Rousseauvian words, predictably, Lamennais said that he did not like that kind of "Italian" music which lacked the union between words and music so evident in medieval chant and classic Renaissance polyphony.[29]

Lamennais's aesthetic was essential to his philosophy of the *sens commun*, a wisdom shared by all people. This dictum seems to combine Rousseau's idea of a general will with the Thomistic—as well as Encyclopedist—doctrine that the good is first apprehended as the beautiful. The purpose of art, said Lamennais, remains "to satisfy the dictates of the moral order, to assist the struggle of humanity toward its End, to raise humanity above materialism, and impart to it a perpetual movement of ascension.[30] There are two implications of this doctrine: first, religious art is humanity's way of grace to ascend the neo-Platonic chain of being in order to attain the eternal source, whence emanates all good, truth, and beauty. And, considered in relation to Enlightenment theories, it implies progress in the arts and society.

Consequently, Lamennais said that "Art sleeps when it yields only retouched copies of ancient models, only cold effigies that have no breath of life."[31] To be consistent, he should have welcomed modern music into his church, whose liturgy he believed was "the complete humanistic drama which combines in one harmonious whole all manifestations of intellectual and moral nature."[32] Lamennais wanted

a music as vast as all creation, embracing all the sounds of creation,[33] and continuing to develop this art closest of all human endeavor to the operations of the spiritual.[34] He believed that recent
composers such as Bach, Haydn, Mozart, and Marcello were making
music more expressive, thus making music history end in progress
and elevation, rather than decadence. But he stopped short of accepting the "dissonances of modern composers" into the temple. For
church music, Lamennais, like Chateaubriand, preferred the art of
inwardness, plain chant, because it had the austere spirit of primitive
Christianity. "For man no longer knows uncorrupted dogma; humanity is isolated from a tranquil heaven, from the contemplation
of truth and beauty in their eternal source."[35]

A decade after his excommunication, Lamennais still thought that
Gregorian chant could help to erase the passionate illusions and vivid
emotions of men who do not contemplate pure Being. Here, again,
we encounter the ultramontane romantics' ambivalence: art—particularly music—is the epitome of communal action; yet this enemy
of the Carlists and delegate to international revolutionary committees[36] would not apply his own democratic principles within his
complete opera. Thus, even the Roman Church's most advanced
thinkers maintained its estrangement from the nineteenth century,
in part because, in spite of themselves, they rejected the artist as a
prophet of a new order.

IV

The populism that Lamennais asserted to be embedded in the
divine natural order had numerous disciples, including Dom Prosper
Guéranger (1805–75), whom we have already noted as an enthusiast of plain chant. He was the restorer of the monastery at Solesmes.
"Music has never said 'odi profanum vulgus' "[37] was at one time the
motto even of those, like him, who later strove to exorcise ecclesiastical symbols of romantic populism. Lamennais deserves much of
the credit for these conservatives' original populism. According to
Dom Guéranger, who later achieved the reputation of having begun
the restoration of an ancient continuous utopian community, Benedictine monasticism, and its music, the congregation need not even
understand, let alone directly participate in, the ceremonies of the
church. The effect of the liturgic chant was *ex opere operato*. Never-

theless, with his mind on his beloved ages of faith, Guéranger had insisted that "plain chant is the sung prayer of the people. . . . Its prosody bears the people's accent, its modes are natural scales, the people's."[38]

Though Lamennais's political liberalism was later condemned by the church, his apologetic traditionalism and ecclesiological ultramontanism were praised. Disciples of his who repented of their errors and remained in the church, and their biographers too, were tempted to announce that they had been attached to him on account of his ultramontanism and traditionalism, and not on account of his liberalism.[39] An example of this is the official Benedictine biography of Dom Guéranger by his successor, Dom Delatte.[40] A book published in 1933, bearing the church's imprimatur, demonstrated in detail both that Guéranger's "ultimate object in founding Solesmes was to create a center for Mennaisian ecclesiastical studies"[41] and that Guéranger did not declare himself against Lamennais until a year after *Mirari vos*, with which Pope Gregory XVI condemned Lamennais in 1832. Ten years later some bishops still thought that Guéranger retained "the allure" of that Mennaisianism which the hierarchy found so repulsive.[42] He never completely lived down the connection with Lamennais,[43] through whom he was linked to the radical side of romanticism.

In 1833 Dom Guéranger led an émigré community of Benedictines—though obviously not all the same monks who had fled—back from their refuge on England's Isle of Wight, where they had spent the revolutionary and Napoleonic eras, to the Priory of Solesmes in France. Here they again lived Saint Benedict's motto *ora et labora* and his *Rule* in a utopian community. They hoped to be a model for a confused modern society as Benedict had hoped his communities would maintain civilization amid the chaotic dark ages which followed the fall of the Roman Empire.

Benedictine, western-style, monasticism is a communitarian total environment, the heart of which is musical.[44] Every sense is offered its view, colors, light, and darkness; its texture; its incense; its kinesthesia; and its sound. The sounds were monophonic chant, which is richer than many know. Little wonder that in the age of Saint-Simon, Fourier, Owen, and Marx, the oldest communism extant in western civilization seemed to some no longer "the denial of humanity" that the eighteenth-century had spoken of, but the "art of arts."[45]

Guéranger and his associates made an aesthetic judgement when they wished to preserve this consummate artwork. Having done this, it was almost inevitable that, in the restoration of Benedictine monasticism, Solesmes should become concerned primarily with its music, the art most thoroughly integrated with the day-to-day performance of the *opus dei*. At first, medieval music seemed the most easily accessible monastic affect because it seemed to depend only on authentic manuscripts and competent performers. Yet music proved to be both the banner and sign of contradiction within the liturgical restoration. Surely Guéranger and his associates made a questionable philosophical judgment when they chained artistry to Roman canon law and thus tried to codify the uncodifiable.

As a disciple of Lamennais, Guéranger was working to recreate a spirit of community and find a dignified living space for religion between superstition and rationalism. With one hand he fought the religious rationalism and individualism which would strike everything nonbiblical—i.e., everything medieval—from the Roman rite and even replace its first-person plurals with singulars.[46] With the other hand, he fought Gallican traditions which were concessions to local custom. These were anathema to any Mennaisian because they suggested that the cosmic authority of Christianity depended upon local bishops, who were now state employees. For Mennaisian ultramontanes, the words "Gallican bishop" conjured up an image of an oversuccessful, self-seeking place hunter like Talleyrand or some cleric out of a Stendhal novel.

So Dom Guéranger worked strenuously to suppress all trace of non-Roman rites.[47] Dogmatic and battle-loving, he was as willing to preserve a false legend in agreement with his theories[48] as he was to destroy local tradition.[49] Some Gallican missals were preserved only by being handwritten.[50] Most were so efficiently proscribed and destroyed by the Romanizers that much music which had equal claim to be born of the church has been destroyed, and researchers today have difficulty even learning about the existence of these rites.

To an ultramontane, Parisian and other Gallican missals and service books were nothing but "an unhappy amalgam of Roman chants and parodies of miscellaneous ancient pieces."[51] For many Gallicans, however, it was an honest artistic difficulty to choose among all the versions which presented themselves as the authentic Roman chant.[52] The Gallicans insisted that an arbitrarily uniform version would confound rather than attract and edify the masses of the faithful, who may have sung their particular Gallican chants for generations. To Guéranger's party, however, community meant uniformity, just as it would to the papal party at the First Vatican Council.

Solesmes's argument was that the oldest extant manuscript is the authentic one and therefore the best. Those who loved Gregorian chant because much of it is fine music or who hoped to restore what they took to be the communal art of the Ages of Faith, yielded to archaists pure and simple.[53] Solesmes's musical archaism became a forerunner of Pius IX's *Syllabus of Errors* of 1864, which seemed to deny any value to modern ideas.[54]

Ironically, Guéranger's study of the words and music of the Catholic liturgy did not restore it in the way he hoped. Insofar as those studies were honest and scholarly musicology, they have helped establish what Guéranger denied: sacred and secular music were not absolutely separate genres in the Middle Ages. Insofar as his studies were rationalizations of the Roman position, they helped to preserve a stifling mortmain over those artists who wanted to compose modern religious music. The church has come full circle as in the twentieth century it grasps at topical and popular forms of ritual, which it hopes will express mass feeling. The tendency to rely more on the judgment of clerics than of musicians is continuous with Guéranger. But direct mass participation in the liturgy is a tradition more in debt to the Enlightenment.

In his own time, the submissive masses within the Roman Church gave Guéranger small comfort. Sophisticated ultramontanes like him urged devotion to Mary because it had been prominent in the rites of the High Middle Ages. When handed over to "manifestations of popular Romanism," as Newman called them, devotion to Mary assured that the austere but rich aesthetic and spiritual diet that Guéranger and the Benedictines proposed was never tasted. The reports of miracles at La Salette in 1846, the definition of the dogma of the Immaculate Conception by Pius X in 1854, and its seeming confirmation by the reports of visions at Lourdes in 1858, helped to maintain the Catholicism of the late nineteenth century in an amalgam of solipsistic devotions and absolutistic papal authority.[55]

V

Solesmes's most respected champion was Joseph d'Ortigue (1802–66). He was both a romantic, for whom art was the way to reach the world, and an ultramontane, for whom art was first of all an insulation against the world. Within and without the church he campaigned incessantly in behalf of modern composers like Beethoven and Berlioz and against the dictatorial mediocrity which limited public music in theaters and churches to what was successful commercially. True freedom, he thought, should mean no slavery to bourgeois taste. Sainte-Beuve reckoned d'Ortigue the wisest and most gentlemanly of all those Catholics who remained faithful to Lamennais.[56]

It was at a dinner at d'Ortigue's that Hector Berlioz—like Sainte-Beuve—met Lamennais, who in a way had an easier life than d'Ortigue. The latter maintained his ambivalence to the end of his life by trying to reconcile freedom and authority in a philosophy of art which discussed all the questions raised here. In several books d'Ortigue elaborated his ultramontane yet romantic aesthetic, wherein the artist is the highest human type, the musician the highest artist, liturgical the highest music, and Gregorian chant the noblest liturgical music. Yet outside the church he was a firebrand.

"Classical music was romantic in its time" was d'Ortigue's motto against academicians like Fétis, who taught that the forms of art are fixed.[57] On the contrary, said d'Ortigue, art is "as limitless as thought, as the soul."[58] He delighted in pointing out that, at one concert of antique music, the musicologist Fétis allowed one of his players to insert a coda obviously from the nineteenth century into a piece of fifteenth-century music.

Most of d'Ortigue's writings attempted to distinguish between the truly dramatic and the merely theatrical.[59] He made all his antagonists fall together by comparing classicist dicta with a despotic government, which in turn is like Gallicanism in religion, that is, a despotism not founded on common consent.[60] Rhapsodizing on Lamennais's theme that music is social instruction, d'Ortigue wrote in 1836, "By means of music one writes on the hearts of all peoples the religious and political laws on which the social order depends."[61]

Mennaisian is d'Ortigue's opinion that "the arts are social by nature and are the essential modes of communication among men. They shall never cease to be an essential tool of civilization, so long as man, *who does not live by bread alone*, has to express the true and the beautiful." But the beautiful is in God. Therefore, among men the love of the beautiful is identical with the love of divinity.[62] Religious music expresses the relation of man to God; dramatic music the relation of man to man; instrumental music, man to nature. Music is the highest art because it sprang immediately from the

Word—from an incarnation of thought united with physical expression. Within this scheme the artist exercises a priesthood and the critic an apostolate. For music, like all art, has in the realm of the emotions, a social mission before God, among men, and between man and the universe.[63]

As did Lamennais, following Chateaubriand,[64] so did d'Ortigue find the Roman Catholic Church democratic at heart because the temple "mediates among all minds, all wills, and all passions. The bell, like the organ, is the voice of the multitude: the *vox populi*."[65] The tower and its bells wipe out class distinctions and tie private lives to the polity by sounding alike for each baptism, wedding, and funeral, not only for those who can pay.

As a critic, d'Ortigue was uncompromising in what he asked of his church. Though he prefaced everything he wrote about Catholicism with a pious credo, d'Ortigue thought that whenever the clergy planned a service, it was poorly done. For the clergy seldom attended public concerts frequently enough to familiarize themselves with the possibilities of music. Moreover, the clergy had the habit of speaking dogmatically and being treated deferentially. Hence they pontificated upon subjects with which they had only superficial acquaintance.[66] The composers among them were even more to blame because, in their zeal to make the church popular, they institutionalized fads. And the faithful believed that music by clerics was better than music by laymen. D'Ortigue related a story about a priest who engaged a string quartet to play at an important service and sent them to their places with an admonition to "do as well as the men we had last year." After the ceremony, the players descended from the loft to receive their pay and, hopefully, a compliment too—for they had played a Beethoven slow movement and some other masterworks. The priest gave them all a pat on the back and referred to the gospel story about the unequal distribution of talent. He condescended to cheer up his hirelings for having only one talent, unlike the previous year's musicians, who had played some show tunes.[67]

Like Lamennais, d'Ortigue began and remained a fiery advocate of Christian civilization. He admitted that Choron had done good work, but asserted that medieval music was superior to the music of the "pagan Renaissance," which Choron featured. Even before the tricolor he hated returned in 1830, d'Ortigue had inveighed against "musical Voltaireanism" in his book *The War of the Dilettantes* (*La Guerre des Dilettanti*):[68]

Now to imagine that church music, which is the inscrutable interpreter of invariable doctrines, should undergo the same metamor-
phoses; to introduce among it the same changes operative in other
music is to exalt forms which are uncertain and frivolous and to
make ephemeral that which is by nature immutable. Apart from a
few convenient concessions to taste, sacred music ought always
to remain the same.

Because, as he put it thirty years later:

Politics, literature, history, and the arts are swimming in a jostling
chaos. Everything is thought arbitrary, indifferent, and at the
mercy of individual impressions. Thus, people avenge themselves
for the absolute submission once demanded in the matter of
dogma. So the ties which bound the eternal verities of religion to
the diverse objects of human consciousness, like the ties which
integrate human consciousness within itself, are ignored if not
destroyed. . . . Thus is destroyed the distinction between right and
wrong.[69]

Others of like mind argued for an exclusive use of Gregorian chant
in the Catholic Church by asserting that "modern music adheres to
a pagan philosophy because it immorally violates the natural law
of harmony by admitting dissonance equally with consonance."[70]

D'Ortigue shared the belief that Gregorian chant is democratic
music, which has great moral and religious—and therefore social—
value because it was natural to the human *sens commun*. He reiterated that plain chant is natural and popular music and insisted that it
still lived among French peasants, as alive as their local patois. In
1852 he denied that trying to teach everyone chant was like trying
to restore a dead language. Surely, he said, both the church *and* the
government should preserve this native, living music for the sake of
both art and archaeology—why, look at all the silly things the government supports![71] He also adduced favorable opinions of chant
by Rousseau, Mesnier, Fossoyeurs, and Lamennais to prove that it
appealed "even to philosophes, Saint-Simonians, Jews, and apos-
tates."[72] Overriding all is d'Ortigue's incessant ambivalence. He campaigned continually for "progress in the arts"; yet, like Lamennais,
he stopped short of admitting modern music into his supreme opus.

Enthusiasts for plain chant believed that diatonic modes and prosody are native to all peoples; therefore the chant seemed a God-given
voice of the people suited to be a universal religious music. These
enthusiasts did not believe that this line of reasoning contradicted
one of their other theses: that chant was the musical idiom peculiar

to the ages of Christian faith. One Catholic scholar of Solesmes's diocese, Mans, reported that a missionary "who had penetrated to the heart of the American desert" found Indians there who sang melodies like those in the *Kyriale*. He reasoned that the Indians could not have absorbed European scales from any outside source. Therefore, the modes of chant must be universal,[73] whereas recent musical and revolutionary creations were not universal but local and ephemeral.

No matter how distinguished the schools or their graduates, the clergy remained as suspicious as Plato's Guardians of these unruly manipulators of the imagination. In direct continuance of neo-Platonic schema like Boethius' and Cassiodorus', the professional musician was treated like a mere tool who should obey the real musicians, the clerical theorists. For their part, the musicians sometimes tried to turn this accusation of sensuality into a virtue. Music, centered on the grand organ at the back of the French church, was said to "speak for the flesh trying to ennoble itself." The altar at the other end stands for the divine. Humanity is caught between.

Though both viewpoints have their eye on the people they are not quite democratic. The hoped-for democratic return to the supposedly more natural organic style of life in the Middle Ages proposed festivals *for* the people rather than festivals *by* the people. Yet there is a touch of rebellion about the whole endeavor from Rousseau to d'Ortigue. The medievalist church found itself alienated from modern civilization and was forced to justify itself in terms applicable to the dominant liberal philosophy. By so doing, traditional religion unintentionally enhanced the cult of the artist heroes, past or present, who seemed also to have contradicted the materialistic ethic. This alliance was a strong support of romanticism. It is continuous with the myth of soul, Gothicism, romance, exoticism, childhood as better than adulthood, androgyny, and the whole romantic syndrome.[74]

In sum, Catholics and liturgical Protestants, who often date the beginning of the Liturgical Movement from 1840, when Guéranger founded his periodical *The Liturgical Year* (*L'Année liturgique*),[75] should notice that the movement's beginnings go much deeper, earlier, and wider. And the romantic character of those beginnings is also their most enduring aspect. Religion, art, psychology, or politics are none of them the whole story. An impulse to combine the supposedly higher and lower functions of each inspired the romantic dream and remains a modern problem.

At the same time, during the Restoration, while the Benedictines were returning to chant the Hours in their cloisters in Europe, the Franciscans were instructing their last generation of Indians at the Spanish missions in California. Nearly fifty years later, in 1876, Robert Louis Stevenson passed by and recorded that the Indians were being driven off by "developers and other thieves." Still, the Indians gathered with their grandchildren on the one day of the year when a priest came to say Mass. They met in the sacristy of the church, for it was the only part still roofed. "You may," says Stevenson, "hear God served with perhaps more touching circumstances than in any other temple under heaven." An eighty-year-old, blind Indian leads the others through a meticulous performance of Latin language and music which was "an experience of culture whereby all they knew of art and letters was united and expressed. . . . I have never seen faces more vividly lit up with joy."[76] Chateaubriand could not have imagined it better.

THE COSMIC OPERA

The Quest for a Total Work of Art in Religion

6

The search for models of the organic wholeness being lost in modern culture eventually ranged beyond the Middle Ages to all places on earth and all times in history. Inevitably, the romantics, who admired artists as rebels, creators, and heroes, were drawn to the Renaissance.

I

When the Renaissance began in the High Middle Ages, long services set to Latin words and music lacked the connection between word and flesh that most Europeans demanded. They were bored. So, parallel to the prescribed chants of the monastically oriented Roman liturgy, the Gothic musicians added some texts they could understand, music that reminded them of things they understood, or simply a musical embellishment. Sometimes they shortened the services by performing many verses of a chant at once. (They knew God could understand.) Thus, in part, began polyphony.

Renaissance musicians continued this practice of syncretizing other-worldly rites and human celebrations. There is a legend of how the bishops at the Council of Trent were about to forbid polyphonic music until they heard Palestrina's *Missa Papae Marcelli*. This legend of how Palestrina tamed the puritanical zeal of the Tridentine Fathers with his *Mass*, thereby assuring a place for music in the

church, probably preserves as much truth as does the scientific de-
bunking of it. For Palestrina was closely associated with Saint Philip
Neri and his oratory, which tried to put into wider practice one of
the aspects of the Catholic reform: reaching the people at large.[1]

Palestrina was in fact trying to combine the elitist thrust of a
Renaissance virtuoso with the needs of an institution that wanted to
popularize itself. Since he was a church musician, he retained the
religious, medieval purpose for his works. He began with medieval
Gregorian themes, just as the visual artists of the Renaissance began
with religious subjects. In the fashion of the humanists he emphasized
intelligibility of the Word—and words. This articulation of the text
was as important to the Fathers of Trent as it would be to the philosophes. By employing themes from Gregorian chant and the popular
religious songs of his day, Palestrina kept his music in close relation
to his libretto, the Roman liturgy. The theologians, however, feared
for clerical status, which Luther was attacking. Hence they refused
to invite any wider popular involvement.

During the century after Trent, the style of classic polyphony
proved to be almost too successful a compromise. Even today, music
students study textbooks of harmony and counterpoint in the sixteenth-century style. As if to give an imprimatur to tradition, in 1903
Pope Pius X in his encyclical on church music placed the polyphony
of the Renaissance second only to Gregorian chant as a model of
balance between restrained declamation of a text and ecstatic outpouring of music.

The philosophical implications of the harmonization of text and
music are essential to an understanding of the secular milieu out of
which the restoration of classic polyphony grew. In the eighteenth
century, as at Florence, Geneva, and Trent, public, that is liturgical,
music had to justify itself in terms of the quarrel between musical art
for art's sake and embellishment of a literary affect such as a play,
scripture, or text of the Mass. Enlightenment humanists were later
critical of secular liturgies set to florid Latinate music, the Italian
opera. Like the Renaissance humanists whose aesthetics resembled
that of the theologians during the contemporary Reformation and
Counterreformation, the philosophes wished to subordinate musical
ideas to the text. A long controversy in the eighteenth century
brought the argument up to date. This debate over the relationship
between the plot and musical or choreographic diversions in opera
was a round in the debate over the relationship between reason and
emotion in human psychology and society. As we have seen, the

literary lights of Paris, which was then the cultural capital of western civilization, were divided between the admirers of Italian opera, such as Rousseau, and the followers of Rameau. Rousseau implied that music could be humanizing in itself. Rameau implied that music should serve rationalistic philosophy. This Bouffon's Quarrel led to the controversy between the Gluckists and Piccinists. The admirers of Gluck stood for uniting music, literature and all the arts in one dramatic composition. The Piccinists, who were often the neoclassical philosophes, wanted as little as possible musical interference with the plot. They thought that the most pleasing effects arose when musical or choreographic diversions were kept separate from the plot, which should be spoken or, at most, declaimed in recitatives. The patriarchs of romanticism usually espoused Gluck's reform. When he integrated music and plot, by implication he made reason and emotion equal citizens of a republic of human faculties.

While romantic poets, artists, and composers were creating new works which integrated various artistic media, as Gluck's operatic reforms seemed to reintegrate words and music, many romantic scholars concluded that the classic polyphonists of Palestrina's time had already achieved a reconciliation not only of the literary and musical media but also of high art and popular appeal. Therefore the romanticists hoped both to create and to restore public music wherein text, tone, *logos*, *ethos*, and *pathos*, were an organic whole. Judging in terms of origins (which may be begging the question) the Rousseau-Gluck romantic insight was correct, because drama—including religious rites—was in most cultures (including the west) originally not a literary but a musical and choreographic ceremony.[2] Such were the philosophic issues which antedated the throne-and-altar nostalgia for Renaissance polyphony as a lost jewel of the Old Regime.

II

Whatever success Renaissance composers might have had, most of the life seemed to have gone out of the polyphonic style by the middle of the eighteenth century. Old and new compositions in the *stylo antico* were usually "pepped up" to conform to prevailing taste and notation by being performed with regular measures in cut time "because the notes were too long."[3] As with the chorales and other

Giovanni Pannini, *A Night of Italian Opera* (1729). The pageantry of the opera house seemed to typify the sensual style of life in the Catholic nations which had created this compendious art form dominated by music. The emotional intensity of opera was often compared to or distinguished from the Roman Catholic liturgy and its music.

early music, rhythmic subtleties were "rationalized" by being forced into a regular meter. Most of the impetus to restore the integrity of classic polyphony did not come first from Palestrina's own church. Those Roman basilicas which one might expect to preserve the music made to match them were cluttered with papier-mâché saints; their music, too, was covered with tasteless decorations. This we know on the evidence of those romantics from north of the Alps who fled into the Roman Church. For example, only a month before Dorothea Schlegel began to recite the Little Office of the Blessed Virgin Mary daily, she complained to her equally ultramontane brother Friedrich that the festive rites in the Italian churches were all show and no substance.[4]

Other admirers of the Roman Church's humanistic treasures made similar complaints during their pilgrimages to Italy. Hester Lynch Piozzi, a patron of Samuel Johnson and friend of the pioneer musicologist Dr. Burney, thought the Sistine Holy Week utterly irreverent.[5] Burney agreed.[6] Nor was the atmosphere in Italian churches any more respectable after the turn of the century. From Venice, Felix Mendelssohn wrote to his teacher, Zelter, one of the founders of popular choral singing, of his joy at seeing in their intended places all the great works of art he had heard and read about. Then he told of his disgust at hearing organists attempt all sorts of tremulando and arpeggiando effects in pseudo-polyphonic style on what they called Gregorian *cantus firmi*.[7] In Rome, Mendelssohn found holiday crowds jamming the Holy Week services, but leaving to stretch their legs during the long recitations of psalmody or Passiontide gospels. He wished that the scripture were either read clearly or set to properly interpretative music. Since the Holy Word had to be sung throughout, Palestrina had been reduced to embellishing the numerals in each chapter-heading of the lamentations with music, while leaving the scripture itself set to monotonous psalm tones.[8] He fondly recalled the straightforward Lutheran chorales he had known in Düsseldorf. These hymns "proved their value by both uniting the congregation in song and educating the taste of people who had no formal musical training."[9] He contrasted these solid chorales with the "silly" performances given many Catholic masterpieces, though these masterpieces were still effective in the huge Roman basilicas.

The Sistine choir, which was supposed to be preserving Palestrina's tradition, seemed just another self-assured vocal display. Like the rest of Rome, it preserved the outward form while neglecting the substance. "Nevertheless," said Mendelssohn, "the effect of chords melting into each other in the great basilicas is so great that he alone may destroy this who can replace it with something better."

Hector Berlioz also visited festivals in the Vatican and had similar reactions. When he entered Saint Peter's, he found it all that he had anticipated—immense, though disfigured by those papier-mâché saints. He awaited the music "which should be the soul of this greatest cathedral." But his hopes were progressively shattered, first by the portative on casters, which was the basilica's organ; then by the choir totally inadequate for the music and the building; next by instrumentalists who tuned and practiced during the Mass when they were not actually performing—and when they did play, that organ denied the established pitch at the end of every phrase; finally, by an outraged woman standing next to him who insisted that the bushy-bearded soprano who so amused Berlioz was her husband and no *castrato*. Berlioz concluded that there was as much cultural life in the churches as in the theaters of Rome: none.[10]

A French priest and music critic, Louis Leclercq, thought that the Roman Holy Week services remained a theatrical display which obscured their meaning for the Italian people. The Sistine choir he thought lost in the vast basilica. Leclercq found the choir still "tastelessly modernizing simple chants and motets."[11] He criticized the "two civilizations" theory reflected in the idealization of Palestrina by the papal choirmaster, Father Giuseppe Baini.[12] It seemed to Leclercq that Palestrina's admirers contradicted themselves.[13] While proclaiming their model divinely untouchable, they mutilated his music to make it ape the all-popular operatic style which had put the old polyphony into the shade.[14] He thought that to follow the example of past greats meant to employ the music of one's own age. Therefore, the church should not restore Gregorian chant and classic polyphony to exclusive use. Palestrina was good art, not above art. He sounded right in a cathedral when performed by trained singers, but his larger compositions were impractical models for ordinary congregations, who needed a clearer melody to follow.[15]

Many ecclesiastics talked about the need for good music. However, those who paid for music usually preferred the contemporary equivalent of pop church music, like the town committee that had hired Bach, which, after admonishing him not to perform any operatic music, admitted that he won the post only because the town had been turned down by a second-rate opera composer.[16]

The novelist Stendhal, who wrote several authoritative books on music and musicians, understood the problem. His hero in *The Red*

and the Black, Julien Sorel, was an ambitious peasant who almost
learned to be the Talleyrand of the democratic era. Having found
that clerical black and civic red both demanded hypocrisy, he used
his "vocation" not for the community but for himself. Sometimes
Julien had difficulty overcoming his natural, romantic inclinations,
as he did at one church festival.

> The deep sound of the bell ought to have made Julien think only
> about the work of twenty men earning fifty centimes each, assisted,
> perhaps, by fifteen or twenty of the faithful. He should have
> thought of the wear and tear on the ropes and the wooden frame-
> work, of the danger to the bell itself, which falls every two
> hundred years, and he should have tried to think of some way of
> diminishing the ringers' wages, or of paying them with some
> indulgence or other favor drawn from the treasures of the Church
> without strain on her purse.
> Instead of being absorbed in these wise reflections, however,
> Julien's mind, exalted by the rich, virile sounds of the bell, was
> wandering in imaginary space. He would never make a good priest
> or a great administrator. Minds that are moved in this way are
> capable only, at the very most, of producing an artist.[17]

"*Imaginary* space." A tragic flaw! Julien was bound ultimately to
fail in the clerisy. He died on the guillotine. Sorel's author, Stendhal,
was an anticlerical who agreed with Chateaubriand, a Catholic apol-
ogist, about the social value of the church's humanistic treasures
symbolized in the ringing of that bell.[18]

III

But the Catholics were slow to realize that their tradition offered
more than a prop for legitimism. Among the first critics to plead for,
and to accomplish, restoration of classic polyphony proper to the
Catholic reformation had been German Protestants of Schiller's
Sturm und Drang generation.[19] These preromantic writers agreed
with the spirit of Lessings *Laocoön*, which argued that each art has
its own demands. If so, music need not be a servant of the words,
for it is their equal.

In 1762 the Prussian Rousseau, J. G. Hamann, had published a
Protest in the Form of a Circular on Church Music,[20] wherein he
proposed to recapture Luther's "sense for music and a holy Protes-

tant enthusiasm" by returning to the "noble simplicity of the old
Italian masters" such as Palestrina.[21] Like the apostles of enlightenment, Hamann thought it ridiculous to break up liturgical texts into
recitatives, arias, and solos. Like Lesueur and the romanticists, he
admired the tight musical and textual continuity with which the great
polyphonists had set the Roman liturgy. In other words, Hamann
recalled that the unity of passion directed by moral intention desired
by the Encyclopedists had been achieved in service of the "grotesque"
Jesuit Catholic reformation.

Hamann's student Herder continued the campaign for the public
performance of sixteenth-century classics. Herder thought that since
the time was past when composers would create solely for the Christian religion, liturgical composers ought to understand the masterpieces of the nearest time when the primary inspiration of art had
been religious. He meant having both humanistic moral intent and
zeal for supernatural ecstasy. Classic polyphony seemed to fit this
definition and was good community music because it was choral
rather than solo. It was not "self-centered," like the elegant background music of the concert style used in Francophile salons or the
opera, where prima donnas paraded their vocal technique.[22] In an
essay, *Caecilia*,[23] published in 1793, Herder said that theater and
church music are as different as sight and sound.[24] He thought that
"worship is the highest," indeed the only, "purpose of music. Sacred
music calms one by its simplicity; it edifies by its majesty." The
Catholic polyphony had simple, pure harmony and majestic movement like the Protestant chorales, which are the greatest German
artworks, ranking with Luther's translation of the Bible in their
ability to make the supernatural accessible.[25] Hence, although the
attitudes of Herder, a religiously oriented German, and his operati-
cally oriented contemporaries seem opposite, both praised the same
musical goal and similar models. Both retained the Enlightenment's
distaste for unrestrained musical entertainment in the mass media of
opera and church, but like the romantics to come, both were skeptical of didactic liturgies. The musical impulse should be "moral"
but transcend moralism.

In the rationalistic quest for "Christian simplicity," the Christian
apostles of enlightenment had virtually discarded music in order to
save the word. In the quest for a total experience, the romantics
wanted to open the priestly cast to nonverbal talents. As Schleiermacher would put it, "In so far as he draws others to himself in the
field he has made his own and can show himself master in, every

man is a priest: every man is a layman, in so far as he follows the skill and directions of another in the religious matters with which he is less familiar. . . . Each in turn is leader."[26] The initial romantic enthusiasm for classic polyphony is therefore understandable not solely in terms of a reconciliation between text and tone, standing for the rational and the irrational, but in terms of the Renaissance and romantic ideal of an aristocracy of talent rather than birth; and in terms of Luther's common sense ideal of a priesthood of all believers.

All the German romantics from Hamann and Herder to Wagner assumed an original identity between music and religious rites which mandated the primacy of religious music among all the arts.[27] The early romantic *Outpourings from the Heart of a Cloistered Brother Who Loves Art* by W. H. Wackenroder (1773–98) made explicit this apotheosis of sacred music. The hero, Brother Joseph, liked to visit churches on great festivals. Before the music began, while he stood in the tightly "packed and faintly murmuring congestion of the crowd; it seemed to him as though he heard buzzing about him, unmelodiously confused, as at a great fair, the commonplace and ordinary life of man. . . . This much is certain—when the music was over and he left the church he thought himself made purer and more noble."[28] Joseph concluded that to be a church musician and thus help men share in the divine was the noblest vocation he could attain. Wackenroder's friend and admirer Ludwig Tieck (1773–1854), in his *Phantasus* of 1812, joined in the assertion that the *old* Italian style was the proper church music, where the eternal *Miserere mei Domine* made one feel the presence of God.[29]

One of the leading writers in the endeavor to awaken interest in the many facets of the human imagination was E. T. A. Hoffmann (1776–1822), best known today as a collector and writer of fantastic, Gothic tales. Nearly all of his works contain at least oblique references to his theory that music is the most spiritual of the arts and the one most capable of arousing the feelings of worship or of the sublime. He composed much and longed to be known as a great musician, though he earned a living mainly as a lawyer. Since he was the most important music critic of his time, his essay "On Old and New Church Music" in the foremost musical journal of the early nineteenth century, *General Musical Journal* (*Die allgemeine musikalische Zeitung*) during 1814 is sometimes mistaken as the first plea for restoration of Palestrina's style. Some Catholic musicologists have said it was the first in a line of writings which led through Cecilianism[30] to Pius X's endorsement of classic polyphony in his

Motu proprio on church music of 1903. As a jurist writing for a comparatively enlightened, middle-class audience, Hoffmann surrounds musical with moralistic arguments. His essay, though it is a plea for recognition of the value of the old masters, avoids antiquarianism for its own sake. Rather, we see a romantic interest in dark and half-forgotten things trying to enlighten minds which would chop away anything not moralistic.[31]

Hoffmann made three points. First, theatrical frivolity is out of place in a communal religious celebration.[32] It is even undemocratic. For it changes the atmosphere of the church into that of the theater, where admission charges and assigned places foster class feeling and arrogance. If such practices continue in the churches, he said, soon we shall have orchestra, parterre, and gallery, just like the opera. "Such improprieties ought to find no place in Christianity, for they militate against all it stands for. They turn a holy place into a concourse of arrogance and ostentation."[33] Hoffmann admitted that when the disendowed churches were restored after the French Revolution, this "frivolous" style was the only one available.[34] The rich, would-be patrons of the arts, who had more money and self-assurance than discernment and educability, understood technical virtuosity better than musical depth.

Second, in the tradition of drama criticism from Rousseau to Artaud, Hoffmann spoke of an original identity between religious rites and drama. This unity, he said, dissolved when drama began to take place outside liturgy and its sacred space. Consequently, less dignified music could be used. Then, when secular drama became normal, its music began to invade the church in the form of oratorios and eventually destroyed its parent. This point had also been Herder's: the Palestrina style is the last one in western civilization to grow up in a society where religious liturgy and communal drama could be thought identical. Therefore it is our most accessible model of sacred music. It is also foreground music without overdecoration; that is, it reconciles text, the symbol of reason, and tone, the sign of feelings.[35] Hoffmann did not include Handel in his strictures against the invasion of secular into sacred drama, but at Haydn's music he drew the line. He thought not only that such eighteenth-century music was operatic, but that even the best of modern church music, Mozart's *Requiem*, was theatrical in its "Tuba mirum."[36]

Hoffmann's third point tempered his second. Modern music should conform to Palestrina's ideal by preserving unity of text and tone, but modern musicians should expect to use modern musical means. Therefore, "Use and adopt new means while preserving the old. . . .

In music, as in painting, we have old Italian masters to follow; but, unlike the technique of painting, that of music and its instrumental resources have greatly advanced. We must not close our minds to the good in the new. Only the false use of modern riches is bad."[37] Using both textual and musical examples, Hoffmann preaches Herder's reconciling gospel of simplicity, majesty, and unity between text and tone. Church music must clothe the text and not yield to frivolous arpeggios and trills. In one of his Gothic novels,[38] Hoffmann wrote that one may pine after this or that church, but the only architect to succeed will be one who knows the spirit, the whole environment, in which the old masters lived. Epigonism is not enough. Words or simple geometrical proportions may have been valid in the old days. In more complicated modern times, music, the more subtle art, will be the most valid communicator of the meaning of life.

Other writers were even more careful than Hoffmann to keep a balance between old and new. In Gustav Schilling's *Encyclopedia of Complete Musical Knowledge*,[39] an article by G. W. Fink complained that those who favor the restoration of polyphony must keep in mind that, merely because most music is no longer church music, it is unfair to say that modern music is unfit for the church.

Every volume of *Die allgemeine musikalische Zeitung* had articles discussing the hows and whys of improving church music as a means of sharing humanism with all people. Usually the gist of these articles was that improvement must combine restoration of masterpieces and recognition of modern composers with the education of public taste. This could be accomplished by formal musical instruction in the schools and by performing outstanding ancient and modern music regularly in the churches.

The general music magazine *Caecilia*, published at Mainz, also carried a running controversy over what music would be religious, edifying—not merely a vehicle for a text, appropriate to changing festivals—and have popular appeal. Some writers relied on the liturgists of the Aufklärung and continued to press for the simplest possible music, "just so the people understand and sing along." They believed that since church music's only purpose is to declaim the text, it departs from this purpose whenever it interprets emotions aroused by that text. The discussion in *Caecilia* was put best in a three-cornered debate in the volume for 1825.

In a book under review, K. Kocher had argued that the old style is best for the church because it "appeals to the intellect and not the feelings." The reviewer, W. C. Müller, argued the middle viewpoint that some fifteenth- and sixteenth-century music is still worth hearing, just as some of today's will always be worth hearing. Restore some of the old; but antiquity is in itself no recommendation. Each period has its own style; the golden age of choral music will not return.[40] In another article, Gottfried Weber held that one dishonors the old masters by copying their technique or by saying that because Palestrina did not use a 6-4 chord, we may not use one in church either.[41] As if, he said, church style came from not using this or that raw material; or as if double counterpoint is more appropriate to the church—actually double counterpoint would seem to express most aptly the contrary striving of human passions rather than the serenity the archaists seek.[42] Weber quoted Rousseau: "Portray the words intelligently—as in Gregorian chant." Who can doubt, says Weber, that more recent music such as Handel's "The Heavens Are Telling" communicates the mood of a Gloria?[43]

Many composers shared these writers' respect for classic polyphony. Beethoven thought that Palestrina's was model church music but that one should not imitate him unless one shared his attitude.[44] Robert Schumann thought that Palestrina "at times sounds like the music of the spheres, and then, what art! I verily believe he is the greatest musical genius ever produced in Italy."[45] During his tenure as Kapellmeister in Dresden, Richard Wagner said he preferred the *a cappella* style to express the inwardness and piety of religious life. Perhaps because the idea complemented his own theories about the necessary unity between music and poetry, Wagner claimed that all the master church works were purely vocal. He wrote that churches ought to get rid of the orchestras, which have made singers imitate instrumental music. Wagner repeated the theory of music as heightened declamation, and echoed Liszt's plan for public education in music through festivals and public performance of great masterworks, especially in the churches.[46]

French musicians and men of letters also projected their ideals onto the existing Catholic Church. Chateaubriand, whose aesthetics were one of the most influential statements of the romantic credo, stated that art "represents the most beautiful nature possible."[47] In his zeal to prove that Catholicism actually did conform to the natural order of human equality, he argued that the Catholic cult is in its way democratic. For it reaches all alike and would not deny the noblest experience to the humblest citizen. Berlioz's teacher, Lesueur, wrote that he modeled his own sonorities on Palestrina's—adding that the Renaissance painter Rafael used the same pigments for both his *School of Athens* and his *Transfiguration*; so should a composer use the same materials for both secular and sacred compositions while employing a different "mood" in each.[48] Cherubini, whose style is sometimes compared to Palestrina's, thought that new music was needed rather than a restoration of the old masters.

The coupling of French and German enthusiasm fostered musicological research into Palestrina's music and a respect for his solemn declamation even among anticlericals.[49] Palestrina and the musicians of his school seemed to have accomplished in their century the reconciliation between text and music toward which the Romantics were groping in their time.

Victor Hugo, whose style—like Schiller's—was definitely not pallid *a cappella*, wrote a poem in 1837 called *Let Music Date from the Sixteenth Century*. Palestrina was Hugo's musical hero "because he communed with nature, like Beethoven." Palestrina's music was, like Beethoven's "natural." Palestrina

. . . saw nothing gaudy,
For his soul, from an immense and teeming world
Swimming before his eyes in blurs and shadows,
Blotted out the color and seized the harmony.[50]

Hugo thought that the great crescendo of a city's carillons at dawn on a feast day excelled any symphony. For all his admiration of antique vocal music, Hugo also organized concerts of modern music.

Lamartine and Balzac, the one content in Catholicism and the other as restless as Victor Hugo or George Sand to decry any obstacle to the accomplishment of human desire, also praised old church music with Chateaubriand's words.[51] They praised the church style and used it as a symbol of what they wished their own new secular art to do. Balzac said of the *grand orgue*: Only this vast choir can speak across the void. The grand organ alone can frame a prayer in music to match man's despair, his contrition, and his every ecstasy of faith.[52] When the organ shook the ancient air within the church, it seemed to resurrect the very spirits of the dead, good and bad, who had walked there. Lamartine thought that no drama on the stage ever gave him an impression comparable "to the sacred voice of the lonely organ whispering around the tombs and altars beneath the arches of a cathedral."[53]

The first attempt at a historical restoration of classic polyphony was made at the turn of the century by a Viennese named Hauber. He failed because his unscholarly editions, *Musica sacra*, reflected the Biedermeier taste for decorative rather than expressive music, because the disendowed churches of the postrevolutionary era claimed to lack funds for projects like scholarly research in music, and because Napoleon's troops melted the plates of his proposed edition of Palestrina into bullets at Leipzig in 1806.[54]

The next step was taken by a Prussian Huguenot who believed that sixteenth-century polyphony was the ideal music for religious rites. Justus Thibault, who was a friend of Schiller's and compiler of the *German Unity Hymnal* to replace the multitude of local hymnals then in use,[55] used the partial editions already prepared by Fétis and Choron.[56] Thibault hoped to combine high art with popular understanding.[57] His work *On the Purity of Music* spoke of religious ritual as an organic whole whose unique qualities would be lost if its traditional language were altered or its music displaced. His contemporaries Zelter, Mendelssohn, Schubert, E. T. A. Hoffmann, and Carl von Winterfeldt were persuaded to support the Evangelical and Reformed Berlin Cathedral choir, which specialized in choral masterworks.[58]

Some Catholics confused their romantic idealization of the church with the actual institution. Giuseppe Baini (1774–1844) published a hagiographic biography of Palestrina[59] in 1828. His book has sometimes been taken as marking the beginning of the Palestrina renaissance within the Roman Church.[60] That distinction belongs in earnest to the circle of Bishop Johann Michael Sailer in Regensburg, Bavaria.

IV

A twentieth-century hero, Mersault[61] in Albert Camus's *The Stranger*, at length throttles the priest who haunts him in his death cell; Camus's natural man is liberated from gods. A romantic hero, Stendhal's Julien Sorel was still Promethean rather than Sisyphean. In his death cell he wished that the old way were true.

> Oh, if only there were a true religion! . . . What a fool I am! I see a Gothic cathedral with ancient stained-glass windows, and my weak heart imagines the priest who goes with those windows. . . . My soul would understand him, my soul needs him. . . . But I find only a conceited fool. . . .
>
> But a real priest. . . . Then loving hearts would have a meeting place on earth. . . . We wouldn't be isolated.[62]

Johann Michael Sailer (1751–1832) probably came as close as anyone of Sorel's time to that church-window priest. Both Sorel and he rose by way of the church in a time when the priesthood no longer attracted so many from the upper economic classes, because benefices were no longer so lucrative.[63] Though Sorel was forever belying his common origins, Sailer tried openly to unite folk wisdom and rational humanism.[64]

Sailer is important for several reasons. First, his ideas combine the Enlightenment's psychological and aesthetic priorities with those of romanticism. Second, the application of these ideas made him a founder both of liberal Catholicism and of liturgical reform. He was the patron both of a program to restore old music and of popular participation in the liturgy. Through his students, among them King Ludwig I of Bavaria, he was also a forerunner of the centrist mixture of Catholicism and German nationalism. Ironically, the work of Sailer, who admired non-Catholic and non-Christian culture, led to the Cecilian Society, which was more Roman than catholic.

Sailer's biographers consider him the most important religious leader of his time.[65] More surprising, they may be right. Having lived and died technically within the Roman Church, he has attracted no liberal historians, as has Lamennais. Since his orthodoxy was suspect, ecclesiastics delayed his promotion during his lifetime and neglected his biography after he died. Out of his circle came researchers and publicists for classic polyphony, who were, at first, like their mentor, delightfully ambivalent. They wished everyone to share in the best human accomplishments and to dignify modern and popular culture. On the other hand, they wished somehow to insulate themselves from a mechanistic century. Later, musicians spoke more of the first wish; churchmen, of the latter.[66] His true role was that of a Catholic Herder.

Sailer was the first Catholic theologian to recognize the importance of romanticism. He appreciated Beethoven's music and was in turn admired by the composer. Sailer's via media between high and dry Josephin Erastianism and ultramontane devotionalism foreshadowed John Henry Newman's later attempt to synthesize artistic intuition and an evolutionary view of history with the traditional doctrines and practices of Christianity. The ideas of both Sailer and Newman concerning the psychology and sociology of the Catholic Church and its liturgy were analogous to those of Schiller concerning opera and those of Herder concerning culture. The ritual and music of the church were organic parts of an all-embracing, though locally adaptable, drama wherein myriad diverse forces were reconciled.

Sailer tried to frame his ideas in a way that dignified both the spontaneous overflowing of a free heart and the closely reasoned learning of a rational system. Above all he was keenly aware of the tension between the liberal thinking emanating from France and the baroque religiosity of central Europe.

Like Rousseau's *Emile* and Schiller's *On the Aesthetic Education of Man*, Sailer's works argue that the development of every human faculty is necessary in the formation of a complete individual just as the development of all human types is necessary in the formation of a good society. Hence simple piety or musical sensitivity are as humanistic as abstract philosophy or political cunning.

Noteworthy among Sailer's works is his *The Union of Religion and Art (Bund der Religion und Kunst)*, the very title of which is revealing. The importance that he attached to art as an expression of the divine in terms of human experience can be seen in the following passage

> If we consider the one, true, eternal religion according to its inner life in a man, we find that it is nothing more than the life of a childlike temper in the one, true God; the life of faith in God as eternal truth; the life of love for God as eternal beauty; the life of trust in God as the one immutable ground of existence. Only this religion, where it exists, is interior by nature and character, spirit and life, invisible. And yet religion, as the interior life of man, has an irresistible impulse to reveal itself, to make itself visible, audible, sensible and to form for itself a body that can be seen, heard, felt, and enjoyed. It is one and the same artistic impulse that sees in the night sky Nature's own great cathedral and conceives and produces Saint Peter's in Rome, Saint Paul's in London, the Stephanskirche in Vienna, and the Frauenkirche in Munich. . . .
> This impulse is never content with the expression of inner life of religion in ever new forms of celestial music and sacred eloquence . . . , does not rest until the deepest feelings have been brought to their full culmination, until other instruments have been combined in marvelous harmony with the music of the spheres and become one celestial music, and the great allelujah of the heavenly choirs is echoed in the human chorus below.[67]

When Sailer's student became Ludwig I in 1825, the king's "deutsch und katholik" sounded like his tutor's balance between the rationalism and nationalism of the Aufklärung and religious tradition. As crown prince, Ludwig had fought the French influence of Montgelas but helped to design and defend the Bavarian constitution. As king he tried to make Munich a showplace of fine art and architecture and a mecca for liberal writers and scholars. A year after his coronation, he brought Landshut University to grace his capital.[68]

At the opening of the University of Munich, Ludwig sounded like Sailer. "Religion must indeed be the basis of life, but I do not like bigots or obscurantists. The youth should take joy in life and not be hypocritical." The rector of the university went even further on the same occasion. "More decisive than all else for the flourishing of the sciences," he declared, "is the freedom of expression and the free exchange of ideas. . . . Abuse of it is indeed possible, but without it there can be no freedom."[69]

What happened to the king as he outgrew his teacher resembled what happened to the music restorers when they too left Sailer's ideas behind. The king became infatuated with power and his mistress,[70] the liturgists with power and the legalistic idea that church ordination alone, not talent, makes one a priest of art.

When Sailer began to administer the See of Regensburg, he found the music in the cathedral "beneath all criticism." In 1825 his secretary, Father Diepenbrock, wrote to another of Sailer's protégés, minister of cults for the new king, Eduard von Schenk:

> Not only does the music contribute nothing to the edifying
> impression which the rites should have, it actually seems to mock
> them. . . .
>   But we have the needed man and could kill two birds with one
> stone by appointing him to this important post. I refer to Dr.
> Proske, who is not only a trained physician and zealous priest but
> is also a musician. . . .
>   For me the only problem is somehow to pension off the young
> lout who now holds the job. Perhaps by careful economy or
> reserving a sinecure benefice you could do this. I am sure that the
> king would wish to do as much for the ear—that organ so inti-
> mately connected with the soul—as he has done for the eye by
> installing new stained glass in our cathedral. Every person in the
> diocese would be grateful.[71]

Dr. Karl Proske had studied music and medicine in Vienna and had become acquainted with the cultural life of Paris while a medical officer in the Bavarian army. In the twenties he decided to become a priest and went to study under Sailer, who ordained him in 1826.

Bishop Sailer and his friends enjoyed themselves in informal sacred concerts under the doctor's direction. Father Diepenbrock always requested Pergolesi's *Stabat Mater*, which usually ranked second only to Palestrina's music in the esteem of most Catholic romantics. When the piece was finished, Diepenbrock would discourse, conflating romanticism and a seminarist's neo-Platonism, on how this music moved his mind to higher things and summed up all reason and religion, especially love of one's fellow man.[72]

Between trying to restore monasteries en masse, rather than one at a time as Sailer urged, and trying to pursuade the king not to reinstate censorship, the minister Schenk did find the resources to support Proske. He made the doctor a canon of Regensburg Cathedral and its choirmaster. The doctor plunged into restoring sixteenth-century music and wrote compositions in what was to become known as the Cecilian style: long notes and slow chord changes, *a cappella*. He traveled to Italy to study at the Vatican Library and Saint Peter's where Giuseppe Baini was choirmaster. In 1834, while returning from a trip to Rome, Proske stopped at the Monastery of Saint Gall to see the famous newly discovered manuscript in both neumatic and solfege notation. "To make these dead bones live," he gave concerts in the cathedral of fifteenth- and through seventeenth-century masters from the manuscripts he had collected.[73]

Proske gathered about him a musical branch of the Nazarene or German Pre-Raphaelite school which included the painter Overbeck, Peter Cornelius, Veit, and Thorvaldsen, who did sculptural paleography by using fragments of Greek statues in his own representations of classical sculpture. In 1852, near the end of Proske's life, he published some new editions of Palestrina and a handbook of choral directing, the *Enchiridon Chorale*—named after the first music textbook by Odo of Cluny in the tenth century. Among the Bavarian musicians associated with Proske were several whose work became synonymous with the Cecilian style: the court organist Kaspar Ett; Hofkapellmeister Johann Casper Aiblinger; and Canon J. B. Schmid. As with some other contemporary revivals of neglected styles of art and life, however, the result was not Sailer's pious enthusiasm but institutionalized epigonism.[74] Proske once declared—as do many who love the title "Doctor"—that the researcher's task is greater than that of the composer who creates new work.[75] In 1837, five years after Sailer's death, Proske brought Georg Mittenleiter to Regensberg to train the cathedral choir. He seemed to like Mittenleiter largely because the latter was self-effacing in the presence of the clergy.[76]

Secular historians who look back on Sailer's era usually have ignored figures like him or classified them as reactionaries. Catholic historians usually employed Ludwig von Pastor's dichotomy between "good" Christian and "bad" pagan civilizations. Such Manichean divisions of reality between the forces of light and the forces of darkness never comprehend a borderline case like Sailer, who was a Catholic and a romantic who continued to appreciate the Enlightenment's drive for intellectual freedom.

Indeed, orthodox religious historians are kinder to the Enlightenment than to the Sailers. Until the turbulent (and romantic) 1960s, the only scholarly monograph on the history of the Roman Catholic liturgy during the romantic era was an article by Arnold Mayer in the *Jahrbuch für Liturgiewissenschaft* for 1930.[77] The author calls the Restoration classical, for this suits his more Roman than Catholic idea that religion should be an articulate, unchanging, rational system. The romanticists are too unpredictable. Consequently, Catholic historians usually decide to split "romantic" and "Restoration," find the latter "classical," and pronounce it alone good.[78]

The romantic enthusiasts for classic polyphony were doing in the aftermath of the pagan Enlightenment what the humanists had done in the aftermath of the Christian Middle Ages. They were trying to redress a lost balance by moving in the contrary direction. The restoration of old liturgical music was one aspect of a widespread sentiment among a new generation. Some believed that the serene music of the ancestors was a common human heritage needed in an age of anxiety. When it appeared that Christianity did not know what to do with this rediscovered spiritual energy, the impulse to create a new society and mentality of organic wholeness was often redirected to utopian socialism, some of whose cults we shall now consider.

The musicians and writers of communal rituals described in the previous chapters projected the ideas of Christianity back upon itself and asked it to live up to them. On the other hand, the utopian socialists, who in general agreed that the Christian myth and cult was good in its own time, believed that Christianity could no longer be made relevant through nostalgic restoration of medieval or renaissance life. What was needed in the nineteenth century was a new style of life and love which would do for the modern world what Christianity used to do. Yet the rebellion against the old style was itself romantic.

Radical schemes to reconcile the antithesis between the tory idealization of the agrarian past and the liberal rationalization of the new industrial society looked both forward and backward. Backward to an idealized organic society whose lost harmony the utopians hoped to recover; forward to enlightened replacements for the formerly Christian-centered moral and social order.

NO MAN IS AN ISLAND

The Liturgical Music of Utopian Socialism

7

"See how they love one another," and "In Christ there is neither male nor female, slave nor master," were supposed to have been marks of the early Christians. *Caritas* and *charisma* kindled the fires which lighted mutual thanksgiving, the eucharist, when Christians embraced one another in the *pax* or kiss of peace, one of the most venerable forms of the ritual. Through the *pax*, brother was to be reconciled to brother before approaching the altar to taste the delights of God. But when individual learning and earning began to supersede the original community of love, the kiss of peace was no longer extended through the whole Christian community.[1] According to the romantic socialists, while individualism dominated from the late Middle Ages to the late eighteenth century, the communalist impulse lay somnolent in western civilization evidenced only by isolated attempts to realize the radical message of the gospel. During times of radical social change, the radical kingdom emerged metamorphosed to suit the modern age.[2]

During the era of perhaps the greatest and swiftest social change to date, socialism became the faith of an important part of the educated and the working classes.[3] Modern socialism began amid the groping for a new morality which would supersede the old religion while retaining some of its better features. By the time socialism made contact with the working class around 1848, capitalism was uprooting the peasantry throughout Europe and consequently uprooting their culture, of which the church was the spiritual center. A translation of their disrupted mythic structure into modern terms was needed. Socialism stepped into the breach by transvaluing the two most important myths of western civilization.

One is the idea of a cosmic harmony transcending all apparent dualities. We share this sort of idea with most other civilizations. The second, which seems peculiar in so virulent a form to the west, is a pervasive messianism, alias utopianism, optimism, hope, progress, or "new consciousness." For better and for worse, the west is a restless civilization looking for salvation in a mythical future to be ushered in by a radical separation from the present reality. This restlessness was synthesized and taught first by Christianity, which united the Greek idea of cosmic harmony with the Hebrew idea that history is a progression of unique events. The Renaissance and Enlightenment taught that an earthly, not a heavenly, city is our goal. But the Renaissance and Enlightenment were still elitist. To cope with the needs of a mass, democratic, technological culture in the *novus ordo saeclorum* prophesied on the Great Seal of the United States of America (pictured on the back of every dollar bill) a new faith was needed. The idea of salvation for all in a mythical future was spread to all classes of the West and to all peoples of the world. The socialist religion was an attempt to understand and guide the new reality by new theoretical formulations. Naturally these theories were created by those who had the leisure to think. Their radical solutions to the new problems are in many ways functions of their thoroughly western education. A similar mythic pattern is reincarnated in today's counterculture, which favors a radical separation from the entire civilization and all it stands for. The more one rejects the old city, the more one is true to its "happy ending" theory of history.[4]

The emotional energies which still help to propel the many-faceted socialistic movements today owed their initial intensity to appeals formulated in the romantic era. Like the admirers of simple piety or grand ritual, the first socialists were partly inspired by a nostalgia for a lost harmony. The writing of young Karl Marx and the communes of utopian socialism, whether religious or secular, were driven by a romantic passion to present the possibility of a new society beyond the suffering caused by alienation. Young Marx wrote of this hope. Many of the utopian socialists acted it out, some on the American frontier, others in the suburbs of Paris.

I

The doctrinal metamorphosis within one of the most influential utopian schemes, Saint-Simonianism, exemplified the progression described thus far in this book. Claude-Henri, Comte de Saint-Simon (1760–1825), was born of the Enlightenment and witnessed the revolutionary rites.[5] For him, as for the revolutionaries, art, music, and the imagination were tools to assist moral instruction. The testament of his final year, *The New Christianity* (*Le nouveau christianisme*),[6] became the starting point for his disciples who proceeded to apply it in the new, romantic fashion. For them, art must still "regenerate mankind," but they hoped to have the artistic imagination lead rather than contain itself within the hothouse of a master ideologue. Saint-Simonian theories about triadic forces at work in history recalled the Trinity and foreshadowed Marxian socialism's Hegelianism; his disciples' exaltation of nonrational psychological realities recalled medieval myth and foreshadowed Freud's complex view of man. The utopian socialists began with the Enlightenment's premise that art must teach, an axiom of the French Revolution and of most revolutionary dogma.[7] They tried to combine this premise with a dogma and a ritual that would supersede Christianity through attraction rather than legislation or violent revolution. Their goal was a communal—"retribalized" is the fashionable term today—emotional and spiritual life valid in the industrial age and capable of withstanding enlightened criticism. Their ceaseless ejaculations about "from each according to his abilities, to each according to his capacities" labored to combine the Protestant ethic of laissez-faire capitalism with a Catholic religion of communal works.

Though Saint-Simon's earlier theories about the social value of the creative imagination had been fashioned according to the priorities of the eighteenth century, his followers recognized some sort of "thirst for the sacred." So, while other romantics were also exploring the effect of art,[8] the socialists studied the most successful cult they knew, Catholicism, not for its beauty as did Chateaubriand, but because they believed that it had been an admirably subtle and complete educational tool.[9] When one thinks of Saint-Simon's first division of society into three types—administrators, scientists, and inspirers—one thinks not of three coordinate human types but of a hierarchy, like that in the Roman Church, a production-oriented

The Universal Social and Democratic Republic (artist unknown). While the symbols of monarchical despotism lie broken, all peoples advance under tricolor banners to gather before a statue symbolizing human rights. Christ and the cross bless the new brotherhood of all humanity. Despite the disillusionments of 1848, the emotional energies of political romanticism helped to found and propel socialism. (Musée Carnavalet, Paris.)

corporation, or the Encyclopedists' educational theory: the executives and their administrators decide which product is needed, the applied scientists check to make sure everything is done rationally and efficiently, and public relations men sell whatever has been made. The skills of the artistic inspirer are those of a servant. He is a propagandist.

In keeping with the nascent romantic Zeitgeist and with the increasing realization that creation not production, leisure not scarcity, might be the problem of modern industrial society, Saint-Simon reversed the ranking in his trinity. *The New Christianity* declared that the banquet spread before man is so sumptuous that dwelling upon material rewards, characteristic of a world of scarcity such as had emerged from the Middle Ages, seemed beside the point.[10] He decided that society needed some "pervasive emotion." Hence, the religious-imaginative inspirers became the initiators atop the trinity, because it seemed that only they could provide the noble and pervasive drives society needed.

When Saint-Simon died in 1825, his disciples exalted their master's last phase and made the artist the "child of light." However, the Saint-Simonians thought that the arts lacked "that which is essential to their energy and to their success, namely a common drive and general ideal."[11] The Saint-Simonian social movement was supposed to furnish that drive and idea because liberalism, which is individualistic and therefore selfish, could not. According to their prophet, the good society will be achieved "only when egotism, this bastard fruit of civilization, has been pushed back to its last defences, when literature and the fine arts have put themselves at the head of the movement, and have finally filled society with passion for its own well-being. . . . What a beautiful destiny for the arts, that of exercising over society a positive power, a true priestly function, and of marching forcefully in the van of all the intellectual faculties, in the epoch of their greatest development! This is the duty of the artists, this is their true mission."[12]

In 1830, the year of the second French revolution that was supposed to open careers to talent, Emile Barrault, a former professor of rhetoric, was commissioned to write a Saint-Simonian aesthetic. His program for motivational psychology proposed that "henceforth the fine arts are the religion and the artist is the priest."[13]

After the revolution of 1830 turned out to be merely a coup of the moneyed over the titled class, the Saint-Simonian "pope," Barthélemy Prosper Enfantin (1796–1864), decided that the time had arrived to fuse belief and action, to cease being stuttering academics and become eloquent apostles. The believers set up a monastic community at Ménilmontant outside the city of man, Paris, lately become a citadel of bourgeois doctrine under Louis-Philippe. Medieval monasticism had not been a mass movement, but Benedict's counsels gave a millennium its ideal. Nor did nineteenth-century utopian communities, from Ménilmontant to New Harmony, Indiana, attract whole nations, but they formulated many of the questions still asked about polities and economies.

The Benedictines had their motto *ora et labora* (pray and work); the Saint-Simonians were to "work and meditate";[14] chant hours; raise calluses; wear a habit (of red, white, and blue for the Saint-Simonians); and perform rituals celebrating the virtues of work for the community rather than for oneself. The Saint-Simonian master's vest, for example, laced in the back, so that he required the help of another man to don it completely. Marriage was to the whole Saint-Simonian family in order to abolish the "selfish, patriarchal bourgeois family" and foster an androgynous sexual freedom and equality.

The purpose of the Saint-Simonian philosophy as developed by Enfantin was to emancipate the flesh, thereby showing that the material world is in no way inferior to the intellectual and moral world, nor labor to philosophy.[15] Thought and matter, as in Goethe's *Faust*, were two aspects of one evolving existence whereby humanity participates in the evolution of divinity and thus continues the work of creation. Communal industry, therefore, becomes the true form of worship. The ideal "monk" of the New Christianity would not be antiworldly.

Though they never studied Hegel's dialectical trinity, the Saint-Simonians strove for a different synthesis, whereby two seemingly opposed principles of religion, medieval spiritual generalization and Protestant-Enlightenment empirical individualization, might coexist. Theologians have usually dismissed such ideas as "mere pantheism," although it is fashionable today to identify sacred and secular modes. Like Schiller, Zinzendorf, Wesley. Pestalozzi, and Rousseau, the utopians thought that education must begin with sensual attraction. And so, like *the* romantic hero, Goethe's Faust, they translated *logos*, the expression of the infinite, not as "word" but as "deed." "In the beginning was the deed," as Faust put it.[16] Like Faust's critic, Mephistopheles, they insisted that the person who could bridge the dualities between passion and reason would be an ideal man, "Mr. Microcosm."[17]

The new utopian man would also balance the masculine and feminine sides of human nature. A complete individual person, like a complete human community, must combine them. Hence, the Saint-Simonians said that the social individual is bisexual or a couple; God was described in androgynous images. Before receiving their symbolic necklace, Saint-Simonian disciples made this profession of faith: "I believe in God, the Father and Mother of all men and women, eternally good [bon et bonne]. . . ."[18] The most successful Saint-Simonian rite seems to have been a *pax*, a kiss of peace, between members of opposing classes. "At meetings of the Saint-Simonian family 'members of the proletariat' who were one moment burning with hatred against the privileged orders found themselves overcome by love as they embraced young nobles before the whole assembly, all joined as children in Saint-Simon."[19]

Enfantin required individuals to "sympathize," whose Greek roots mean "to experience together":

If one takes away the sympathies which unite men to their fellows, which cause them to suffer of their sufferings, take pleasure in their joys, in a word live their lives, it is impossible to see anything else in society but an aggregate of individuals without ties or relationships, having nothing to motivate their conduct but the impulses of egotism.[20]

My life is one, he said. It manifests itself in me, outside of me, and in the *union* of the me and the non-me. This last respect is, properly speaking, the unity of my being but all three are indispensable for me to love, to understand, and protect life. . . .

A union of love, a union of spirit, a union of matter. Such is the life of a man. Such are the phenomena Divine unity is constantly revealing to him, toward which he can advance only if he had a love coitus (the word is too beautiful to be avoided) of intellect and matter with all that is.[21]

Today radical social reformers and progressive theologians employ a similar language. And even Catholics suggest that the thus-far celibate clergy ought not to avoid the most natural union of me with non-me. One of the few times when the ultramontane Catholics and doctrinaire liberals agreed since the Revolution was when the respectables of Paris sent the police to close the Saint-Simonian community at Ménilmontant. Some of the leaders were arrested for having "outraged public morals by suggesting free love." Among other things, Enfantin had suggested the Laurentian idea that some personal crises might be mitigated sensually. For example, intercourse with a priest or priestess could offer more to a penitent than could a celibate confessor (or an analyst).[22]

At their trial, the "children of Saint-Simon" assured their conviction by declaring that their plans for a society based totally on relationships of love were moral and Christian, whereas bourgeois marriage merely facilitated the accretion and exchange of property—women foremost—among the owning classes and kept property out of the hands of the working class. Love had no part in it. Therefore, a bourgeois marriage was itself covert prostitution, which in turn corrupted poor women, who could not raise a family on their man's wages, and drove them into overt prostitution. Continuing with arguments more familiar today from the underground press or the works of Marx and Freud,[23] Enfantin said that he wished to rehabilitate the flesh and sanctify physical beauty, both of which had been crucified in the Christian and bourgeois eras.[24]

Though many of those who had been attracted to Saint-Simonianism during their early maturity were later to become technocrats, there were a few who became artists. Some progressive musicians and composers found the doctrine congenial because of its emphasis on the value for society of art in general and music in particular.[25] About the time that Carlyle and Mill across the Channel, Heine and the Young Germans across the Rhine,[26] and Mazzini across the Alps were feeling the Saint-Simonian influence, Charles Duveyrier, "poet of God," persuaded Hector Berlioz that the "social question" was paramount. Later Berlioz wrote from Rome: "Tell me what I can do and I shall give you my ideas on the ways in which I can be musically useful to the great work when I return to Paris." The "great work" meant betterment of the "most numerous and poorest class, the natural ranking of talent, and the abolition of privileges of every kind."[27] Berlioz directly applied the Saint-Simonian precepts concerning sosial utility, especially communication among humanity, as the aim of art in his *Song for the Opening of a Railroad*,[28] when he set a song celebrating Peace, the Nation, and Workers.[29]

Berlioz and Liszt, who were among the musicians who composed in the religious and revolutionary tradition of music for popular and national occasions as opposed to courtly and sociable ones, attended Saint-Simonian meetings. Their professional work complemented the democratic feelings at work in the amateur choruses.[30] In the same spirit, Saint-Simon, Fourier, Lamennais, and other thinkers provided for communal music in their schemes for social reintegration.

One composer dedicated his life to the Saint-Simonian system. Félicien David (1810–76) was educated as a choirboy in the Maî-trise du Saint-Sauveur at Aix and at the Jesuit Collège de Saint-Louis, whose fathers drew no distinction between sacred and secular music, expecially opera in the "Jesuit" baroque tradition perfected by Calderón but attempted at Jesuit schools even in the twentieth century.[31] When in 1828 the government closed the college, young David became *maître* (master) of his old Maîtrise. But Aix did not satisfy him; so he went to Paris in 1830, where Cherubini was per-suaded to admit him to the Conservatoire. David's first pronounce-ment on music recalls the classicism of Lesueur and the French theorists in the previous century:[32] "One of the most difficult and important qualities of composition is unity"[33] of idea and emotion; of profound and popular meanings.

When a rich uncle ended his subsidy to David, a painter named Justus persuaded him to leave the conservatory and join the Saint-Simonians. He was among the first to join the band of apostles at Ménilmontant,[34] coming the week after Emile Barrault, their aesthe-tician, pedagogical theorist, and liturgist.

David wanted to be "the Saint Ambrose"—that is, the artful pop-ularizer rather than the Byzantine professional—of the new cult by creating, or at least inspiriting, its liturgies. The composer doubled as chapelmaster. Assisted by an ex-violinist of the Opéra-Comique, Tajan-Rojé, he trained forty choristers, who much impressed the thousands who came when the Saint-Simonian rites were held pub-licly twice each week. After the community was dissolved, David published his Saint-Simonian hymns in 1833. He was careful to tell the respectable public that these hymns now belonged to history, but, he said, they had given him a foretaste of the "music of the future."[35]

The titles of David's songs and choruses describe the monastic office they graced: *Prayers for Morning and Evening, Before and After Meals,* and *The Taking of the Habit.* For the latter ceremony the monks chanted a new style *Ecce Sacerdos—Salut au Père*—after which the novices and their "abbot" sang a responsory about avoid-ing the selfish mores of the Parisian bourgeoisie. Then the habits were distributed. They were tricolored as befitted the new order, but redolent of the ancient theological virtues: white for faith, red for love, and blue for work.[36] (A gospel of work is a gospel of hope in the future; hence the Saint-Simonian theological virtues are like the Christian.)

The last major festival of Saint-Simonianism was the Commence-
ment of the Works of the Temple on Friday, 1 July 1831. Two
thousand spectators saw the brethren assemble on the lawn; salute
Père Enfantin; sing antiphonally of the life to come; hear Emile
Barrault chant an oration on how future perfection will come through
toil in the present vale of tears; and conclude by intoning a song
To Work. Work then commenced in dignity.[37] Liberals were irritated
by the Saint-Simonians; Catholics were enraged at being patronized
as members of a worthy but deceased medieval ancestor. One further
communal rite was held on July 17 to bury Edmond Talbot, one of
the family, who had died of cholera. At Père-Lachaise cemetery,
Barrault followed the logic of Christian and all teleological burial
rites by speaking first of death and having the choir sing a *Song of
Death*; then he concluded by speaking of life, whereupon the choir
sang a *Song of Life.*

In addition to composing formal pieces, David improvised during
sermons—as the musicians in gospel tabernacles do today. (The
Gradual of the Mass had once been such a rhapsody interrupting
readings and homilies.) The sermons were also interrupted by visions, witnessing, faintings, and glossolalia.[38] David resisted a rather
schoolmasterish suggestion by one of the brethren that he set to
music the community's motto, "From each according to his ability,
to each according to his needs."[39] His music for an astronomy (perhaps astrology) lesson, in which some of the students acted out the
movements of the stars with torches, later became the basis for a
secular *Dance of the Stars.* His therapeutic piece *Accompaniment
during Cholera*[40] was later employed in a successful cure by music
of the French consul, M. Damiani, at Jaffa, near where Saul and
David (as well as Napoleon) are said to have practiced similar medicine, and where the apostle Félicien David now journeyed with the
newest Covenant.

After Ménilmontant had been dissolved, some of the remaining
apostles took a trip to the east. They set out for Egypt "to help restore that ancient beacon of civilization to its former eminence"[41]
and appropriate some wisdom as yet uncorrupted by technology. On
their way to their ship at Marseilles, a quartet sang Saint-Simonian
songs to win converts and earn fees to augment the travelers' chest.
In industrialized Lyons, a M. Charan, who was an admirer of David
and a piano builder, gave him a portable piano. Fashionable Avignon
laughed at their habit, but the proletarians of Marseilles gave the
"left wing" socialists a tumultuous welcome, which is a practice they

have continued in elections. On 22 March 1833 they left for the
Orient on the brig Clorinde, whose mate was Giuseppe Garibaldi.[42]

In the Orient, the family, typical western categorizers in spite of
themselves, hoped to find the eternal feminine, a "liberated woman"
or "the Mother" to be a mate for Enfantin, "the Father." David
hoped to gain direct inspiration from folk singers uncorrupted by
civilization. After being detained for a while in Istanbul, the party
convinced the Sublime Porte that their doctrines were not dangerous
and proceeded toward Egypt. On the way they visited the Ionian
Isles, Jaffa, and Jerusalem—where they were banned from the Catholic monastery's hospice after an admirer described their sexual
doctrines to the father superior. After their stay in Jerusalem, they
returned to Jaffa, thence to Alexandria and Cairo, where David
made friends by giving music lessons.[43] After journeys in the desert
and encounters with bandits, the apostles sailed back to France in
June 1835.

Back from the trip, David worked in retirement for several years
trying to put his reactions into music. He believed that eastern music
was an uninhibited cry of the folk soul and devoid of harmony,
which was a western complication. His success was at first so small
that he had to pay for publication of his Oriental Melodies. But in
1844 the friends who had encouraged him were parading and singing
his songs on the boulevard to celebrate his musical conquest at the
Conservatoire.[44]

A metaphorical trip to the east or to the wilderness had long since
become a standard feature of romanticism. Delacroix and Victor
Hugo, to name only two, had accustomed the public to "Oriental"
subjects, which had usually been merely devices in previous French
art; so audiences were prepared for David's Symphonic Ode, The
Desert. In it, David employed themes from Levantine folk songs,
chants of Muezzin, and music written for the Saint-Simonian chapel.
His preference for simple musical means in music intended for a
mass audience resembled the Encyclopedists' similar doctrine and
practice for a similar purpose. Though David said that he eschewed
both the Italianate aria-recitative and Berlioz's programmatic format,
his work did resemble the musicodramatic technique of his more
famous contemporary. Both used narrative strophes to accompany
restrained action or sketch the scene and relied on the music of an
orchestra as their "grand emotive force."[45]

The Desert was taken as a Saint-Simonian's rejection of civilization. One of the work's best-received parts was its Hymn to the

Night, further exemplifying the familiar romantic interest in the exotic and the night side of the mind.[46] Night in the desert has often been thought a poetical revelation of celestial harmonies—as priests of Chaldea, Mohammed, and Chateaubriand well knew. Despite the work's success, receipts fell short of expenses by 1,200 francs. But David was now fortunate in his Saint-Simonian connections, for Père Enfantin, now of the bourgeoisie, found him a financial angel.[47]

David's continuing quest to combine his religion and his recollections of the east led to several oratorio-like and operatic works in which he followed the normal composers' practice of taking the music of one liturgy into another. Once, he expanded a tableau from his biblical melodrama, *The Last Judgment*, into an entire work on ancient Roman rather than biblical history.[48] None of his later works achieved the success of *The Desert*, and he lived the rest of his life in relative obscurity. He was buried in a civil funeral because he still adhered to Saint-Simonian doctrines. There was no official rhetoric, nor the prescribed number of soldiers from the Legion of Honor, "only," his biographer says, "very impressive, simple rites."[49]

There were hundreds of other attempts to discover alternative styles of life. Some of them were based on the ideas of François Marie Charles Fourier (1772–1837), who died the same year as the revolutionary musician Lesueur. Though he insisted that he was not one of Saint-Simon's disciples, his aesthetics developed like theirs. He agreed that art could provide the catharsis which would divert mass feeling from fanaticism to love. Fourier's phalansteries, where communal music was to be an integral part and symbol of the daily routine, remind one of monasteries brought up to date. His thoughts about participation in communal activities like choruses show that "he was far from averse to the cultivation of intermediate loyalties —to the work group in which one labored for an hour, to a phalanstery in which one lived, to the nation, the continent, the planet— but how different these were from the fixations of ordinary men in civilization. Their loyalties might be intense, but they were usually fleeting; they were like team spirit in the best sportsmen's tradition, and left behind no rancor in defeat, no arrogance in victory."[50] Fourier's fundamental mythos resembled the *felix culpa* (happy fault) sung of by the Christian church when it wishes to teach optimistic teleology to its children in adversity: One tree bore the fruit by which Adam fell and another tree gave the wood whereby Christ redeemed us, runs the ecclesiastical hymn. Fourier, enlightened and post-Newtonian, had four apples to juggle in his prophecy: two, those of

Hebraic Adam and Hellenic Paris, sowed discord; two others, the
one which fell upon Newton and another whose price in a Parisian
restaurant shocked Fourier into work on his theories, were to create
concord.[51]

As we might expect, Fourier believed that concord of passions
and intellect within the individual lay anterior to concord of individuals and groups. Since artists, who educate the animal as well as
the rational side of man by harmonizing intuition and calculation
were great benefactors of mankind,[52] Fourier thought they should
be paid by all mankind. According to his book *Théorie de l'unité
universelle*, if everyone in the world would remit one *sou*, the composer of a symphony would not have to endure penury in order to
practice his art. Fourier was optimistic that an official jury would
make enough good decisions to balance their prejudiced ones.[53]

Phalansteries based upon Fourier's ideas were tried in one form
or another all the way around the world from Rumania to New
Lanark, Massachusetts, to New Harmony, Indiana. Where they were
successful, they were envied and destroyed by force from without.
In all these communities, making music together was to be part of
education and a symbol of community life.[54]

Although these utopian communities have disappeared, their religion remains to create new ones. Like other utopians—the monks
of the Middle Ages, the radical Christians of the sixteenth century,
and the philosophers of the eighteenth—their ultimate influence has
been to reinforce the peculiar western myth: progress, teleology, salvation, history—and its many other aliases. If Christianity was a
Pauline blend of the Hebrew idea (that history is linear) with Plato's
doctrine (that present suffering is but a lapse from eternal bliss),
Christianity's ultimate lesson was the belief in a unique and purposeful existence for each man *and* for mankind.

As for the contemporary order, the utopians were as sure as Voltaire had been that contemporary society was wrong. But Candide's
individualistic advice to "cultivate your garden" seemed no longer
sufficient. Rather than the nascent laissez-faire jungle, the utopians
wanted a heavenly city wherein the lion would lie down with the
lamb. To begin fulfilling this prophecy, one must be saved psychicly;
art can do this, they thought. To achieve the heavenly city, all must
contribute according to their ability; art, especially ensemble music,
symbolizes this contribution. To make the heavenly city worth having, it must be worthwhile in itself; this, again, is found in art. Such

rhapsodizing about the public role of the artistic imagination corresponded to what romantic musicians like Carl-Maria von Weber were saying of themselves: "What love is to man, music is to the arts and to mankind . . . [an] ethereal language of the emotions, containing all their changing colors in every variety of shading and thousands of aspects; true only once, but to be understood simultaneously by thousands of differently constituted listeners."[55] Such philosophies of art and music in turn correspond to the theory of worship in liturgical churches: the congregation creates something greater than the sum of their numbers by uniting through the mediation of their minister or music; everyone shares in this communal action according to his capacity. Thus it is that some romantics found an affinity for organized religion when they addressed themselves to whole human beings—to persons not only as individuals but as members of the whole.

Church and revolutionary musicians had thought that mass music made one communal work out of many individual efforts. So did the first socialists, who grew up after the Revolution, suppose music to be a universal language, giving to all who made or heard it unity and a common spiritual life or group consciousness. Men might no longer find God, but they would find sympathy for their fellows. By such a performing art could the lone mystic be united with the whole creed. In the words of Dilthey, "the musician will set the tone of life better than any meditation or introspection. Thus he will find new dignity as a priest in the holy temple."[56] Stripped of its romantic ebullience, such a statement could be agreeable to Lamennais, Voltaire, Aquinas, and Aristotle: the good is first apprehended as the beautiful.

In the later nineteenth and early twentieth centuries, socialism seemed more closely associated with the programs for democratic reform which it fostered in the Protestant and more liberal northern Europe. In the infancy of socialism its first attraction was the dazzling possibility of a new religion. As republicans and Jacobins occasionally asserted in the revolutions of forty-eight: "Socialism is the work for which Jesus Christ died, it is the Good News proclaimed by Saint Paul."[57] As such, it has accomplished its stated objective of uniting the romantic mystical vision with the Enlightenment's social science. One aspect of this large and complicated case is beyond dispute: the utopians have had much to do with all subsequent ideologies and their communication.

Among its permanent influences Saint-Simonianism can count the young Karl Marx, and therefore all Marxism, the young Dostoevski, and therefore modern literature and psychology, the young Italians of the early Risorgimento, and the leaders of many new nations in the twentieth century. Marx discarded their utopian wish for a society based upon love stemming from emotional attraction and posited a more deterministic system.[58] His followers' belief in determinism has been proven a chimera, and we are back trying to educate the emotions anterior to action. Dostoevski eventually thought of Saint-Simonianism as the typical western heresy of rationalism, but his daring analogies have nourished, not Russian Orthodoxy, but the existentialist underground men of the twentieth century. Similarly, in the Risorgimento, the cultural nationalism of the first half of the nineteenth century yielded to the power politics of the second, but the first kind is still motivating new nationalistic movements today.

Perhaps the one undying idea that unites all of the reforms and counterreforms proposed in behalf of a new community of love is the wish to improve the quality of life for everyone. Since the romantics believed that the artistic imagination is the highest human faculty, their reforms usually included plans for helping everyone everywhere to share artistic inspiration. Since the romantics also wanted art to be a metaphor of a heightened and improved sense of community, they needed an art to which everyone might contribute according to his ability and receive according to his needs. They found such a metaphor of community in mass participation in music. Choruses, glee clubs, bands, orchestras, concerts, lessons, lectures, and general mass enthusiasm for music at home or in festivals are a legacy of revolutionary mass action enhanced by the romantic cult of the artist.

DILETTANTES, AMATEURS, AND LOVERS

Romantic Designs for Popular Aesthetic
Education through Music

8

"Dilettante" and "amateur" both derive from Latin roots meaning "to love." Through popular aesthetic education the romantics hoped to make dabblers in the arts into whole-hearted lovers. Through whole-hearted lovers they wished to evolve a society where citizens would be more sensitive than acquisitive. Soon, participation in music came to symbolize the aspiration for a better—morally, politically, and culturally—as well as more comfortable life. (In the twentieth century, with more to spend but little more to love, we confront the same problem of combining a quality life with mass consumption, except that our problem is multiplied.) Designs for popular aesthetic education are an intersection of the cult of free genius with the habits of the man in the street.

The challenge to make art for a mass audience became a necessity in many places during the eighteenth century. After the French Revolution and Imperium, a more democratic style was spreading to most aspects of culture, while the bourgeoisie continued to replace the nobility as arbiter of taste.[1] A rising standard of living and of secular interests in England, North America, and western Europe was accompanied by the rise of a mass audience which became a ready market for the commercialization of leisure via newspapers, gardening, travel and tourism, sports, and the arts.[2] Musicians were both part of and limited by this thirst for advancement of the middle class. Musicians thought of their work as expressive in itself, rather than as a symbol of affluence or a background to something more important. Yet they were individualists, like the middle class, asserting their liberty. But they were limited by the musical intelligence of their new audience, which continued to understand only the forms of music that gave a composer little room for expression in depth. In a word, the artist was liberated from paternalistic lords and prelates only to find himself hemmed in by commercialism.

The individualistic, bourgeois ethic promised to liberate art, music, and the whole range of the human talent from servitude to the artificial standards of the nobility and the superstitions of religion. But by diminishing the demand for music as part of the tradtional liturgies of church and court without offering a reliable democratic alternative, this ethic turned the arts into a product whose worth is measured by its sales. And those sales might best be increased by a planned obsolescence in which art moves best as a gaudy package whose minimal content is quickly consumed and discarded, thus assuring continued demand but perhaps ignoring any human need for profundity, craftsmanship, or permanence. Moreover, the liberal members of the middle class were likely to be trained in the Enlightenment, neoclassical canon that music is at best a pleasant vehicle for conveying something really important. Therefore, any artist who would wrap up his soul in his work might find it judged by the same standards as a work made to titillate for the moment. (Oddly enough, he might not have felt this disappointment under the more repressive Old Regime because individual self-fulfillment was not then expected.) The classic reaction to such a situation is alienation from essentially meaningless work.[3] But artists could not take that short way out and be true to the individual human dignity which they now supposed it their destiny to teach.

As if to increase the difficulty, art and artists had become the repositories of the ideals of the Revolution. The romantic artist wanted to be a man of the people who rises from them against all odds, creates a noble environment out of their common humanity, and shares the achievement with his brothers. The romantic vision of the artist as prophet of a new democratic order stemmed from the insight that folk, high, and popular culture were in reality parts of one human environment and should fecundate one another. When the institutions of the post-Napoleonic era proved politically reactionary, the aspirations of their musical life helped to preserve the ideals both of Christianity and of the Enlightenment. Workers for universal education, suffrage, temperance, abolition, and socialism shared the same romantic emotional energies.

Meanwhile, constitutions, reform bills, the Risorgimento, the Frankfurt Assembly, Jacksonianism, anticolonial revolutions, and the Orleanist coup all formally recognized a political role for the bourgeoisie, already dominant economically. The new arbiters of public life wanted their art and music to do two seemingly contradictory things. On the one hand, they preferred simple, realistic styles and sober moralism to any suggestion that they were wasteful and therefore decadent; on the other, they liked works which proclaimed that the new aristocracy was as opulent as the old.

As one might expect, aristocratic connoisseurs found the new style bourgeois, meaning gauche. The new music seemed bombastic and afraid to trust restrained or subtle effects. The open box office and subscription policies of the entrepreneurs seemed designed to inconvenience the dedicated patron while catering only to the moneyed or the numerous—both of whom were likely to be the ignorant.[4]

In addition, the comfortable classes of Restoration society began to realize through their conscience or through revolts like those of 1848 that education and political life would eventually have to be democratized, if only to increase the economic efficiency of workers in modern industry. Coordinate to manifestoes forecasting that the despised of the earth would one day control the means of production there emerged an increasing respect in European high culture for the formerly despised human faculty, music. A signal rationale for the new attitude had been given in Rousseau's novel *Emile*, in which it is assumed that music is a natural part of a complete education. Virtually all the belles lettres of the romantic era share the same attitude. Educational reformers were soon proposing the translation of a holistic picture of human nature into designs for education which would integrate rather than alienate the individual and society.

Part of the romantic program for a democratic culture was public aesthetic education, often through amateur musical ensembles under a professional's direction. Sometimes these grew out of rejuvenated congregational singing in covenanting churches or out of musical ensembles which formerly had served liturgical churches. In other places, secular music making arose independent of ecclesiastical ensembles. In most places music-for-the-masses began as an enhancement of religion or education, then burgeoned into an independent movement. In almost every instance we see a picture of that thing so rare in history books—people enjoying themselves. We can also see how these enjoyments were exploited.[5]

I

In the mid-eighteenth century many respectable burghers needed a religious excuse before they dared to enjoy spending time and money on luxuries like the theater or music.[6] To dramatize a passion directly seemed too daring. Except in Italy, opera and its conventions were felt to be the residue of an aristocracy and unsuited to rational, middle-class ways.[7] Yet, the burghers had their price. One man who knew it was Handel, the greatest composer of eighteenth-century opera before he came to England, the model bourgeois country—and he did not compose for the Anglican liturgy while there.[8] He was too good a dramatist to misplace the sermon by dragging it out of the meeting house and into the theater; so he persisted in the style of the opera house, not the choir loft, for his oratorios. The *Messiah* is entertainment, not preaching, because Handel knew what he could sell to the British middle classes. They wanted not the Nazarene humility of the carpenter's son, but the confident expression of the triumphant rulers of a world empire,[9] free of conventional plots and kow-towing. Sometimes Handel exceeded the wishes of the Britannic oligarchy. The sociopolitical bent of Handel's oratorios can be judged from the fact that the performance of *Israel in Egypt* was questioned in England and not sanctioned in Germany until long after his death, because it and his *Samson*—the story of a hero who died for the people—might incite the masses against the ruling classes.[10]

Originally, Handel's oratorios were composed for and performed by the small, professional ensembles normal during the Old Regime. A generation after his death, monumental performances of his music were well established in England. As in the contemporary monumental French style, soon to be put into the service of the Revolution, the number of performers was multiplied and new metal instruments were added to maintain proper tonal balance in vast ensembles.[11] Thousands came, and special arrangements, ancestors of the huge Royal Albert Hall with its Promenade concerts, had to be constructed to hold them. The eminent Charles Burney, a correspondent of Jean-Jacques Rousseau, proclaimed in his *General History of Music*:

> The year 1784 was rendered a memorable aera in the annals of Music by the splendid and magnificent manner in which the birth, genius, and abilities of HANDEL, were celebrated in Westminster Abbey and the pantheon, by five performances of pieces selected

from his own works, and executed by a band of more than 500 voices and instruments in the presence and under the immediate auspices of their Majesties and the first personages in the kingdom. This event, so honourable to the art of Music and an illustrious artist, and so worthy of a place here, having been minutely recorded already in a distinct work, I shall only add, that this celebration has been since establishment [*sic*] into an annual musical festival for charitable purposes, in which the number of performers, and perfection of the performances, as well as favour of the public have continued to increase. In 1785, the vocal and instrumental band amounted to six hundred and sixteen. In 1786, to seven hundred and forty-one. And in 1787, to eight hundred and six vocal and instrumental performers.[12]

Like the musical levée en masse during the French Revolution, such festivals were signs of a trend to make art music for mass expression and consumption where it had formerly been a professional's métier. Music by and for the masses became an almost universal sign of a new Zeitgeist.

Likewise, Haydn's popular oratorio *The Seasons* reflected bourgeois attitudes. The music is not meditative; the text, as in the final chorus of part 1, "Spring," is not ecclesiastical but an optimistic bourgeois interpretation of the deist ethic about the Master Planner's design evident throughout the universe.[13] As an oratorio, this ethical but worldly work is like a revolutionary fête more in honor of agriculture than of the Good Shepherd: a love duet of peasants, a spinster song, storm scenes, the sunrise, the laborer's song.[14] Pious Haydn was syncretizing the sacred and the secular.

The public was demanding a whole new fabric of art to clothe its imagination. Fiction in prose, the novel, began to eclipse the aristocratic convention of fiction in poetry which had flourished since long before Homer.[15] Musicians had to create new music to reach the new audiences who read realistic novels and could not accept the antique conventions of Italian opera. The new square-cut, lusty singing of the concert style ended the folk, aristocratic, church traditions native to England, Spain, and France. The economics of music changed, too. By the turn of the century one could buy a subscription or a ticket rather than have to "own" the players in order to enjoy a concert. Since the audience was now buying music for its own sake and not as an embellishment of some other ritual, one might think that musicians were raising their status. There was as yet, however, no new large class of discerning listeners. Music there-

Caricature of Berlioz, by Gustav Doré (1850), conducting one of his massive works. Amateur choruses drawn from all classes and conditions of society were one of the most widespread attempts to democratize culture and enhance the quality of life for everyone. Observers of the popular concerts later organized by Jules Pasdeloup at the Cirque Napoléon remarked that the audiences at these packed Sunday morning events had an almost religious intensity.

fore became a business, dignified by earning its way in middle-class fashion; demeaned by having to cater to numbers. Concerts "could not do without the great mass and its money contributions; thus a *free art*," complained one musician, "has been changed into a servitude. . . . Taste *for* music is spreading more rapidly, but taste *in* music is growing all the more slowly."[16] Therefore, the cleavage between art and society continued into the nineteenth century despite the romantics' aspirations.[17] The musician remained cut off from the independent and prophetic role he yearned to play.

For their part, the clergy, who were still major patrons of music, continued to "expect the musician to exhibit high emotion but not to expect earthly recompense."[18] When W. H. Wackenroder wanted to personify the romantic artist struggling against philistinism institutionalized, he wrote as a church musician trying to make his way in a more democratic and rational but utterly prosaic society.

> Feeling and understanding for art have gone out of fashion and become unseemly; to feel, in the presence of an artwork, is considered quite as odd and laughable as suddenly to speak in verse and rhyme in company, when one otherwise gets through one's life with sensible prose, intelligible to all. Yet for these souls I wear out my spirit and work myself up to do things in such a way that they may arouse feeling! This is the high calling to which I had believed myself born. . . .
> [Yet I am hemmed-in by] petty customs and usages—a hundred empty-headed fellows put in their word and demand this and that.[19]

Wackenroder's hero, who had longed to be an organist, found that "he is of no use to the world; less influential than any tradesman." A sense of frustrated spiritual vocation continued to suffuse the image of the artist.

French critics blamed the Italian opera for setting a tone of mere pomposity and diversion, though they might have criticized their own grand opera. Original musicians found it hard to get their works mounted because the mass media—then concert halls and choir lofts —were clogged with a few standard items. Berlioz's friend Joseph d'Ortigue thought that musical taste had declined since the time of Gluck, despite all the fine music and musicians of the age of Beethoven. In an alienated moment Berlioz wrote that the new tastemakers were no aristocrats: "Let the partisans of public opinion say what they please. If this sublime inspiration arouses only polite and infrequent applause, there is something about it that is nobler, higher, and worthier for a man to take pride in having created than there is in a graceful Tyrolienne, even though it be applauded by a hundred thousand and sung by the women and children of all Europe. There is a difference between the pretty and the beautiful."[20] Music is not made for everyone, nor everyone for music.

So uninterested in Beethoven, for example, was the greater part of the French affluent class, that a campaign to raise money for his monument in Bonn did not even meet advertising expenses in France.[21] Music journalists in Germany, meanwhile, continued to complain about their public's stolid preference for standard devices: lusty final choruses, contrapuntal amens, and maudlin solos.[22] Wagner grumbled in 1841, when he was still a bit of a revolutionary, that "society" had demanded and got a performance of Rossini's *Stabat Mater*, instead of Mozart's *Requiem*, to celebrate Napoleon's birthday because "the philistines thought that the Rossini work would be a better vehicle for vocal display, even though the Mozart music was superior."[23] Even the well-born aesthete Chateaubriand, whose *Genius of Christianity* had apotheosized the romantic philosophy of art,[24] showed that he did not fully understand the active nature of listening to music when he wrote that in an ideal park there should be musicians playing *background* music![25]

In the hands of the new opulence, music was more than ever a diversion from weighty matters of the day. The few festive public or religious celebrations in the nontitled classes' life were frequently neglected so that music became more of a private amenity, wider and shallower.[26] Instead of an expression of sincere if simple religious feeling, as had been the case when they were pietistic, the newly-risen classes preferred, as they did in their businesses, a good technical performance rather than a search into the ultimate meaning of existence.[27] It was something to "fill up empty hours" rather than "instruction in the harmony of the spheres," as one romantic journalist lamented. Music journalists, themselves a sign that the musician's image had changed from servant to teacher, complained that music was dominated by dilettantes who wanted only to tap their foot, which is something circus horses can do, rather than be united to their fellow men, which would be a properly human response.[28]

So, although some burghers had been taught Italian opera in a form acceptable to their moral sensibility, and although some of the affluent had learned to like the monumental style sprung from the Revolution by calling it "grand opera," serious artists and musicians were becoming alienated. Without knowing it, they felt Marx's analysis of industrial society. Mass production for an increased market seemed to minimize musical craftsmanship. Too, no sooner had musicians taken their place among the burghers than they were ostracized, for their ideas outran those of the moderation-loving bourgeoisie or stationary clergy. To less imaginative citizens, artists are bohemians taking the easy way out. Busy people could learn all they needed to know about such frivolity from books like Fétis's *Music on Everyone's Doorstep: Concise Explanation of Everything Needful to Judge this Art and Speak about it without Study.* No wonder Berlioz spoofed him! Music critics and musicians, as we know, were not describing a phenomenon to which only their peculiar prejudices made them allergic. The existentialist strain in modern philosophy is descended from a like irritant: One recalls how musical philistinism spurred Nietzsche to impugn the cult of Holy Mediocrity in his essay "The Case of Wagner." As a forgotten musician put it earlier in the century, "A time that loves the mechanical will hate the romantic. That time is now." Individualism, in short, leads to populism and thereby creates obstacles to its own survival.[29]

II

The romantic response was Faustian, and, when necessary, Sisyphian: to complain, but try to educate public taste. And try again.

Uncertain of how their aesthetic offensive might go, the musicians and their publicists prepared second lines of defense. They anticipated the worst, as did Mendelssohn in 1830 when he said, "Everyone is becoming a narrow-minded philistine." In reserve they held an even more democratic aesthetic: the greatness of a musician does not depend upon contemporary acclaim. It depends upon how many of all ages admire his work.[30] Thus began the confused war with and against the dilettantes. Mendelssohn, in a more confident mood, believed that "this very dilettantism . . . plays us many a trick, because of its two-fold nature: necessary, useful, and beneficial, when coupled with sincere interest and modest reserve, for then it furthers and promotes all interests; but culpable and contemptible when fed on vanity, and when obtrusive, arrogant, and self-sufficient. For instance, there are few artists for whom I feel so much respect as for a genuine dilettante of the former class, and for no single artist have I so little respect as for a dilettante of the latter class."[31] Mendelssohn believed that good musicians could bridge the gap between music for the people and music for connoisseurs. He liked to write to his friends and tell them how his recitals of neglected masters had done just that.[32]

Musical periodicals of the first half of the nineteenth century were preoccupied with the same problem. Nearly every issue of the *General Musical Journal*, of bourgeois Leipzig, carried articles describing how musicians could improve the taste of the dilettante as well as of the maestro.[33] School, state, and church were to work together in general education, not asking which is "correct style," but how each style adds to man's awareness of the world. To this end, applied music should be dignified by a place in the university curriculum. Evidently some of these articles were written by church musicians eager to have the shoe pinch the other foot for awhile, for they insist that professors of music should judge the fitness not only of candidates in music but also in theology! Some suggestions were more businesslike: these agreed that improved public music, especially in churches, would achieve general aesthetic education. But the way to do this, they said, was to talk less about music and concentrate on adequate salaries for musicians. Everything else would take care of itself.[34]

A few reformers actually did get public support for public aesthetic education. One of these was Alexandre Choron, who thought that he could educate the public to styles other than the light opera prevalent in church and concert hall. His theories were analogous to those of Lamennais, who also tried to reconcile the new and the old.

Before settling on his vocation to preach music as "civilizing," Choron had studied civil engineering. His first interest remained general education according to organicist educational theories like Rousseau's; among Choron's writings is a *Method for Learning to Read and Write at the Same Time*. Since artists were to be the teachers of humanism, they should have a complete humanistic education themselves. In the old choir schools (*maîtrises*), Latin and music had been the only subjects regularly taught to the *ancillae liturgiae*, "handmaidens of the liturgy," as musicians were called by the church. Students in the music schools modeled on Choron's (like those in Lesueur's proposed curriculum during the Revolution) were to study all the liberal arts.

Choron was interested in finding a public place for something more profound than light opera, and his proposals found a few political and ecclesiastical friends. Although the upper classes of the Empire were indifferent to religion for themselves, they thought it necessary for the masses and their morality. According to some authors, before Napoleon's Concordat, the French people missed the old rites enough for a kind of lay priesthood to grow up in remote villages, where a layman would read scriptures and the people sing hymns.[35] After the Concordat of 1801, Napoleon's ministers of cult reported in 1807, 1809, and 1813 that people were avoiding the restored church's services because the music was so bad.

Napoleon commissioned Choron, Director of Music for Public Festivals, to do for the Empire what other musicians had done for the Revolution. He kept this post under the Bourbons, who allowed him to restore and update the choir schools, which he thought "had been the cradle of French musical culture since Charlemagne and Pepin."[36] Choron was probably paraphrasing Rousseau, whose article on plain chant in his *Dictionnaire* recounted Charlemagne's reputed bringing of singers from Rome to teach the authentic Roman chant in France.[37] In 1817 Choron founded a School of Classical and Religious Music, which was to train directors for local *maîtrises*. So few dioceses actually did attempt to attract the people back into their churches by improving their music that in 1826 the Bourbon government gave up the project. Charles X turned seminary education over to the Jesuits and reduced Choron's subsidy to a permit for the occupancy of some unused buildings. Choron's submissively renamed School of Religious Music struggled on, thanks to his energy and personal funds, until 1832, when the Bourgeois King's government found another use both for the buildings and their maintenance fund without bothering to repeal the school's charter. Though Choron died two years later, his zeal for music as civilizing survived.[38] The concerts he gave demonstrated and inspired all manner of musicological investigation. His collection of Renaissance choral masterpieces, published in 1820, was one of the sources used by Thibault in his *On the Purity of Music*.[39]

Hector Berlioz, who never praised anything merely because it was traditional, mourned "the sad end of Choron, who with his slender resources had already obtained such important results in his school for choral music, and who died of grief when, *for the sake of economy*, the July Monarchy cut off his subsidy."[40] The important results Berlioz alluded to were not limited to circles of professional musicians.

Choral music, more than other forms, was suited to be the musical love feast wherein Choron and the romantic educational reformers hoped to reconcile amateur zeal and professional discernment. This seemed logical because choral music is necessarily communal and

therefore might teach the "sentiments of association"[41] that seemed
a good and necessary part of democratic culture.[42] Choral music also
has the largest repertoire, both in size and variety of styles, of any
musical medium—far larger than any instrumental combination.[43]
It is also the amateur's métier, for Mendelssohn's open-minded,
modest dilettante would actually be a better chorus singer than many
a professional prima donna. Important for historically minded romantics was the fact that choral music had been the interpreter of
every cult from Orphic Thrace to the Champ de Mars.

Choral religious music was also program music. Historically so-
called absolute music has usually enjoyed a much smaller number
of competent listeners than choral music with words, opera, or the
rites of a familiar cult—even one in a dead language. Since the latter
three are "program music," they combine the most lyrical art, music,
with a text or some other extramusical association. Franz Liszt, for
example, believed that to enjoy absolute music "requires genuine
artistic insight and a more active and experienced sensitivity. . . .
[This is] something not to be expected of a whole audience no matter
how select it may be—it will never listen to a symphony, quartet,
or other composition of this order without outlining a program for
itself during the performance."[44] That reasoning may be questionable, but choral music persists as a bridge between avant-garde styles
and lay appreciation even in the twentieth century.[45]

Popular aesthetic education was also implicit in Liszt's revolutionary *Manifesto on the Sacred Music of the Future*,[46] even though
the nineteenth-century church was suspicious of allowing democratic
tendencies into its symbolical language. In place of the town choir
composed of a handful of present and past choirboys—lifelong musicians—composers had to accommodate amateur choral societies,
often with the treble turned over to women, which was a blow at
the forever-masculine clergy. Meanwhile the older markets for music
were drying up because blooded patrons were becoming less wealthy
relative to the bourgeoisie; nobles sometimes imitated burgeois rationality and austerity by diminishing their musical establishments.[47]
Again, musicians had to reach the middle class to survive.

III

Choron and the others who strove to deepen French musical life
envied the Germanies. There, it seemed, people took music seriously

and were also successful at preserving bonds between high and folk art.[48] Among these bonds, when the arts were being laicized at the turn of the century, were the *Liedertafeln*, singing societies, which spread through German lands in two complementary streams, one patrician, the other plebeian. Both were attempts at adult education flavored with the "first the heart, then the head" educational theories of the day, which were, as we have seen, in debt to Rousseau, Schiller, and the Moravian Brethren for their idea of music as catalyst of humanity's good instincts.

In northern Germany, singing societies tended to be patrician groups which grew out of the liberal Masonic lodges and secular collegia recruited among the enlightened upper middle class and civil servants. Some of these groups appear to have been ready-made substitutes for the declining traditional religions. The lower middle class continued a generation longer to supply the church-based choir schools. During the wars with the French, the purpose of the Prussian elite was more national than artistic—at least until the romantic movement overtook them in the person of Carl Maria von Weber, who had studied with choirmaster Michael Haydn, and Carl F. Zelter, who had studied with Frederick II's court musician C. F. Fasch, and taught Mendelssohn.[49] German bards were welcomed in place of French if they composed Prussian military songs. During the Napoleonic wars, many leaders of *Turnvereine* were members of *Liedertafeln* or the Lyre and Sword, which concentrated on musical propaganda against the French.[50] Mendelssohn's teacher, Zelter, had to please the king, who ordered male choruses established throughout the Prussian army "in order to build morale, educate the soldiers musically, and build emotional attachment to the established religion." Yet Zelter was not a lackey. He tried to shift the emphasis in these choruses from musical decoration of Prussian propaganda to music for itself; he was also music director at the Berlin Cathedral. After the Congress of Vienna, north German singing societies remained an appendage of the Old Regime having little to do with those outside the official caste. By 1830 other north European sovereigns were imitating Prussian practice; meanwhile, the Prussian model began to mingle with the less exclusive south German practice. Sharing music proved to be a way of overcoming sectarian theological disputes.

The southern *Liedertafeln* combined musical folk customs among Catholic Germans and educational theories like Pestallozzi's dictum "through the heart and feelings to the intellect."[51] Informal singing groups in Swiss towns were the germs whence grew an organization of 200,000 choristers during the nineteenth century. Their best-known director was Hans Georg Naegeli (1773–1836), who worked to apply Pestalozzi's theories to general education. He was careful to give equal suffrage to all styles and avoid the cult which was turning the Palestrina style from music into aural iconography. *Liedertafeln* in southwestern Germany, that is, in relatively liberal Bavaria, Württemberg, and Baden, were attracted to the Swiss model. Singing societies here were mass organizations with broad membership and aimed at enriching the life of all classes of society.[52]

Reactionaries thought these singing clubs were a subversive cult. The king of Holland established a Musical Society in 1829;[53] the next year, half his kingdom rebelled. No cause and effect there, but the guardians of public morals were not so sure in other instances. Singing together *is* a potent symbol. Mass organizations open to anyone who could hold his part, effusive texts about what good men could accomplish when they made up their minds to do it, and songs about human freedom and equality were properly diagnosed and anathematized by reactionary patricians. Who were Orpheus and Apollo, the patrons of these singing clubs, but collaborators with Bacchus, whose Mystery, like the pietists' Christian Eucharist or the rationalists's Cult of the Supreme Being, knew no born privilege?

Patrician societies could use their own Masonic halls; commoners needed permission to use the local church for their concerts and sometimes brought female singers into the chancel for the first time. In Bavaria they required permission from the king himself to lift a police suspension of singing societies in Regensberg.[54] Metternich refused to allow "this poison" into the domains he controlled. He deemed it akin to the immense dinners and petitions subverting the established order in France and England.

Choral societies became a public way to combine the enlightened belief that anything, including art, is learnable and romantic enthusiasm for native culture. In Leipzig, while their women were safely closeted with the new rationally mechanical, yet subtly responsive, pianos (which were displacing aloof harpsichords), the merchants appropriated choral music for themselves. During the *Vormärz* between the Congress of Vienna and the revolutions of 1848, the businessmen of Leipzig gave bigger receptions to German musicians like Mendelssohn than they did to princes and generals.[55] Also during the *Vormärz*, the Old Regime's secular musical estate disappeared. The town piper guilds dropped out of existence while music in the churches often shriveled to a few congregational hymns or disappeared. The lower middle class, who used to provide the personnel for public music in the churches and town squares,[56] either elbowed their way into the concert of the upper middle class or sank into the proletariat, with consequent loss of their small leisure. So the son of the Master Town Piper yielded, in company with the chancel full of tonsures and the liveried orchestras at court, to amateur societies in which everyone might participate regardless of status.[57]

Meanwhile, vast civic music by and for masses continued to grow. A *Te Deum* mounted to celebrate the dedication of the Gutenberg monument at Mainz in 1835 reminds one of the Festival of the Supreme Being during the French Revolution or the huge *Messiahs* becoming traditional in England. Similar musical precautions were taken to mass the trained choruses of the district and teach the refrains to a throng, said to number a quarter million.[58]

Unwittingly echoing his contemporary de Tocqueville[59] on the United States, the music journalist who reported the celebration around Gutenberg's new monument proclaimed the time an "age of association."[60] There are, he said, spontaneous combinations being formed to promote all sorts of things. In the time of their prophet, Gutenberg, burghers had symbolized their claim to the clerks' promised land of leisure with intimate communal song—madrigals and Protestant chorales. Now they held triumphs. But the gates were swinging open to more than the middle class, for miners' diaphragms were stronger and more numerous than bankers'.

Every political opinion wanted the muse on its side. Massed choral music was used as music and exploited for propaganda by the French Revolution, Methodism, Chartism, singing societies of both patrician and plebeian bent, socialists, and reactionaries. It seemed a means of moral improvement and influence best denied to one's opponents. When the bishop of Manchester praised the itinerant choral instructor Joseph Mainzer, he did not know that the musician had eulogized the Jacobins in music. The bishop cautioned Mainzer not to let any of the choral music "fall into socialist hands."[61]

After the revolutions of 1848, the German choral movement became one organization which combined the north's nationalism with the south's populism. At pan-German choral festivals, including the largest in 1861 at Nuremberg, singers from every German land met at an historic source of German culture.[62] (I hope that the Nazi rallies held many years later on the same site are ascribed more to the spirit of those autocrats who would have banned popular singing societies than to our choristers.) The success of evil men in exploiting mass emotion is a warning to respect its reality and a challenge to humanize the sentiments of ordinary people, not sneer at them.[63]

In the early eighteenth century, Germans had been called to head the aristocracy of birth in Europe's most productive colony, England. By the end of the century, Germans were beginning to dominate the aristocracy of musical talent in what had been an Italian musical province. Before the continental teachers came, the natives were already evolving from ecclesiastical to secular forms of celebration. As we have seen, oratorio in England was sometimes opera in biblical disguise. It appeared religious and was therefore judged a safe import which did not violate local taboos. Moreover, it encouraged mass consumption of surplus cultural wares and services from the metropolitan Continent.

Amateur group singing had strong precedents in England. Glees and catches, together with church music, were probably the most viable remnants of the English musical tradition.[64] In times past, a number of cathedral choirs would join at festivals to perform oratorios. The amateurs who now joined the cathedral professionals for such celebrations included women, who first joined the soprano section and then worked their way into the previously all-male alto section. At the same time, while Catholics and workers were asserting their political rights, "sensuality"—music to enjoy—was allowed even into the nonconformist Calvinist churches. In dissenting churches the modicum of choir singing that did exist had never been sharply distinguished from congregational singing. During the first quarter of the nineteenth century this tradition grew so rapidly that by the time Victoria was crowned in 1837, some dissenting congregations had long been practicing congregational anthems scarcely less difficult than choir music.[65] In these churches, choral music was a new Protestantism because it made weight against domination of the service by the cleric's sermon. The Kirk of Scotland ran full circle from 1750, when the squeak of a pitch pipe in church was deemed a near sacrilege; through the Mainzer movement of the 1840s, when whole congregations worked to learn sight-reading; to the 1850s, when only conservative congregations did their own singing.[66]

Joseph Mainzer was the "music man" of the 1840s and well experienced at appealing to the sympathies, aspirations, or morbid interests of the time. First he was a Catholic priest, then a composer of two topical operas, *Triumphs of Poland* and *La Jacquerie*, both "entirely in the key of D," Berlioz sneered. As a musician, Mainzer has been rated among those fraudulant dilettantes who disgusted Mendelssohn; as a pitch man, he was faultless. He came to England in a seller's market, when every merchant and miner wanted to share in the fun of singing those peppy oratorios newly published by Novello and his competitors at a price any glee club could afford.[67] Mainzer had all sorts of "scientific" rules and gadgets for sale to anyone ready to pay for the chance to "take lessons."[68] His avowed intention of "music for the millions" seemed achieved in his evening schools thronged by men of all classes. Meanwhile, composers were rising a millimeter or so to the challenge of composing something that sounded familiar, but not familiar enough to be confused with last year's offering by the same choral society. Liszt, Brahms, Dvořák, Gounod, the more limited Horatio Parker, John Stainer, and Sir Arthur Sullivan in his "serious" music were all prolific for this widespread combination of adult education and mass entertainment.[69] In this market, Mendelssohn was the most successful at composing "something both scholarly and for the people," as some fans in Munich said.

One example of English music "both scholarly and for the people" appeared in the musical education of British orphans, whom Hector Berlioz admired in a vast choir festival by 6,500 charity children in Saint Paul's Cathedral. He reported in *Evenings with the Orchestra* that the children were serving in parish choirs and thus able to enrich the musical life of the Church of England. Berlioz described the orphans' "entering with joy and pride" and their impression on the hushed spectators.

> After a chord on the organ, there arose in a gigantic unison the first psalm sung by the incredible choir:
>> All people that on earth do dwell.
>> Sing to the Lord with cheerful voice.
> It would be useless for me to try to give you an idea of the musical effect; the strength, the beauty were to those of the best choir you have ever heard as St. Paul's itself is to a village church and then a hundred times more. . . .
> I was electrified. I had to count many rests [Berlioz was sitting in on the cathedral choir's bass section], in spite of the kind attention of my neighbor, who kept pointing out to me in his part the bar we had reached in the belief that I had lost my place. But when we came to the psalm in triple time . . . sung by all the voices to

the accompaniment of trumpets, kettledrums, and organ—nature, under the shattering effect of this inspired and glowing hymn, so grand in its harmony and of an expression as noble as it is touching—nature asserted her right to be weak, and I had to make use of my vocal score as Agamemnon did of his toga, to veil my face.[70]

Berlioz then moved about the church to delight in the musical monument from many acoustical angles. He concluded with a barb for the niggardly government of Louis-Philippe, which had cut off all subsidies which might make such festivals possible in Paris. Indeed, he observed, Parisian orphans did not even seem well fed in comparison with the English, let alone well educated.

The growth of musical education was connected with one of the most important advances of the time, universal public education. Schools had been largely a charitable activity of churches. In workers' neighborhoods worse than any pictured in Hogarth engravings the teachers were attempting to civilize a rootless and brutalized folk, half of whom could scarcely write their names. School inspectors often remarked that the only schools which were more than mere holding pens for the young were those which used music. Whether to give variety to the school day, to sweeten moral uplift, enhance religious catechism, or as a joyful study in itself, singing was a happy mitigation of the stern righteousness of Manchester-style liberalism and other well-meaning attempts to bring the good life to the masses.[71]

In spite of continuing admiration for English ways, Paris, where both Joseph Mainzer and Hector Berlioz spent the most notable parts of their careers, remained the cultural capital of the western world. By mid-century, Paris saw the birth of two institutions which relied on music to assist in supplying the rites of community and the invitation to the sublime formerly dispensed through the church. The first was grand opera, which exploited everything good and bad about the romantic era. Grand opera was lavish commercial escapism. Like the film in our time it was also a seemingly magic trip to wider worlds which purport to explain our narrow existence. Historical or traditional roots, topical issues, and the Gothic thrills of visualized fantasy were at least celebrated, if not analyzed. The form was conglomerate. Moralism from the Enlightenment, full-voiced singing from the Italian opera, and vast actions featuring the chorus as representative of a nation (as the chorus had been during the musical theater of the Revolution) were standard. New stage technology and orchestral techniques helped the works of Giacomo Meyerbeer set the theatrical standard for the world. But, according to the romantics, grand opera was an ersatz cult because it repressed music, the arts, and therefore the quest for the sublime. Under Louis-Philippe, the Bourgeois King, the same liberalism which freed the arts from state control also freed them from state subsidy, in effect preventing any creation which might not make a profit.[72]

More democratic and typically romantic were the concerts and mass choruses which attracted many people who could not afford tickets to the opera. The choruses "covered the earth of France" with seekers after the divine spark through music. In the capital after 1848, popular concerts at low prices ministered further to the thirst for spiritual nourishment. Often the choristers and their friends shared the satisfaction of performing or hearing the vast and lofty works which nineteenth-century composers from Beethoven to Mahler wrote for them. Berlioz and other critics noted the "profound religious silence" which reigned at the Sunday morning *concerts populaires* frequented by the workers—in contrast to the idle chatter of the society audiences at the opera and the frequent self-important busy-ness in churches. Looking back, another observer told how the five-thousand listeners packed on uncomfortable plank benches in a circus amphitheater reminded him of "the grandeur of ancient classical theater for the community." This was no perfunctory Sunday congregation. "The audience was in search of comfort for the soul, edification, and a better life. In this vibrating mass of humanity you will find pious and restless souls, tired of their narrow church and zealous to communicate with living humanity. There you will see philosophers tired of their systems, who recover amid this intent crowd a type of religious emotion and pray that the accents of the great music bring a wind from on high."[73]

As the founder and director of these popular concerts, Jules Pasdeloup, said, they were—like grand opera—business ventures. He played everything from polkas to Mozart. Both the original *concerts populaires* at a vast arena, the Cirque Napoléon, and their imitators all over the western world were also part of a romantic dream of democratizing leisure, education, and pleasure. Pasdeloup desired that art be above all a moral factor in civilization more than the decoration of a fête. He was a priest of the sort of religion that issued from nineteenth-century schools of thought.

The interest in music also spread to the strongest cultural institutions of America, its Protestant churches. Alas, two hundred years after their ancestors had fled to assure that they need suffer no popish deviltry like choirs, organs, part music, or anthems, whole American congregations lapsed into music. But Jehovah let the devil chastise them. When English churches habitually paid more for continental musicians than for natives, Americans also over-valued imports—the English discards. American congregations would have only an English music master—until the German article flooded the market in the late forties. When an immigrant music master could not find a church willing to hire him, he sometimes set up a singing school in the local tavern, rather than sail back to the whims of his prelatial masters in the Church of England. Such goings-on aroused puritan wrath against replacing the word of God with the works of the devil.[74]

Contemporaneously, in formal theology, Emerson and the Transcendentalists were introducing a native strain of romanticism.[75] But until almost mid-century in New England, respectable churches eschewed art music and sang only the metrical psalms.[76] The Unitarian halfway house between Protestantism and secularism, and the then-reactionary theologians of the Princeton Seminary, were musically conservative. The Unitarians, who had evolved from the older forms of Arian, Socinian, and Presbyterian dissent, were rooted in the middle class and seem to have retained a strong verbal sense of community without formalizing it in musical ritual.[77] They were the ultimate Protestants: nonliturgical, bound to books, and haughty toward groups less "liberated" than themselves. When the Unitarians employed music in their rites, it was not congregational singing, which they considered lowbrow, like revivalism. Rather, what music they did eventually employ tended to suit their highbrow clientele: the thing to say on Sunday morning in Boston in 1847 was, "Let's hear Beecher and [his organist] Zundel."[78] The Unitarians were equally suspicious of the aberrations of "popery" and of chiliastic sects, for both were thought strong on emotion and weak on reason.

The most Dionysiac sect peculiar to the century before the Civil War was probably the celibate Shakers. Their ritual was a true folk art, wherein the believers sublimated their suppressed desires into a worship which was at once play and autointoxication. By songs and dances which had begun as ecstatic outcries and developed into elaborate ritual, the Shakers hoped to achieve "that self-forgetful union with the non-self which the mystic ever seeks." The Shakers also had their own system of musical notation.[79]

Except for the Unitarian and puritanical fringes of the theological spectrum, most American Protestant congregations were soon converted to "regular" singing—that is by note or rule, *regula*, rather than by rote imitation of a precentor.[80] They hired music teachers, imported or built organs, and soon were exporting their own contribution to popular musical education: simplified systems of musical notation based upon differently shaped note-heads for each tone of the diatonic scale. Starting in New England in 1805 and reaching their greatest extent and longest life in the frontier states of the newer South during the next fifty years, shape notes and revivalism became the first mass media to penetrate Appalachia and our other frontiers.[81] The German Moravians had taught Wesley to use music, he taught the Methodists, their preachers taught the Americans, and the Americans fed their shape-note systems back into the Methodist Sunday Schools in England.[82] A veritable triangular trade in music to express mass feeling.

With conventicles practicing music, it seemed that either God or the devil—or perchance Jean-Jacques Rousseau, who had labored over a scheme to simplify musical notation—had triumphed. Yet when the "Sacred Harp" tune books and popularizers like Lowell Mason expanded American musical taste, they also limited it.[83] Competition to get in on a good thing diverted musical education from its original goal of mass culture to moneymaking alone. The constantly changing tune books assisted the tendency to leave all singing to the choir or ignore it after the first enthusiasm for music passed. Consequently the dragging and confusion which had destroyed the covenanters' metrical psalms returned to the popular churches.

Hard behind the meetings of religion which offered Dionysian communion to isolated frontiersmen came cleared forests and cities with another wave of music as a sign of the new community. Cities were founded in the Old Northwest after the American Revolution. They multiplied after the Continental revolutions and ostracisms of 1830 and 1848 sent more immigrants, many of them musically serious, to the New World to make a living. Singing societies followed the cities. There has been a Handel and Haydn Society in Boston since 1815. This and the Chicago Sacred Music Society, founded in 1842, sound English. Clearly German were the Männerchor of Philadelphia, 1835; the Milwaukee Musikverein, 1849; and the Cincinnati Sängerfest, 1849.[84] Other choirs, such as the male choruses which our grandfathers might remember, Chatauqua, and college (i.e., seminary) choirs would continue the list. "They represent the highest development of a tradition which had its roots in the congregational singing of Protestant churches. With few exceptions, the singers in these societies and festivals, apart from the soloists, were amateurs who had acquired a knowledge of and enthusiasm for part singing at their religious gathering. . . . Congregational singing did prepare the more gifted for the musical discipline and better training that they received as members of the more advanced singing groups."[85]

"Folk music" collectors today delight in digging up "spontaneous expressions of the soil" from the Appalachians and other areas isolated until recently. These "spontaneous folk expressions" often sprang originally from the skill of a cultivated musician be he Elizabethan entertainer extending the ballad tradition or German immigrant rejoining a singing club or church choir in the new country.

Even though popular musical education was limited by the necessity to impress a majority of the congregation or audience on the first hearing, it was an attempt to attain the sublime in America. Like revivalism, it was part of the romantic movement. The effect of revivalism and of making music together, not always intended, but generally welcomed was to blur denominational distinctions.[86]

Further analysis of American religious practice based upon musical form as well as theological content would blur some and establish other distinctions. Afro-American religion we now realize continues a total vision of life found in the liturgical dance and play of African tribes.[87] Music, the seemingly spontaneous outpouring of feeling, is just as important as the often coded, seemingly escapist, words of spirituals in conveying a sense of ecstatic communion with all being. Many white preachers of the gospel were at first suspicious that Negro song and dance were demonic. They shared these opinions with their fellow clergy and the enlightened philosophers who also thought that the enthusiasm of conventicles and revivals were as satanic as the elaborate and sometimes refined emotional stimuli of Catholicism. In retrospect the Christian doctrine of the resurrection of a glorified and liberated body seems aptly portrayed by having the god and the devil within used to set dry bones to rattling. Ironically, descendants of the whites who were so worried about black demonism welcome the prospect of living in an age of "consciousness" led by Afro-American music. The new generation of musico-social critics is almost shouting its zeal for the New Day when even the white bourgeoisie will not preach but dance its religion.[88]

V

The religion of music and dance, of feelings, as a needed way of lighting out for the Territory with Nigger Jim because "sivilisation" has gone just too far, owes something to the intercourse between a continuing African consciousness, Mediterranean Catholicism, and American evangelism whose verbal images it borrowed. The expressive identity which the black man formed in spite of slavery was also influenced by the peculiar situation in New Orleans, a uniquely festive-minded outpost of Latin Catholic culture within the Protestant United States. It was the most important American city where the white Anglo-Saxon Protestant establishment was an intrusion. Just as Protestant evangelical fervor could give and take from the blacks; so did the frankly emotional and musical celebrations of "Mediterranean" New Orleans.

In polyglot New Orleans, music was communication, not only among the people there, but also among the various high and popular aspects of their arts. Dancing was the readiest form of social intercourse and may have always remained the greatest in terms of effort and quantity.[89] But the earliest sustained musical activity probably was church music.

Although the theologies governing the use of music in New Orleans varied all the way from Catholic or African animism to secular humanism and nationalism, music there kept a fairly constant appeal to the human psyche. During the passage of Louisiana from French and Spanish Catholic dominion to Protestant and secular American control, life in New Orleans partially succeeded at the romantic ambition of integrating the arts and thereby integrating men and their talents. All Atlantic races were present and found something in the city's rituals to suit their tastes.

Pagan rites had competed with Christian from many sides in the eighteenth century. In 1786 a law forbade slaves to dance in the public squares on Sundays and holy days until after Vespers. Early in 1799, a visitor to the city took a stroll after his Sunday dinner and saw on the edge of town "vast numbers of Negro slaves, men, women, and children, assembled together on the levee dancing in large rings."[90] In 1817 such dancing was restricted to daylight; from about 1820 until 1845 it was forbidden altogether. About mid-century, the northerner Frederick Law Olmstead—a landscape architect whom we thank for making some of the great parks in American cities close to a useful state of nature—found Christianity being Africanized. The spectacle conjured a vision of primitive Hebrew rites. "The congregation sang; I think everyone joined, even the children, and the collective sound was wonderful. The voices of one or two women rose above the rest, and one of these soon began to introduce variation . . . Many of the singers kept time with their bodies accordingly. Before long the preacher raised his own voice above all, clapped his hands, and commenced to dance . . . first with his back, and then with his face to the audience. So danced the Hebrews in their worship long before."[91] Such pre-Civil War music and dance is a visible root of jazz and Afro-American music. The spirit of such churches—and we are fortunate enough to be able still to witness them—is, like that other favorite of old New Orleans, opera, a formalism dealing with deep psychic realities, which frees the musical spirit for full play.

Throughout the pre-Civil War period, visitors observed that "the luxury and ways of the white people were impudently imitated by Negroes," both slave and free.[92] The most convenient occasions for mingling the races were balls. For a time, no celebration could be held without an all-night ball. Balls were often "tricolor, all races and conditions of servitude mingled too freely."[93]

However, Terpsichore had Orpheus to herself no more than Mother Church did. La Patrie was also wooing him. A devout Episcopalian found that when church services and sermons were not finished early on Sunday, they were drowned out by the bands of the militia parading outside.[94] Other reports seem to indicate that patriotic rituals were absorbing some of the more popular ecclesiastical customs, as they had in France during the Revolution. In 1802 Dr. John Sibley witnessed a Corpus Christi procession, which was a major summer festival of popular Catholicism. It occurs in the same season of the year as the Independence and Bastille days of the nationalistic creeds founded since the de-Christianizing eighteenth century. Bands, fireworks, and parades with the Consecrated Host would be normal on Corpus Christi. However, the procession Sibley witnessed seems shrunken if one thinks of the grand Spanish *auto* or French *Fête Dieu* it once was. "Five or six friars and four or five boys, all habited, walked as fast as they could," chanting at intervals.[95]

Some commentators speculated that religious processions were an ancestor of elaborate secular funeral processions. Six years later, when a wealthy Creole planter and militia officer, Colonel Macarty, was buried, his procession was led by twenty militia officers, mostly Creoles, and followed by a band, the clergy, flag bearers, the governor of the territory, legislators, militia officers, army officers, the mayor, and the council in that order.[96]

In a city so taken with bands and parades, what more fitting means could there be to honor the dead? When the architect Benjamin Henry Latrobe, designer of Baltimore's Catholic Cathedral among other neoclassic designs, came to New Orleans in 1819, he was "struck by the funeral parades which he said were 'peculiar to New Orleans alone among all the American cities.' He described two such funerals, both of them Negro burials. In one he estimated that there were at least two hundred people in the procession. 'All the women and many of the men . . . dressed in pure white.' At the grave he noticed some boys nearby cutting up and tossing skulls and bones which had been dug up; 'the noise and laughter was general by the time service was over.' "[97]

Perhaps this was not an ancestor of "When the Saints Go Marching In," but it was a congenial antecedent. Another antecedent of lively funeral processions, which later added jazz bands, was the Catholic burial ritual itself. The mood of funerals like the one Latrobe described also resembles some customs which have accompanied the Latin burial rites. In the Roman rite, after the funeral Mass, the coffin is rotated so that, if the deceased rose, he would be walking to God's Acre in a position of honor second only to the clergy. At this moment, the musicians intone the *In paradisum*, whose joyful text and major-mode music set the tone for the burial procession. They efface the mood of those parts of the Mass for the Dead built on resignation (*Requiem*), terror (*Dies irae*), and supplication (*Libera me*). The remaining pieces suggested for the graveside are the confident antiphon *Ego sum resurrectio* and the *Canticle of Zachary*,[98] which is an exultation over the Messiah-arrived—a Christmas mood.

The Roman Church has often winked at folk customs in a joyful mood inserted during the burial procession which follows the strictly prescribed liturgy of the Mass. Vernacular songs and music by outdoor bands could still be heard mixed with the official Latin in the eastern and southern European Catholic ghettoes of most American cities until a few years ago. Therefore, in a city where Catholicism was once the dominant religion, it need not be a long step from the spirit of the Roman rubrics and its associated popular customs to the later New Orleans funeral processions with Dixieland bands.[99]

It seems no further a step than those whereby the regalia of tide-water planters united with cakewalks, or those whereby the carnival and Mardi Gras have reverted to early-spring Bacchanalia. Scholars now think that there is much evangelistic hymning in Negro spirituals and vice versa. Blacks and whites blended the spirit of the African, Franco-Spanish Catholic, and Southern American Protestant old regimes in New Orleans.

Memorial parades also had antecedents in the Catholic liturgy for All Souls Day,[100] which long remained an excuse for a parade in New Orleans,[101] as it still does for American children on Hallowe'en. New Orleans turned such commemorations into patriotic festivals, in which even Masonic lodges (which would have been anathema at a strictly Catholic service) participated, to memorialize Lafayette, Jefferson, and Napoleon, three "patron saints" of American Louisiana.

New Orleans's most lavish funeral, however, was for a musical hero, John Davis, the patron of the best of their three resident professional opera companies, the Orleans Theatre. In 1839 "a grateful populace turned out in an 'immense crowd,' and numerous companies of the Louisiana Legion marched in the procession. At the St. Louis Cathedral a special requiem composed for the occasion was sung by the entire company from the Orleans Theatre. New Orleans was honoring this day the man who had raised its theater from a 'wretched condition to prosperity and excellence.' "[102]

Like religious and patriotic rites, opera in New Orleans was an unusual integration of arts and peoples. Manifestly, Negro patrons were expected by all three houses in the thirties—the French Orleans Theatre, the Anglo-Saxon Camp Street, and the Italian Saint Charles.[103] The works performed included many melodramatic thrillers by composers who had helped to develop the monumental style of the French Revolution, Grétry, Dalayrac, Méhul.[104] As this city, which had been small and geographically isolated but commercially active, was absorbed into the more segregationist ways of the United States, Negro music began to separate from white music; art music from popular. "The colored" were limited to "reserved" sections at concert halls and were forbidden to attend balls for white people, except for the girls invited to the quadroon balls. Negroes responded by organizing or demanding balls and concerts for "persons of color."

For a time the city's public festivals allowed a kind of syncretism impossible where one or another ideology, language, or culture was the unquestioned creed of all. Northern Europeans sometimes found that this cultural miscegenation confirmed their prejudices. An unbusinesslike preoccupation with the music of operas, churches, parades, and dances was a sign of the Mediterranean races' decadence, just as singing and dancing was a sign of the dark man's shiftlessness. But the stone that the builders rejected became the cornerstone of the continuing romantic search for a new consciousness. In the early nineteenth century, New Orleans was a unique place where trade made for plenty of money to spend. Geography concentrated the people behind levees and made for a life more urban than in most of the United States.

Outside New Orleans virtually the only other operas performed in the United States before the Civil War were brought here by two excellent popularizing musicians. Manuel Garcia, Senior, brought an Italian operatic troupe to New York in 1825. He also toured the entire western hemisphere and brought to the cities he visited their first glimpse of the standard European repertoire plus a few of his own operas. Manuel Garcia, Junior, a star tenor, carried on his father's work. (He probably came as close as any teacher of singing to the creation of a scientific method for the voice when he invented the laryngoscope, which allowed direct observation of one's own vocal apparatus while singing.) The younger Garcia taught generations of opera singers. Amateurs and professionals alike studied his *Metado di canto*, which went through dozens of editions and translations before its author died at the age of one hundred in 1905.[105] Like its author and his father, it mediated between the sublime or esoteric and the popular.

In a neoromantic theory of culture, John Kouwenhoven argues that in earlier, more vital periods, the "classical" and the "vernacular" tradition in the arts were closely allied. By "classical" he means the art of tradition and training; by "vernacular," the functional art of the people. When the two are not isolated they draw from and benefit each other. But when the classical is cut off from its roots in the vernacular, it tends to harden. Kouwenhoven thinks that American art had made many good beginnings by the eighteenth century, but that the classical then separated from the vernacular and these beginnings could never properly develop a new formal art.[106]

Such a theory ignores the fact that "vernacular" culture often lags behind the "classical." For example, English "folk" ballads about Lord Randall and Sir Patrick Spens sound as though they were originally sung in aristocrats' halls. Nevertheless, it is intriguing to apply this theory to music in New Orleans. "Here for a substantial time, the vernacular (dance music) and the classical (opera) were close in many ways. Had they remained thus, who knows what might have ensued? To some extent opera in New Orleans was always close to the community, but as the opera gained prominence it did draw away from the baser dance activities. Especially was this true from 1890 on, when the character of dance music was changing. Ironically, in 1918, when the French opera house burned down, marking the end of resident opera in the city, New Orleans Dixieland dance music was carried abroad for the first time."[107]

Kouwenhoven's hypothesis seems worth applying further to the problem of mass antihumanism in the twentieth century. In a careful article which attempts to synthesize historical opinion on the roots of Nazism, Wolfgang Sauer hypothesizes "that the diversion between the educated and uneducated may have developed in the nineteenth century into the true dividing line between the ruling oligarchy and its subjects. . . . If this is true, subjects seeking emancipation had two ways to respond: either forming a subculture or resorting to barbarism. The first was the solution of the socialist labor movement; the second was the way of the Nazis, and it was the true revolutionary way. . . . Hitler's prestige with the masses . . . appears to have been supported by the fact that Hitler succeeded again and again in defeating and humiliating members of the old oligarchy."[108] Sauer does not insist upon his hypothesis, but, if it is true, it means that romantic reconciliations, whether imaginary androgynes, utopian phalanxes, or tricolor balls, were very much to the point.[109]

Yet another crossing of the streams of high and popular culture were the religious controversies in England during the industrial revolution. These were "Gothic revivals" in every sense.

GOTHIC REVIVALS

The Rebirth of Religious Lyricism in Britain

9

"I consider music as a very innocent diversion, and perfectly compatible with the profession of a clergyman," spake the Reverend Mr. Collins in Jane Austen's *Pride and Prejudice*.

> I do not mean however to assert that we can be justified in devoting too much of our time to music, for there are certainly other things to be attended to. The rector of a parish has much to do.—In the first place, he must write his own sermons; and the time that remains will not be too much for his parish duties, and the care and improvement of his dwelling, which he cannot be excused from making as comfortable as possible. And I do not think it of light importance that he should have attentive and conciliatory manners towards everybody, especially towards those to whom he owes his preferment.[1]

Wherever there was a Mr. Collins, religion was a bore. In such places the establishment was resting on a negative force, lethargy and indifference—and this force would soon be exhausted.[2]

To save itself, religion would at least have to be interesting. It would have to carve out a living space separate from lazy habits, self-assured rationalism, and two types of insensible clerics. Sometimes of a perfunctory sort were the clergy of the establishment. They performed parochial rites to suit the taste of the squirearchy, like Mr. Collins' ill-bred patron, Lady Catherine de Burgh, who thought church quite necessary for the morality of humble folk, no matter how careless the ritual or dry the sermon. In the cathedrals

of the Church of England some prelates continued the courtly fol-
derol of their continental peers, but most of them altogether ignored
making the rites artistic because they counted money and effort spent
on such things a waste. Under George III few provincial cathedrals
maintained their choral establishments.[3]

In the churches of the left—the Dissenters or the now-respectable
Methodists and Evangelicals—many clergy were of an eager sort,
long-winded preachers who were righteously certain of their personal
inspiration or superior reason. With evangelistic gush or long, boring
theodicies in imitation of Alexander Pope's *Essay on Man*, they
dominated their congregations from those thronelike pulpits which
overwhelm the east end of many churches built in the eighteenth century.[4] The clergy did not see that if religion relied on reactionary
inertia or liberal "proofs," the England of the industrial revolution
would overwhelm or just ignore Christianity more surely than did
France in its Revolution.

Against those negative forces, the spiritual revival in England re-
acted, like that on the Continent, with a sympathetic reevaluation
of everything from monasticism to glossolalia. A romantic impulse
called the establishment away from its harlotry to the state to revive
the riches of the Christian heritage elaborated in the Gothic Middle
Ages. The same romantic impulse called the nonconforming sects
away from their middle-class smugness to revive their Gothicism, an
intense enthusiasm based upon respect for the individual as a temple
of inner light. While the prophetic Swedenborgian poet William Blake
cried out for a spiritual rebirth, a changing conscience was evident.
The old, preindustrial folkways, including religion, were collected
and advertised as something fresh; next came theories and movements
which attempted to recapture Christianity's primitive zeal; finally
the revival was institutionalized and proceeded in two directions. In
the one, those who followed Newman into the Roman Church metamorphosed their personal and aesthetic perception into a dogmatic
and legalistic one. In the other direction the lyrical impulse was subsumed into Matthew Arnold's Broad Church, for which religion was
defined as man's best poetry and the church as a public aesthetic
educator. A similar impulse informed some new charismatic sects,
such as the Salvation Army, which were the popular analogue of
Arnold's high culture. Together they all contributed to the romantic
cultural revolution which insisted that true religion or art is a sense
of honesty or beauty rather than a thing of legalistic privilege or
scientific proof.

I

Like most revolutions, English romanticism seems to have begun
with some atavism or at least a glance backward into history. Wesley, for example, had thought he was resurrecting primitive Christianity; so did Blake; so would Newman think; so thought the revival
within the Church of England. The formal revival began linked to
the results of research and writing on English folkways, especially
the lyrics of those times when England was "still merry, and musical." A common ancestor of both the secular catches and glees, sung
in meeting halls from Wales to the Hebrides, and of the *Hymns Ancient and Modern* in the high church, was Bishop Thomas Percy's
Reliques of Ancient Poetry of 1767. Percy apologized—perhaps
ironically—for collecting such trifles in an era of Augustan literary
giants. Soon all manner of lyrical "reliques" came into fashion,
among them MacPherson's epic, *Ossian*, that best-selling "expansion" of some ancient Celtic fragments. Meanwhile English musicians like Samuel Arnold, organist at Westminster from 1793 to
1802, and Samuel Webbe, the most prolific composer of his time for
church and community choruses, began to collect musical reliques.[5]

   Poets and philosophers were joining the scholars with praise for
lyricism and folkways. Wordsworth and Coleridge's Preface to the
Lyrical Ballads of 1798 was a manifesto of this tendency. In those
years when the two poets left behind overt sympathy for the Parisian
form of the democratic revolution,[6] Wordsworth enunciated a co-
vertly radical aesthetic. In much the same way, Edmund Burke's
evolutionary establishmentarianism was disestablishing faith in ver-
bally-definable absolutes.[7] His *On the Sublime* was a banner of liberation for the underground side of the human mind. Wordsworth
thought that since human nature was everywhere the same, a univer-
sally intense feeling should be a natural truth and vice versa. Thus
a child or a savage is as appropriate a subject for a poem as Achilles
or Queen Elizabeth I. Therefore, the truest picture of man is the one
most rid of artificiality.[8] In sum, like the Methodists, Wordsworth
and the other English romantics became politically conservative but
remained psychologically democratic—even radical—because they
glorified that which had been thought undignified.

   Wordsworth's partner in the *Lyrical Ballads*, Coleridge, attempted
the philosophical synthesis which reinforced a galaxy of ecclesiastical
movements in the next generation, ranging from Newman's Catholi-

cism through Matthew Arnold's Broad Church and F. W. Maurice's Christian Socialism to humanistic psychology in our own time. What Schleiermacher was to Protestant Germany and Lamennais would be to Catholic France, Coleridge was to via-media England. Zealous to reconcile Hebrews and Hellenes, he insisted that "there is no chasm between God and man, between the religious and the natural; the religious life is the natural life of man in the highest sense."[9] Thus man could measure the supernatural. So far we have a mind of the eighteenth century, like Pope's. But Coleridge adds that the measure of human possibility is the poet's imagination, which is no longer the mere power of receiving images, the *phantasia* of the Greeks; or of Locke; it has become and remains the voice of God in the artist.[10] In this way did Coleridge try to reconcile "belief in the complete autonomy and the unique originality of the individual work . . . with a confidence in universal principles of value."[11]

He sidestepped collision with the rationalists by declaring that reliques—for example the Bible and religious lyrics—remained valid not because of an institution's precept or a philosopher's proof but because they were expressions of the "natural life of man in the highest sense." Coleridge's priorities were therefore contrary to those of that overestablished Mr. Collins. Not tithes and livings but human integrity was the heart of Christianity. And *anyone* could achieve this integrity.

Now the one who shall achieve this, said Coleridge, is he who penetrates by an immediate insight into the core of whatever is being considered. This penetration he called "imagination," a faculty which is vouchsafed to artists more often than to theologians and metaphysicians. Hence, the poet, who might be a very plain man, is the truest philosopher.[12] Thus far Coleridge sounds individualistic, "Protestant," but his tendency is more high church.

As for religion and its practice, Coleridge taught that their task is to comprehend the "total intellectual and aesthetic life of the nation"[13] and see to its distribution throughout the nation. For the plain man needs to know something of the best that has been thought, said, and done in the world.[14] Squabbling over contracts for livings and "proofs" of God's existence or nonexistence were equally obtuse. As Coleridge's liberal follower, Matthew Arnold, would say, "the strongest part of religion today is its conscious poetry. A religion which is merely ethical, or merely theological, has no power to move the soul and is no religion at all."[15] Coleridge noted that where customs and rites he supposed to be Gothic inheri-

tances had been exorcised during the Enlightenment, morality was
no better.

Even in the hands of a political conservative, such a theology is
essentially populist, for it can deny neither divine immanence in
every earthly man nor evolution of creeds to suit the needs of every
time and place. Coleridge's "sense of divine immanence has almost
wholly submerged his sense of divine transcendence, and he likes
to think of God, man, and nature as interfused in one great cosmic
harmony. He believes in natural goodness, the moral sense, the inner
light, the powers of genius. He likes to think of his imagination as a
creative force akin to that which has thought the universe into being.
Creeds, rules, logical formulas, sharp distinctions, external controls
of every sort, are repugnant to him. Shunning the permanent and
normative elements of life, he revels in spontaneity, diversity, uniqueness and individual expansiveness."[16]

Though Coleridge did not write at length about music, when he
approached the subject he reversed the eighteenth century's prefer-
ences. His short poem *Music* found even the minimal music of a
country church precentor and his bawling congregation Dionysiac.[17]
His theoretical writing on music applied his unclassical dictum that
all the arts are communication and that the immediate object of a
poem is pleasure, not truth. In meter, the most obviously musical
aspect of poetry, he found not a supernumerary charm but an organic part of the whole communication.[18]

Romantic theory therefore complemented research into folklore.
So did the popular Methodist movement toward a religion of feelings. With contemporary Methodist success and competition to spur
on the existing churches, it was only a matter of time before lyricism
penetrated the establishment. For example, well into the nineteenth
century, the species of lyric poetry called hymns was suspected of
a tendency to dilute the Anglican liturgy with Methodist pietism.
When Bishop Heber of Calcutta could get no imprimatur from the
Archbishop of Canterbury for his *Hymns*, his widow published the
work posthumously in 1827 as private poetry.[19] Concurrently,
the Reformed churches, which did not require the imprimatur of
bishops, tested their tradition by turning from exclusively biblical
texts to "hymns of human composition." Also in 1827, John Curtis,
a Baptist, published a *Union Collection* as an "addition to Dr.
Watts." He included some texts by the romantic poets, Coleridge,
Scott, Byron, and Moore, and hymns from all denominations. Curtis
explicitly denied the dictum of Dr. Johnson in the previous century

The Bard (1796), a painting by John Martin in interpretation of a poem by Thomas Gray. The romantics often pictured the poet or artist as an ecstatic prophet or singer. Although alone—at least in his imagination—in a wild, natural setting high above the rest of humanity, the bard remained in touch with the instincts of his people. Of all the arts, music was often thought the most sublime, offering a direct path to the most elusive side of human nature. (Laing Art Gallery of Tyne and Wear County Council Museums, Newcastle upon Tyne.)

that poetry interfered with true religion. That year saw a few psalms for congregational singing and a few hymns bound into the back of an edition of the Anglican *Book of Common Prayer*. These first hymns with an official sanction were the forerunners of *Hymns Ancient and Modern*, which appeared in the 1860s.[20]

Through its Methodist offshoot the hierarchical Church of England had had a more radical reform in the eighteenth century than had the nonconformists or other Reformed, who had only to adjust a cult that always had been by and for the congregation. Wesley had intended his adjustment of Anglican rites to be a mixture of the formal and the free, the clerical and the charismatic. Through emotional preaching, singing, and crying-out, the Methodists had reopened the expression of religious experience to laymen. Accompanying the lay-oriented religion of John Wesley were the hymns of his brother Charles, the poet of Methodism. And where lyric poetry led, music was soon to follow. Though John Wesley had first abhorred the use of professional music in his services, his followers were permitting oratorios in Methodist chapels within a generation after his death.[21]

A similar progression from the preaching of words to the hearing of music marked the history of Evangelicalism, which remained within the Church of England. The contrast here is more marked because the Evangelicals opposed not only musical professionalism —which is an unordained clericalism—but all manifestations of the spirit of music, that is, all private frenzy in public rites, save preaching. More forceful than the Reverend Mr. Collinses of the realm, the Evangelicals thought that music was a snare of the devil to interfere with and subvert the formality which should rule outside the sermon. For a strict Evangelical, "wine itself, though a man may be guilty of habitual intoxication, does not more to debauch or befool the natural understanding than music, always music; music in season and out of season weakens and destroys the spiritual discernment."[22]

As we shall see in the last chapter, the supposedly ritualistic Tractarians were sons of these seemingly anti-aesthetic Evangelicals. The Tractarians wedded biblicism from the Protestant side of Anglicanism to a whole range of aesthetic expressions from its Catholic side. Their goal was to widen the meager circle of Evangelical writing and preaching, which had been totally biblical and narrowly verbal, to include all facets of the human psyche.[23] Many of these could be called Gothic.

The connection between Evangelical or Methodist Protestantism and Mediterranean Catholicism, which Newman would discover in the nineteenth century, had been found earlier by John Wesley's nephew. Catholicizing was a matter of refining and enriching, not denying, the religion of feelings. Samuel Wesley, son of the poet Charles, became a Catholic in 1784 at eighteen, "seduced by the Chant of the Portuguese [Embassy] Chapel,"[24] and repelled by "crude" evangelistic hymnody. Charles's other sons and his grandsons also became eminent church musicians. One grandson, Samuel Sebastian Wesley, whose surname kept him—but not his music— out of the best posts in the Anglican Church, maintained a born Methodist's enthusiasm superior to the nostalgia of his chosen Anglicanism. He thought that the acoustics of a cathedral covered a multitude of sins, especially the one of saying that only music written in square notes[25] is acceptable. He thought that setting up chant as model church music was "like telling Michaelangelo to imitate Stonehenge."[26] But for other Church of England men in the new century, Gothic was not only a question of deep musical feeling. It was a passion for organic continuity and ethical integrity.

For many Anglo- and Roman Catholics, Gothic seemed good because historically correct. It was native to England and antedated the national state.[27] Contrarily, Graeco-Roman styles seemed "essentially pagan" and redolent of Erastian authoritarianism from papal Rome or Bourbon Paris.

The architects and writers of the Gothic revival seconded that historical argument with an assertion that Gothic was natural and therefore ethical.[28] Echoing political liberals like Viollet-le-Duc (1814–79) in France, dogmatic Catholics like Augustus Welby Pugin (1812–52) agreed with liberal Broad Church men or nonconformists like Matthew Arnold and John Ruskin that there was a happy coincidence between the Gothic style and English freedoms.[29] Christianity seemed the proper religion for a democracy, which England was becoming, and Gothic seemed the most Christian style because "it had been made by humble craftsmen, not princely designers."

To turn the tables for a moment, there may really have been a quite natural, historical reason behind the affinity for the Gothic felt by those aesthetes who supposed they were escaping the age of democratic and industrial revolution. In both the Gothic and the roman-

tic eras, that which had been the province of a few aristocrats and
clerks became more of a mass phenomenon because of an economic,
political, and psychological revolution. The rise of cities, the chance
to be a free bourgeois, and the scholastic assertion that natural reason is reliable were dramatized in Gothic church buildings and liturgies, which delighted in the city of man. Gothic religion "humanized
and emotionalized Christianity."[30] A new tolerance of the noble
heathen, one of the few indubitable effects of the crusades—in the
eighteenth and nineteenth centuries, read "of the exploration and
colonization of the world"—expressed the new religious feeling, freer
and more inward, which is characteristic of the age. The mysticism,
the mendicant orders, and the heresies of either century are symp-
toms of the same trend. The professionalized architectural engineering and dramatic music of the Gothic cathedrals might also be read
as a declericalizing preferment of talent over status.

Both Gothic and romantic were unstable equilibria of world-
affirming and world-denying impulses. High medieval chivalry and
modern liberalism were both permeated by an inner contradiction
between the law of the jungle and the golden rule. So, too, the religious life of both periods fluctuated between dogma and inwardness, between clerical creeds and lay piety, between idealism and
sensuousness, between orthodoxy and subjectivism.

A striking manifestation of the wish to overcome this dualism is
the peculiar feeling for nature found once in Gothic and again romantic poetry and art. After the Franciscan movement "any creature
can be counted as brother." Five hundred years later, landscape
painting, "English" gardens, a belief in the wisdom of the unlearned,
and, above all, a belief that reality is inseparable from sense experience manifested the same tendency. All testify that even those on
the lowest rung of the neo-Platonic ladder have their chance of rising
to complete humanity. There may be an order to the universe, but
one must face it existentially. This is the message of the episodic
montage found in passion plays or pageantry and consummated by
that patron saint of romanticism, Shakespeare, in his unclassical
juxtapositions and unlikely chronologies.

In sum, both Gothic and romantic tried to reconcile opposites.[31]
Too, in Gothic and afresh in romantic art, the lyricism of modern
art and also its cult of virtuosity begins.[32] Both styles added the element of confession of personal experience to the styles that preceded
them. According to classical aesthetics, music is the confessional art
par excellence because it is supposed to be the spontaneous outpour-

ing of feelings. Music is "being natural and honest." Some romantics found a similar confession of truth in the Gothic exposure of the structural elements of a building.

The leading architect of the Gothic revival in England, Pugin, deplored "mere decoration and false fronts," or the concealment of important structural and decorative features, such as the flying buttresses hidden in Wren's Saint Paul's. "In such cases," it seemed to him, "the laws of beauty and morality coincided; an attempt to deceive produced a building architecturally deplorable."[33]

These aesthetes, the English Catholics and Anglo-Catholics of the nineteenth century, were also sacramentalists desiring that religion give them a mystical experience, not a lecture. They put the altar at the focal point of their churches, just as the previous century had been homiletic and put the pulpit there.[34] But their sacramentalist theology and antiquarian interest in Christian symbolism were governed by an aesthetic righteousness. Apropos of the priests who were required for the sacraments, Pugin wrote:

> Do not deceive yourselves, . . . the Catholics will cut their own throats, the clergy will put down religion. These are hard sayings, but they are twice mad fools; straining at gnats and swallowing camels, the very men who do not hesitate to violate rubrics every day to suit the convenience of their pockets, now swelling with indignation and horror at the idea of an ample surplice or flowing chasuble such as almost every saint in the Calendar wore. Administer baptism out of an old physick vial; reserve the blessed Sacrament in *dirty cupboard*; say mass in vestments made out of an old gown; burn gas on the altar; have everything as *mean*, as *pitiful*, as shabby as you please; hire protestant performers to sing; leave out every ceremonial in the ritual; do this and you will be right.[35]

To be truly right demands theology *and* artistry; therefore the mystical essence of a sacrament is partly aesthetic.

If clerical indifference was an annoyance to the Gothicizers, laissez-faire liberalism was an enemy. Yet, even in the negativism of the later Gothic revival, which seemed to see nothing good in an England growing industrial and liberal, there was at least a paternalistic concern for what the industrial masses were being deprived of. The plates in Pugin's book *Contrasts*[36] are in their way socialist. On the left page he sketched a medieval town. The best things in it were community property—churches, bridges, parks, hospitals, wells, gates, and vistas. Facing each of those sketches was a plate of the same town in the middle of the nineteenth century. The use of any good thing now depended upon one's ability to pay. There are toll gates on the bridges, gas works and factories where the common land had been along the river, and workhouses where the hospices had stood. Pugin's idea of what a medieval town looked, sounded, and smelled like were idyllic, to say the least. Nevertheless, behind his contrast between Gothic fancies and endless boxes is the philosophy that people are better off when one's income does not determine the quality of one's life.

For his Gothic churches, Pugin wanted Gothic music, which he thought was unaccompanied Gregorian chant—hardly the operatic repertoire sung in Newman's Oratorian churches, where it was said lady vergers wearing feathers took up the collection, while others of their sex—perhaps also with feathers—chirped and warbled in the loft near the ceiling. Pugin wanted a tonsured, male choir in the sanctuary behind a rood screen.

> A man may be judged by his feelings on Plain Chaunt [sic]. If he
> likes Mozart, he is no chancel and screen man. By their music ye
> shall know them.[37]
>   There exists a *want of reality* in the present service of the
> Churches in this land and many other countries; and from what
> does it proceed but the corrupt and artificial state of ecclesiastical
> music? The clergy and people have been precluded from taking
> any real part in the service of Almighty God. They are reduced to
> the position of listeners instead of worshippers . . . so that in
> lieu of clergy and people uniting in one great act of adoration and
> praise, the service is transferred to a set of hired musicians, who
> perform in a gallery while the congregation is either amused or
> wearied.[38]

Pugin has acquired his taste for Gregorian music from a circle of Anglo-Catholics who had been initiated into the aesthetic riches of the Roman *opera* by a French émigré priest. One of these Anglo-Catholics, Ambrose Phillipps,[39] was converted to Catholicism at sixteen, about twenty years before Newman. In 1830 Phillipps's father installed him in an ancient manor house in Leicestershire named Grâce-Dieu, where the entire menage acted the cosmic Roman *opera*, with every detail from the stitching of their costumes to the landscape architecture well-regulated for the greater glory of God.[40] Close to Phillipps was Kenelm Digby, whose encyclopedic apologia *Mores*

Catholici (1831–42) drew material from every conceivable source to explain the "Ages of Faith."[41]

Other enthusiasts began to twist the aesthetic step which was or would be so crucial for the Wesleys, Newman, and Pugin. One of those who erected an artistic preference into a theological dogma by favoring the exclusive use of Gregorian music was the Reverend Henry Formby. Father Formby would follow Newman from the Anglican to the Roman clergy and was the author of a church history reminiscent of Chateaubriand's *Genius of Christianity*. He was as fervent a Gothicizer as Newman, in spite of his disclaimers, would be an Italianizer. According to Formby, musicians were now less religious. "The chief authors and singers of Plain Chant upon earth are among the Saints of the Church, who are known to be in heaven, and to intercede for us; on the other hand, the chief authors of harmony and figured music, are not only *unknown* to be in heaven, but in no few instances, to judge from their lives, are under considerable improbability of being ever admitted there."[42] In a pamphlet on the chant, Father Formby spent most of his text urging monks to perform chant well, for only through a good performance of the office will non-Catholics be attracted to the church. Though he seemed to believe in the romantic (and Aristotelian-Thomist) dictum that the good is first apprehended as the beautiful, Father Formby subscribed to an *ex opere operato* philosophy of church music: "Another reason [to prefer the chant] arises from the known hatred of the devil to the Plain Chant; to any other kind of music, supposed to be sacred, he will grant a truce. To the song of the Divine Office alone, he will grant none. Why? Except that in it he sees what he so much fears and hates, the most engaging manifestation of our Blessed Redeemer."[43] We recognize reasoning like that which Chateaubriand had or Newman would use to praise the aesthetic riches of Catholicism, but we miss their enthusiasm for the art itself. Authoritarian aesthetics cannot supply the inner light.

Perhaps the most romantic of all English aesthetico-religious ideas was the Broad Church, which attempted to justify religion through plain social utility. This church—or rather, proposal—refused to concede that, once a religion begins to step down from dogma, there is no place it can stop. The Broad Church hoped to do without miracle, mystery, and authority—as Dostoevski named them in his Grand Inquisitor[44]—to maintain itself. Its leaders, like their opponents, the Tractarians, were educated in a combination of righteous Evangelicalism and the protean philosophy of Coleridge.

> They sought to overcome scepticism and irreligion, but were not opposed to liberal thought. They emphasized not the institution and the Church, but the individual: they minimized sacramentarism, sacerdotalism, and traditionalism.
> From Coleridge they got their drive toward comprehensiveness, toward seeing the Church as the organized religious life of the whole nation; they sought unity by inclusion. . . . [for] the Church is not the only means of fostering religious life.
> Bishops should not lord it over the Church and [there should be] a variety of rituals.[45]

The Broad Church, like Tractarianism, was a response to the Reform Bill of 1832. The father of the Broad Church idea, the eminent liberal educator and reforming headmaster of Rugby School, Thomas Arnold, was the father of Matthew Arnold, its leader, and godfather to John Keble, the Tractarians' founder. Both the Broad Church men and the Tractarians dreaded disestablishment. However, Arnold, Senior, put the blame not on liberalism, but on the dogmatism of the Church and the curious fact that the church of Jesus Christ had become incensed in earnest only when its purse was threatened by the possible extinction of ten Irish bishoprics in communion with Canterbury. To protest, as the Tractarians did, this act of simple justice for the Irish seemed as blindly establishmentarian as Jane Austen's Reverend Mr. Collins.

Arnold was right. Among the Tractarians, W. G. Ward thought "social improvement of slight importance to those who looked to heaven"; Newman thoroughly despised the necessary banalities of popular movements; Hurrel Froude disliked " 'niggers' for being the symbols of Whiggery, cant, and Dissent"; and Pusey, personally a charitable man, thought the "abolition of slavery absurd because it involved the expenditure of twenty million pounds for 'an opinion.' "[46] Workers saw the church's condescension and the middle class its economic power as the last citadels of feudalism. Following his admired historians Vico and Michelet, Thomas Arnold argued that the "church's chief function is education, to be administered in behalf of the state." This education would be most useful when it developed the heads and the hearts of all citizens as well as it trained their hands for the factories.[47] Within the state, the primary job of religion was to assure everyone a taste of the sublime.

Since the Broad Church was conceived as a species of general education rather than doctrinal reform, the conscious emphasis of the Broad Church Party was at first more liturgical than the Tractarians', who announced that they were concerned with doctrine anterior to practice. In the end, the leading Tractarian, Newman, joined the most dogmatic branch of western Christianity, and the leading intellects of liberalism, John Stuart Mill and Matthew Arnold, carried romantic assumptions to their logical conclusions. Religion was to be socially useful, but as poetry;[48] poetry was to be socially useful as the highest perception of any truth. In other words, religion, art, and education were to be scientifically united to form useful citizens.[49]

Thomas Arnold had been a doctrinaire rationalist to the point of ignoring the Rousseauvian insights of romanticism in his zeal for an aristocracy of talent. Conversely, his son Matthew had a passionate dislike of systems. For example, his partisanship for or against the various French revolutions varied according to how much revolution he thought England needed at the time.[50] From among the Middle Ages, Reformation, and revolutionary eras he desired to conserve the best of each, and consequently got his drubbings from all parties —many of them deserved.[51] To reconcile all these—ultimately to resolve the tension between the creative imagination and the critical intellect which lay at the heart of the romantic philosophy—became Arnold's life work. He wished for "integration, of the individual, of the work of art, and finally of the social order."[52]

Since theological agreement was unlikely, unity of ritual or charitable work became the only conceivable and practicable way for religion to "recognize and appreciate that which is true and good under all varieties of forms."[53] Only by broadening its doctrine to include all Englishmen could the Anglican Church dare to claim the right to administer the endowments which had been put into its trust for the moral and intellectual—one used to say spiritual or ghostly —improvement of the people. But while Matthew Arnold was urging absolute openness, "the Tractarians were demanding both that the Church be further 'purified' in point of doctrine and that its right to Establishment not be questioned. Their position seemed to Arnold an arrogant challenge to the nation, tempting one to demand disestablishment and withdrawal of the Church's right to its property."[54]

As for the cult, which should be public education: "What is done and said in a public place, and bear[s] with it a public character, should be done and said worthily. . . . They are a kind of schooling, which may educate gradually such performance into something better, and meanwhile may prevent it from standing forth, to its own discredit and to that of all of us, as public and representative. . . . No one will say that the common Englishman glides offhand and by nature into a strain pure, noble, and elevated. On the contrary, he falls with great ease into vulgarity. But no people has shown more attachment than the English to old and dignified forms calculated to save us from it."[55] Arnold refused to countenance revision of the Anglican ritual because "profound sentiments are connected with them; they are aimed at the highest good, however imperfectly apprehended. Their form often gives them beauty, the associations which cluster around them give them always pathos and solemnity. They are to be used as poetry. . . . The eternity and universality, which is vainly claimed [by Newman] for Catholic dogma and the ultramontane system, might really be possible for Catholic worship."[56]

That is, the mystical value of the sacraments has become aesthetic; they are poetry. The leading clerical theologian and liturgiologist of the Broad Church movement was not formally in it. Frederick Dennison Maurice (1805–72) tried to meet the liberals, scientists, and Tractarians on their own ground by combining a devotion to theology, social justice, and ritual.[57] His method for applying his theories was liturgical, in that he thought that even the Broad Church party had too much concern for theology, whereas the success of Anglicanism from Elizabethan times onward had been its liturgical inclusiveness rather than its theological definitiveness.

Maurice looked upon Anglicanism and its *Book of Common Prayer* as Lamennais would have had men look upon the Papacy. It should continue to be broad, inclusive, and should prescribe forms of worship conformable to the needs of the human community before it prescribed doctrinal formularies. He thought that the Anglican prayer book struck the right balance between an excessive number of mediators between God and man, as found in the Roman rite, and flat deism, which looked upon worship as flattery. Hence, he was for a modernized via media.

Maurice asserted that the primary need of man in what was becoming the age of Darwin, was the recognition of utter dependence upon God or the need for obedience to God, rather than theories about him.[58] In that assertion we recognize the familiar pietist predilection for a mystical intuition of God found throughout romantic religion in Schleiermacher, Lamennais, and Newman. Maurice thought that the eighteenth century had erred by limiting faith to what could be understood through Lockean reflection upon sensation.[59]

Out of Maurice's circle "Christian Socialism" began in 1848 as a response to the widespread threat of revolution in that year and lasted about six years. Where the Broad Church men had assumed that the state was identical with the nation, Maurice's circle minimized the role of the state in favor of purely voluntary cooperation.[60] The Christian Socialists condemned the use of religion as an opium dose for keeping the people quiet,[61] although they were probably unaware of Marx's similar remark. They hoped for a new social order based upon cooperation rather than competition.

Such doctrines gained them striking success in slum parishes[62] and earned Maurice a place alongside the Saint-Simonian Thomas Carlyle in Ford Madox Brown's realistic painting "Work." In the background could be seen a billboard advertising one of Maurice's "workingmen's colleges." Maurice himself was inspired by a Roman Catholic version of Saint-Simonianism practiced in France by Philip Buchez after the debacle at Ménilmontant.[63] Another eminent Victorian, John Ruskin, who called Carlyle "Master" in social matters, taught in one of Maurice's workingmen's colleges for a time. Ruskin's Gothicism was the typical conservative-radical hope for a new order based upon the cooperation which seemed to contrast medieval and modern times.[64]

Maurice's theories were in the spirit of the times. He began his lectures on "social morality" by stating that "Rousseau's line of investigation was the most fruitful educational speculation" and that the subsequent revolutionary and romantic eras had taught men the value of "common" themes.[65] He concluded the book with a chapter in the vein of Comte: humanity needs a worship without dogma,[66] where "Hellenic art and Hebraic truth" will be reconciled by an artistic language which is true to the soul and therefore true entirely.

Even the thoroughly Protestant nonconforming churches appropriated some Gothic liturgical practices.[67] During the eighteenth century, as we have seen, rationalism had caused the widest liturgiological quarrels within the most liturgical church—the Roman. In the nineteenth century, things changed. Now the austere Reformed churches were more troubled by the latest liturgical style, which seemed the very idol that John Calvin had toppled in the sixteenth century. There were some schisms in certain Reformed churches when the critical, analytical spirit, which had not arrived among

them on time in the eighteenth century, overlapped the new currents
of organicist thinking in the German style. Across the Channel, liberalism became dominant in the Dutch Reformed Church, while
traditionalist groups—who held to the strict views of the Synod of
Dort—split away.[68]

Just as both rationalists and romantics within the more liturgical
churches deplored perfunctory ritualism and groped either toward
new creation or toward the restoration of viable old forms, so too
in the Calvinist churches there was a reaction against repetition of
prescribed formulae. Reformed Christians had always used "nothing
but God's word" as liturgical songs.[69] These were the psalms in some
hallowed metrical translation which fitted one or another of the few
long-meter tunes surviving in the congregation's musical memory.
The words of the psalms were so sacred to the Reformed congregations that the precentor, who was usually the local schoolmaster, did
not even dare to rehearse the sacred text with its tune. He used
nursery rhymes or anything at hand when not actually "lining out"
the psalm for his congregation to imitate. Occasionally this led to
comic lapses of memory when, say, a grocery list emerged during a
particularly inspired performance.

Reformed congregations had forgotten most of the original tunes
and corrupted the rest; finally, everyone devised his own "graces"
to enliven the tortured tunes. Sometimes it took half a minute for
the Covenanters to reach a consensus on a single note; a whole verse
might take fifteen. One eyewitness described a contest between some
elect and their precentor, who held forth from the lowest level of a
three-decker pulpit, in which the minister occupied the top deck:
"They made such a discord as quite defaced this noblest part of
divine worship. . . . [There was] screaming, dogs barking, babies
crying. When the minister could bear it no longer he popped up
again, leaned over, touched the precentor's head, and instantly all
sound ceased."[70] Jean-Jacques Rousseau, exasperated by such strug-
gles, had proposed that the citizens of Geneva keep together in their
psalmody by following a visual, rather than an aural, director, "for
light is incomparably faster than sound."[71]

To a staunch Calvinist, however, the psalms, even thus chanted,
were as sacred as the popery they had displaced two centuries earlier. Like liturgical prayer everywhere, the paraphrases of psalms
were in general, third-person terms, as in Watts's

People and realms of every tongue
Dwell on His love with sweetest song.[72]

Again, as in the liturgical churches, so in the Reformed, rational-istic reformers had reckoned the psalms "too poetical," even super-stitious. Romantics would think that the lyrics attributed to David were the "ne plus ultra of holy joy, which would raise even an un-willing heart on high." Hence, they meant to restore the psalms to the central place they had held in the Hebrew and Christian tradi-tions.[73] While the psalms were being banished and then recovered in the liturgical churches, biblically oriented churches such as the Reformed began to allow "hymns of human composition"—usually paraphrases other than the familiar one—into their rites. Though, for example, most Huguenots did not want to sing other than Holy Writ when hymns were introduced in 1805,[74] Calvinists in the fast-nesses of Scotland were already installing organs.[75]

Sir Walter Scott offered the Scottish Kirk some paraphrases of the psalms—that is, hymns—rather than the new version of the Psalter he was asked to produce. He thought that the old version should be retained in the homely, plain, and "forcible accents of our church fathers."[76] Sir Walter added that he thought the people needed the sense of an ancient and living tradition.[77]

The result of these adjustments of Reformed rites paralleled the critical spirit which the Enlightenment had asserted in the liturgical churches. Both traditions loosened their rubrics and gained greater variety in their ritual. Though not always intended, such changes made for rites which blurred the distinctions among the sects within European religion.

Besides the revivals based upon historical or philosophical argu-ments, there were some new sects which were Gothic in a third sense. Barbarous though they seemed to some; they seemed to others a usefully Dionysian liberation amid an excessively Apollonian mi-lieu. The Disciples of Christ and other evangelistic sects combined the Protestant idea of the gathered church with Anglican tradition-alism and sacramentalism.[78] Most dramatically eclectic was the Cath-olic Apostolic Church. Dour John Knox would have regretted that the fanciful ecclesiasticisms he had once fought were now proposed again in the Scottish Kirk by followers of Edward Irving (1792–1834). Irving had probably gained breadth and comprehensiveness from his study of Coleridge, but gradually his chief interest in Cole-ridge's philosophy centered on that which was mystical and obscure. This probably accounts for his adoption of the doctrine of mille-narianism.[79] His favorite reading included a work by a Jesuit posing as a Jewish mystic; in 1830 Irving was deposed from his pulpit for teaching heresy about Jesus' humanity.

Sophisticated critics like William Hazlitt[80] thought that Irving was bombastic for bombast's sake. Certain "enthusiasts," who had been driven out of various Christian churches in the British Isles, took him for a modern John the Baptist. Though the Scottish Kirk had expelled him, his followers increased and the church he founded still exists. He added Gregorian chants and other ancient music to the Calvinistic service because he thought that glossolalia, "when the speech utters itself in a way of a psalm or spiritual song, is likest to some of the most simple and ancient chants in the cathedral service. The heart and sound of the speaker are moved [and] far from unmeaning gibberish, it is regularly-formed, well-proportioned, deeply-felt discourse."[81] After Irving died in 1834, the Puritan and Calvinistic elements in his church diminished to the point of reserving the Eucharist in a tabernacle at all times, as is the custom in the Roman Catholic Church.

In July 1835, Irving's admirers elected twelve apostles of a Catholic Apostolic Church.

> For the service of the Church a comprehensive book of liturgies and offices was provided by the "apostles." It dates from 1842 and is based on the Anglican, Roman, and Greek liturgies. Lights, incense, vestments, holy water, chrism, and other adjuncts of worship are in constant use. The ceremonial in its completeness may be seen in the church in Gordon Square, London, and elsewhere. The community has always laid great stress on symbolism, and in the eucharist, while rejecting both transubstantiation and consubstantiation, holds strongly to a real (mystical) presence. It stresses also the "phenomena" of Christian experience and deems miracle and mystery to be of the essence of a spirit-filled church.[82]

Meanwhile, another Scottish evangelical, Robert Haldane, had preached in Geneva against the rationalism of the ruling Venerable Company of Pastors there.[83] Haldane influenced the Swiss orientalist and hymn writer, Solomon Caesar Malan (1812–94). The latter came to England armed with knowledge of several European languages and of Tibetan, Armenian, and Georgian. He opposed transliterating or otherwise tampering with the look or sound of the original text, which he deemed an integral part of any literary expression.[84]

So to insist that the form is integral with the content was typical of the romantic quest for truth to natural feelings. Though this insistence was often led by traditionalists or religionists, their mentality reflected and fostered the cult of feelings in society at large, not just within formal religion.

To view the century as a whole, perhaps the most successful combination of the charismatic and sacramental liturgical styles within English-speaking Christianity came after 1870 in the Salvation Army. They believed, like the Quakers, that one could retain the essence of a sacrament without the canonical form, and so the Army dropped the sacramental forms but apotheosized music.[85] Many a man's grudging admiration of the Army was expressed by George Bernard Shaw, who put into the mouth of the man who loved its Major Barbara:

> I am a sincere salvationist. . . . It is the army of joy, of love, of courage; it has banished fear and remorse and despair. . . . It marches to fight the devil with trumpet and drum, with music and dancing, with banner and palm; is become a sally from heaven by its happy garrison. It picks the waster out of the public house and makes a man of him; it finds a worm wriggling in a back kitchen, an lo! a woman! . . . It takes the poor professor of Greek, the most artificial and suppressed of human creatures, from his meal of roots, and lets loose the rhapsodist in him; reveals the true worship of Dionysios to him: sends him down the public street drumming dithyrambs.[86]

GOD AND PEOPLE

The Manifestation of the Risorgimento through Music

10

During the early nineteenth century, Italy reevaluated her culture and decided that she needed a politics to match. This reevaluation was the Risorgimento.

For Italians of the Risorgimento, even more than for Germans of the contemporary age of Hegel, the question of nationhood was a question of *if*. To liberate Italy from "the Austrian" in the north and from the mortmain which gripped her south of Tuscany seemed a utopian dream. And until the politicians found a way, culture—and especially music—was the proudest public expression of the Italian spirit. Indeed, it seemed to non-Italians that the Napoleons of music (as well as the Napoleon of the French armies) were Italian. Like his armies, in other lands their music caused a reaction against its invasion and in favor of native culture. The Germans, French, and English resented that the Italian style bore away all before it and stifled local products. In part, the northerners' antipathy was a reaction against operatic catering to the lowest common denominator of taste. To this much fastidious Italians agreed. On the other hand, even the most critical northern aestheticians did the Italians the honor which the chanceries of Europe had done Napoleon: they wanted to emulate the Italians' success.

But not in war. Having lived through the regime of the Corsican, Europe was used to the romantic posture, but tired of blood. Meanwhile, an Italian musical aggressor Gioachino Rossini (1792–1868), began to capture, one by one, every European capital. The French were disgusted, the Germans angry. Stendhal put his finger on the invader's magic: Rossini seemed to epitomize Italy—the pursuit of beauty and pleasure rather than money and conquest. Love the gorgeous Italian style or hate it, musicians, stage producers, and churches had to meet at least halfway the public's infatuation.[1]

This emulation in music was part of an emulation of all that Italy stood for. Not only the ruins of classical civilization were now admired but every custom strange to enlightened ways was now relished the more, almost as a forbidden fruit. In short, romanticism in romance nations should not be considered a side issue or innovation.[2] It was the mainstream.

The Italians remained essentially the same; only the perception of the romance spirit changed. No longer did travelers come only to research the glories of classical antiquity while tolerating the streets littered with the dung of Christianized superstition. They came on a sentimental journey to southern Europe seeking the sublime and awful sides of life supposedly banished from nations of shopkeepers. Literature, travelers' chronicles, and popular novels alike begin to assume that the Mediterranean—in American novels the darker— races were still masters of the dark side of life—they were more "musical." Love, death and life—in that order—are somehow more real in an Italian city or a malarial swamp than in the Royal Society. Italian politics of the Risorgimento dramatized the power of sentiment expressed publicly.

I

Utopian, romantic nationalism, which was the dominant kind in Italy before the failures of forty-eight attracted the provinces of the defunct Holy Roman Empire to the style of blood and iron, was usually not a xenophobic "my country, right or wrong." Rather, it was often a pantheistic religion of all humanity. Twentieth-century historians may find certain lights of the Risorgimento, like Rosmini and Gioberti, pleasantly archaic for having maintained that the "primary operation of the intellect is a direct intuition of 'being' identified with God." But such mild Platonism then seemed a Spinozan (which meant pantheistic or romantic) heresy. And so it was opposed by the rising influence of the reconstituted Jesuits, who were politically reactionary and philosophically committed to scholasticism; eventually various writings of Gioberti and Rosmini were condemned.[3]

In any case, it would be impossible to disengage the Italians from
symbols and attitudes handed down to them through the Roman
Church, no matter how much the reformers might wish to do so.
One must compare the Risorgimento not with John Stuart Mill's
On Liberty, but with Stendhal's *The Charterhouse of Parma*.[4]

Upon the two foremost prophets of the Risorgimento, Garibaldi
and Mazzini, the utopian socialists' influence was direct, strong, and
lifelong. On that voyage of Saint-Simonians to the east in 1833,
Giuseppe Garibaldi (1807–82)[5] was a mate on the *Clorinde*. His
memoirs speak of admiration for Barrault, the Saint-Simonian aes-
thetician, and the other "persecuted apostles of a new religion."

> Then, during those transparent eastern nights which, as Chateau-
> briand says, are not darkness, but only the absence of day, beneath
> that sky all spangled with stars, afloat upon that sea whose sharp
> breezes seemed full of generous aspirations, we debated, not only
> the narrow question of nationality, to which, up till then my
> patriotism had been confined—questions restricted to Italy, to
> discussions about province and province—but now we went
> further, we discussed the great question of the human race.
>   First of all, the apostle proved to me that the man who defends
> his country, or attacks the country of others, is simply a soldier;
> but he declared that a man who, by becoming cosmopolitan,
> adopts some other country as his own and makes offer of his
> sword and his blood to every people struggling against tyranny, is
> more than a soldier; he is a hero.[6]

Giuseppe Mazzini (1805–72), too, was of the generation which
matured during the thirties. Orthodox catholic and doctrinaire liberal historians alike warn us that Mazzini was a heretic because his
new religious synthesis, "God and People," sprang from the Saint-
Simonians' interpretation of New Christianity.[7] Like the Saint-Simonians, Mazzini exasperated the Catholics by not throwing down
the gauntlet to them as to a worthy adversary. He patronized the
church as an honorable ancestor whose work had been done.[8] Neither could Mazzini give the Piemontese liberals credit for the moral
integrity he possessed because he had seen them snuff out the independence of his birthplace the Republic of Genoa in order to add it
to Savoy.

In the spirit of the utopians, Mazzini, the inspirer, wrote works
on aesthetics which are a synthesis of ideas present in the post-
Napoleonic world. His *Philosophy of Music* argues for a reunifica-
tion of all arts in public performances, which are best described as

rites which will reconcile and sublimate all temperaments and ideas, the sort of festival Rousseau hoped would inspirit the general will of a post-Christian era. Mazzini acknowledged that it was Schiller who inspired a good part of the *Philosophy*. Like Schiller, Mazzini was a lover of music; in fact, he loved music best of all the arts. Unlike Schiller, he wrote no works for the stage, which might have given him a chance to demonstrate his theories. He had what Schiller lacked. He played the guitar and had a resonant speaking and singing voice. With Mazzini, more than most authors, one might be tempted to find his monumental rhetoric tedious. The *Philosophy of Music* oscillates between supplying with rhetoric what Mazzini lacked in musical knowledge[9] and the straightforward persuasion of Italians to be aware of their possibilities. In retrospect, one realizes that Mazzini was using his treatise on music as an underground political tract. Music stands for society.

Mazzini began his *Philosophy* in Hegelian fashion by asserting that art is the expression of a divine idea which is progressive.[10] Unaware that history would call him a romantic, he disliked the name. Though he thought romanticism was necessary to liberate the spirit from the tyranny of academies and from "bastard Greeks and Romans," it was "unable to produce any fruit itself." What is needed, he said, is a total art which will unite all the arts in a single idea of civilization.[11] Music should return to the public purpose it had among the ancients, when it was the heart of human civilization and progress.[12] Arts and ideas must reunite in order to leave behind the ephemeral music which has fragmented the opera, once the vehicle of one overwhelming effect, into a series of cavatinas, arias, duets, and loud endings. Similar opinions were current among non-Italians like Schiller, Berlioz, Lamennais, d'Ortigue, and many others who complained that "decadent" Italian music dominated the world.

After a snort at the French, who "have little to offer of themselves, except Berlioz, who has not yet realized his potential," Mazzini cautiously allowed that only Germany could dispute the musical crown with Italy. The Teutonic and the Mediterranean temperament, he went on, need each other. Italy's gift, said Mazzini, is melody, which is an individual art; Germany's is harmony, which is social. The problem of music is like the problem of society: how to reconcile individualism and communalism.[13] The Italian school seems always to lapse into melody for its own sake, good solo singing; the German school lapses into religiosity and the ego disappears.[14] Rossini seemed to have initiated the reintegration of a unified, "Teutonic," dramatic

affect with the "Italian" melodic method. But Rossini's integration
had not gone far enough. It will be consummated only when the
communal spirit of northern poetry is fused with Mediterranean
personal lyricism. After calling to mind the kindred spirit of Schiller
from the "Teutonic" side of the Alps and the psyche, Mazzini declared that a European style of music, like a European civilization,
drawing upon the unique characteristics of each member, will be a
cross-cultural language of the utopian Zeitgeist now printing its mark
on every thought and action.

As for the musical devices which could fuse idea and ego, Mazzini
thought that Mozart's *Don Giovanni* and Meyerbeer's *Robert the
Devil*[15] pointed the way. Exposing still more romantic themes like
those that Verdi (and Nietzsche) would develop, Mazzini asserted
that the chorus must be treated as a collective individuality as it had
in Greek tragedy, where it often personified the polis or the cosmos.
Using arguments like those then being used by admirers of organic
wholeness in medieval and Renaissance culture to favor the restoration of Gregorian chant and classic polyphony, he argued for increased use of *recitativo accompagnato*, wherein the demands of the
text, standing for reason, and the music, standing for sentiment, are
blended rather than sundered.[16] Mazzini believed that if music outgrew Germanic pedantry and Italianate venality, it would exercise
tremendous influence on society. "Genius will solve the problem of
the struggle that has gone on for thousands of years between minds
and matter, good and evil, heaven and hell, . . . martyrdom is transformed into immortal life, the tears of the beloved one into the kiss
of holy and eternal love."[17] For a society cannot attain regeneration
without regenerating musical life.

II

Mazzini's populist aesthetic was no mere theory. It described a fact,
for the musical theater was probably the most subtle and most effective propagandist for Italian unity. This is so for two reasons. First,
Italians readily forgot their political and cultural separatism when
appreciating or applauding an Italian musician. Emotion shared
through music was a short cut, as Mazzini pointed out, to consciousness of a national unity existing prior to political unity. Second, the
symbolism of so many operas about heroes languishing in foreign

Lewicki, *Harvest Festival in Poland* (1838). Cultural nationalists in places such as Italy, Germany, and Poland encouraged idealization of the arts and folklore as sources of a common strength and wisdom flourishing even in the absence of a unified political state.

oppressors' dungeons scarcely needed a leap of the imagination before application to Italy's predicament.

A score of years under French revolutionary or Napoleonic influence had temporarily erased the seemingly eternal political divisions of the Italian peninsula. In 1799 the Rome of the popes had been a republic with its pageantry supplied by civic festivals modeled on those of revolutionary Paris. When the Restoration tried to recover the status quo ante, trouble was inevitable. In the opera houses, which were as numerous as cinemas today, popular nationalistic manifestations began overtly in 1814, while Napoleon was on Elba. On 18 July at the Teatro Carlo Felice in Genoa during a performance of the melodrama *Atar* by Donizetti's teacher, Mayr, the audience, who felt betrayed by the allies, exploded into a spontaneous demonstration upon hearing the chorus

Liberty! Arise and forever
Endure in thy glory.[18]

The following year in Bologna, a chorus, *Italy, Arise* (*Sorgi Italia*), with music by Rossini, caused a demonstration in favor of Joachim Murat, whom Napoleon had appointed king of Naples. Italian patriots were eager to help Murat salvage a united Italy from the wreckage of Napoleon's system.[19] When Murat was defeated, Francis I of Austria capped his return to Italy with a visit to La Scala in Milan to witness an allegory, *The Return of Astrea*, which flattered Francis the way that Roman court poets had flattered their emperors. He was portrayed as a godlike lawgiver, from whom all of Italy's blessings flowed.

The same Teatro alla Scala remained a symbolical battleground throughout the Risorgimento.[20] During performances there, Italians often applauded patriotic allusions in the operas. The Austrians in the audience, caught up in the enthusiasm, unwittingly applauded revolutionary propaganda. On other occasions, when Italian conspirators were convicted, sentenced, and executed, the theaters were virtually deserted as a sign of mourning.

Meanwhile, Spontini—whose *The Vestal Virgin* is said to have epitomized the French Imperial style in music[21]—Rossini, Bellini, and Donizetti conquered Europe musically with operas and melodramas about heroes languishing in tyrants' prisons. How strange that the historian of liberalism, Guido de Ruggiero, says that Cavour was the "only truly European figure of the Risorgimento."[22] Strange even if one agrees with him and discards Garibaldi, Mazzini, and all artists, writers, and musicians of lesser rank than Dante or Michelangelo. One "dreamer" must stay. For he did combine "God and people" *and* died an honest man—some would say unlike Cavour.

Giuseppe Verdi's (1813–1901) credentials were good among "real" politicians, for he was among the signers of a despairing plea for help to France from the provisional government of Venice in 1848.[23] Several of Verdi's operas were allegories of Italy's agonies while she freed herself.

Since opera is not a popular mass medium in the United States, much of Verdi's daring is lost to us.[24] But many of his works which now live on account of their music were first applauded for their patriotism. Better and more often than any other artist, Verdi seems to have attained Schiller's[25] and Mazzini's romantic desiderata of fusing the arts; better and more often, he fused a mass feeling with art at once serious and popular—like the ideal romantic dramatist, Shakespeare. Verdi's beliefs were inseparable from his artistic and political actions, which in turn articulated the aspirations of his countrymen during the Risorgimento.

Verdi received his early musical education within the church. His youth was spent directing music for the week by week unfolding of the church year for his home villagers, who delighted in the *opera Dei* as interpreted by Verdi. Later he ceased to be a Catholic according to the precepts of the church, but his biographers agree that he remained "in the ideal, the moral, and the social sense, a great Christian,"[26] charitable in word and purse; a man who forgave his enemies. Though he did not call his mixture of melancholia and optimism Faustian, such was his temperament from the time he failed of admission to the Milan Conservatory, was refused a post he desired as a cathedral organist, and suffered the loss of his first wife and their children.[27]

Alessandro Manzoni, the principal spokesman of the Catholic revival in Italy and the man in whose honor Verdi composed his awesome Requiem, was the principal influence upon Verdi's mature religious beliefs.[28] These included a romantic interest in the past. Even during the thirty years when Verdi composed no formally religious music, there was scarcely an opera of his that did not contain a prayer scene, a chorus of monks or nuns, or a final ensemble expressing faith in a future life. Of course, Verdi had the showman's sense for situations which would appeal to his audiences, most of whom happened to have been trained as Catholics.

More to the point, almost every one of Verdi's operas from *Nabucco* through *Simon Boccanegra* contains thinly veiled patriotic references mixed with religious sentiments. Indeed, Verdi helped communicate to the Italian people the drive previously shared only by a small minority of liberals, Illuminati, Carbonari, and literati.[29]

Verdi's *Hernani*—based upon Victor Hugo's bombastic work— dramatized the coming history of his art and his country. It is probably the first opera in which the hero rejects society and sticks to his decision. In his third opera, *Nabucco*, premiered at La Scala in Milan in 1842, Verdi succeeded in transforming the rather static traditions of religious oratorio and secular melodrama into a new type of biblical drama with realistic conflict, action, passion, the clash of contrasts, and elaborate stage effects.[30] The heart of its plot is the yearning of the captive Jews to repossess their fatherland.

I Lombardi, Verdi's next opera, presented crusaders who had set out to recover their Holy Land from infidel invaders. It is generally reckoned an inferior work except as a foretaste of the Verdi to come, but it does show us scenes of the kind he liked—love and death against a religious background. The censors disapproved of his handling of religious ideas. But he ignored them and persevered.[31]

Verdi continued the Rossinian evolution of opera as a ritual of the community by expanding its form and content to express the ideals of the middle and lower classes. The chorus was made an integral participant in the dramatic action and pronounced judgments, not in the name of the Olympians but of the people. Frequently the people were portrayed as oppressed and struggling to claim their rightful freedom. The chorus in Italian romantic opera thus functioned more like the chorus in Greek tragedy than like the less important choruses in the aristocratic *opera seria* of the preceding period. The mood of Verdian music drama was undoubtedly more religious than the intended ritualism of earlier opera full of classical myths and heroes. Although the censors forbade literal representations of Christian rites on stage, these could be rendered unnecessary by proper musical effects. Triple invocations in rising keys captured the mood of the most solemn moments of the rituals better than a few realistic vestments. Historical plots about real people were more exciting than mythology for most people. In fact, nineteenth-century opera was like the prose novel in literature, more realistic on the surface. Just as journalistic-looking prose succeeded poetry in belles lettres, historical situations and the elimination of castrato roles became normal on the stage. In both cases, however, the increase in apparent realism was an actual increase in the repertoire of systematic illusion and allusion available to depict the supernatural, historical, or psychological forces that ordinary people believed in.[32]

On the political level, under the eyes of the censors, musical interpretation of outlawed heroes, oppressed peoples, and self-immolated
heroines was an exacting though unliteral school for revolutionary
values.

Verdi's opera was, therefore, democratic. His populist devices also
manifested the style of thought that lay behind Mazzini's philosophy
of music. These devices were consonant with the philosophy of a
writer whom Mazzini and Verdi both admired, Friedrich Schiller.
Many of Verdi's works were based upon the plots and the methods
of Schiller's plays. Dramatization of elemental themes such as fate,
love, death, jealousy, and sacrifice were intended to create an atmosphere at once religious, didactic, and subtly attuned to the yearning articulated by the classical and Judeo-Christian mythic systems.[33]

Today, a historically inclined traveler who might frequent the
streets, churches, piazzas, and few remaining opera houses of Italy
for the full circle of a year could still see why Verdi's operas were
recognized as potent celebrations of solidarity among the varied
Italian peoples. However, more than the ersatz Napoleonic pomp,
revolutionary bombast, or nouveau riche pretentiousness of some
grand opera, Verdi's work invites comparison with other rituals that
flourished before and since the age of popular opera in the nineteenth
century. Among the monuments erected before Verdi's time, the
Counterreformation splendor of the church buildings calls to mind
the fervent religious festivals which were still widespread when Verdi
was a youthful church music director. Purists have often warned that
opera, like the rites of the Roman Church, was dangerous. Indeed,
Italian opera does tremble with the pagan ferocity and arabesque
inventiveness of the Holy Week dramas of suffering and death still
played out by whole towns in the south and in Sicily. On the modern
side, one might venture to compare the earnestness of Giuseppe
Verdi, who made spectacles to appeal to the middle class rising to
take its place in history, with the moralizing earnestness evident in
the rallies whereby the communists work so diligently to produce
rituals of community.[34]

The Verdi operas of the mid 1840s contained choruses which
were encored at their premiers and became popular because they
epitomized the sorrows and aspirations of Italians during the Risorgimento. "Va, pensiero, sull' ali dorate" from *Nabucco*,[35] which became nearly a second national anthem for Italians, expresses nostalgic longing for the Chosen People's native land by paraphrasing
psalm 138. "O Signore," a chorus from *I Lombardi*,[36] is a prayer

which earned a great popularity, in part because it was a unison aria for the entire chorus—really a folk hymn. Verdi's use of the chorus in these and other instances shows the maestro as consistent in his dramaturgy as he was in his conscience. The choruses were not extraneous decoration or thumping *stretti* to invite bravos; they were integrated with the dramatic action and musical logic of Verdi's *Gesamtkunstwerk*. Even when bringing his whole cast on stage, he avoided the grand "liturgical" scenes done only for theatrical effect which were so popular in contemporary French grand operas like Meyerbeer's. Neither did Verdi strive for an archaic "ecclesiastical" style in his music for religious scenes.[37]

Other patriotic operas composed by Verdi in the forties were *Giovanna d'Arco* and *La Battaglia de Legnano*. The latter dropped the veil and, in forty-eight—the year of revolution—appealed boldly and openly to patriotic sentiment. Incidentally, Verdi's patriotism was more than musical. He helped to buy and smuggle guns for the patriots and raised money to aid the wounded and widows. These activities would have meant prison if the Austrians had returned. Verdi was called to Rome during the war of Liberation to mount *La Battaglia*; by that time *Viva V.E.R.D.I.* had been in use seven years as an anacrostic for "Viva Vittorio Emmanuele Re D'Italia."[38] When that graffito became a governmental motto, Verdi served in the Italian parliament at the invitation of Cavour, who wished him and Manzoni—respectively Italy's greatest musician and greatest writer—to grace the new regime.

Some of Verdi's greatest operas were written during the last years of the Risorgimento—the sixties—when relations between church and state were at their nadir. Though Verdi remained a Christian and used his fortune generously to aid ecclesiastical charities, he thought that, as a class, priests were dangerous, ignorant, and un-Christian. He was pleased to note something providential in the fact that the popes' intransigence produced the opposite result of that intended.[39] In two operas of that decade, *Don Carlo*, with its malevolent Grand Inquisitor, and *Aida*, with its pitiless Egyptian priests, the clergy are portrayed as inhumane representatives of an inhumane establishment. The analogies in the latter work are even more telling because the ancient Egyptian religion's ideals about the afterlife symbolize Christianity's: immortality of the soul, purgation after death, and final, complete felicity in the effulgent kingdom of light. In *Aida*, as in so many other of Verdi's works, Christian-like optimism in the face of death is taught in a romantic fashion consistent with the Catholic cult as it emerged from the Middle Ages: the eternal feminine—a prayer by the lyric soprano—teaches a belief in the redemptive value of suffering.[40]

Von Bülow and the Wagnerians said that Verdi was just an Italian show-off; the archaist Cecilians stopped just short of calling him a sinner. Regardless of those probably green-eyed critics, Verdi wished "to base his art, his music on no other proposition than truth to his feeling. And that is precisely the factor that differentiates him. . . . He distinguishes himself by his earnestness."[41] Like Palestrina and the other great Italian composers, whom Verdi admired as much as the Cecilians did, he was at his best drawing together the emotions of poetry and music. Like the classic polyphonists, an essential unity of style pervades both his sacred and secular pieces.[42]

"Verdi's greatness as a religious artist, then, consists in the fact that he made the distinction between sacred and secular styles meaningless. And in so doing he was, of course, far closer to the spirit of Palestrina—or Bach or Pergolesi—than any of those who consciously set out to imitate them."[43] He transmuted the liturgical bases of the past into modern metal.

III

Complementary to the art of the opera house, popular *inni*[44] spread the ideals of the Risorgimento on the *piazza*. These songs were mostly for group rather than solo singing. As elsewhere, amateur group singing in Italy, even when done with ephemeral texts and music, proved a potent language for blending local dialects, parties, and individuals into one mass feeling. The texts of the *inni* published between 1796 and 1848 spoke of Italy's aspiration to arise. Some writers proposed that *inni* drawn from Paisiello and Cimarosa operas would inspire the Italians as songs had "inspired the Israelites in Egypt."[45] While informal songs favored the unification of Italy and called for clever assassins to rescue brave heroes, the constitutional monarchy of Sicily adopted an *inno* which imitated *God Save the King* in both words and music.[46]

Fratelli d'Italia, which was to become united Italy's *Inno Nazionale*, was written during this time. Like the anthems of France and the United States, Italy's was composed during a time of war and revolution. All three enshrine a moment of fervent action rather than a ceremony of contemplation (as do the text and music of *God Save The King*, which was adopted in Britain and imitated, at least in music, in several other lands during calmer times).[47] The Italian, French, and American anthems strain amateur vocal resources with wide intervals and a range that runs over an octave. Most anthems outside the musical tradition of *God Save the King* have followed the revolutionary tradition of the *Marseillaise* by beginning with an up-beat and continuing with a borrowed dance meter and a topical text about a particular battle.

The texts of most songs were not folk poetry but conventional compositions produced by the educated liberals of the middle class who led the Risorgimento. For example, the text of *Fratelli d'Italia* was involved and remote from popular experience. The Italian brothers are told to don "the helmet of Scipio" and remind "Victory that she is the slave of the goddess of Rome." In the refrain all are told to join the "cohorts of Rome" (which was then ruled by the pope). Many songs addressed Mother Italy, *la Patria*, with images of censure and suffering borrowed from the literature of romantic love. Others pictured her as a weeping slave girl able to free herself only by serving other potential tyrants. Still others speak of Italy as the mother of disloyal children.[48] The texts were sometimes dryly didactic, but it was the singing of the equally unoriginal but pleasantly dancelike melodies that drew Italians together across provincial and class boundaries.

When the *Musikalische Zeitung* (the Italians called it the "Teutonic" *Gazetta Musicale*) of Berlin scoffed in 1848 that the Italians had no patriotic music, only precious barcaroles and pastorales, Ricordi's *Gazetta Musicale* of Milan retorted that when Italy does reach the moment for independence, her music and her patriotism will unite easily.[49] Droll Heinrich Heine, like Mazzini, a romantic in spite of himself, thought he noticed vitality in Italian music and believed that a people so alive in song was on the verge of a resurgence.[50] Italy had ceased to be a remnant of classical order and became the sign of a new Europe. The moment of truth soon arrived.

During the Five Days of revolution in forty-eight, the Italian rebels armed with reams of *inni* called upon the pope, Sardinia, and Naples to help them—at least they did so until the pope turned from them. Many cities where the patriots achieved power mounted festivals of liberation which were usually accompanied with balls, opera —often Rossini's *Gugliemo Tell*—and melodrama.[51]

On the walls and behind the barricades, obscenities and doggerel, such as plays on "Pollo-Pollaco" against the Austrian general Radetsky, swept aside verses by the literati.

After forty-eight, poetic images of filial devotion gave way to images of *la Patria* as the beloved woman sacrificing herself for her beloved or shut up in marriage to an undesirable husband. A happy outcome was prophesied for the unfortunate lady. There was, of course, a transfer of imagery directly from religious to patriotic songs. The last verse of the national anthem sounds almost liturgical. In less august songs pious legends began to enfold some of the more popular leaders. One Sicilian song, no doubt with the sentimental tune of an Italian religious *inno*, immortalized Garibaldi. It described how the author had been assured of Garibaldi's sainthood by a pious nun who had heard of it during a vision of the patron saint of Palermo, Santa Rosalia.[52]

As for religious rites proper, historians argue whether Mazzini endeavored to maintain the Roman ritual or to substitute something like the Saint-Simonians' New Christianity for Catholic ritual during the Roman Republic in 1849, when Pius IX had fled.[53] On one occasion, a Republican army chaplain, Father Spola, said Mass at the altar reserved for the pope in Saint Peter's and blessed the crowd from the pope's balcony; then Mazzini put in a brief appearance. A Mazzinian priest reported, "There lacked the vicar of Christ; but by no fault of ours; and though he was away, we had the people, and we had God."[54] The former Saint-Simonian, Ferdinand de Lesseps, who was then in Rome as an observer for Napoleon III, suspected "Mazzini—a remarkable and very influential man—of wishing to favor a religious schism: his writings ought to make one fear it. He has frequent conferences with English travelers; he sees Protestant missionaries of all nations."[55]

When the risings of forty-eight all had been put down, the Moderate or Liberal party replaced the *piazza*—utopian radicals like Mazzini and Garibaldi—as the leaders in the task of turning the dream of a united Italy into reality. After forty-eight, the *inni* speak not of the possibility but of the certainty of the new nation and exalt the weapons, assaults, and revolts whereby the unification will take place.[56]

In 1859 at La Scala, during the chorus "Guerra, guerra," which concludes the last act of Bellini's *Norma*, some patriots began to echo loudly "War, war." Their challenge was answered by "War,

war" from two rows of Austrian officers at the front of the theater.[57] After the Franco-Piemontese victories of that year, Victor Emmanual II and Napoleon III attended a special performance at La Scala which included pieces from *La Muette de Portici* by Auber[58] and Verdi's *I Lombardi*.

Those historians who describe the Risorgimento as primarily a literary movement seem to have a crypto-scholastic preference for verbal formulae over other kinds of experience. Such a bias ignores much of the best Italian creation of the last century. For most people, feelings remained more real than journals of opinion. By de Ruggiero's own admission, the average Italian understood Cavour's political and economic calculus even less than he understood Mazzini's idealism.[59] But Italians did understand Verdi.[60] It was precisely musical culture, not politics, wherein humanism lay preserved and united with popular culture. Hence, a more hard-headed generation should not smile at the *Gazetta Musicale*, which wrote in 1854 that music should be "thought of as an instrument of civic education."[61]

The beauty of the music of the Risorgimento is that it tried to share the best of human creation with all Italians, and with all men. The Mazzinis and the Garibaldis of history may never have succeeded without the Cavours. We shall never know. But we can know that the adroit lies of the Cavours have no justification whatsoever unless some idealists and martyrs propose a decent goal. This we know even if the devious order described in Stendhal's *Charterhouse of Parma* could be cured only homeopathically, by a "realism" more devious than itself.

FORMULAS

The Artist as Servant, Music as Insulation

3

Such poetry is not even found
among the more respectable
Greeks, but among those only who
sing songs over their wine, with
noise and revel.

John Henry Newman,
quoting Saint Athanasius on
Arius's songs

SPIRITUAL MATERIALISM

An Attempt to Legislate Aesthetic Standards

11

During the Age of Democratic Revolution, the churches, like other "legitimate" institutions, had felt their very existence threatened. Their usual response was an increasing preoccupation with unity and readiness for self-sacrifice, which they combined with a desire to flee or abolish the modern world. And so, in response to the revolutionary mass movements, the churches themselves became mass movements far more purposeful and dogmatic than they had been during the Old Regime. Hence all the talk about the need for an official, not merely an appropriate, art and music.[1]

Like the nobility, the churches became and remained exiles in their former lands. As with émigrés before and since, whether their exile had been in fact or only in the mind, adversity taught "unquestioning acceptance of loyalties which they thought were old, but which were really new and high-powered abstractions drawn from their recent experiences in the arena."[2] Their aesthetic, as well as their political and moral, ideas were more rigid, narrow, and bitter than they had been before the revolutionary era.

There is nothing to indicate that the composers from Haydn and Mozart through Beethoven and Berlioz to Bruckner were less religious than their forebears. Worthy music did not die out. It was merely ignored by the churches or driven elsewhere. Independent of institutional decrees, scholars and musicians continued to restore and create liturgical forms which they thought might be both communal and edifying.[3] Yet the Roman Church—and to a lesser degree other ecclesiastical bodies—rejected the best music of the eighteenth and nineteenth centuries for being "contrary to the fixed practice of the liturgy" and "too worldly and lacking in seriousness."[4] Since the dramatic and rhythmic attractions of modern music were links to the humanism of the new age, they were condemned.

The ecclesiastical predilection for reviving ancient styles or for art *d'intériorité* to insulate the churches from an unfriendly century may seem like a part of the nascent religion of art. Actually such epigonism was a rejection of that side of romanticism which made the artist a prophet. The churches modified the general romantic premise that art, especially music, is the highest form of social expression into the belief that only the music of a formally Christian society— such as had existed from Constantine or Charlemagne to Luther —could express the holy. This belief contradicted the romantic belief in the democracy of the artistic impulse. Although the scholars and musicians soon realized that religious music has always been a twin of secular music, the churches denied this kinship. They asserted that there was a uniquely Christian music which must be employed to the exclusion of "frivolous" music sprung from the revolutionary era.

This rigidity, which asserted that theological definitions must precede artistic creation, may have been an offspring of romantic nostalgia. But it more nearly resembled its grandparent, classicism. Though it took the arts seriously, it regarded them as the decoration rather than the expression of life. Like classicism, it believed in rules independent of time and space.[5] Rather than accept the redeeming individualism and historicism of the revolutionary and romantic eras, the churches accepted only their respective banalities and archaisms. In spite of all the condemnations of modern music, imitations of the rejected masterpieces in the guise of second-rate, formularized compositions by dilettantes from among the clergy and legitimist salons filled the churches.[6] Far from achieving a sense of community with one's fellows past and present, far from giving talent the freedom to show what it can do, ecclesiastical rites relapsed into symbols of social division.

As among the French revolutionaries, art was now to be propaganda, closely watched lest it depart from the words of whatever dogma was in control. The best musicians of the day, even when their music was too profound for the congregations, were a barrier to the psychological passivity demanded by such unthinking mass movements. For the musicians sought freedom to interpret or even transcend the text. The theologians refused to allow "emotional" interpretation or individual development any more than Guéranger would allow local Gallican rites.

The ultramontane theologians of music were spiritual materialists because they taught that grace, the spark of the divine, comes mechanically *ex opere operato*, "whenever the action is performed." They taught that the spiritual effect of a human action does not depend upon how artfully—how well—the human action is performed. Thus they taught that the universe is a mechanism. In contrast, for the despised, "pantheistic" romanticists, whether they believed in organized religion or not, "supernatural" results also include an element *ex opere operantis*: Mephistopheles' preternatural tricks could not save Faust without Faust's own human effort.

From the single-minded émigré mentality, it was only a step to the argument that Gregorian chant or Counterreformation polyphony was automatic grace. Other music was of uncertain worth. D'Ortigue's generation of liturgical theorists had still tried to balance the two arguments. Now the liturgists were busy excluding not only the toleration born of the Enlightenment, but also romantic evolutionism and individualism from the music and rites of the Catholic Church. Hector Berlioz had observed the trend and reduced its arguments to absurdity:[7]

> The *O Salutaris* is a prayer, isn't it? In it the Christian prays to God for *Strength*, he implores His help; but if he begs for them he obviously does not possess them; he feels the lack of them. Hence he who prays is a weak creature, whose voice, when pronouncing the *Da Robur*, should be as humble as possible. . . .
>
> Compositions in which sacred texts are treated in this would-be expressive style are overrun with similar nonsense. It is this nonsense, undoubtedly, that has given pretext for the founding of a new sect of the strangest kind, which keeps alive in its conventicle a delightful proposition on the agenda. According to this innocent heresy, the object is to preserve a truly Catholic music; actually, it tends to the total suppression of music in the divine service. These Anabaptists of art would not tolerate violins in their churches, because violins suggest the music of the theater—as if the double basses, the violas, and the other instruments, together with the voices were not in exactly the same position. Still according to this doctrine, the new organs have been provided with too many stops and are too expressive. They conclude next that

melody, rhythm, and modern tonality are damnable. The moderates will still accept Palestrina; but the perfervid ones, the Balfours of Burleigh of the new Puritanism, will have nothing but plainsong, raw. . . .

One of these puritans of church music attended a funeral.

While abominating modern music "which excites the passions," he was comically passionate about plainsong, which I must admit is far from possessing that grave defect. He managed to control his feelings fairly well until the middle of the ceremony. A rather long pause having occurred and the congregation being sunk in deep and solemn meditation, the organist inadvertently let a key [sound]. . . .

The puritan went into ecstasy over such mono-tone-ous music.[8]

He was at any rate a good logician, since according to him sacred music must contain neither melody, nor harmony, nor rhythm, nor instrumentation, nor expression, nor modern tonality, nor ancient modes (for these recall the music of the Greeks, who were pagans).

Much as the ultramontane Catholics longed for a return to that imagined golden age when all had been as orderly as a Thomistic proof for the existence of God; much as they might try to resurrect that Golden Age by reviving the music of "the thirteenth, the greatest of centuries," during the nineteenth century independent historical scholarship moved toward the conclusion that medieval life was a "constant interchange of sacred and profane terms. . . . Nothing is more characteristic in this respect than the fact of there being hardly any difference between the musical character of profane and sacred melodies. Till late in the sixteenth century profane melodies might be used indiscriminately for sacred use, and sacred for profane."[9] But nineteenth-century theologians moved in the opposite direction. They deemphasized the romantic belief that medieval art had depended on talent and taste. When speaking of music, the ecclesiastical "generation of materialism" continued to accept the argument that "We have preserved the architecture of the Ages of Faith and recognized that these buildings are eminently suited to religion, and to religion alone. Religious music also has its rules. These rules produced the Gregorian chant."[10] Despite the fact that such an aesthetic is quite mechanical, Felix Clément wrote a book arguing that "modern music has plunged the art of the church into the abyss of mate-

A nineteenth-century engraving of Rafael's *Saint Cecilia*. Interpretations of
this picture corresponded to varying interpretations of the role and worth of
music (see page 74).

rialism."[11] He labeled all postmedieval music "theatrical" and lauded
the medieval liturgical dramas, where the faithful had joined in the
singing or were represented by actors, over the "silly cavortings of
modern opera,"[12] which, since the Renaissance, is "full of passions."
Clément admitted that Bach was an outstanding religious composer
but "complimented" the composer of the *Saint Matthew Passion* for
being "insensitive to the effects of dramatic music"![13] He ignored
modern composers, like Berlioz, who were as put off by theatricality
as he was.

Strangely, after arguing that religious music is a special genre
unrelated to its environment—an escape rather than an involvement
—Clément pronounced the version of Gregorian chant by Father
Louis Lambillotte, S.J., the best. Lambillotte's version, he said, was
better than Solesmes's, "whose work does not suit modern taste."[14]
Clément then spent several chapters arguing that Lambillotte's work
would suit the taste of modern congregations, that they would like
to sing it, and that they would enjoy learning good music through
it. Clément did not see that Lambillotte's versions of chant "achieved
a modern rhythmical structure" by eliminating melismas more ruth-
lessly than had the discredited Medicean version of Palestrina's
time.[15] Lambillotte's results were therefore closer to Victorian hymn
tunes than to the Gothic *Gesamtkunstwerk*.

Clément asserted that Father Lambillotte's original compositions
for the church were healthy antidotes to the transplanted operatic
arias from Adolphe Adam that were so often heard in churches.
Other admirers of medieval musical tradition disagreed and called
Lambillotte an example of the "false, evil, pagan, and worldly tendency in art."[16] The ultramontane but musical d'Ortigue said "his
works would not rank him above a tenth-rate dance hall composer,"
and "priest-composers often go astray."[17]

According to Jules Combarieu, the subsequent history of musical
paleography in the nineteenth century resembled any other human
quarrel. The commentators around Saint Gregory acted "like so
many crows around a wounded eagle."[18] Every editor of the several
versions of the chant[19] wanted the church to make an infallible musical judgment—accompanied by the lucrative privilege of publishing an official edition—by declaring his version to be the Catholic
Church's universal music.

Both Solesmes and its competitors came to rely upon extramusical
arguments. Solesmes eventually began to consider the chant a fixed,
unchanging thing. Their paleographic method was to consider the

oldest manuscript the most valid one.[20] "Yet," one of Solesmes's critics pointed out, "these sticklers for antiquity did not hesitate to introduce into their notation all sorts of modern and hybrid signs in order to make the chant easier to sing."[21] The critic asserted that the later developments of the Solesmes theories actually made the chant *harder* to sing. Hence it became more esoteric rather than more popular.

On the other side, the critics of Solesmes proved themselves anti-romantic in their preference for authority over musicality. The same critic asserted that "it is surely a startling proposition to put before the faithful that the settlement of the Plain Chant must be dependent upon the studies and decisions of a school of archaeologists and not upon Rome."[22] A German rival of Solesmes, F. X. Haberl, and his publisher, Pustet of Regensberg, also used the argument from authority when they attempted to maintain the privileged and lucrative position of their Ratisbon Edition of the chant.[23] This edition was based upon the *Mechlin Graduale*, which had appeared in 1848. In turn, the *Graduale* rested upon the seventeenth-century *Medicean Graduale*, which, among other things, had made the musical solfege conform to the syllables of the Latin text wherever possible. For example, if the word "sola" occurred, then *sol-la* was given as the melody, the ultimate in mechanical music-must-follow-the-text rules. The Mechlin editors also used another peculiar device of musical paleography. After comparing several antiphons having similar modal and melodic characteristics, the "corrector" would retain only those notes common to all versions. The others were rejected as false additions.[24]

In 1878, over the scholarly and nationalistic objections of Solesmes, Pope Leo XIII maintained the privilege of Pustet to publish the Roman Church's official music. This privilege was eroded until 1905, when the Solesmes *Vatican Edition* was made official. Pustet had already ceased claiming his privilege in France, and the Vatican had ceased trying to enforce it.[25]

In 1903, Pius X, the first pope of the twentieth century, did for Catholic music what Leo XIII, the last pope of the nineteenth, had done for Catholic philosophy. Pius' *Motu proprio tra le sollecitu-dini*[26] affirmed the belief that the style of music dying when Aquinas was born should be the model for all music. Yet in the same document, which called for the people to sing the chant, Pius X began the twentieth-century liturgical movement with its bias toward direct popular participation. This movement has eliminated Gregorian chant

from most Roman services for the very reason which first inspired
its restoration in the nineteenth century. By desiring popular participation, Pius X reopened the door to an aesthetic which values musical efficacy more than supposedly canonical "correctness."

Pius X was completing the work encouraged by various "Societies
of Saint Cecilia." Pope Pius VIII had founded a Saint Cecilia Society in 1828 at Rome "to practice the ideals of the Council of
Trent."[27] The next pope, Lamennais's nemesis Gregory XVI, urged
the society to "correct abuses in church music."[28] The society dispensed with the romantic primacy of aesthetic values, for reform
was to be done first on the authority of the church, "which is infallible in faith and morals and therefore knows what kind of music
she needs"; second, on the authority of scholars whose opinions the
church might consult; third, on the authority of the centuries, for
the liturgical chant is born of the church.

In the Germanies, dozens of diocesan synods were promulgating
legalistic versions of romantic ideas about the revitalization of church
music. Their decrees followed a pattern: after praising the chant and
the Palestrina style as models for church music, the hierarchy reiterated that "all theatrical and profane influences were to be excluded
from the churches," the organ must only support the singing; all the
rubrics about sung services were to be observed. Instruments other
than the organ were to be tolerated only with the approval of the
bishop of the place, and then only to support the voices. Among
the "theatrical" instruments usually forbidden are flutes, oboes,
brasses, and all percussion instruments.[29]

Throughout central Europe there had been a curious liturgical
alliance. The Jesuits had begun and the Enlightenment fostered—
sometimes required[30]—a High Mass with the choral parts of the
Ordinary, hymns, responses, and prayers in the vernacular. By about
1860, in the face of rising nationalism, such local customs were being
expunged in favor of at least outward conformity to the Latin Roman
rite.[31] The High Mass in German and modern music were alike
deemed "tampering with the textual order," which was declared fixed
for all time. The community was to watch the rites, not make them.
Although these decrees called for many of the same things that the
romantics had desired, their thrust was not to respect and hence
liberate the musical element in religion. Rather, as in the dogmatism
of the *Aufklärung*, music became something to be legislated against
and contained, lest it prove the opening wedge of further freedom.

In Regensburg, Bavaria, the tolerant and populistic spirit of Bishop Sailer[32] was exorcised by 1858, when Bishop von Senestrey, his successor, decreed that church music was to be limited by what he believed was done during the "Ages of Faith." Church music is a liturgical art, said the bishop, not a form of individual expression. He was sure that Gregorian chant "awakened piety better than other more worldly music," and he wished *no* vernacular used in his diocese at liturgical functions.[33]

One of Bishop von Senestrey's diocesan priests was Francis Xavier Witt, who believed that his vocation was to assure the triumph of the cleric over the Reformation in church music. Father Witt, who had studied under Sailer's protégé, Father Proske, thought that priests made the best choir directors because they understood the Breviary better than laymen.[34] Witt might remind one of the morbid side of romanticism. He "loved nature," but rain on the windows made him nervous; thunder drove him to the cellar. In 1859 he began his writings on church music by stating his desire to reintroduce the mystical element and popularize serious music in the church. These plans were inspired by the example of Johann Michael Sailer's circle in Regensburg a generation earlier. Witt's journal *Church Music Circular (Fliegende Blätter für Kirchenmusik)* was complemented by his campaign to assure that music became part of the curriculum in Catholic gymnasiums and seminaries. He also urged the founding of church music commissions in every diocese and a school for musicians, who were to receive a general as well as musical education. In 1867 he added to the worldwide growth of musical societies and adult education by founding a society for improving church music, the influential Cecilian Society.[35]

Its leaders included Franz-Xaver Haberl, then choirmaster of Regensburg Cathedral, and the publisher, Pustet. The society's musical activities included issuing editions of Gregorian chant and classical polyphony. Because Witt and his friends were skeptical of any immediate possibility of improving congregational singing or popular music, they concentrated on educating choir directors to Cecilian standards. Paradoxically, these standards were based upon the Platonic and patristic tradition used to justify the earlier insistence of the apostles of enlightenment upon congregational singing in preference to professionally directed music. The hymn tune High Mass in the vernacular inherited from the Enlightenment was now attacked in favor of plain chant. Since classic polyphony was also thought to clothe the Latin text, it was granted a place second to that of the chant. "Figured music" might be tolerated, as long as it imitated the chant and polyphony. The classical and operatic style of Catholic Europe in the eighteenth and nineteenth centuries were condemned.

The Cecilian argument that specific musical standards could be legislated proved to be congenial to the Roman Church following the First Vatican Council. This rationale found its way into the writings on music of subsequent popes, especially Pius X.[36]

"Down with the instrumental mass of the Viennese school" was the motto of Witt's followers. They insisted that music be drawn only from those works previously approved on liturgical grounds, rather than the other way around. In the long run, this amounted to "down with music" and contributed to the legalistic, rationalistic resurgence in the church which has helped it to jettison its artistic and symbolical tradition. Ironically, those who believed that they were combating a Josephin lack of fervor returned to Joseph II's philosophy of music. The Cecilians believed that they could design and legislate music that would be holy and universal. Rather than echoing Herder's century-old call for a return to the spirit of music in religion, the Cecilians helped to stifle it.[37]

Although the Cecilians and Solesmes were competing publishers, they were at one in trying to contain the lyrical excrescences of romanticism within the limits of theological propositions. The first volume of the *Cecilian Almanac*, published in 1876, had as its frontespiece a portrait of Dom Prosper Guéranger. The first full-length article in the *Almanac* was a translation from Guéranger, "The Life, Works, and Sufferings of Saint Cecilia."[38]

Like Solesmes's ally, Joseph d'Ortigue, the Cecilians were musically broad-minded outside the church. Most issues of the *Cecilian Almanac* tried to mix high art with popular perception. There were cartoons showing viola players eating sausages during rests and half-scholarly, half-fanciful articles about the Masters. One of these articles, "Chopin und Berlioz in Paris,"[39] included portraits of Berlioz, Meyerbeer, and Liszt. It told how Chopin was bewildered by the City of Light until Berlioz showed him how to find good music there. The Cecilian family tree included musicians and scholars who might have been expected to apply musical standards inside as well as outside the church.[40] Indeed the Cecilians' purely musical work was often eminently successful at achieving the romantic desideratum— a junction of the artful and the popular. Music historians from outside Germany have to admire both the wide repertoire which the restorers made available and the workmanlike service music "for country choirs" which the Cecilians published.[41] Gebrauchsmusik it was, but well-made and *simplex munditiis*. Their theories, however, were dourly devoid of any musicianly pragmatism.

When it came to church music, no quarter was asked or given in reviews of religious works by non-Cecilian authors and composers. Only the sacrifice of aesthetic values for the unity of the church mattered. There was but one eternally correct way, the way of canon law. Latin only; no non-Catholic tunes or texts; no harmonic progression Palestrina hadn't used; nothing faster than a quarter note.

Some of this narrowness was due to political conditions. Fear of Bismarck's Kulturkampf led Catholics to emphasize ultramontanism, for, they said, a higher principle than the state was needed.[42] Somewhat like the Irish in the British Empire or the Poles in the Russian, Catholics in the Prussian Empire tended to see everything from a Roman viewpoint. Vernacular singing was deemed too Protestant for use except in paraliturgical services. When a Jesuit priest, Guido M. Dreves, reasserted a romantic schema, "A song should first be a song, then a folksong, and lastly church music,"[43] the Cecilian periodical called Dreves's hymnal "heretical-Protestant; secular-Josephin; vernacular, not liturgical."[44] For their part, the Cecilians were sure that "episcopal scrutiny would improve both the poetry and the music used in the churches."[45]

Under these circumstances, lyricism was divorced from the Catholic liturgy. Within it, music was supposed to conform to the letter of antimusical laws. Outside the liturgy, in the "missions" and popularized services, unbridled sentimentalism imitated the most accessible musical fads of the day. Prelates and people affected sentimental devotions to the Sacred Heart and the Blessed Virgin accompanied by hymns composed in 6/8 time but sung in 3/4, which made them conformable to the musical tastes acquired in music and dance halls. The Cecilians take much of the credit—or blame—for driving the vernacular out of the formal rites of the Catholic Church until 1964. Bäumker credited the Cecilians with improving the hymnals in music as well as text.[46] The credit or blame that they should take is for establishing the aesthetic categories which Roman Catholic theorists still take for granted: in matters musical, one consults clerical theologians prior to performing musicians. Because of this antiromantic premise, when the liturgical theorists look back at the nineteenth century, they see it filtered through the *Motu proprio* of Pius X,

which is still said "to reflect the general thinking of the most enlightened musicians of the time"![47]

Among the late nineteenth-century writers of, and commentators
on, vernacular religious songs, one misses the romantic admiration
for heaven-storming achievement no matter what its origin, an admiration that had served to moderate even the most dogmatic statements of d'Ortigue, Sailer, and Schleiermacher. Instead, one finds a
longing to be cut off from a hateful and unfriendly century.

In the seventies the Protestant hymnologist, Knipfer, employed
the romantic jargon about how the heart is just as or more important than the head; how feeling for the whole is more important than
individual virtuosity. But he hated Klopstock, who he said wrote
"the art songs of rationalistic Christianity. For rationalism is nothing
other than pietism, an error, moved from the heart to the head."[48]
Knipfer's favorite hymns exude a Bismarckian confidence in the
power of Germany to overcome her troubles by force.[49]

Catholic hymnologists were so eager to exclude influences from
outside the church that they ignored all previous efforts and dated
the beginning of musicological restoration from the beginning of their
own generation.[50] Their ignorance amounted to a determination to
have the worst of both the baroque-romantic and the classical-En-
lightenment world views. Moralism like that of the Enlightenment
appeared in admonitions meant to scold musicians into obeying antimusical rules. The romantic dissatisfaction with the limitations of
moralism yielded to a fatalism which said that since the world is evil,
there is nothing one can do but complain about a lost golden age.[51]
Caught between this neoclassic Scylla and postromantic Charybdis,
artists seldom try any longer to create for organized religion.

It would of course have been a prodigy to combine any set of
theological propositions with creative music. But Berlioz, Franck,
Liszt, and Bruckner—to name only a few—did try.[52] Their music
is undoubtedly more "religious"—if there be such a category—than
the epigonous brand fostered to guard against romantic ecstasies.

Like the "scandalous" Berlioz, the "devout" Anton Bruckner
(1824–96) was formed by the folk and liturgical music which he
heard in his home village, Ansfelden, near Linz in upper Austria.
On festival Sundays, trumpets, horns, and trombones joined the regular Sunday ensemble of soli, chorus, strings, and organ which performed Mozart's and Michael Haydn's settings of the annual liturgical cycle.[53] Little wonder that Bruckner, pious though he was, never

forced his muse into the Cecilian straitjacket. The same is true of César Franck.[54]

While Bruckner and Franck were maturing, Franz Liszt, a revolutionary of music, was growing old. Perhaps influenced by the religious zeal of the women who were his friends in later life, the prodigy who had insulted Louis Philippe, hushed the Emperor of All the Russias, and issued a manifesto calling for a blend of the *Marseillaise* with the *Kyriale*[55] was retreating into orthodoxy. Liszt was becoming an ultramontane; he had already become a Wagnerite. There is a similarity between his theological and his musical development.

Liszt's friend Richard Wagner, when a young man, had been ducal Kapellmeister in Dresden. While thus employed technically as a church musician, Wagner wrote—as did so many romantics—that classic polyphony is the ideal church music. He who was later to speak of the poet's primacy in *The Artwork of the Future* was then speaking of the musician's primacy in the extant ecclesiastical liturgy. Although Wagner, a musician, was not allowed to write the text for the church, he wished, nevertheless, to master the church. For "all the other arts bring their own images and 'allegories': to be true art they must be heterodox. But music speaks emotion without images such as a painter or poet might need, therefore it can live by communicating its emotion through the setting of a prescribed text. But it is no longer the prescribed text which is living, but the music."[56]

Theologians, who have been verbalists ever since Plato anathematized singers, will insist that such an Orphic cult should yield to verbal allegories. If Wagner is correct, the theologians must crush music in order to assure that the priest's allegory be the only one conveyed through the liturgy. Wagner believed this and continued his remarks on music by saying that music itself is an allegory which, in connection with drama, can represent moral laws and the ideal. Therefore music is a subtle way of dissolving worn out allegories, such as those of the old Jewish and Christian priests, and the new pretenders, the physical scientists.[57]

According to Wagner, Judaism and its offspring, Christianity, had had a reprehensible influence because they had made God extra-human. Since Christians had to please a supernatural, nonanthropomorphic Jehovah, who did not really "enjoy" music, art fell from its high mission and became a means instead of an end.[58] So Wagner hoped to emulate the classical Greek liturgies where music had been no mere distraction to kill time but "the expression of the deepest and most profound group consciousness." At these festivals of public art, the gods themselves had moved on the stage and to be a musician was to share in divine life.

Wagner presented his ideas of a synthesis of art, philosophy, and religion as something brand new, despite the writings of Gluck, Grétry, Lesueur, Schiller, and the preceding century.[59] For both Wagnerites and Cecilians "artistic faith became dogmatic and authoritarian; it hurled anathemas, condemned former beliefs as erroneous or allowed them as a preparation for the reign of the new law."[60]

"In opera," the mature Wagner said, "the musician must surrender unconditionally to the poet."[61] Contemporaneously, in church music, as in Wagnerian opera, the "literarization" which had threatened since the end of the baroque era now triumphed over the temporary ascendancy of the spirit of music during romanticism (which began with Haydn and Mozart, according to some important critics such as E. T. A. Hoffmann). Musical church music was roundly denounced because it was not the "humble handmaiden" of the text.[62]

Liszt's Mass for the Dedication of the Cathedral of Estergom (the Gran Mass), began the "Gregorian Wagnerism" which in 1855 began the close of his romantic, revolutionary phase. Liszt announced his satisfaction. "It is," he asserted, "of pure *musical water* (not in the sense of ordinary *diluted* church style, but like diamond water) and living Catholic wine."[63] When the Mass was revived in Paris ten years later, two divergent but still romantic critics, d'Ortigue and Berlioz, disagreed with the composer. The ultramontane wrote "Transeat a me calix iste" ("Let this cup pass," from Jesus' agony in the garden); the Gallican, "What a negation of art!"[64] Most critics have agreed with d'Ortigue and Berlioz and say either, "The poignant melody line is barely able to sustain itself . . . ; even Parsifal seems better structured alongside,"[65] or, "too eclectic: more a summary than an essay on a theme."[66] However, one critic has admired Liszt's casting off romantic organicism in favor of the Wagnerian system and praised the Mass's Wagnerism for "attempting to give a musical exigesis of the text. . . . For Liszt characterizes God the Father by triads, God the Son by melody, and God the Holy Spirit by a fusion of the two."[67] Thus passed Gluck's, Rousseau's and the romantics' theories that music portrays one's perception of an event rather than the event itself. Liszt was now trying to give us not an interpretation of reality, but a surrogate for it. We seem in retreat to the pre-

Kantian naiveté that wishes music might someday approach the condition of painting or geometry.

The Gran Mass was supposed to offer a way out of Cecilian epigonism by applying Wagner's theories of a new *Gesamtkunstwerk*.[68] Yet Liszt soon was sanctioning Cecilianism and its ideal of a static music. He had always been a political conservative and he now took from the Princess Carolyne of Sayn-Wittgenstein the "conviction of the futility of so much effort" and lost faith in everything but the consolations of religion.[69]

Liszt spent much of his last three decades in Rome contemplating projects to rival the musical monuments of the sixteenth and seventeenth centuries. One of his idiosyncrasies after middle age was to praise virtually all music submitted to him for a judgment. He praised F. X. Witt, founder of the Cecilian Society, for "acting as admirably in practice as in precept, as is evident in your own compositions."[70] Witt's pieces were imitations of Palestrina's.

Edified by the zeal of the Cecilians, Liszt missed the point of their music-by-legislation:

> It seems singular that they should stumble on obstacles. What is in question? Innovations . . . ? By no means. The noblest conservatism remains the essence and aim of the Cecilian Society; it merely demands a serious study and proper performances of the most dignified classical authors in church music, Palestrina and Lassus at their head. Nothing can reasonably be objected to this, and you may confidently maintain, dear sir, that "recognition must take place and the good cause prove victorious."[71]

Still, Liszt was not quite a religious recluse. Borodin described a concert by Liszt at a church in Jena in 1877 thus: he entered with a handsome woman on each arm; when his turn to play came, he strode to dazzle everyone and spent the moments between numbers conversing in four languages.[72]

Rome could not take such a man seriously, although he did take Minor Orders in the mid-sixties, perhaps to remove the temptation to marry Princess Carolyne. Rome bracketed him with his contrary, Verdi: a theatrical and oratorical, Mennaisian and Saint-Simonian wolf in a shepherd's cassock. Meanwhile, Liszt's power of composition had begun to fade. The values which he had once relied upon failed.[73]

Despite his disappointments, Liszt somehow remained true to his romantic youth. When he moved to Rome from Weimar in 1861, he announced that he "would not praise the so-called classics from Palestrina down to Mendelssohn" in order that some would pardon the pecadilloes of his youth. He would not accommodate himself to formulas "which praised the pseudoclassics" and cried out that art is losing itself and that all art is lost."[74] When his patron, Frigyes Podmianszcky, banned Liszt's *King Song* from the inaugural performance of the Royal Hungarian Opera at Budapest "because its motifs are borrowed from the well-known Rákóczi song directed against the sovereign dynasty,"[75] Liszt lectured the director with a succinct explanation of how sacred art had always absorbed its seeming opposite, secular art, and vice versa.[76]

While the Roman Church's liturgiologists were insisting that the church possessed all the music it would ever need, its theologians and philosophers were insisting that it possessed all truth and could learn nothing from perceptions outside those listed in canon law. The supposed distinction between two musics, the one moral and the other evil, is the aesthetic analogue of the theology in the *Syllabus of Errors*, issued by Pio Nono in 1864, which asserted that there are two civilizations in the nineteenth century which must destroy each other.

Perhaps one might apply the words of Sir Kenneth Clark on the Gothic revival in England to the musical restorers. Their great mistake was that, over the long run,

> they tried to revive a style which depended on sentiment as if it depended on rules. . . .
> Indeed as long as they based their argument on subject matter they were bound to be in trouble, for though the Saints in a modern Catholic image shop are extremely virtuous, they are obviously the products of an utterly worldly civilization, whereas the gargoyles of a medieval cathedral, though monsters of vice, are alive with the spirit of a truly religious age.[77]

The liturgiologists trapped themselves into a supposed distinction between musical effort undertaken within and that undertaken without a predominant religious spirit. By denying the connection between religion and lyricism they denied romanticism. By denying romanticism they denied that at the bottom of every theology is poetry.[78]

The mistaken prejudice of the Cecilians was similar to the rationalistic strain in the Enlightenment; both believed that one could legislate aesthetic standards. We have thus come full circle, so that a new romantic rebellion will be required to assert and continue the impulse to freedom once symbolized by the musical impulse. And so a discursive, reflective summary is appropriate now to balance this essay. Finally, a short conclusion will point the way to the twentieth century, whose antirationalistic, seemingly anticultural trends are a renaissance of romanticism.

COR AD COR LOQUITUR

John Henry Newman's Nostalgia for an Absolute

12

There were two criticisms which John Henry Cardinal Newman took as compliments: "That Methodist!" and "He mixes and confuses everything." These jibes he regarded as apt characterizations of the vitalizing effect of genius on the tidy and uninspired. Such characterizations are also apt summaries of tidy and uninspired opinions about romantic religion and psychology. Newman's own opinions are summed up in the motto he chose for his arms as a cardinal, *cor ad cor loquitur*, "heart speaks to heart." These words could well have been a motto for romanticism. Newman's intellectual development articulated problems like those faced by Johann Michael Sailer who also tried to combine tradition and modernity. Both perceived religion as a total psychological and cultural system in constant evolution.

Newman's long life (1801–90) charts the rise and fall of the romantic rebellion, dream, and failure. Born of the Age of Reason's doppelgänger and dying in an attempt to transcend the Age of Materialism, his life is a mirror of the nineteenth-century romantic cycle and foreshadowed the postromantic style which still informs our culture. Like Diderot's philosopher he—and we—still seek to combine intellectual precision with a free heart.[1]

Like most of us, Newman found the romantic absorption in continual struggle too demanding. At length, he took his craving for a secure mythopoetic system literally and joined the religion which seemed most clearly continuous with its progenitors. He assented to the Christianized Platonism which avowed life is a once- and art a twice-removed mirror of another world. Religion was an explanation and exploration of a revelation embedded in the world from its creation. Religion was not, he said, a human arrangement, an art. It was an absolute.

Yet he never assented to the corollaries of the rationalistic tradition. Rather than the primarily static and visual metaphors preferred by rationalists from Pythagoras to Pufendorf, he preferred to think in terms of a process or movement, not a static diagram. He took analogies for explaining himself and models for structuring his thoughts from his favorite recreation, music.

I

In Newman's childhood there were two preferred modes of expression, pietistic religion and music. Both should be thought of romantically as the spontaneous overflow of the inmost desires. Both manifested a mystical feeling, a hint of something transcendent. Throughout his life, they were sometimes separate, sometimes in conflict, and often "mixed and confused." Ultimately, his craving for interior justification and his aesthetic sophistication were reconciled. In the Roman Church he found infinite possibilities for expressing every human faculty and situation. For him the church provided a total environment wherein the cult of self-expression and the knowledge born of historical experience could be united.

Some say this fascination with the splendors of religion was Protestant bibliolatry converted to Roman idolatry. A more generous critic must allow to Newman's theology and the prose that expressed it what is denied to his poetry. It is the work of a consummate artist, of a violinist who might have wanted to rival Paganini.[2] Biographers pro and con may call Newman what he said he was, the apostle of dogma. He was at heart the apostle of lyricism, muse-ic. Throughout John Henry's life, whenever he communicated with others, he did so in the lyrical spirit of "Heart speaks to heart."

His interest in music in the strict sense was inspired by his father. His brother Frank remarked that there was "nothing beyond natural pride and affection in common between father and son except their love of and skill in music." In finance, politics, and religion, father and son quarreled. The failure of Mr. Newman's bank during the crucial years of John Henry's teenage seems to have diminished the respect which the son might have had for his father. The boy presumed to offer some arch advice and to console his mother that, had he been there, all would have run smoothly and solvently. On another occasion, John Henry's will to have reliable assurances led him to take the part of the ministry in Queen Caroline's trial for adultery. Mr. Newman chided, "Well John! I suppose I ought to praise you for knowing how to rise in the world. Go on! Persevere! Always stand up for men in power and in time you will get promotion."[3] The father was a little put off, lost even, in the atmosphere of religiosity which Mrs. Newman fostered. He preferred Shakespeare to the Bible, whose psalms and epistles he thought disfigured by uncharitable language.[4]

In matters musical, father and son did not quarrel. The boy took up the violin at ten; the next year he was good at it. At fourteen, he composed words and music for a comic opera. The rest of the family were musical too and participated in the mounting of this sophisticated exercise of the imagination.[5] Father was immensely amused by his son's ability to express himself through music.

When the lad went to school, the students who came to meet and haze him were introduced to "Mr. Newman and his fiddle."[6] Bending his peculiar talents to the curriculum of a proper young scholar, he set some Greek choruses to music. He preferred Aeshylus's lyrical strophes to the "dry, stiff, formal, affected, cold, prolix, dignified Sophocles," whose tightly plotted plays were favored by the schoolmasters. Did young John Henry know he was choosing sides in the ancient battle between the rationalists, who usually prefer Sophocles, and the lyricists, who usually prefer Aeschylus, whose plays are closer to the origins of tragedy in music and religion?

Religion in the Newman household came formally from his mother, a thoroughgoing Evangelical. Christianity was enthusiasm, a mystical communion with God. The converted sinner was to be filled with the presence of the Ineffable and let his convictions of God's presence flow into every moment of his daily life.[7] For John Henry, the spiritual world was more real—including the serried ranks of angels milling about him—than the rough-and-tumble world of most boys his age.[8] "Life," he thought, "might be a dream." For Mrs. Newman and her son, the dream of God's immediate presence was made explicit in the King James Bible, whose poetical language he reveled in. He read it at home and heard it rolled out through the year according to the lectionary in the *Book of Common Prayer*.[9] Evangelical rites employed little professional music, but the Bible was a pageant to challenge popish liturgies and match any grand opera. John Henry wanted the pageant to continue.[10]

Many of his later sermons were autobiographical; we hear the child speak through the man—as Wordsworth and Proust as well as Freud and Erikson have reminded us he does—of the cosmic drama in the Bible. Indeed, Newman's sentiments in his sermons are often like Wordsworth's on the passage from childhood to adolescence in his "Ode on Intimations of Immortality from Recollections of Early Childhood."

Heaven lies about us in our infancy,
Shades of the prison-house begin to close about the growing boy.

Newman continued to adhere to such a romantic belief in the primacy of the intimations of childhood and childlike impulses.

While John Henry was still a schoolboy, he and a few other boys formed a secret brotherhood with its own newspapers, *The Spy* and *The Anti-Spy*, to authenticate their game.[11] Newman was Grand Master, of course. The charade was at length broken up by a *profanum vulgus* of uninitiated boys. Before he passed from school to the university, and thus—in those days—nearly out of the reach of that "common herd," he capped the religion of his youth with a proper Evangelical conversion. This event of his fifteenth year occurred during a summer when he remained virtually alone at boarding school because the family was in turmoil after his father's bank had failed. Perhaps these coincidences were a rite of passage, a defeat of the father accompanied by the claiming of spiritual maturity by the son. The clergyman who facilitated the conversion, through which John Henry felt assurance of his salvation until he was twenty-one, offered many arguments.[12] Yet it was not the arguments which won the lad so much as the fervor with which they were advanced. Newman again proved himself aesthetic in the literal sense of the term. A feeling led to a belief to an action in religion as in music.

Newman seems never to have learned the tough, emotionless exterior which northwestern European civilization demands of its men. The slow maturation of this boy adept in the arts and imagination was not rudely fractured.[13] His childhood world of the imagination —music and pietism—was continuous with his youthful world of the intellect—a university education in classics and mathematics.

At Oxford, John Henry Newman was able to sublimate the masculine instincts which his mother had cauterized and somehow reassemble his intellect and emotions to the body from which they had been divorced. Perhaps his yearning to be a poet and his continuing love of music were sublimations of his yearning to be a part of the wider masculine world of contest and conquest. Women usually are encouraged to spend their emotional capital in familial or other intimate relationships. Public spear-wielding or the equivalent is usually expected of men. The satisfaction which Achilles achieved from deeds of glory persists in sports, invention, economic competition, and the performing arts. Newman's satisfaction came privately through music and publicly through religion, as we shall see. A psychologist might see in Newman a sublimation of his sense of frustration and isolation expressed in a grand mythopoetic design.[14] Similarly, a historian or cultural anthropologist might see in the modern humanities' clinging to romanticism a continuing reaction to a world perceived as coldly mechanistic.

II

When Newman went to Oxford at seventeen, he was a bit of a liberal for those days. More than a bit of musicianly pragmatism lingered in his "Everything must be believed in its own way": science and theology would get along. A seeming collision between them was merely discord between two different temperaments. "Doubt," he said, "was like the discrepancy between a tuned piano and the ideal scale; you cannot exclude it, but you must, nevertheless, tune the piano." There was, however, never any question for him but that the revealed scale put doubt in its proper place.[15]

Newman also did plenty of musical tuning, for he was in demand to play first violin in quartets with the dons and students.[16] A musical club gave him recreation throughout his Oxford career,[17] and it was to music that Newman retreated while waiting word of the results of his examination for a fellowship in Oriel College. When the butler came to announce Newman's success, he scarcely looked up from his fiddling. For he was in despair and afraid of repeating the poor performance he had given a year before in Trinity College after too much cramming.[18]

Newman's biographers sometimes point out that, superficially, John Wesley was to the eighteenth century as John Henry Newman was to the nineteenth.[19] Both started within the established church and ended without; both were fellows of Oxford colleges and ap-

An aisle of the Cathedral of Syracuse built into an ancient Greek temple. John Henry Newman, the paladin of the Oxford Movement, was fascinated with religious practices in Sicily, where, he observed, "the Roman Church had scraped up the lore of ancient paganism." (From Sandro Chierichetti, *Masterworks of Sicily*, 1973, p. 87. © S.A.R.—Usmate [Milan].)

pealed to the early church for the purest example of Christianity; both were intense students of the Bible; and both were ascetic Christians who had a friend who died young because of too much fasting.

Newman sensed that the resemblance was not superficial. For, although as an Anglican and later as a Roman Catholic he was expected to call Wesley and the Methodists heretical for excessive enthusiasm and insufficient theology, he never called them heretics. His statements about them praise their zeal, condemn their persecutors, and liken John Wesley—whom Newman thought personally unattractive—to a Catholic saint.[20]

In the eighteenth century, the Methodists had shown how to sublimate emotions through religion. But, as an individual or a class grows in intellect and discernment, fantasies that were once a liberating sublimation—so to speak, in the childhood of a cult or culture —can become repressive, superstitions, unless they are combined with a richer intellectual and aesthetic diet. Newman and his friends, the Tractarians, provided this diet for themselves and tried to provide it for others. But for those without the Tractarians' or the Wesleys' sensibilities, the aesthetic often reverted to the sentimental; the architectonic to the merely ritualistic. In a word, popular culture without high art becomes kitsch.

In addition to the English analogue of pietism, Evangelicalism, many of the ways which Newman and the Tractarians used to feed their imaginations were either drawn directly from other romantics or learned through similar circumstances. Newman, for example, was not a disciple of Coleridge, but, when he read him, he was surprised to find so many similarities to ideas which he had long been nurturing.[21] He continued to admire Wordsworth's "Intimations on Immortality," and frequently referred in his writings to Sir Walter Scott's historical novels for moral as well as aesthetic examples.[22] Organic theories of society, such as underlay the writings of Wordsworth, Coleridge, and Scott were a strong influence upon him and his friends.[23]

When Newman wrote as a social philosopher, he intended to sound like the conservative organicists Coleridge, Burke, or Chateaubriand.[24] However, some ears might detect the timbre of radicals like Schiller, Michelet, Mazzini, or Rousseau. "As individuals have characters of their own, so have races [i.e., nations]. Most men have their strong and their weak points, neither good nor bad, but idiosyncratic. . . . Proper to each [is] a certain assemblage of beliefs, convictions, rules, usages, traditions, proverbs and principles; some political, some social, some moral; and these tending to some definite form of government and *modus vivendi*, or polity, as their natural scope. . . . This then is the constitution of a State."[25]

So to treasure idiosyncrasies is a form of historicism. By becoming historical, Newman and the Tractarians-to-be were adding a dimension to their youthful Methodism or Evangelicalism. They were supplying a continuity between nature and grace. This implied a movement away from the Platonically-based all-or-nothing dualistic theology of strict Protestantism that stressed a radical discontinuity between divine grace and human nature.[26] In spite of themselves, the young Tractarians were moving toward a religion of works. Thus, they built a bridge between two species of romantic religion of heartfelt experience. Pietistic personal conversion and Roman institutional ramification could now be satisfyingly harmonized.

Their search for theological and hence psychosocial reintegration moved the Tractarians in the direction of Catholicism, whose sacramental system offered the missing link between visible signs and invisible grace. It is hard to tell just how much of the Tractarians' original attraction to the Roman system came directly from thinkers like Chateaubriand or Lamennais who made much of the historical and geographical scope or reputed aesthetic richness of Catholicism. There is good evidence that Richard Hurrell Froude introduced the Tractarians directly to the thought of Lamennais and the French ultramontanes.[27] Newman's travels in Catholic countries and his friendship with some émigrés had already disposed him favorably to some Catholic practices.[28] When Froude died, Newman took his Roman Breviary as a keepsake. The book had been given to Froude by the Anglican Bishop Lloyd, who was a scholar of the Roman liturgy and a teacher of the Tractarians. Therefore, although Newman's friends may not have participated in the Continental Catholics' discussions, they profited by them.[29]

Orthodox religious writers have until recently denied the name religion to the "religious sentiment" of the Continental romantics Chateaubriand, Lacordaire, and Lamennais. Even for Newman's biographer Father Bouyer, that French trio are "mere amateurs."[30] He does not wish to conclude that Newman was, like them, an aesthete. But when Newman himself later looked back over his life, he did not scholasticize or claim to deduce his belief from a postulate grasped by reason. In the climax and conclusion of his *Apologia pro Vita Sua*, Newman declared himself an amateur theologian and went on to say; more in the spirit of Pascal than of Descartes, "I feel it quite impossible to believe in my own existence without believing in the existence of Him."[31] If one grants Newman the truth of his "I feel," Newman will demand that one grant him every detail of his vision. One might think of this assertion as the poetico-religious analogue of a scientist's hypothesis, a science since matured enough to be thought of as play, not dogma.

III

"That Methodist," as a curate in his and the century's twenties, was the contrary of the flatulent smugness evident in clergy like Mr. Collins in Jane Austen's *Pride and Prejudice*. Vivid preaching was Newman's forte. To complement the preaching we would expect of a good Methodist or Evangelical, Newman made his Sunday school flourish[32] and convinced his parishioners to keep a near-puritanical Sunday reserved for study of the Word. Outside the services he was careful to remove all barriers between the theological and psychological. He visited everyone in his parish, and personal contact was decisive in all his successes. His religion was becoming a romantic work, which did not intend to mean but to *be*. He hoped that the initial religious experience would become a habit, as patient as water on stone and, therefore, certain of winning more than the short volcanic upheaval of a momentary conversion. His theory was more evolutionist than cataclysmic.

Newman's drift toward a religion of habits and works progressed far enough for him to declare that the strict line of demarcation between the converted and unconverted did not exist.[33] Miracles were less a proof of the divinity than the church itself—or at least, than his idea of the church. "Were a being who had experience only of a chaotic world suddenly introduced into this orderly system of things, he would have an infinitely more powerful argument for the existence of a designing Mind than a mere interruption of that system can afford."[34]

Everything in the parochial service was orchestrated and performed by Newman. "In art less is more" says Mies van der Rohe, and so it was with Newman. He kept the standard Anglican ceremonial—no elaborate vestments, lights, flowers, or posturing—though he did increase its frequency.[35] But, "restraint in the communication of religious knowledge" notwithstanding, in the hands of John Henry Newman, preaching and puritanism became music and dance, stylized and subtly attractive. Again and again in his parochial work Newman fell back not on dry doctrine but on poetry, that is, music in its largest sense. When the choir at his first curacy, Saint Clement's, did not satisfy him, he dismissed them and said, "We now sing en masse."[36] Very Evangelical.

The enthusiasm which the Reverend Mr. Newman created in his parish reminds one again of how methodically John Wesley, the patriarch of British lyrical religion in modern times, worked while he remained within the Church of England. Where a half-dozen or so communicants a couple of times each year out of a cathedral full of worshipers had been normal in the eighteenth century, Wesley's communicants numbered thousands. So, too, did Newman enthuse his charges. Many differences between the Methodists and Evangelicals on one side and the Tractarians on the other did not emerge until debates over points of doctrine began in the thirties. Until that time, all were united—and dismissed—as enthusiasts.[37]

"Enthusiasm" continued when Newman became vicar of Saint Mary's, Oxford. He seemed quite sure that his professional competence as a musician excelled that of the director and even that of church tradition. He wrote to his sister Jemima that "Mr. Gould, who is perhaps somewhat conceited . . . not only disapproves of the Chant we fixed on, but attempted to convict me of making discords and mistaking keys in certain alterations I suggested, and lastly suggested a melody which I cannot approve of."[38]

At Saint Mary's, Newman remained as attentive to the Sunday school for the local working-class children as he was to the expectations of university Fellows. After near despair over the Sunday school he at last reported to his sister Jemima: "The children are improved in their singing. I have had the audacity to lead them and teach them some new tunes. Also I have summoned out a violin and strung it . . . [and] begun to *lead* them with it, a party of between twenty and thirty, great and little. . . . I have just begun chanting . . . Gregorian chant which the children seem to take to."[39] The children were soon coming punctually, and surprisingly clean.

The doctrinal side of Newman's religion continued ancillary to the musical, lyrical side. From his first sermons to his last, Newman was a spellbinder in the pulpit.[40] From the university parish his virtuosity became renowned. Those repelled by his ideas were as afraid to put themselves under his spell as the early Evangelicals and Puritans had been afraid to expose their feelings to the popish blandishments of music in the house of God. But the sermon was only a part, although a great part of the total work of art that Newman built in his mind, his parish, his university, and his universe. His *opus* touched and moved all who heard him. Newman's voice "like a silver bell" was heard first in the lessons. He was reader, preacher, and celebrant; the music and ceremonial were his also, for if others ever filled these departments, "they faded from the memory which has settled down on him alone."[41]

As season followed season, his listeners looked forward to certain lessons as special examples of Newman's power: the sacrifice of Isaac, the story of Joseph, the passage of the Red Sea, the history of Balaam. Looking back after thirty years, Canon Oakeley saw in those afternoons at Saint Mary's "that sublime idea which the Church has embodied in the quasi-dramatic recital of the Passion in Holy Week."[42] Newman's critic and admirer Matthew Arnold once commented on how the greatest part of Newman's sermons was the voice, manner, and appearance of Newman himself.

> Who could resist the charm of that spiritual apparition, gliding in the dim afternoon light through the aisles of St. Mary's, rising into the pulpit, and then in the most entrancing of voices, breaking the silence with words and thought which were religious music— subtle, sweet, mournful. I seem to hear him still saying, "After the fervor of life, after weariness and sickness, fighting and despondings, languor and fretfulness, struggling and succeeding; after all the changes of this troubled and unhealthy state at length the white throne of God, at length the beatific vision."[43]

Like a great actor who forgets himself and is intent upon the action of the drama, so Newman was intent upon the action of worship —in his eyes the greatest action man can perform. "The boy had thrown himself into his part in Latin plays, but for the man, only the Creator's drama was real, was truly dramatic."[44] Albeit in the manner of a Victorian divine, Newman was David dancing before the Ark.

Above all, Newman combined the liturgical system with a personal touch. The touching memory of one woman was that, in burying her baby, Newman had *added* some additional words to the service to express his conviction of the child's blessedness. The repeated remark of another woman soon after his departure was, "We don't seem so comfortable now as we used to, I thinks."[45]

The earnest young Anglican clergy who were to join Newman at Oxford were of two backgrounds. Some, like him, had been bred in Evangelicalism and ramified its psycholigical implications until they evolved to the High Anglican threshold of Catholicism. Others, like John Keble, Hurrell Froude, Isaac Williams, and R. W. Church, spent their entire lives in the via media, the Church of England. These achieved through a sense of historical continuity the certainty of salvation which the Evangelicals had sought through a semimystical conversion. For the born via media men, the Christian Church, as it had been erected in patristic times and remodeled since, was not merely a collection of ideas, customs, and artifacts. It was the structure of time willed and unfolded by Jehovah. Historical study would, they thought, yield a truer biblicism and a surer contact with God than could the isolated enthusiasm of an Evangelical conversion. The romantic religion thus sought to combine interior feeling with a sense of organic continuity.

The Tractarians-to-be began their historical studies because they hoped to remind the English that the church was older than the state which was now threatening it with disestablishment. Their problem was to convince the English to value reliques older than the state. In order to argue that the church was at least the equal of the state, the Oxford men laid out for themselves an ambitious program of historical study and theological argument[46] which widened the range of historical and emotional attractions employable by Christianity. Consequently, they repeatedly eschewed the simple conversion-or-no-conversion of Evangelicalism and thus moved naturally toward complexity and hence subtlety. But this subtlety, this "reserve in communicating religious knowledge," as they were wont to call it,[47] led to an elitism, which fostered the recurrence of the individualism which had caused Evangelicalism and Methodism in the first place. True, this individualism was quite stylized in the minds of the Oxford Movement. Nonetheless, by developing the lyrical side of the mind, the movement remained a place to find a personal, emotional grip on a cold universe of "hard" facts and to communicate this vision to one's brothers and sisters.[48]

The Tractarians' attitude toward hymn singing, which they thought to be a religious folk tradition, is a good example of how they thought historical research would recover the spirit of primitive

Christianity more surely than could pietistic enthusiasm alone. Although they were avid hymn writers, the early Evangelicals had persisted in the long-standing custom of the Anglican and Reformed churches by allowing "only God's word"—paraphrased psalms—to be sung in church. Once the Tractarians discovered that the early Christians—like the ancient Greeks—had sung contemporary hymns, they too allowed such lyrical effusions. Once more, like Wesley, Hamann, or Lesueur, they wanted hymns which would make a critic turn believer, rather than a believer turn critic.[49] Scholars or no, they liked sentimental songs.

The Tractarians were much like John Wesley's Holy Club of about two dozen at Oxford a century before. They were "all one body, and, as it were, one soul; zealous for the religion of the Bible, of the Primitive Church, and, in consequence, of the Church of England; as they believed it to come nearer the scriptural and primitive plan than any other national church upon earth."[50]

These heirs to Wesley's band and Chaucer's clerk who clubbed together at Oxford around 1830 were, as Fellows of Oriel College, required to be celibate. All had an unusual capacity for sharing emotional perceptions. After summarizing the attachments among the movement's leading men, including their sexual implications, Geoffrey Faber avoids either piety or ridicule: "To most modern readers the capacity [for strong emotional friendship] will probably seem unusual, and even indecent, except in the very young."[51] These men remained, in a good sense, childlike. "Perhaps a conventionalized and devitalized conception of friendship provides us with a poor standard of comparison. It might be no less foolish to write the Tractarians down as fundamentally unbalanced, than to think they were specially equipped for their providential purpose by a peculiar emotional sensibility. It might be better simply to observe that they were not ashamed of being emotional, and that in consequence, few as they were, and contrary as their aim was to the intellectual tendencies of the time, they were able to produce a lasting impression upon their own century and possibly even upon ours."[52] Since many of these sensitive youths had learned to avoid sexual fulfillment, they were so much the more ready wholeheartedly to accept a *Weltanschauung* wherein virginity and celibacy were positive virtues rather than deprivations.

The aesthetic sensibilities which the Evangelicals and Newman learned from music and religion, the other members of the movement learnt from English religious history and directly from the English countryside, as Wordworth might have wished. The two inspirations were combined, as Coleridge or Chateaubriand might have wished. All the Tractarians "possessed the moral earnestness and religious emotion of the early Methodists and Evangelicals, but combined them with an intellectual power of analysis and exposition."[53] They were dreamy, but as rhapsodists with a clear theme in mind. It was inevitable that their aesthetic urges needed a dogmatic apologia to justify their cosmic opera.

Their love of a religious culture organically linked to the past was of a piece with their love of a nature untouched by the noise and manipulations of the modern age. Among those born to such sentiments in the High Church party, Hurrell Froude retained the most intense reverence for a religion which seemed an integral part of a perfectly idyllic cosmos. "We had our father, our mother, brothers, sisters: and the old faces of the old servants, and the sheep and the cows in the meadow, and birds upon the trees, and the poultry in the bushes, and the sky, and God who lived in it, and that was all. And what a beautiful all."[54] And that was all? Froude continued to relish nature and the outdoor life. Like most of the other Tractarians he was personally quite informal, but grew argumentative whenever anyone dropped in his hearing such phrases as "the Dark ages, superstition, bigotry, right of private judgement, enlightenment, march of the mind, progress, or laws of science."[55]

Another born High Churchman was Edward Bouverie Pusey, who came from a long line of successful commercial men, divines, scholars, and nobility. His most fervent recollections were of an unchanging cosmos symbolized by the view from the manor house on the Pusey lands, whence stretched the living landscape and the unchanging outline of *their* town.[56]

Two other tories shared Newman's enthusiasm for music. William George Ward, who preceded Newman into the Roman Church and began his family's career as Catholic apologists, used to twist the common room furniture into kindling in accompaniment to the passion of his arguments. At other times, he sang whole operas and accompanied them with appropriate action while a friend played the piano.[57] Blanco White, whose theology was growing in an opposite direction—from Spanish Catholicism through Anglicanism to Unitarianism—appropriately complemented Newman's frenzied and excited violin technique with a calm and serene secondo.[58] It was for

White's journal, the *London Review*, that Newman wrote his essay on poetry[59] in 1828 and had promised a second essay on music, when the paper failed.

In the thirties the more or less private writings and sentiments of the Oxford men became a political movement. Historians, following Newman's and the Tractarians' own chronology, usually date the beginning of the Oxford Movement from the politically antirevolutionary, but psychologically incendiary, Assize Day Sermon on 14 July 1833 by John Keble.[60] At first glance, Keble's theology and poetry may appear to be little more than a lament over a pious antiquarianism disrupted. The Second French Revolution in 1830 and the First Reform Bill in England, which abolished electoral privilege in principle, were giving Englishmen the "sense of living in a new era when great changes could safely be made."[61]

To Keble and the High Church tories, as to Lammenais and Dom Guéranger, every institution of value seemed in danger and was only to be saved by heroic exertions. The tories admired Charles X of France and his minister Polignac, who wished to punish sacrilege by death. At home in England, the Reform Bill abhorred by tories had been passed by a king coerced into threatening the House of Lords with a majority of liberal peers. Moreover, Irish Catholics were already sitting in parliament, and Jews too soon would be voting on ecclesiastical matters. It seemed that if the Church of England were to survive, it must rediscover for itself a principle of identity and authority other than the mere fact of establishment by the state.[62]

Complementary to political liberalism, new drives for industrial progress and economic success were engulfing the old institutions. The Tractarians thought that all this was bad, in part because "poverty and subjection were good for the soul." They won. The liberals had only remotely threatened disestablishment and state control of the church by proposing to diminish the insult which was the Irish (Episcopal) Church and to put the revenues of ten paper bishoprics to socially constructive, charitable uses. This threat forestalled Englishmen from coming to their senses in this Irish matter for generations. The political attitude that Keble fostered among the Tractarians must sound reactionary to twentieth-century ears. Yet, in his personal life, Keble was charitable, close to saintly.[63]

Keble's Tractarian blend of personal with institutional religion stood out in the conclusion of his Assize Sermon on "National Apostacy." No Calvinist ever steeled his heart more solidly against an evil visible world and in favor of the invisible Kingdom of the Elect. The High Anglican Keble achieved from this resolve the same result as the Puritan elect—personal consolation. The good churchman "may have to wait long, and very likely pass out of this world, before he sees any abatement in the triumph of disorder and irreligion. But, if he be consistent, he possesses, to the utmost, the personal consolations of a good Christian: and as a true Churchman he has that encouragement which no other cause in the world can impart in the same degree:—he is calmly, soberly, demonstrably SURE, that sooner or later, HIS WILL BE THE WINNING SIDE, and that the victory will be complete, universal, eternal."[64]

Under his pious and diffident surface, Keble hid some of the time's most sensationally radical psychology.[65] His *Lectures on Poetry* might as well have been written by a priest of Dionysios as by a priest of Victoria. Though Keble was a persecutor of political freedom, he was an apostle of psychological freedom. All the arts, he said, are linked by the expression of one feeling in diverse media. To support his Rousseauvian theory, he instanced fragments of "natural" song from the rites of "primitive" people the world over —Lapps, characters from Norse sagas, American Indians, and archaic Greeks. All the examples were said to have their origin in "the desire to relieve thoughts that could not be controlled."[66] The passionate outcry of the noble savage poet—Rousseau named this music—reveals those things hidden to the conscious mind and is therefore oracular—prophetic. The passionate outcry is thus a concrete example of a spark of divine grace which momentarily fuses the fragmented psyche, senses, and environment. Musical poetry is a miracle, our only miracle.

Keble's *Lectures* praised the frenzy of those initiated either into the Dionysian *mysteries* or the Christian sacrament, where message and medium, outward sign and inward grace, are one. He said the goal of life is to liberate repressed feelings. Such a commonplace of mystical theology is more stylish today when called a way of liberation from civilization's discontents. Or, as we now hear a similar aesthetic applied to politics by radicals like Marcuse, poetry is doing what a repressive society forbids; when society is no longer repressive, we shall live erotically, in a state of heightened sensitivity.

Strangely, Keble's own poetry (like Marcuse's political advice) is scarcely frenzied, but an assertion of dogma, as in

Enough, I eat His Flesh and drink His Blood,
More is not told—to ask it is not good.[67]

Unlike the rest of the Tractarians, Keble had no ear for the Dionysiac art, music.[68] Like the rest of them, Keble had the unfortunate
habit of ennunciating approved sentiments tricked out with ornament
and metaphor according to shopworn recipes for religious poetry.[69]
Their verse hardly fits their own definitions of poetry as an uncontrolled, passionate outcry. They were writing religious propaganda.
Their real poetry was in their performances of the *opera Dei* or in
their sermons, where, under the ancient (primitive, childlike?) mask
of religious ritual, they could turn loose their rhapsodic instincts.[70]

The Tractarians were named for the way they advertised their
views from the pulpit and in the *Tracts for the Times*, a series of
anti-Erastian polemical pamphlets. The Tractarians were all vivid
preachers, whose impact rivaled that of the Evangelicals.[71] They
argued passionately for maintenance of the ancient cult and dogma
and for historical research to acquire a clear idea of what Christian
antiquity was like. Still, the nonverbal aesthetic riches of religion
seemed at first to concern them but little.[72] The aesthetic link between the "beautiful all," which these men had known as children,
and their dogma as adults was present in the early thirties only sub-
consciously. Nonliturgical "music meetings" and the Handel festival,
which the dean of Westminster allowed in the hallowed Abbey, were
thought an abomination.[73]

Newman heard of the danger to Anglican privileges while he was
touring in the Mediterranean. Consciously, he was still a strict Evangelical Protestant skeptically touring gaudy Catholic territory. He
was not opposed to the pleasures of a good house, but was suspicious
of public pleasures like alcohol and the theater.[74] Despite the operatic diversions he had known at home, he was still afraid to attend
a playhouse. While on the Greek island of Zante he yielded enough
to go and "see what it is like."[75] If Newman's Evangelical prudery
would not let him enjoy under its true label the pleasures he craved,
was he not bound to find them elsewhere?

William James understood what it was that Newman craved:

> Although some persons aim most at intellectual purity and sim-
> plification, for others *richness* is the supreme imaginative require-
> ment. When one's mind is strongly of this type, an individual
> religion will hardly serve the purpose. The inner need is rather of
> something institutional and complex, majestic in the hierarchic
> interrelatedness of its parts, with authority descending from stage
> to stage, and at every stage objects for adjectives of mystery and
> splendor, derived in the last resort from the Godhead who is the

fountain and the culmination of the system. One feels then as if in the presence of some vast encrusted work of jewelry or architecture; one hears the multitudinous liturgical appeal; one gets the honorific vibration coming from every quarter. Compared with such noble complexity, in which ascending and descending movements seem in no way to jar upon stability, in which no single item, however humble, is insignificant, because so many august institutions hold it in its place, how flat does evangelical Protestantism appear, how bare the atmosphere of those isolated religious lives whose boast is that "man in the bush with God may meet." What a pulverization and leveling of what a gloriously piled-up structure! To an imagination used to the perspectives of dignity and glory, the naked gospel scheme seems to offer an almshouse for a palace.[76]

I date Newman's conversion to the Roman Church not from his announcement in the sermon "The Parting of Friends" in 1846, but from his trip to the Mediterranean in 1833. As far as a Protestant might be concerned, Newman's tragic flaw was revealed now on those islands and peninsulas where the original tragedies had been sung. Fate willed that his abhorrence of the Babylonian Woman was not strong enough to repel the attractions of that church which Newman said had "scraped up the ancient lore of the Mediterranean." In Sicily he found "the religion which is around me—statues of the Madonna and of the Saints in the streets, etc., etc.—a more poetical but not less jading stimulus than a pouring forth in a Baptist chapel."[77] What Newman thought was a distinction between bad poetry and bad religion was soon to seem a likeness among all that he thought good. The heir of paganism, as Newman called the Roman Church, was making its appeal. He did not resist the emotional appeal of the preacher when he was fifteen. He could not resist now. The pagan worship had had a perfect setting, Newman said; the new Roman Catholic paganism also seemed to combine nature and art in a total work of art produced by one Creator.[78]

His aesthetic impulses assailed his doctrine. Doctrine lost. He was bound to be driven into the religion which offered the most complete combination of aesthetic richness and systematic doctrine. If he had named his sentiments art rather than dogma, he might have been driven in a different direction—toward a career in music or toward something like Matthew Arnold's religion of culture.

"Dogma has been the fundamental principle of my religion,"[79] wrote Newman later in defense of his seeming changeability. On this foundation of dogma, said Newman, was erected the teaching of the

Roman Church to be found in her creeds, her great divines, and above all, the Fathers of the early, undivided church.

> Some portions of their teaching, magnificent in themselves, came like music to my inward ear, as if the response to ideas, which, with little external to encourage them, I had cherished so long. These were based on the mystical or sacramental principle, and spoke of the various economies or Dispensations of the Eternal. I understood these passages to mean that the exterior world, physical and historical, was but the manifestation to our senses of realities greater than itself. Nature was a parable. Scripture was an allegory: pagan literature, philosophy, and mythology, properly understood, were but a preparation for the Gospel.[80]

That was the old cardinal in his *Apologia.* At the time of his formal conversion to the Roman allegiance, he explained how he thought the Master Composer's organic work had been tampered with by mediocre editors and performers:

> The Anglican system [was] all but destitute of this divine element, which is an essential part of Catholicism—a ritual dashed upon the ground, trodden on, and broken piecemeal;—prayer clipped, pieced, torn, shuffled about at pleasure, until the meaning of the composition perished, and offices, which had been poetry no longer even good prose;—antiphons, hymns, benedictions, invocations shovelled away;—Scripture lessons turned into chapters;—heaviness, feebleness, unwieldiness, where the Catholic rites had the lightness and airiness of a spirit;—vestments chucked off, lights quenched, jewels stolen, the pomp and circumstance of worship annihilated; a dreariness which could be felt and which seemed to token of an incipient Socinianism; . . . huge ugly boxes of wood, sacred to preachers, frowning on the congregation in place of the mysterious altar; and long cathedral aisles unused, railed off, like the tombs (as they were) of what had been and was not.[81]

"The absence of positive teaching drove men to prayer and Bible meetings," as well as to the "solemn captivating services whereby Popery gains its proselytes." Men, he was saying, were driven to allegiances which fully recognized man's aesthetic dimension. As he had done while a boy, Newman again had to reconcile music and religion. This time, though his inspiration was aesthetical, his conclusion was theological. No longer able to compose an opera for his father, he would sing in the *opera* to the Father.

For a religiously and historically inclined aesthete like Newman, Catholicism will often seem more attractive than Protestantism. Protestantism or its successors will never make many converts among Catholics such as Newman was already at heart. William James again:

> [Catholicism] offers a so much richer pasturage and shade to the fancy, has so many cells with so many different kinds of honey, is so indulgent in its multiform appeals to human nature, that Protestantism will always show to the Catholic eyes the almshouse physiognomy. The bitter negativity of it is to the Catholic mind incomprehensible. To intellectual Catholics many of the anti-quated beliefs and practices to which the Church gives counte-nance are, if taken literally, as childish as they are to Protestants. But they are childish in the pleasing sense of "childlike,"— innocent and amiable, and worthy to be smiled on in consideration of the undeveloped condition of the dear people's intellects. To the Protestant, on the contrary, they are childish in the sense of being idiotic falsehoods. He must stamp out their delicate and lovable redundancy, leaving the Catholic to shudder at his literal-ness. He appears to the latter as morose as if he were some hard-eyed, numb, monotonous kind of reptile. The two will never understand each other—their centres of emotional energy are too different. Rigorous truth and human nature's intricacies are always in need of a mutual interpreter.[82]

The *opus Dei* and the opera possess those minds which come to know their elaborate business, their formalism, their magnification, their absurdity, their liturgicality, and their fantasy, which so per-fectly rebels against a simplistic notion of human nature.

IV

"What then does Dr. Newman *mean?*" asked his liberal theological opponent, the Reverend Charles Kingsley, and thus provoked the *Apologia pro Vita Sua.*[83] On the surface, Kingsley was merely using a debater's ploy. In fact, the question went deeper than this or that definition in one sermon by Newman. The style of all Newman's works declares a man striving to combine the clear meaning of ra-tional exposition aimed at the head with the allusiveness of emo-tional attraction aimed at the heart. Because of the Tractarians' zeal for theological exposition, their best poetry is their prose. (The same may well be true of many eminent nineteenth-century writers who were zealous for historical or critical reconstruction.) Newman's writing owed its rhythm and harmony as much to the great and constant recreation of his home, music, whereby he became familiar with the chamber music of Handel, Beethoven, and Mozart, as well as of the masters of the Italian school—such as Corelli—as to sedulous cultivation of periodic sentences in imitation of Cicero.[84]

When Lytton Strachey called Newman an artist *manqué*,[85] he struck a nerve which some biographers are at pains to shelter, just as respectable historians and critics were once expected to denigrate romanticism. To them it seemed disreputable to have been an artist —especially during Newman's formative years when artists were romantics. So, the majority of Newman's biographers, whatever their theological tack, are at pains to make him "no such idle dreamer."[86] Likewise, some biographers have been deceived by his hanging everything on the neo-Platonic tree of Porphyry implicit in the writings of the church fathers whom he admired. For example, one biographer dares to assert: "It is significant that the reader will have to search long in the sermons of Newman to find any evocations of the beauty of Nature. Strongly theological minds (unless of the Platonic and Alexandrian cast), with an overwhelming concern for ethics, do not readily lend themselves to the allurements of aesthetics in a fallen world. They turn to the pageantry of Grace rather than to Nature; or if to nature as to a veil behind which stands God."[87]

Such distinctions, so often applied to the romantics, are inaccurate because, for Newman as for all romantics, nature reveals rather than veils the Ultimate. As a result of such tenuous distinctions, most of Newman's admirers protest too much against "the sentimental myth."[88] They fail to distinguish between, as well as connect, the sentimental and the more deeply emotional, that is, between the ephemeral whim and the artistic creation. They do not, therefore, recognize Newman's appeal to man's aesthetic sense for what it is. A historian must recognize it in his idea of education: "The first step in the conversion of man and renovation of his nature is his rescue from that fearful subjection to sense which is his ordinary state."[89] What remedy does Newman propose? The same as proposed by so many European thinkers from Rousseau to Freud. To be liberated from slavery to the senses means knowing how to use them. "We need a remedy which we can make our own . . . a sort of homeopathic remedy for the disease," which Newman found in "natural culture."

Supernatural culture, explicit theology, was never for Newman the only instrument through whose note God sounds His harmonies.

In his youth, he had recognized that poetry was the mysticism of the age, and music remained for him supreme in that "whole series of impressions made on us by the senses" in which he saw a "Divine economy suited to our need and the token of realities distinct from themselves." Perhaps, as he took up his violin by himself or in ensembles, he tried to learn through it the unknowable and to utter the unutterable.[90] Thus did Newman once use music to prove the existence of a divine economy:

> Let us take another instance, of an outward and earthly form, or economy, under which great wonders unknown seem to be typified; I mean musical sounds, as they are exhibited most perfectly in instrumental harmony. There are seven notes in the scale; make them fourteen; yet what a slender outfit for so vast an enterprise! Shall we say that all this exuberant inventiveness is a mere ingenuity or trick of art, like some game or fashion of the day, without reality, without meaning? We may do so; and then, perhaps, we shall also account the science of theology to be a matter of words; yet, as there is a divinity in the theology of the Church, *which those who feel cannot communicate,* so is there also in the wonderful creation of sublimity and beauty of which I am speaking. To many men the very names which the science employs are utterly incomprehensible. To speak of an idea or a subject seems to be fanciful or trifling, to speak of the views which it opens upon us to be childish extravagance; yet is it possible that that inexhaustible evolution and disposition of notes, so rich yet so simple, so intricate yet so regulated, so various yet so majestic, should be a mere sound, which is gone and perishes? It is not so; it cannot be. No; they have escaped from some high sphere; they are the outpourings of eternal harmony in the medium of created sound; they are our echoes from our Home; they are the voice of Angels, or the Magnificat of Saints, or the living laws of Divine Governance, or the Divine Attributes; something are they besides themselves, which we cannot compass, which we cannot utter,—though mortal man, and he perhaps not otherwise above his fellows, has the gift of eliciting them.[91]

"Those who feel" may not be able to argue their opponents into religion, but Newman thought music could communicate the meaning of religion. People, he asserted, who don't like the piled-up externals of religion are "like the man in one of Miss Edgeworth's[92] novels, who shut his ears to the music that he might laugh at the dancers." The beauties of religion convey its meaning. "The pious feeling which accompanies the sight of the image is the music . . .

As music incites to dancing, so religion would lead to images; but as dancing does not improve music to those who do not like dancing, so ceremonies do not improve religion to those who do not like ceremonies." Or, more concisely, "beautiful spires are not a sham just because you cannot see their foundations."[93]

In a more formally philosophical mood, Newman assayed a proof of the ultimate through what he called the Illative Sense. He asserted that "the jejeune generalizations which treatises can give" supply no rules for conduct. Dismissing Aristotle's *Ethics*, Newman asserted that "properly speaking there are as many kinds of 'high mindedness' as there are personalities." Rather, "In no class of concrete reasonings, whether in experimental science, historical research, or theology is there any ultimate test of truth and error in our inferences besides the trustworthiness of the Illative Sense that gives them sanction."[94] The sanction of the Illative Sense seems to have been what William James called the Sentiment of Rationality. It was an introspective proof of design, a proof such as might have been devised by Descartes or Anselm, had they been Methodists or some other species of pietist. Taking himself as the ultimate Baconian, Newman found no way to escape from the idols of the mind. But this limitation he turned into a proof of the Illimitable. "As the structure of the universe speaks to us of Him who made it, so the laws of the mind are the expression, not of mere constituted order, but of His will. I should be bound by them even were they not His laws; but since one of their very functions is to tell me of Him, they throw a reflex light upon themselves, and, for resignation to my destiny, I substitute a cheerful concurrence in an overruling Providence."[95]

Of course, Newman reminded himself that the imagination does not create anything real; that poetical creation is real only insofar as it reflects an ideal order. Even with such a Platonic viewpoint, Newman, like Edmund Burke, drifted nonetheless into an evolutionary, and therefore relativistic, social philosophy: "While nature physical remains fixed in its laws, Nature moral and social has a will of its own, is self-governed, and never remains any long while in that state from which it started into action."[96] Still, in explicit theology, he fell back upon dogmatism: "I have resisted to the best of my power the spirit of liberalism in religion, the doctrine that there is no positive truth in religion . . . that revealed religion is not a truth but a sentiment and a taste; not an objective fact."[97]

At bottom Newman was not defending religion against a charge of aestheticism; he was defending the aesthetic against the charge that it is not real. If Newman's devotion to the invisible—which

could make him say that all human suffering would be a fair price
for the avoidance of one venial sin—disappoints, turn to a writer
with a lively social conscience, who was also devoted to the invisible.
In *Hard Times*, Charles Dickens stated that the *mal du siècle* was—
is—that mediocre minds limited the definition of fact to what they
could weigh and measure. "Between the lying-in hospital and the
cemetery, what you couldn't state in figures, or show to be purchas-
able in the cheapest market and saleable in the dearest, was not, and
never should be, world without end, Amen."[98] If Newman's high
price for the avoidance of "sin" still cloys, compare it with the bloody
penances some of our philosophers are ready to impose on humanity
in order to assure a radical moral conversion.

In common with the fantasies of idyllic youths and the compas-
sion of writers like Dickens, Newman shared an "astonishing capacity for visualizing the abstract and invisible."[99] This is how he combined the high-and-dry with the Evangelical sides of Anglicanism.
Newman's sermons were poetry, wherein the rhapsodist outshone
the logician, great though the logician was.

Newman's sermon "Omnipotence in Bonds" is an epic example
of his poetical incarnation of catechetical formulae. Upon the paradox of divine grace, strongest when apparently weakest, Newman
played variations upon one theme, one sustained image,[100] of the
humiliation of the Son of God in the Incarnation, buttressed with
scriptural citations from beginning to end. The sermon is also a
summary of the life of Christ from the bondage of the Virgin's
womb, in the confines of the swaddling clothes of infancy, in the
chains of parental authority, under the restraints of temptation, beneath the servitude to man's needs, manacled on the cross, to the
ultimate cramping of the shroud in the tomb. When we are prepared
for the liberation of the Resurrection by Newman's phrase "He tore
open the solid rock," the sermon surprises us by a deceptive cadence. "Christ is ever in the bonds of the Eucharist by which he
made provision for perpetuating captivity to the end of the world."
Newman wished "to teach us our place in His wide universe and to
make us ambitious only of that grace here and glory hereafter, which
He has purchased for us by his own humiliation."[101]

Like most thinkers since romanticism, Newman thought that truth
was palpable in idyllic nature. When he grew enamoured of the
drama in the yearly cycle of the Roman rite, he lamented that
some of its principal architects, the medieval Benedictines, had had no
Vergil to describe their rural labors. So Newman, who admired Vergil's *Georgics*,[102] decided to combine his classical training and his

lyrical impulses and become the Benedictine's nature poet. He wished to fulfill Vergil's lyrical side in Christian terms as Dante had fulfilled his epic side.[103] There is, however, an autumnal irony in Newman's romanticization of the Benedictines, for they already had fulfilled the georgic idylls not by nostalgic writing but by living the harmonious life, working and singing the *opus Dei.*

> How could he [a Benedictine Vergil] have portrayed St. Paulinus to St. Serenus in his garden, who could draw so beautiful a picture of the old Corycian raising amid the thicket his scanty pot-herbs upon the nook of land that was not good for tillage, nor for pasture, nor for vines. He who loved the valley, winding stream, and wood, and the hidden life which they offer, and the deep lessons which they whisper—how could he have illustrated that wonderful union of prayer, penance, toil and literary work, the true *otium cum dignitate,* a fruitful leisure and a meek-hearted dignity, which is exemplified in the Benedictine! That ethereal fire which enabled the prince of Latin poets to take up the Sibyl's strain and to adumbrate the glories of a supernatural future, that serene philosophy which has strewn his poems with sentiments that come home to the heart, that intimate sympathy with the sorrows of human kind, and with the action and passion of human nature, how well would they have served to illustrate the patriarchal history and office of the monks in the broad German countries, or the deed, the words, and the visions of a St. Odilio or a St. Aelred.[104]

Nature poetry that is, albeit without piles of apostrophes.

One commentator says of that passage, "Never did a Beethoven or a Mozart orchestrate a theme with more telling effect; the triumphant clash of the strings in 'The ethereal fire . . .' the soothing notes of the flutes and oboes in 'that serene Philosophy.' "[105]

Also in nature poetry did Newman hail the actual rearising of the cosmic opera—the *opus Dei*—in England in his sermon "The Second Spring." The story was sung in an A-B-A sonatina.

First the theme:

> Each hour, as it comes, is but a testimony how fleeting, yet how secure, how certain is the great whole. . . . Spring passes into summer, and through summer and autumn into winter, only the more surely, but its own ultimate return, to triumph over that grave, towards which it resolutely hastened from its first hour.

Next, a modulation and development in a different key:

Such is nature; such is not Man.

Man rises to fall; he tends to dissolution from the moment he
begins to be; he lives on indeed in his children, lives on in his own
name, he lives not on in his own person; he is as regards the
manifestations of his nature here below, as a bubble that breaks,
and as water poured out upon the earth. He was young, he is old,
he is never young again. This is the lament over him, poured
forth in verse and in prose, by Christian and by heathen. The
greatest work of God's hands under the sun, he is all the manifestations of his complex being, is born only to die.[106]

Then Newman recapitulated the first passage by speaking of a second youth or spring in heaven.

V

What Newman wrote specifically on music must be pieced together. Though the specific references to music in the "Essay on
Poetry" are small, one can infer that, had he written an essay on
music, he would have changed its place in the Aristotelian hierarchy
of dramatic—including liturgical—expression. Newman would have
raised music from the next to last place among plot, acting, sentiment, poetic diction, music, and settings, to the first place.[107]

Newman almost begrudged the putting of a poem on paper,[108] for
this might "tend to withdraw it from the spontaneous exhibition of
pathos or imagination to a minute diligence in the formation of a
plot."[109] Now, composers plan their works every bit as much as
writers. But this plan—"form" they call it—is usually perceived
posterior to the emotional impact of the music by most listeners. A
nonmusical play is often the other way around, its plot—a musician
would say its "form"—is often perceived anterior to its emotional
impact.

Newman liked plays which he thought approached music. He did
not care for Sophocles' tightly reasoned *Oedipus rex*, which Aristotle thought was the best play ever written because it has the best-
wrought plot. Newman preferred plays where the "workmanship"
that went into a tight plot was less evident. He preferred Aeschylus,
who "in four out of seven plays had hardly any plot at all," or even

Euripides, "who is careless in the construction of his plots." Among
Aeschylus's works Newman preferred the lyrical nature poetry of
the choral strophes. He even thought them among the best of all
poetry.[110]

Aristotle saw a play as an exhibition of ingenious workmanship;
Newman saw it as a free and unfettered effusion of genius.[111] Romantically, Newman found poetry in the seemingly chaotic pages of
Shakespeare, equally in the often wordless minds of young people—
especially in the season of spring,[112] and in the crannied ritual of the
church[113] where "there are no mute, inglorious Miltons," because
God sees and understands every man's "poetry." Granted that Newman thought most moments of poetic greatness come in contemplation or solitude. After all, he was brought up a rather introverted
lad. Had he been a professional, rather than an amateur, musician,
he might have realized that music was for him the primary way out
of himself and into contact with the whirl of the world. At any rate,
for Newman, the thing to be is a poet, by which he means something
closer to a performing musician than a closeted writer. And of all
musics, Newman prefers the least plot-ridden. "We may liken the
Greek drama to the music of the Italian school."

Good poetry—which is to say, good music, the true expression of
honest feelings—is also a sign of good morality. Lest such a sentiment seem bigoted from a religionist like Newman, let us again recall
Dickens—or almost any artist of the past two hundred years—kick-
ing against the same dismal goad of laissez-faire classical liberalism.
Of some circus performers who were nearly illiterate, totally uncal-
culating, and thoroughly disreputable, because nothing they did
seemed to produce anything which added to England's gross national
product; who seemed immoral because economically unsuccessful,
Dickens said, "Yet there was a remarkable gentleness and childish-
ness about these people, a special inaptitude for any kind of sharp
practice, and an untiring readiness to help and pity one another,
deserving often of as much respect, and always of as much generous
construction, as the everyday virtues of any class of people in the
world."[114] To better make his point, Dickens had their spokesman
lisp. The reader will recall that the good life—the enjoyment of the
aesthetic—was also the moral end of life for Marx and Mill, the two
complementary high priests of social evolution, who—like the Tractarians—preached a kind of salvation through their teleological theories of history.[115] If today one would categorize philosophers according to how strongly they believed that more perfect consciousness is

more perfect sensitivity, Newman would belong in both the most radical and the most conservative category. Like Johann Michael Sailer in Beethoven's Germany (see chapters 2 and 6 above), Newman has been praised and condemned from all sides. For both Sailer and Newman, music was crucial in their development, which led them beyond theology to religion.

A case can be made à la Nietzsche that all philosophers of history during the nineteenth century shared a vision which satisfied their aesthetic sensibilities. In the light of more recent theories of evolution, their schemes were not world explanations, but—as Nietzsche said—world arrangements, which satisfied their will to power, their will to impose their vision on the world.[116] For instance, the Tractarians shared the teleological myth with Darwin, Marx, and Mill. However, the Tractarians retained the Christian terminology for a philosophy of history that the others expressed in secular terms.

To survive, the Tractarians had to discover for the Church of England a principle of identity and an authority other than the mere fact of establishment by the state.[117] In their search for a non-Erastian foundation for the Church of England, Newman and the others were surprised to learn that the familiar and venerated *Book of Common Prayer* was a remnant and reflection of medieval and primitive devotion still embodied in the Roman service books.[118] Soon they were examining and publishing the writings of the fathers of the church. Newman tells us that his conclusions after a systematic reading of the fathers was that primitive Christianity and the Roman Catholic Church were one.[119] Naturally, this assurance of an historical anchor amid counter claims of church and state satisfied his aesthetic sense, "when the Fathers' teaching came like music" to his inward ear.[120]

Most of the Tractarians remained anti-Roman because they were anti-Erastian and the Roman Church seemed to have sold itself into the bondage of jesuitical power politics. Later Newman became pro-Roman because Rome seemed to reach beyond Erastianism to a time when Christianity was pure, for "the notion of doctrinal knowledge absolutely novel, and of simple addition from without is intolerable to Catholic ears, and never was entertained by anyone who was even approaching to an understanding of our creed. Revelation is all doctrine; the Apostles its sole depository, the inferential method its sole instrument, and ecclesiastical authority its sole sanction. The Divine Voice has spoken once and for all, and the only question is about its meaning."[121] This is a favorite passage of commentators

pro and contra Newman. Whatever its meaning, it shows a man in
love with the integrity of a work of art and, if this be not admitted,
at least a man for whom the artist's "inferential method" is crucial.
Had he but the daring of Nietzsche, to say of religion as well as
science: it is "not a world exposition, nor a world explanation, but
a world arrangement."[122]

Newman and the Tractarians found God inferred in ceremonial
worship because it is aesthetic in the literal sense. "Ceremonial worship uses rhythm and gesture, contact, sight, and speech, not only
the bit of us called spiritual in the approach to God. Whilst we are
in this life we can never, of course, get rid of the close partnership
of body and spirit: in the doctrine of the incarnation Christians find
this partnership blessed and endorsed by God."[123] In Tract XXXIV,
Rites and Customs of the Church, Newman did mention music, but
emphasized the acceptance of those customs—which I call art—to
the point where customs become dogma. He meant they become
sacraments, mysteries.[124] In Newman's novel *Loss and Gain*, the
Catholic religion is real because it is like a total music drama, the
varied yet coherent reintegration of every human mode of expression.
A Catholic—obviously the *persona* of the author—says to an Anglican:

> The idea of worship is different in the Catholic Church from the
> idea of it in your Church; for, in truth the *religions* are different.
> . . . I declare, to me, he said, and he clasped his hand on his
> knees, and looked forward as if soliloquising, to me nothing is so
> consoling, so piercing, so thrilling, so overcoming as the Mass. . . .
> It is not a mere form of words—it is a great action, the greatest
> action that can be on earth. It is not the invocation merely, but, if
> I dare use the word, the Evocation of the Eternal. He becomes
> present on the altar in flesh and blood, before whom angels bow
> and devils tremble. This is that awful event which is the scope,
> and is the interpretation, of every part of the solemnity. Words
> are necessary, but as means not ends; they are not mere addresses
> to the throne of grace, they are instruments of what is far higher,
> of consecration of sacrifice. They hurry on as if impatient to
> fulfill their mission. Quickly they go, the whole is quick; for they
> are parts of one integral action. . . . Quickly they pass; because as
> the lightening which shineth from one part of the heaven unto the
> other, so is the coming of the Son of Man. . . . So we, all around,
> each in his place, look out for the greatest Advent, "waiting for
> the moving of the water." Each in his place, with his own heart,
> with his own wants, with his own prayers, separate but concordant,

uniting in consumation . . . like a concert of musical instruments, each different, but concurring in a sweet harmony, we take our part with God's priest, supporting him, yet guided by him. [Like a conductor and his ensemble?] There are little children there and old men, and simple labourers, and students in seminaries, priests preparing for Mass, priests making their thanksgiving; there are innocent maidens, and there are penitent sinners; but out of these many minds rises one eucharistic hymn, and the great Action is the measure and the scope of it.[125]

The *opus Dei* is a total work of art.

Or, as Newman phrased his sentiments in the *Apologia*:

The contrast was presented to me by the Catholic Church. Then I recognized at once a reality which was quite a new thing with me. Then I was sensible that I was not making for myself a Church by an effort of thought; I needed not to make an act of faith in her; I had not painfully to force myself into a position, but my mind fell back upon itself in relaxation and in peace, and I gazed at her almost passively as a great objective fact. I looked at her;—at her rites, her ceremonial, and her precepts; and I said, "This *is* a religion;" and then, when I looked back upon the poor Anglican Church, for which I had laboured so hard and upon all that appertained to it, and thought of our various attempts to dress it up doctrinally and esthetically, it seemed to me to be the veriest of nonentities.[126]

Once inside the Roman Church, Newman did not try to recover the visions of Augustine or the logic of Aquinas. Nor did he retire to the bucolic Benedictines whom he so greatly praised; rather, he helped to organize in England the thoroughly Italianate Oratorian Fathers. Therein he sought the spirit of their baroque founder, Saint Philip Neri, the only bona fide musical entrepreneur ever canonized.[127]

One orthodox Catholic commentator found it a "curious illustration of the strange ways of providence that 'that Methodist' would receive a welcome from the patron saint of humorists."[128] "Whether or not I can do anything at all in St. Philip's way," Newman said, "at least I can do nothing in any other."[129] He wished to "take men by surprise"; we might say "inferentially," "aesthetically," or "musically." Newman wrote a Latin Litany of Saint Philip—"Man of the ancient days; holy light of joy; you, who have experienced great ectasies." He liked the paradox Philip used for a motto: "Scorn the world, scorn nothing, scorn yourself, scorn being scorned."[130]

There is nothing strange in the youthful "Methodist's"—if one may continue to stretch the meaning of Evangelical—later following the baroque Philip Neri. For Newman thereby traveled back to the pageantry of his youthful imagination and back to the bittersweet isolation from and communication with the world he had known by way of a soul more poetic than most. If the boy had been satisfied with familial pageants and personal conversions, the man was bound to be satisfied only with a cosmic pageant and patron saints who knew how to be friends.

Newman stated that he wanted to retain those intimations of immortality he had known in his youth. "Old men are in soul as stiff, as lean, as bloodless as their bodies, except so far as grace penetrates and softens them. And it requires a flooding of grace to do this. I more and more wonder at *old* saints. [But, even the youthful] St. Aloysius or St. Francis Xavier or St. Carlo, are nothing to St. Philip. O Philip gain me some little portion of thy fervour. I live more and more in the past, and in hopes that the past may revive in the future. My God, when shall I learn that I have so parted with the world that, though I may wish to make friends with it, it will not make friends with me?"[131] The world was much bigger now, but in relation to it, John Henry Newman at sixty was still childlike.

On one occasion, when lauding the mission of Saint Philip Neri, Newman longed "for the fervour which is itself the proof of fervour."[132] Returning to the past and to the youthful spirit of Saint Philip meant a return to the religion of the Mediterranean which had captivated Newman in 1833. The style of music and ritual favored by Newman, and even by the rest of the English Catholic hierarchy, was not the properly English and medieval Gothic style favored by the Anglo-Catholics. Newman's Catholic style resembled Italian opera and Baroque religion, quite close to the popular style of devotions he once had felt obliged to condemn, in his *Difficulties of Anglicans*, as "calculated to prejudice inquirers, to frighten the unlearned, to unsettle consciences, to provoke blasphemy. . . . I prefer English habits of belief and devotion to foreign."[133] For a while, converts like Newman out-Romanized those who had been Catholic from birth. Italian opera stars were welcome to display their wares in the churches during the London season. Father Faber of the London Oratory held those Catholic services which were numerically the most successful. These were popular evening services with uninhibitedly passionate prayers, similar English hymns, and a flamboyant sermon.[134] The stone that the liberals rejected was used by the Catholics—as it was by the fundamentalist sects and by the Socialists.

Born English Catholics and Anglicans might have their Gothic, but for Newman, Gothic music did not match Gothic architecture. Gregorian (Gothic to him) music was not elaborate enough for him. It was fine in ancient basilicas, "because both were of non-Christian origin and not very elaborated." Gothic architecture was elaborate enough; cathedrals in that style expressed one idea "infinitely varied and elaborated in its parts; so is a symphony or quartet of Beethoven."[135]

Although Newman venerated the Mediterranean style, which hereditary English Catholics found so flamboyant, the essence of his religion remained the inward conversion experienced in his boyhood.

> And I hold this still, I am a Catholic by virtue of my believing in a God; and if I am asked why I believe in God, I answer that it is because I believe in myself, for I feel it impossible to believe in my own existence (and of that fact I am quite sure) without believing also in the existence of Him who lives as a Personal, All-seeing, All-judging Being in my conscience. Now, I dare say, I have not expressed myself with philosophical correctness, because I have not given myself to the study of what others have said on the subject; but I think I have strong true meaning in what I say which will stand examination.[136]

"Feeling," this time music itself, remained the attraction which at length reconciled Newman to those Anglican friends he had once inspired at Oxford. Near the last, he and his Oxford friends dared to meet again. Two of them presented him with a violin. Newman, who had given up playing "lest it interfere with the graver duties of life," returned to it with delight. He wrote to thank Dean Church "in terms of almost boyish glee that recall those happy times at Oxford, and to say how delighted he was at thus regaining his friend and his music."[137] Before Newman died, he met Keble and Pusey again; his most vivid impression that day was of the woodland setting on the way to Keble's parsonage. Finally, in the year of Newman's death, Mr. W. Wood, an Independent minister, wrote to the cardinal to express his gratitude; he concluded: "I feel that I have very inadequately stated my experience of benefit, but that precious and profound doctrine which you teach us, viz., that the best part of Christian life remains hidden, leads me to hope that from this very impoverished utterance you may be able to understand how rich and, I hope, lastingly rich you have made me in that inward life according to which we are accepted."[138] *Cor ad cor loquitur.*

Yet in Newman's idylls there is romanticism's autumn. The end is in sight. Art is no longer the way to reach the world, but an insulation from the world. The critic D. G. James compares Newman on the Arcadian Benedictine with Wordsworth on the pastoral life.

> The priest of the Roman Church, brooding over a world lapsed by an awful catastrophe from God, will pay, in the security of his freedom from foolish illusions, a kind of homage to a pretty romanticism by speaking of the monastic state as a return to "that primitive age of the world, of which poets have so often sung, the simple life of Arcadia in the reign of Saturn, when fraud and violence were unknown." But Wordsworth, the Romantic poet will not sing of these things. His shepherd is no Saturnian or Arcadian figure. Newman can safely take the risk of speaking of his monk in this fanciful manner; Wordsworth will take no such risks with his shepherd. The priest may indulge fancy; the Romantic poet sticks to the facts.[139]

By metamorphosing his illation into a dogma, Newman at length was hoist with his own petard.

Newman, like Matthew Arnold, attempted to combine romanticism and Christianity (as Diderot and Schiller had tried to combine the classical with the romantic). Arnold was perhaps the more romantic for he tried to live with a contradiction between dogma and freedom. But Newman was the more tragic, for he had farther to fall. His old age was also the age of the First Vatican Council. After them, Christianity kept to sober and fastidious paths, "in which it [successfully] resists the vulgarities, attractions, and dangers of Romance."[140]

CONCLUSION

Thou askest, is life worth living—
O hark!: the song of the fisherman
  across the sands.

Wang Wei
Gift of Thanks (T'ang dynasty)

Sweet songs of heaven,
  keep sounding forth!
My tears well up,
  I belong once more to earth.

Goethe
Faust I

CONCLUSION

The strength of romanticism lay in its possibilities. Its sources and influences extend so far beyond the confines of the cenacle which nurtured it originally that it is hardly comprehensible in terms of lexical formulas but well understood in terms of its historical functions. Let us consider three of these. First, romanticism as the torch in the cave, continuing the exploratory enterprise begun by modern paganism, the Enlightenment. Second, as a complementary movement, the spoils of the Christians, translating into modern terms the heritage of the millennium-and-a-half between the fall of Rome and the rise of romanticism. Finally, as the reformulation of two basic questions concerning man and society: how to foster the reintegration of the human individual and how to build a sense of community.

I

Like prisoners bound in a dark cave and able to see only flickering shadows on the walls, we are accustomed to living in the dark. So thought Plato. A wise man, he said, would want to free the prisoners in order to show them how things looked outside the cave in the clear light of day. But habitual prisoners would prefer to stay and listen to the charms of sibyls and superstition, rather than see by the clear light of reason. Despairing of the possibility of finding truth in the dark cave of sensory phenomena, Plato, the chief articulator of the rationalistic tradition, taught that reality belongs to a superior world, accessible only to the mind. Such doctrines became the mold into which Christianity was poured.

The Enlightenment took issue with this other-worldly legacy by insisting that there is no outside realm to which we may escape. We should, therefore, concentrate upon bringing light into the cave. As a continuation of the Enlightenment, the romantic movement devoted itself to illuminating those dark corners of ourselves and our environment that most needed exploration. Just as new historical sciences and organicist philosophies were instrumental in this exploration, new aesthetic and psychological theories redefined the relationship between ideas and experience.

Before the late eighteenth century, the west still lived more in the tradition of rationalism, tending to believe that in the achievement of clarity, definition, or abstraction one attained the truth. So to identify reality with the contents of acts of understanding is to emphasize definition. And behind definition lies the metaphor of a visual diagram, *l'esprit géométrique*.[1]

This metaphor was central to the rationalistic tradition. If ideas —acts of understanding—constitute reality, as the rationalistic tradition believed, reality cannot be located in richness of experience. Ideas, and thus reality, are found in some superior world. Although the Enlightenment assaulted the belief in a superior other-world, the Enlightenment, if only by reason of its self-chosen name, was part of the old intellectual regime. For the rationalistic tradition was dependent not so much upon theological arguments as upon a hierarchical structure of consciousness implicit in the rationalistic faith. The Age of Reason may have been a great pivotal period, but it continued to measure itself by the standards of the past, matched with a still-vigorous champion—theology—and embedded in a hierarchical picture of human nature and society. Only after this hierarchy had been toppled could a new attitude emerge truly based on freedom and equality.

The economic and political, as well as philosophical, battering of the old regime gradually made such a new attitude inevitable. For the more one accepts the enlightened precepts "dare to know" and "dare to do," the more one becomes reason's doppelgänger, curious always to go one step further into the how, the why, and the taboo.

To put it another way, the imagery favored by the Enlightenment proved inadequate to explain the implications of its discoveries. This inadequacy was most evident at the very core of its thought, in its picture of how human beings perceive, are motivated, and communicate. Precisely here the didactic, hierarchical, and even mechanistic assumptions inherited from the rationalistic tradition proved least sufficient.

According to the rationalistic tradition, music and musicians manifested our sensual and irrational "lower" faculties. In the age of democratic revolution, such elements—which had been rejected as the least transcendant aspects of human consciousness and society—became the cornerstones of a new cultural edifice. Quite reasonably, the rebellion against the rationalistic tradition eventually came to favor these supposedly inferior sides of humanity.

Contrary to the suspicions of music inherited from philosophy and theology, the leading thinkers of the latter part of the eighteenth century began to take music for the model human activity. This fresh viewpoint tended to think of truth more as an intuitive epiphany than as a deductive geometry, more as a unique moment than as a reflection of uniform principles. The supposedly least geometrical endeavors and persons such as music and musicians now seemed to be not the barrier but the key to understanding the connection between the noumenal and the phenomenal.[2] In short, the modern evaluation of full reality and the significance of feeling amounts to a revolution against the rationalistic belief in the supremacy of sight. This revolution was not complete until a new metaphorical picture of the world emerged based upon *l'esprit de musique*, the kinesthetic flow of experience, process rather than stasis, organicism, chance, change, and evolution. By substituting the musical for the geometrical metaphor the romantic movement finished relocating reality from heaven to earth.

II

Whereas the Enlightenment schooled the west in analysis, romanticism schooled us in synthesis. This function of romanticism in the modernization of western culture is analogous to that of earlier syntheses, such as the Christian appropriation of Hellenistic culture during the decline of the Roman Empire. To explain and justify the Christian synthesis, Augustine, in his *City of God*, compared the Christians to the ancient Hebrews, who had taken the "spoils of the

Egyptians" on the journey toward the Promised Land. He argued
that the "spoils" of pagan culture were similarly licit and necessary
for the Christians in their pilgrimage toward salvation. In modern
times, the Enlightenment undermined the Christian synthesis by revitalizing pagan attitudes that had been carried dormant through
history with Christianity. Thereupon, when it became evident that
the west could escape from Christian domination, the question arose
of whether and how to utilize the Christian mythopoesis in a new
synthesis. The romantics answered that question by deliberately taking enormous "spoils of the Christians."

During the decline of the Old Regime, the transporting of reality
from the other world to this was expected to destroy religion, just as
the rule of reason was expected to employ the muses in useful work.
Theology did decline, but religion perdured and art declared its independence of patronizing restraints. Yet the experiences in whose grip
one is transported beyond experience remained unexplained.[3] For
the Enlightenment probably fell most short of its goals in aesthetic
matters, especially music, whose origins and effects were likened to
that most dangerous opiate, religion. Paradoxically, by suspecting
music and religion at once, the Enlightenment inadvertantly reinforced their historic intimacy.

Regarding the possible utility of supposed superstition, the romantics usually believed that if secularization threatened historic
religious mythic patterns and ritual practices, it thereby threatened
the means by which countless human beings gave voice to their
deepest feelings about the ultimate meaning of living and dying.
Several brilliant scholarly works have elucidated how romantics used
the traditional mythopoetic patterns to formulate a modern world
view.[4] One of the most outstanding such works, M. H. Abrams's
Natural Supernaturalism, emphasizes literature, as is appropriate in
a work centered upon the bibliocratic tradition of England and northern Germany, "two great Protestant nations." Since the present study
emphasizes music, it has been appropriate for me to give equal
weight to the Catholic tradition, whose ritual was the locus for much
of the nonliterary framing of the western mentality.

The key to understanding the role of music in society is in fact
an understanding of the close relationship between music and religion, not necessarily religion in a strictly ecclesiastical sense, but in
the sense of a set of primary symbols which harmonize diverse experiences. The impulse which created religious and quasi-religious
music from the time of the French Revolution to the later nineteenth

century continued even in cultural situations where God and ecclesiastical religion were rejected. In such situations the impulse was— and is—translated into related forms of activity such as revolutionary cults, utopian rituals, idealization of art and artists, nationalism, socialism, or educational designs intended to enhance the quality of life.[5]

Understanding the relationship between music and religion requires attention to the complex religious geography of Europe. For example, pietism was as important to the German musical tradition as it was to the quasi-Protestant character of the Aufklärung which was metamorphosed into German romanticism. Likewise, Catholicism was as important to the music of Austria, France, and Italy as it was dialectically bound to the liberal, statist, and socialist rivals of the church in those countries. Each relationship is further reinforced and complicated by the relations between popular and establishment religions.

Such religious and quasi-religious fusions of transcendant reality with sensual experience were meant to arouse human consciousness to the possibility of a more pervasive sacredness incarnate in this world. However, in the minds of some religious conservatives such syncretism evidenced only a failure of nerve. Nevertheless, religious tories did come close to defining the historical significance of romanticism by defining it in phrases such as T. E. Hulme's "spilt religion." For just as romanticism was a continuation of the Enlightenment's exploration, so too, was it the reinterpretation of the Judeo-Christian tradition, albeit often in a nonliteral, inferential, artistic mode.

III

Among the differing romantic formulations of basic questions concerning human society and the human psyche one can discern a coherent theme. Its gist is that all things are implicated with one another.

Socially, the romantics were above all communitarians. It is only by a historical oversimplification that they are stereotyped as individualistic, egocentric, aesthete and effete, antisocial misfits and dropouts, preoccupied primarily with their personal feelings. In fact, such a narrow interpretation overlooks some major results of the era. The concern with the alienation and frustration engendered by civilization reinvigorated historic sources of communal solidarity. The romantics also founded new institutions and movements to liberate and enfranchise all of humanity. The study of earlier customs revealed that music always had been an integral part of public celebrations and a means of combining free individual expression with social regulation. Music was therefore an apt metaphor of community. Furthermore, although music is expressed and perceived differently by each individual who is performing or listening, it does seem to unite everyone present into a unique entity greater than the mere sum of its parts.

Psychologically, the romantics taught the reintegration of the psyche by insisting that the constant reciprocal influence between the conscious and the subconscious is normal. Amid the disintegration of the old mythopoetic interpretations which had harmonized one's perception of divergent phenomena, the romantics taught the reintegration of the human person through artistic imagination and activity. New designs for educating a healthy personality used music to exemplify and train a harmonious interplay among every aspect of human nature whether it be conscious, subconscious, mental, physical, internal, or environmental.

Since music seemed to embrace a whole complex of otherwise irreconcilable juxtapositions, it became the favorite metaphor of the balanced psyche and community. Because of this complexity and uniqueness, music remained the most elusive of the arts in the face of literal analysis. Hence many intellectual and cultural historians who have convincingly examined other art forms within the framework of social and political development have neglected music. Studies that rely mainly on the silent, private medium of printed literature rather than the vocal, public, arts may minimize the essentially communitarian and integrative functions of romanticism. Since virtually all the leading thinkers of the romantic epoch agreed on the social significance of music, the relative void in its scholarly treatment as a cultural phenomenon is unfortunate.

IV

Like the children of immigrants in a new land, the scholars of the post romantic century often seemed ashamed of idols of their parents.

Romantic patterns of thinking and creating seemed either to be barriers against further progress of technology, sources of dangerous antirational insanity, or not tough-mindedly irrational enough. The fact is that the west remains dialectically embraced in romanticism. For we are more often struggling to cast off the clichés used to oversimplify it than we are actually operating outside any known limits of the romantic synthesis.[6]

For us in the late twentieth century, romanticism has become ancestral rather than parental. It should therefore be easier to see in perspective. The romantics were in a position like ours—following wars of previously unthinkable violence, living through revolutions accomplished or invited in politics and economics, outliving their gods, and on the waning margin of surrogate faiths such as (in those days) the Enlightenment and (today) Marxism, psychoanalysis, and social science.

Thus the romantics have become the useful and beloved past of the industrial world. Today one hears of the debt which the current generation of social thinkers owes to the generation of Freud and Wittgenstein, who in turn stand in debt to the generation of Marx, which was, as we have seen, in debt to the romantic generation.

Each autumn of romanticism has therefore become a second spring. For we still attempt to live astride that line between the high and the low; to mediate between the rational and the irrational; to make explicit the decisive role of subconscious motivations in conscious behavior; to stand at the point where all sources of data, internal and external, impinging upon the human psyche, intersect prior to being formed into intellectual constructs; to combine the sublime and the grotesque, the formal and the free;[7] and to balance the positivistic spirit of the times, whose apparent success is quantified daily on the map and in statistics, with a whole-making concern for the qualitative side of life. This romantic concern with balance was symbolized most succinctly in the idea that the complete human being is androgynous. Our enlightened reasoning, stereotypically masculine, geometrical, and conscious "day" side and our romantic, dreaming, stereotypically feminine, musical, and subconscious "night" side, are but two aspects of the same thing.

If insights cross, as they do, although in disguised form, from one aspect or locus of the human psyche to another, then the explorers, restorers, and rebuilders of western myth and ritual were forecasting, educating the next epoch's "cluster of geniuses,[8] from Marx to Freud, who have since continued the exploration and made a transvalued science follow where *mousiké*—the musical instinct—leads. The first explorers, therefore who grasped the torch of enlightenment in the time of Diderot's *Rameau's Nephew* and Jean-Jacques Rousseau, carried it deeper into the cave, and passed it to that new cluster of geniuses who lived astride the line between the traditional eastern and progressive western, Catholic and Protestant, amateur and academic, Christian and Jewish, southern and northern cultures of Europe, that cluster of geniuses who began as humanists and who have formed our modern ego and its consciousness.

APPENDIXES

APPENDIX 1

Cultural Anthropology and the Translation of Values

The psychic revolution included a transvaluation of old beliefs to the extent that the new religion of humanity and human feelings might be said to continue rather than to abolish the old. This thesis can be clarified by employing the methods of definition used in structural anthropology. For example, Clifford Geertz states that "a religion is: (1) a system of symbols which acts to (2) establish powerful, pervasive, and long-lasting moods and motivations in men by (3) formulating conceptions of a general order of existence and (4) clothing these conceptions with such an aura of factuality that (5) the moods and motivations seem uniquely realistic."[1]

We note that there is here nothing necessarily supernatural or of "God." Second, the definition is purified by being abstracted from society. Third, it defines *a* religion, not religion. That is, it defines that which is religion within a cultural system. Religion is synoptic and will contain symbols from other social and psychological aspects of a culture. The big question is whether this definition and under what circumstances this definition applies to any pervasive ideology. But perhaps that puts the question backward. The true thrust of the structural approach to religion would be to say that if an ideology or way of looking at things becomes pervasive enough, we should look for ways to understand how it expresses the unconscious patterning of thought that occurs in a culture and, therefore, in minds nurtured within it. For example, the values and viewpoint of Christianity might be internalized and effective long after its conscious observances cease in an individual. Just as an acute listener can recognize the work of a composer or performer after only a bar or two of music, so should the cultural historian or anthropologist be able to ascribe the proper source of an example from the system of axioms and postulates which encode and define a particular culture.

A cultural historian should, of course, avoid two extremes. One, that iron laws of cause and effect determine everything in history, as if Napoleon's invasion caused Beethoven's music. The other extreme is to think that there is no reason for things to be together, as if Beethoven's music would be the same had he composed it while at Columbia on a Guggenheim grant. Rather, the cultural historian assumes and concludes that things are not together unless they belong together, but he should not pontificate. Things being together include sequential relationships forward and back in time as we inherit and entail the past. Things together obviously also include lateral relationships with contemporary realities. Therefore, while we try to dissect the layers and parts of a cultural system, we must always keep our eyes on the whole.

Of a total cultural system, which cannot be defined otherwise than as a religion, we must always ask the question, What did this mean to the believers? If we keep in mind that people of common sense do not throw away all that their environment has taught them even when they say they do, but keep the code of their old languages even when they spell new communications with its symbols, we may be on our way to understanding cultural language.

The most translatable part of a cultural language is myth, according to Lévi-Strauss.[2] Myth is part of an arbitrary language in which one can write many equations which reach the same conclusion: Although the specific expressions of myth may be poetry, art, or life styles which cannot be translated except at the cost of serious distortions, myth is almost the contrary. If there is a meaning to be found in mythology, it does not reside in the isolated elements or ritual which incarnate myth but in all expressions, wherever and whenever. And so, secondly, myth is part of language where the formula *traduttore, traditore* (translator, traitor) reaches its lowest truth value. Third, these special properties of myth are to be found above the ordinary linguistic level. That is, they are more complex than the features found in any other kind of linguistic expressions. Just as in languages there are phonemes, units of sound, pitch, length, etc., are there *mythemes* in myths? Yes, according to Lévi-Strauss. These gross constituents of a myth consist of relationships, not isolated but "in bundles."[3] One of the conclusions which Lévi-Strauss reaches is that although the growth of a myth is a continuous process, the structure of a myth remains discontinuous. That is, different versions may have very different nomenclature and still declare the same relationships. For example, in western culture, Freud's telling of the Oedipus complex in terms of upper-middle-class Vienna of 1900 is a part of the myth along with Sophocles' Athenian version. So, too, the New World "new consciousness" is part of the Christian myth.

Another conclusion is that the kind of logic exhibited in mythical thought is as rigorous as that of modern science, and that the difference lies not in the quality of the intellectual process, but in the nature of the things to which it is applied.

This is well in agreement with the situations known to prevail in technology: What makes a steel ax superior to a stone ax is not that the first one is better made than the second. They are equally well made, but steel is quite different from stone. In the same way we may be able to show that the same logical processes operate in myth as in science, and that man has always been thinking equally well; the improvement lies, not in an alleged progress of man's mind, but in the discovery of new areas to which it may apply its unchanged and unchanging powers.[4]

An application of the structural anthropologist's approach to the language of myth can be seen in my investigation of the recurring structure lying beneath the apparent change occurring in any period of western civilization.

APPENDIX 2

A Provincial Fête

A revolutionary morality play in the Gallican-Gothic style at Perpignan, capital of Roussillon, in February 1790 demonstrated a degree of formality somewhere between spontaneous demonstrations and the elaborate festivals in Paris. The play was a lesson for the aristocrats of the town.

One hundred and twenty men of the Garde Nationale, led by their officers carrying a banner inscribed "Long live Liberty," began the procession. "The soldiers carried wreaths of flowers and garlands of laurels all the while singing, in a martial spirit, a song suitable to the occasion." The first wagon of the pageant carried garlands, inscriptions, and a cask of "wine for the people." On the front of the cask one could read "It flows only for good patriots." A second wagon bore a staved-in barrel inscribed "Repository of feudal rights" and addressed to the princes of Germany, whither so many *émigrés* had already departed.

After this second wagon walked an elegantly dressed man, supported by a pair of enchained slaves; he represented an aristocrat, and wore as an emblem a two-faced mask. Following was a numerous court. When all this throng had arrived at the most popular square in the town, the order to halt was given, and a toast was proposed to the health of the good King Louis XVI, father of the people, and restorer of French liberty. A unanimous cry of "Long live the good King!" was heard, and thirty musicians sounded a fanfare. The aristocrat gnashed his teeth, and made an effort to disturb this solemn moment. . . . A royal courier, perfectly garbed, appeared on the scene and delivered a dispatch to the commander: it contained the speech which the King had given at the memorable session of the fourth, and a letter supposedly written by the President of the National Assembly to the good people, of Roussillon. These the second in command read in a loud voice. At each comforting word for the people, the aristocrat grew pale, and at the moment when he heard these words [of the King], "Let us profess . . . . attachment to the Constitution, "he fell over backward. People rushed to his aid. A doctor having examined him, cried "*He is dead!* It is the effect of sudden grief." Immediately he was placed on the second wagon, and a great number of people of every description, dressed in black and wearing mourning ruffles, came forward to follow the body. The commander thereupon cried out "Since no more enemies exist, let us drink to union, peace, and concord!" People drank lustily, and the band played an air suitable to the occasion.[1]

More than ten thousand persons are said to have witnessed "this truly comic scene."

NOTES

INTRODUCTION

1. Leslie Fiedler, *Love and Death in the American Novel* (New York, 1966), passim.
2. *Aisthanomai*, the Greek root of "aesthetics," means "I perceive," "see," or "learn"; "I feel," in the physical sense. Thus, aesthetic perception was not a mere sentiment but part of the objective cosmos.
3. M. H. Abrams, *The Mirror and the Lamp: Romantic Theory and the Critical Tradition* (New York, 1958), passim.
4. Sylvia L. Thrupp, ed., *Millennial Dreams in Action: Studies in Revolutionary Religious Movements* (New York, 1970), p. 13.

CHAPTER 1

1. Peter Gay, *The Enlightenment: An Interpretation*, I: *The Rise of Modern Paganism* (New York, 1967), p. 26.
2. Gay, *The Enlightenment*, II: *The Science of Freedom* (New York, 1969), p. 25.
3. Fiedler, passim.
4. Abrams, 1–46.
5. Jean-Jacques Rousseau, "Imitation," in *Dictionnaire de la musique, Ecrits sur la musique* (Paris, 1839).
6. Some of the philosophes delivered diatribes against "absolute music," as Rousseau did in his article "Sonate" in his *Dictionnaire*.
7. Gay, I, 178.

8. A. R. Oliver, *The Encyclopedists as Critics of Music* (New York, 1947), p. 4.
9. Joseph Kerman, *Opera as Drama* (New York, 1956), p. 13.
10. Oliver, p. 49.
11. Kerman, p. 61.
12. Oliver, p. 48.
13. "Grand opera is a visual art for a large audience. Obviously, subtle gestures and facial expressions will not carry to such an assembly eager for spectacle. . . .

    "To generalize, in operas—as in all public displays—convention rules and petty realism does not matter. Ritual makes clear the intention, which is why opera calls for gorgeous costume, costume magnified beyond credibility and the power to sit down, as in the real life of the eighteenth century.

    "In earlier centuries, and notably in the age of Shakespeare, the playhouse used to afford this same spectacle of gorgeousness." Jacques Barzun, "Why Opera?" *Opera News*, 28 January 1967, pp. 7–9.
14. Jean-Philippe Rameau, *Démonstration du principe de l'harmonie* (Paris, 1750), Préface, pp. vi–viii. Oliver, pp. 100ff.
15. Michael T. Cartwright, "Diderot critique d'art et le problème de l'expression," *Diderot Studies*, XIII (1969), 247–56; Paul Henry Lang, "Diderot as Musician," *Diderot Studies*, XI (1968), 95–107; Oliver, p. 167.
16. See Charles B. Paul, "Music and Ideology: Rameau, Rousseau, and 1789," *Journal of the History of Ideas*, XXXII (1971), 396–99. The life and work of Jean-Jacques Rousseau revolve so completely around an attempt to answer this sort of question that I must allude to his influence in almost every subsequent chapter.
17. Denis Diderot, *Le neveu de Rameau*, in *Oeuvres complètes* (Paris, 1876), X, 330. Cf. Herbert Josephs, *Diderot's Dialogue of Language and Gestures* (Columbus, Ohio, 1969). *Le neveu* was completed in 1761 but circulated only in manuscripts until 1805, when Goethe published a German translation. Versions in French and other languages soon followed, although a manuscript in Diderot's own hand was discovered only in 1891. See Arthur W. Wilson, *Diderot* (New York, 1972), pp. 415–24, passim. Jacques Barzun, Preface to his translation *Rameau's Nephew* (Indianapolis, 1956), pp. 3–4.
18. Diderot, p. 361.
19. Ibid., p. 377.
20. Ibid., p. 385.
21. Fiedler, *Love and Death*, passim.
22. Mme. de Staël, *De l'Allemagne* (Paris, 1958), V, 357–66.
23. George M. Frederickson, *The Black Image in the White Mind* (New York, 1971).

24. Edmund Burke, in *Philosophical Enquiry into the Origin of our Ideas of the Sublime and Beautiful* and *Reflections on the Revolution in France* (New York, 1958).

25. R. M. Longyear, *Schiller and Music* (Chapel Hill, N.C., 1966), pp. 7, 15.

26. Ibid., pp. 8ff.

27. Ibid.

28. M. G. Flaherty, "Opera and Incipient Romantic Aesthetics in Germany," *Studies in Eighteenth Century Culture*, III: *Racism in the Eighteenth Century* (Cleveland, 1973), p. 207. Schiller may have been angry that Italian operas were more popular than his German plays.

29. Longyear, p. 124. Gluck's opera was first performed in 1778; Goethe's play on the same subject was completed in 1787.

30. Longyear, p. 123.

31. Flaherty, p. 214. Perhaps the enthusiasm for Shakespeare, which we still share, received its first impulse from Gottfried Lessing (1729–81). He dared to rank Shakespeare ahead of Corneille, Racine, and Voltaire as a dramatist. For this insult to Voltaire, Frederick the Great of Prussia denied Lessing an appointment. In *Laokoön* (1766) Lessing asserted that each art has its peculiar function. Such a statement tended to abolish the classical hierarchy which had ranked music low among the arts because it was deemed the least verbal, and therefore the least exact and rational.

32. The Greek derivation of basic terms in Christian theology and, therefore, in western thought is essential for comprehending the roots of the western intellectual tradition. When these terms were first employed *koine* (colloquial Greek) was still the middle eastern *lingua franca. Leitourgia* (liturgies), in the sense of "things or actions done for the community = Latin *opera* (singular: *opus*).

33. Act II, scene vii.

34. Longyear, p. 34.

35. Ibid., pp. 36–47.

36. Ibid., p. 30. See chapter 2.

37. Longyear, p. 104.

38. Friedrich Schiller, *On the Aesthetic Education of Man in a Series of Letters*, trans. Reginald Snell (New York, 1965), p. 105.

39. Leonard P. Wessell, Jr., "Schiller and the Genesis of German Romanticism," *Studies in Romanticism*," X (1971), pp. 187–190; Longyear, *Schiller*, pp. 196–197.

40. Schiller, p. 16.

41. Longyear, p. 103.

42. See Ilse Graham, *Schiller's Drama: Talent and Integrity* (New York, 1974), passim.

43. Schiller, p. 105.

44. Friedrich Schiller, "Über naive und sentimentalische Dichtung," *Sämtliche Werke, Säkular-Ausgabe* (Leipzig, n.d.), XII, 209.
45. Cf. Paul F. Marks, "The Application of the Aesthetics of Music in the Philosophy of the *Sturm und Drang*: Hamann and Herder," *Studies in Eighteenth-Century Culture*, III: *Racism in the Eighteenth Century* (Cleveland, 1973), pp. 219–38.
46. Longyear, pp. 110f.
47. Ibid., p. 118.
48. Ibid., p. 127.
49. Ibid., p. 19.
50. Ibid., pp. 20f. See also Romain Rolland, "Goethe's Interest in Music," *The Musical Quarterly*, XVII (1931), 157–94. Neither did Goethe care for what Beethoven and other eminent musicians did to his lyrics or the old German chorales. "Certainly not anti-Christian, not unchristian, but assuredly non-Christian," Goethe once described himself in a letter. Karl Viëtor, *Goethe the Thinker* (Cambridge, 1950), p. 87. Goethe also said: "The so-called improvements done on our songs repel me. They are all right for those with plenty of head and little heart. A hymn is worth singing only if it lifts my soul to the rapture which was the poet's. This will happen but rarely should our pedants make us sing like snobs more worried about footnotes than music." Knipfer, *Das kirchliche Volkslied* (Bielefeld and Leipzig, 1875), p. 232. Of the irrationalities found in hymns he said: Superstition is the poetry of life; the poet, therefore, suffers no harm from being superstitious." Goethe, *Sämtliche Werke, Jubiläums-Ausgabe* (Stuttgart and Berlin, 1902–7), XL, 168.
51. Longyear, p. 126.
52. Ibid., p. 21.
53. *Encyclopaedia Britannica*, X, 470; Longyear, p. 18.
54. See chapter 10.
55. Longyear, p. 117.
56. W. H. Bruford, *Culture and Society in Classical Weimar* (London, 1962), pp. 365–66.
57. Paul Henry Lang, "The Patrimonium Musicae Sacrae and the Task of Sacred Music Today," *Sacred Music*, XCIII, (Winter, 1966–67), 124.
58. Walter Emery, "Bach and his Time," in Arthur Jacobs, ed., *Choral Music* (Baltimore, 1963), pp. 122ff. Otto Ursprung, *Restauration und Palestrina-Renaissance in der katholischen Kirchenmusik* (Augsburg, 1924), p. 14.
59. Francis Fergusson, *The Idea of a Theatre* (Princeton, 1968), pp. 1–12, 95–142.
60. Paul Henry Lang, *Music in Western Civilization* (New York, 1941), p. 702.

61. Mosco Carner, "The Mass—from Rossini to Dvořák," in Jacobs, *Choral Music*, p. 232.
62. Romano Guardini, *The Spirit of the Liturgy*, trans. Ada Lane (New York, 1935), pp. 171–84. The Viennese school of classical composers were in a sense pupils of the eighteenth-century Italians. E. J. Dent, "Italian Opera in the Eighteenth Century, and its Influence on the Music of the Classical Period," *Sammelbände der Internationalen Musikgesellschaft*, XIV (1912–13), 509.
63. Roger Fiske, "The Viennese Classical Period," in Jacobs, *Choral Music*, p. 165.
64. Adam Gottron, "Musik in sechs mittelrheinischen Männerklöstern im 18. Jahrhundert," *Studien zur Musikwissenschaft*, XXV (1962), 230.
65. Cf. Jean Starobinski, *The Invention of Liberty* (Geneva, 1964).
66. Paul Henry Lang, "The Enlightenment and Music," *Eighteenth-Century Studies*, I (1967–68), 108.

CHAPTER 2

1. Jules Michelet, *Histoire de la Révolution Française*, II (Paris, 1952), pp. 543ff.
2. Cf. Antonin Artaud, *The Theater and Its Double* (New York, 1958), passim.
3. Cf. Alexander L. Ringer, "J.-J. Barthélemy and Musical Utopia in Revolutionary France," *Journal of the History of Ideas*, XXII (July-September, 1961), 356; James A. Leith, *The Idea of Art as Propaganda in France, 1750–1799* (Toronto, 1965), pp. 15ff.
4. Robert R. Palmer, *The Age of Democratic Revolution*, I, (Princeton, 1964), 356. See also Leith.
5. Georg Knepler, *Musikgeschichte des 19. Jahrhunderts* (Berlin, 1961), I, 111–210. Julien Tiersot, *Les fêtes et les chants de la Révolution Française* (Paris, 1908), p. 37.
6. Cornwell Burnham Rogers, *The Spirit of Revolution in 1789, A Study of Public Opinion as Revealed in Political Songs and Other Popular Literature at the Beginning of the French Revolution* (Princeton, 1949), pp. 5–17.
7. Alphonse Aulard, *Le culte de la raison et le culte de l'Etre suprême* (Paris, 1892), pp. vii–viii.
8. Gay, *The Enlightenment*, I.
9. Cf. Albert Soboul, "Sentiment religieux et cultes populaires pendant la Révolution: Saintes patriotes et martyrs de la liberté," *Annales historiques de la Révolution Française*, XXIX (1957), 193–213.

10. Ferdinand Brunot, "Le culte catholique en français sous la Révolution," *Annales Historiques de la Révolution Française*, II (1925), 208–9.

11.   Vive ce moment fortuné
      Où tout ainsi qu'un nouveau'né,
      Le Royaume est régénéré! [Quoted in Rogers, pp. 57–58.]

12. Ibid., p. 11.

13.   Les vignes qu'on croyait être gelées,
      Présentent des grappes en quantité;
      Ah! quel miracle que celui-là!

14. Constant Pierre, *Musique des fêtes et cérémonies de la Révolution* (Paris, 1899), p. iii.

15.   Après avoir été
      Longtemps dans la misère
      Et près de succomber
      Dans nos pauvres chaumières;
      LOUIS, notre bon Père,
      Pour guérir tous nos maux,
      Convoque, en cette affaire,
      Les Etats-Généraux. [Ibid., p. 88.]

16.   Sans doute le grand Necker
      Est vainqueur de l'enfer [*bis*]
      Car il foule aux pieds Lucifer,
      La Discorde et l'Envie
      Ah! c'est un bras de fer
      Qui rompt la Calomnie. [*bis*] [Rogers, p. 97.]

17.   Parmi le trouble et la fureur,
      Effet d'un Ministre oppresseur,
      Necker parut comme un Sauveur.
          Alleluia. [Ibid., p. 94.]

18.   Beati qui non viderunt,
      Et firmiter crediderunt,
      Vitam aeternam habebunt. Alleluia. [*St. Gregory Hymnal*, Philadelphia, 1947, p. 247].

19.   Cette auguste Assemblée
      De Héros, d'Immortels
      Gémit, et desolée,
      Lui dresse des autels. [Ibid., p. 118.]

20.   Notre S. Père est un dindon,
      Le calotin est un fripon,
      Notre Archevêque un scélérat.
          Alleluia. [Ibid., p. 200.]

21. Knepler, I, 111.

22. Rogers, p. 211.

23. Ibid., p. 16.

24. Ibid., p. 212.

25. See the psalms usually sung at Compline, the evening rite of the Roman Catholic Latin Office: "Deus in adjutorium meum intende," etc.

26. Marvin Carlson, *The Theatre of the French Revolution* (Ithaca, 1966), p. 45.

27. See Appendix 2 for an example of a provincial rite which changed the content but retained the style of a medieval morality play.

28. Michelet, I, 423–24; David L. Dowd, "Art as Propaganda in the French Revolution: A Study of Jacques-Louis David" (University of California, Ph.D. Thesis, 1946), p. 69.

29. Dowd, pp. 70–82.

30. Peuple, éveille-toi, romps tes fers
    Remonte à ta grandeur première,
    Comme un jour Dieu du haut des airs
    Rappellera les morts à la lumière,
    Du sein de la poussière,
    Et ranimera l'univers! [*La Révolution Française* (Paris: Guilde internationale du disque), p. 29 of the booklet which accompanies the six records.]

31. See, for example, Jacques Ellul, *La technique* (Paris, 1954), passim.

32. Carlson, p. 109.

33. Dowd, pp. 17–20.

34. Brunot, passim. The sacramentary is a liturgical book which contains only those parts of the Mass which pertain to the priest or celebrant of the service. Presumably, if the sacramentary is translated, the rest of the missal, which also contains those prayers, readings, and actions pertaining to the assistant ministers, choir, and people, would already be translated.

35. Brunot, passim.

36. Jean-Jacques Rousseau, *Lettre à M. d'Alembert sur les Spectacles* (Geneva, 1948), p. 168; Paul Landormy, *La musique française de la Marseillaise à la mort de Berlioz* (Paris, 1944), pp. 7–12.

37. Tiersot, xxvi. See also Romain Rolland, *The People's Theater*, trans. Barrett H. Clark (New York, 1918), pp. 63ff. and passim.

38. Knepler, I, 115; cf. Dowd, pp. 131ff. See also: Warren D. Anderson, *Ethos and Education in Greek Music: The Evidence of Poetry and Philosophy* (Cambridge, 1966), passim; Werner Jaeger, *Paideia* (New York, 1962–63), I, 299ff; II, 227–29; III, 250f; Harold T. Parker, *The Cult of Antiquity and the French Revolutionaries* (New York, 1965), passim; Leith, pp. 158ff.

39. Montesquieu, *De l'esprit des loix* (Paris, 1950), I, 84ff.

40. Voltaire, *Œuvres complètes* (Paris, 1877), "L'orphelin de la Chine," V, 320; "Les Guèbres ou la tolérance," VI, 490.

41. Jean-Jacques Rousseau, *Œuvres complètes* (Paris, 1824), V, 264.

42. Denis Diderot, *Œuvres complètes* (Paris, 1876), "Essai sur la peinture," X, 502–4; "De la poésie dramatique," VII, 313. Diderot omitted music in his survey of the fine arts and architecture (cf. "Essai").

43. Montesquieu, *De l'esprit des loix*, I, 44.

44. J.-J. Barthélemy, *Voyages du jeune Anacharsis en Grèce dans le milieu du quatrième siècle avant l'ère vulgaire* (Paris, 1788), II, 150.

45. Cf. Ringer, pp. 360ff.

46. Jules Combarieu, *Histoire de la musique des origines au début du XXᵉ siècle* (Paris, 1920), II, 383.

47. Dowd, p. 8.

48. Pierre Trahard, *La sensibilité révolutionnaire* (Paris, 1936), p. 43.

49. Ibid., p. 42.

50. François Benoit, *L'Art française sous la Révolution et l'Empire* (Paris, 1897), p. 3.

51. J. W. Mackail, "Patriotism," *Classical Studies* (New York, 1925), p. 241.

52. Julien Tiersot, "Notes sur les chansons de la période révolutionnaire," *Revue musicale*, 1904, p. 180.

53. Cf. Dowd, pp. 131–34.

54. Palmer, II, 124.

55. Ibid., p. 358.

56. Jean Leflon, *Pie VII* (Paris, 1958), p. 434. The translation is from Palmer, II, p. 316.

57. James A. Leith, "Music as an Ideological Weapon in the French Revolution," *The Canadian Historical Association, Annual Report*, 1966, p. 133.

58. O Liberté, Liberté sainte!
    Déesse d'un peuple éclairé!
    Règne aujourd'hui dans cette enceinte,
    Par toi ce temple est épuré!
    Liberté! devant toi, la raison chasse l'imposture;
    L'erreur s'enfuit, le fanatisme est abattu,
    Notre évangile est la nature,
    Et notre culte est la vertu.

    .   .   .   .

    Aimer sa Patrie et ses frères,
    Servir le Peuple souverain,
    Voilà les sacrés caractères,
    Et la foi d'un Républicain.
    D'un enfer chimérique
    Il ne craint point la vaine flamme;
    D'un ciel menteur
    Il n'attend point les faux trésors;

Le ciel est dans la paix de l'âme,
Et l'enfer est dans les remords. [*La Révolution Française*, p. 30.]

59. Soutiens contre de vils esclaves
La République et ses enfants.
Notre cause est juste, ils sont braves,
Fais-les revenir triomphants.
Quand par eux des tyrans
La rage impuissante est punie,
Veillons pour eux,
Et que la France, à leur retour,
Leur offre une famille unie
Par la nature et par l'amour.

[Ibid.] Judging from a recording, Lesueur was probably fitting old music to new words, some of which are accommodated only with difficulty. His melody in a minor key—an "ancient" mode?—and ⅜ time repeats the last line of each stanza three times before resting in its final cadence. See Leith, "Music as an Ideological Weapon," pp. 127ff. for examples of songs which mingled familiar Latin words like *te deum* with revolutionary jargon like *maximum*.

60. Dowd, pp. 90–110.
61. Rogers, pp. 26f, 224ff.
62. *La Révolution Française*, p. 30.
63. Rogers, pp. 26–27; Jean-Baptiste LeClercq, *Essai sur la propagation de la musique en France* (Paris, an IV), p. 11.
64. Rogers, pp. 26–27.
65. Octave Fouque, *Les révolutionnaires de la musique* (Paris, 1882), pp. 73–86.
66. His brother, the great poet, André Chénier was executed in 1794.
67. Rogers, p. 262. Patriarchal gave way to matriarchal images like *la Patrie, la Liberté*, or *la Raison*; *Dieu* to *Déesses*.

Some primitive religions, such as those of the pre-Homeric Greeks, were evidently matriarchies, whose religions were fertility rites replete with female goddesses. Perhaps this underground, pre-Christian myth had been tacitly acknowledged in the medieval cult of Mary, Mother of God, and was now modernized in the revolutionary goddesses.

One strange such manifestation was the sect of la Mère de Dieu during the terror. It revolved around the visionary, Catherine Théot. Cf. G. Lenôtre [Louis Léon Théodore Gosselin], *Le mysticisme révolutionnaire, Robespierre et la "Mère de Dieu"* (Paris, 1926), passim.

68. Dowd, pp. 17–20 and passim.
69. During the Revolution the commune of Beauvais invited local musicians to place themselves at its disposal. So few volunteered that *l'Assemblée municipale* voted the musicians pay to attract them.

Since even that did not yield enough candidates, Beauvais founded a conservatory "with four professors." Maurice Dommanget, *La déchristianisation à Beauvais et dans l'Oise, 1790–1801* (Paris, 1922), p. 47. From the National Assembly to the Directory, sundry politicians issued proclamations commending musicians for their contributions during the Revolution. But one is little impressed with such eulogies or with paragraphs in music histories about the social role of revolutionary music in edifying the masses. Music histories are all written by musicians, who, like other artists, have to serve the dominant cult in order to survive during revolutions. The theorists and cults of opposing ideologies can seem almost identical from an artist's viewpoint. Ideological theorists often tell the artist to consecrate himself to tasks which preclude creativity.

70. Rogers, pp. 23–25.
71. Arthur Loesser, *Men, Women, and Pianos* (New York, 1954), p. 322.
72. Rogers, pp. 22ff; Pierre, pp. 122, 129.
73. Leith, "Music as an Ideological Weapon," p. 133.
74. Cf. Alphonse Aulard, *Christianity and the French Revolution*, trans. Lady Frazer (Boston, 1927), p. 107; Marie-Joseph Chénier, *Poésies* (Paris, 1844), p. 112.
75. Palmer, II, 150, 167, and passim.
76. J. H. Elliot, "The French Revolution: Beethoven and Berlioz," in Jacobs, *Choral Music*, p. 201.
77. Jules Combarieu, *Music, Its Laws and Evolution*, trans. F. Legge (New York, 1910), p. 200.
78. Combarieu, *Histoire*, II, 419.
79.   Père de l'Univers, suprême intelligence,
          Bienfaiteur ignoré des aveugles mortels
          Tu révélas ton être à la reconnaissance
          Qui seule éleva tes autels.
          Ton temple est sur les monts, dans les airs, sur les ondes
          Tu n'as point de passé, tu n'as point d'avenir;
          Et sans les occuper, tu remplis tous les mondes
          Qui ne te peuvent contenir.
     Constant Pierre, "L'Hymne à l'Etre Suprême enseigné au peuple par l'institut national de musique," *La Révolution Française*, I (1899), 53–64.
80. *Procès-verbaux du comité d'instruction publique de la Convention Nationale*, ed. M.-J. Guillaume (Paris, 1907), VI, 479.
81. Leith, "Music as an Ideological Weapon," p. 135. Barrel organs were available in some country churches even into the twentieth century.
82.   Unissez vos cœurs et vos bras,
          Enfants, citoyens, magistrats,
          Plantons l'arbre sacré,

L'honneur de ce rivage!
Que ton emblème, ô liberté
Soit le signal de la gaieté;
La tristesse en ce jour n'est que pour l'esclavage.
Les jeux, les chants sont un hommage
Pour les succès
Des Français! [*La Révolution Française*, p. 32.]

83. Paré de verdure et de fleurs,
Prairial aux champs nous appelle,
Des prés que sa faux renouvelle
Au Ciel consacrons les primeurs!
Nos autels sont leurs pyramides,
Leurs simples parfums notre encens.
L'abondance aux joyeaux accents
Chante sur leurs sommets humides.
Fille de la Nature, ô mère des vertus,
Lien des cœurs, sainte reconnaissance,
Viens, sur l'ingratitude et l'orgueil abattus
Fonder les lois et leur douce puissance! [Ibid.]

84. Jacques Barzun, *Of Human Freedom* (Philadelphia, 1964), pp. 56–59.

85. Cf. Dowd, p. 119, passim.

86. Barzun, *Of Human Freedom*, p. 55; Julien Tiersot, *Rouget de Lisle, son oeuvre, sa vie* (Paris, 1892), pp. 153–80.

87. Hermann Eichborn, "Studien zur Geschichte der Militärmusik," *Monatshefte für Musikgeschichte*, XXIV (1892), 93–118; Knepler, I, 137–42.

88. Anderson, passim; Théodore Gerold, *Les pères de l'Eglise et la musique* (Paris, 1931), passim.

89. See Barry Ulanov, "Music in the Church: A Declaration of Dependence," in *Crisis in Church Music* (Washington, 1967), p. 90.

90. Cf. Gay, pp. 352–55.

91. For example, much of the harpsichord music of the seventeenth century, Bach's "Sonata on the Departure of his Beloved Brother" with its post horn calls, and the "Musical Sledge Drive" by "classical" Mozart's father. Frederick Jackson Turner, *Mozart, The Man and His Works* (New York, 1966), pp. 4–5.

92. Arnold Schering, *Geschichte des Oratoriums* (Leipzig: 1911), pp. 9f.

Complete clericalization of the church's rites paralleled papal assertion of clerical supremacy over lay political officials in the High Middle Ages. According to the papal theory, laymen received status only by delegation, not by right.

Though some of these dramas were retained in the monastic liturgies of the later Middle Ages, all the roles were now performed by and for clerics in standard ecclesiastical vestments, as they now are in the Easter Vigil Service—complete with special props and several costume changes.

93. Wilhelm Dilthey, *Von deutscher Dichtung und Musik* (Berlin, 1933), pp. 193–96. Cf. Benjamin Hunningher, *The Origin of the Theater* (New York, 1961), passim; Cf. Johan Huizinga, *Homo Ludens* (Boston, 1966).

94. Roland H. Bainton, Review of *Naissance et affirmation de la réforme*, by Jean Delumeau, *American Historical Review*, LXXI (April 1966), 511.

95. Fouque, p. 4. Choir schools were called *maîtrises* in French.

96. Wilhelm Buschkoetter, *Jean François Lesueur, Eine Biographie* (Halle, 1912), p. 39.

97. Ibid., p. 17.

98. Felix Clément, *Histoire générale de la musique religieuse* (Paris, 1860), pp. 244, 252.

99. Buschkoetter, p. 39.

100. Mary Hargrave, *The Earlier French Musicians* (London, 1917), p. 21.

101. Fouque, p. 78; Buschkoetter, p. 35.

102. Buschkoetter, p. 39.

103. Ibid., pp. 38–40.

104. Felix Lamy, *Jean-François Lesueur, 1760–1837* (Paris, 1912), p. 126; Hector Berlioz, "Inauguration de la statue de Lesueur à Abbeville," *Journal des débats politiques et littéraires*, 27 août 1852, p. 1.

105. Berlioz, ibid.

106. Lamy, p. 127.

107. Jean-François Lesueur, *Exposé d'une musique, une, imitative, et particulière à chaque solemnité* [sic]; *où l'on donne les principes généraux sur lesquels on l'établit et le plan d'une musique propre à la fête du Noël. ... Pâques. ... Pentecôte* (Paris, 1787), p. 28.

108. Donald H. Foster, "The Oratorio in Paris in the Eighteenth-Century," *Acta Musicologica*, XLVII (1975), 67.

109. Parker, pp. 8–36.

110. Fouque, p. 47.

111. Lesueur, p. 21.

112. Karl Nef, "Die Passionsoratorien Jean-François Lesueurs," *Mélanges de musicologie offerts à M. Lionel de La Laurencie* (Paris, 1933), p. 266.

113. At Mass the Kyrie would intervene, but this would likely be shorter and more somber, a diversion which renders return to joyful music all the more forceful.

114. At Mass the gospel recitative and perhaps a sermon would intervene between the Sequence and the Credo. Still, a leitmotiv from the

Easter Sequence on Easter Day, sung to a congregation taught to regard its text as the justification of their corporate existence, would be no artificial thing.

115. Lesueur, pp. 28, 38, 65.
116. Ora Frishberg Saloman, "The Orchestra in Lesueur's Musical Aesthetics," *Musical Quarterly*, LX (1974), 620; Lang, "The Enlightenment and Music," p. 105; cf. Kant, *Kritik der Urteilskraft*, Par. 53. "The attraction of what generally can be conveyed in music seems to rest on the fact that every expression of speech is connected with a tone. This tone designates more or less an affect and elicits from the hearer the same idea that the composer had in mind, therefore all this takes place according to the law of associations." (Lang's translation.)
117. Combarieu, *Histoire de la musique*, III, 240.
118. Nef, p. 261.
119. Buschkoetter, p. 22.
120. Fouque, p. 132.
121. Ibid., p. 65.
122. Buschkoetter, p. 48.
123. Ibid., p. 41.
124. M.-J. Chénier, "Epître au musicien Le Sueur," *Poésies* (Paris, 1844), p. 112.
125. Buschkoetter, pp. 52ff.
126. We have noted his composition for the *Hymne pour l'inauguration d'un Temple de la Liberté* of 1793.
127. Knepler, I, 188–90.
128. Buschkoetter, pp. 59ff.
129. Ibid.
130. Tacitus, *Annales*.
131. Now the Church of La Madeleine in Paris. William Fleming, *Arts and Ideas* (New York, 1963), pp. 430–31, 622.
     The production that best caught the spirit of the new Empire, however, was Spontini's *La Vestale* (The Vestal Virgin). In 1807 Europe saw itself mirrored in an opera full of battles, full-voiced singing, maidens oppressed by tyrants, and a Roman setting.
132. Nef, p. 261; Paul Huot-Pleuroux, *Histoire de la musique religieuse* (Paris, 1957), pp. 300ff.
133. Combarieu, II, 438–41; Jean Mongredien, "La musique du sacre de Napoléon Ier," *Revue de Musicologie*, 1967, no. 2, pp. 137–74. Mendelssohn's later overture *Fingal's Cave* is a familiar example of the enduring influence of Ossian.
134. Fouque, p. 114; *Ossian*, exhibition at the Grand Palais, Paris, 15 February–15 April, 1974.
135. Fouque, pp. 136–63.

136. Hector Berlioz, *Memoirs, 1803–65*, trans. Holmes, rev. E. Newman (New York, 1935), p. 25.
137. Hector Berlioz, *Les musiciens et la musique* (Paris, n.d.[1903]), p. 59.
138. Nef, p. 261.
139. Berlioz, "Inauguration de la statue de Lesueur," p. 1.
140. Frédéric Hellouin, *Gossec et la musique française à la fin du XVIIIe siècle* (Paris, 1903), p. 188; Louis Dufrane, *Gossec, sa vie et ses œuvres* (Paris, 1927), pp. 199f.
141. Paul Huot-Pleuroux, *Histoire de la musique religieuse* (Paris, 1957), p. 289.
142. Schering, p. 516.
143. Cf. Dowd, pp. 34ff.
144. Combarieu, *Histoire*, II, 385.
145. Cf. Ringer, p. 367; Barzun, *Of Human Freedom*, passim.
146. Clément, p. 352; Joseph d'Ortigue, *La musique à l'église* (Paris, 1861), p. 244.
147. Combarieu, *Histoire*, III, 183ff.
148. Lang, *Music in Western Civilization*, pp. 734ff, 754ff.
149. Deryck Cooke, "Chorus and Symphony: Liszt, Mahler, and After," in Jacobs, *Choral Music*, p. 248.
150. Crane Brinton, *The Political Ideas of the English Romanticists* (Ann Arbor, 1966), p. 58.
151. Loesser, p. 261. See also Professor Barrows introduction to Hester Lynch Piozzi, *Observations and Reflections Made in the Course of a Journey Through France, Italy, and Germany* (Ann Arbor, 1967), pp. x–xii and *passim*.
152. Lode VanDessel, *The Influence of the French Composers of the Nineteenth Century on the Music of the Catholic Church* (unpublished Master's thesis, Wayne State University, 1953), pp. 11f.
153. Clement Greenberg, *Art and Culture* (Boston, 1965), p. 18, n. 5.
154. Gottfried Weber, "Ueber das Wesen des Kirchenstyls," *Cäcilia* [Mainz] III (1825), 125ff.
155. Lang, *Music in Western Civilization*, p. 769.
156. Ludwig van Beethoven, *Letters, Journals and Conversations*, Translated and edited by Michael Hamburger (New York, 1960), p. 168.
157. See chapter 6; Martin Cooper, *Beethoven: The Last Decade* (London, 1970), pp. 105–20; 276–348; see also Donald Mintz, "Mendelssohn and Romanticism," *Studies in Romanticism*, 1963–64, pp. 216–24.
158. Cooper, p. 119.
159. Beethoven, *Letters*, p. 82.
Paul Bekker, *Beethoven*, trans. Bozman (London, 1925), p. 148.

160. Arnold Schmitz, "Zum Verstaendnis des Gloria in Beethovens Missa Solemnis," in Abert, ed., *Festschrift Friedrich Blume* (Basel, 1963), p. 320.
161. Ralph Vaughan-Williams, "Some Thoughts on Beethoven's Choral Symphony," in *National Music and Other Essays* (London, 1963), pp. 82ff.
162. Lang, *Music in Western Civilization*, p. 758.
163. Combarieu, *Histoire*, II, 686.
164. Bekker, p. 265.
165. Ibid., p. 268.
166. Jacques Barzun, *Berlioz and the Romantic Century*, 2-vol. ed. (Boston, 1950), I, 104.
167. Joseph d'Ortigue, *Le balcon de l'opéra* (Paris, 1833), pp. 363ff.
168. Clément, p. 353; Fan Stylian Noli, *Beethoven and the French Revolution* (New York, 1947), passim.
169. *Correspondence of Liszt and Wagner*, trans. Francis Heuffer (New York, 1889), II, 92ff. Wagner was, of course, trying the same thing.
170. Cooke, in Jacobs, p. 248.
171. Ibid., pp. 257ff.
172. Fouque, p. 114.
173. Ibid., pp. 164–83.
174. French musicians theoretically governed themselves as professionals through the Conservatoire, which Napoleon I erected out of the musical sections of the Garde Nationale. Its first inspectors were the musical revolutionaries Méhul, Gossec, Grétry, Lesueur, and the aloof and anti-Napoleonic Cherubini. Louis XVIII and Charles X disliked the idea of servants achieving independence under revolutions and usurpers; the Bourgeois King, Louis-Philippe, thought that a Conservatoire for musicians was a needless extravagance. All three trimmed its budget until Napoleon III again found it a source of *gloire*.
175. Jacques Barzun, *The Energies of Art* (New York, 1962), pp. 302–3.
176. Ibid., p. 301.
177. Hector Berlioz, *New Letters*, ed. Jacques Barzun (New York, 1954), pp. 43–44.
    The *Te Deum* was first performed in 1855 after the restoration of the French Empire. Berlioz intended to portray the glory of the First Consul, greeted by armies, choirs, bells, and organ when he entered the church. Sacheverell Sitwell, *Liszt* (Boston, 1934), p. 194.
178. Elliot, in Jacobs, p. 213.
179. Jacques Barzun, *Berlioz and His Century, An Introduction to the Age of Romanticism* (New York, 1956), p. 323.
180. Franz Liszt, *Gesammelte Schriften*, trans. L. Kamman (Leipzig, 1881), II, 55–57.

181. Barzun, *Berlioz and His Century*, p. 104.
182. Liszt, *Gesammelte Schriften*, II, 53. See also Wilfred Mellers, *Man and His Music*, IV: *Romanticism and the Twentieth Centutry* (London, 1957), p. 45.
183. See chapter 1.
184. Jacques Poisson, *Le romantisme social de Lamennais, 1833–1854* (Paris, 1931), p. 152.
185. Franz Liszt, *Letters*. Comp. and ed. La Mara. Trans. Constance Bache (London, 1894), I, 15.
186. Raymond Leslie Evans, *Les romantiques français et la musique* (Paris, 1934), p. 136.
187. Poisson, p. 373.
188. Liszt, *Gesammelte Schriften*, II, 245.
189. Paul Charreire, *Aperçu philosophique sur la musique* (Paris, 1860), pp. 113f.
190. Sitwell, *Liszt*, p. 325.

CHAPTER 3

---

1. Immanuel Kant, *Die Religion innerhalb der Grenzen der blossen Vernunft*, in *Immanuel Kants Werke* (Berlin, 1923), VI, 302.
2. Such investigation was the explicit purpose of several periodicals and books published in the late eighteenth century. In 1784 the initial article in *Seilers Liturgisches Magazin* (Published at Erlangen in northern Bavaria) stated that it would circulate all opinions about religious rites because public debate would be good for liturgical studies. Though most of the articles in this and similar German periodicals were by and for Evangelicals, issues usually included articles on Catholic, Reformed, or Jewish rites. Eight issues of Seiler's quarterly were published; other magazines soon took up the same study. By the turn of the century, there were periodicals by and for musicians, as well as theological journals, to treat these questions. Meanwhile, Germans of every ideological persuasion were offering suggestions about how public rites, festivals, and schools might help to make the still-feudal Germanies into a nation-state.
   Judging from the number of published proposals suggesting improvements in the liturgies of the various churches, the year 1811 was the climax of the controversy over liturgical reform. The remaining neoclassical reformers' careers then overlapped those of the romantics. For further titles of liturgiological periodicals, most of them short-lived, cf. the notes and bibliographies in Anton L. Mayer, "Liturgie, Aufklärung und Klassizismus," *Jahrbuch für Liturgie-*

wissenschaft, IX (1929); Burchard Thiel, O.F.M., *Die Liturgik der Aufklärungszeit: Ihre Grundlagen und die Ziele ihrer Vertreter* (Breslau, 1926). See also the detailed study by Ottfried Jordahn, "Georg Friedrich Seiler—Der Liturgiker der deutschen Aufklärung," *Jahrbuch für Liturgik und Hymnologik*, XIV (1969), 1–62.

3. Since England and Scandinavia lay to the Protestant side of Christianity, which was more hospitable to the Enlightenment, their liturgical tradition received its strongest shocks later during the romantic phase of the democratic breakthrough, which is the subject of later chapters.

4. Robert R. Palmer, *Catholics and Unbelievers in the Eighteenth Century* (Princeton, 1939), passim; Gay, I, passim.

5. Joseph A. Jungmann, *The Mass of the Roman Rite*, trans. Francis A. Brunner (New York, 1950), p. 140.

6. Benedict Maria Werkmeister, *Beyträge zur Verbesserung der katholischen Liturgie in Deutschland* (Ulm, 1789), p. 396; Albert Vierbach, *Die liturgischen Anschauungen des V. A. Winter* (Munich, 1929), p. 336.

7. The Common of the Saints contained generalized liturgical prayers for various categories of saints, such as Widow, Martyr, Virgin, Virgin-Martyr, Confessor, Confessor-Bishop, Doctor of the Church, etc., with scarcely any reference to the particular person whose festival was celebrated that day.

8. Thiel, p. 8. Cardinal Heenan spoke in a similar vein at the Second Vatican Council: "The Faithful are without pastors because perfectly healthy monks refuse to come to the aid of their bishops." *Commonweal*, LXXXIII (December 1965), 326.

9. Quoted from F. X. Turin's diary in Rupert Giessler, *Die geistliche Lieddichtung der Katholiken im Zeitalter der Aufklärung* (Schriften zur deutschen Literatur für die Goerresgesellschaft), X (Augsburg, 1928), 164.

10. *Liturgisches Journal*, VI (1806), 14.

11. Ulrich Leupold, *Die liturgischen Gesänge der evangelischen Kirche im Zeitalter der Aufklärung und der Romantik* (Würzburg, 1933), p. 55. Most experiments remained in the parsonage library, some reached the pews of the local parish church, and a few were published.

12. Heinrich B. Wagnitz, "Über das Verhältnis unserer protestantischen städtischen Kirchen zu den verbesserten liturgischen Formen des 19ten Jahrhunderts," *Liturgisches Journal*, III (1803), 1–3.

13. Karl Fellerer, *Beiträge zur Choralbegleitung und Choralverarbeitung in der Orgelmusik des ausgehenden 18. und beginnenden 19. Jahrhunderts* (Strassburg, [1932]), passim. This carried to its logical conclusion the folksinger's convention of using the same tune for

several texts. *O Sacred Head* still uses a tune which was originally a love song, and the venerable Palestrina employed profane *cantus firmi*, often disguised in Masses *Sine Nomine*. An eighteenth-century hymn writer, Ignaz Franz, used the same tune for *Von der Todesangst am Ölberg* and for a German version of the *Te Deum*.

14. These choir schools, which were sometimes part of a foundling home, were sometimes the only school at hand. This situation could make church musicianship the key to education and the advancement it could bring.

15. Knipfer, p. 237; Leo Schrade, "Herder's Conception of Church Music," in *The Musical Heritage of the Church*, ed. T. Hoelty-Nickel (Valparaiso, Ind., 1946), pp. 83–95.

16. The entente between rationalism and liturgical reform which began in the last quarter of the eighteenth century flourished until the French excesses under Napoleon, and the rebelliousness manifested at the Wartburg celebrations in 1817 frightened the upper classes. For example, Metternich's Catholic and Hapsburg Vienna celebrated the three-hundredth anniversary of the Reformation in company with the rest of Germany. At the celebration, Luther's *volkstümlich* line "Ein' feste Burg ist unser Gott" was changed to the more abstract "Ein starker Schutz ist unser Gott." The notes of the melody were chopped in half to fit the wordy new text. Hans Joachim Moser, *Die Musik im frühevangelischen Österreich* (Kassel, 1954), p. 98. See also the same author's *Die evangelische Kirchenmusik in Deutschland* (Berlin, 1954), pp. 202–4.

17. Knipfer, p. 239.

18. Prediger Bonitz, "Ist die Einführung neuer Gesangbücher unbedingt zu empfehlen?" *Liturgisches Journal*, V (1805), 377.

19. *Liturgisches Journal*, II (1802), 85; Leupold, pp. 38–52; Theobald Schrems, *Die Geschichte des Gregorianischen Gesanges in den protestantischen Gottesdiensten* (Freiburg, 1930), passim.

20. Horton Davies, *Worship and Theology in England, from Watts and Wesley to Maurice, 1690–1850* (Princeton, N.J., 1961), pp. 41ff.

21. Again, the meaning of certain Greek and Latin terms is crucial to an understanding of western thought. The reference to Christ as the *Logos* in the beginning of Gospel according to John implied a multifaceted Incarnation. *Logos* became *verbum* in Latin. Subsequent translation into English (and other languages) as "Word" or even "preaching" sometimes tended to restrict the implications of the original term. The confusion of "the Word" with "words" implied a denigration of the nonverbal, in particular music. See also chapter 1, the Conclusion, and the discussion of Goethe's *Faust* in chapter 4.

22. P. 68, quoted in Thiel, pp. 17–20.

23. Giessler, pp. 72–89.

24. Herr! deine Allgegenwart hebe *jetzt unsere Andacht.*
    Dann wollen wir deiner Güte fröhlich singen.
    Und deine Wahrheiten seien der alleinige Gegenstand
       unseres Denkens.
    Quoted in Mayer, "Liturgie, Aufklärung," p. 91.
25. *Liber usualis*, (Tournai, 1950), p. 1. An English translation might
    have run:
    Thou wilt turn, O God and bring us to life,
    And thy people shall rejoice in Thee.
    Show us, O Lord Thy mercy.
    And grant us Thy salvation.
    Saint Andrew Daily Missal (Saint Paul, Minn., 1953), p. 540.
26. Kommt, ihr Winde
    Wählt gelinde
    Breitet eure Flügel aus:
    Tragt die Mutter eures Herren
    In des Zacharia Haus.
    Berg und Tale,
    Allzumale,
    Kleidet euch, sie zu beehren,
    Heut mit manchem Blumenstrauss. [Giessler, p. 96.]
27. Lass uns die Tugenden besingen
    Die Zierden an Mariae Bild!
    Lasst uns mit ihr Gnade ringen,
    Nach Ehre, die im Himmel gilt!
    Es muntre uns ihr Lebenslauf
    Zur Freude und zur Tugend auf! [Ibid.]
28. The same thing happened in America in the sixties. An old standard
    hymn in sentimental 6/8 was "Bring Flowers of the Rarest" from
    the *St. Basil's Hymnal* (Chicago, 1935), p. 90:
    Bring flow'rs of the fairest,
    Bring flow'rs of the rarest,
    From garden and woodland and hillside and vale;
    Our full hearts are swelling,
    Our glad voices telling
    The praise of the loveliest Rose of the Vale.
    A streamlined Marian hymn, akin to Werkmeister's, comes from
    The People's Hymnal (Cincinnati, 1964), p. R–10. Properly ecu-
    menical, it is set to a seventeenth-century Protestant American folk
    tune:
    Sing of Jesus, son of Mary
    In the home at Nazareth
    Toil and labor cannot weary
    Love enduring unto death.
29. Heilig preisen wir die Guten,
    Deren Geist fuer Wahrheit rang—

Siegreich kämpften die nicht ruhten,
Wenn der Ruf der Pflicht erklang—
Die, fürs Heiligtum zu bluten,
Gingen mit Triumphgesang. [Giessler, p. 103.]

30.   Den Nächsten, wer er immer sey,
Türk, Jude oder Heide,
Zu lieben stets, vom Stolze frey,
Ist Christenpflicht und Freude!
Er ist ein Mensch, wie ich,
Und ist oft besser noch, als mancher Christ.

Benedict von Werkmeister, *Einleitung zum Gebrauche des neuen
Gesang und Melodienbuches bey den Gottesverehrungen der Cath-
olischen Kirche* (Tübingen, 1808), p. 50.

Again one finds an equivalent in a recent American Catholic
hymnal: "Where Charity and Love Prevail," *People's Hymnal*,
L–25: Vs. 3:

Forgive we now each other's faults
As we our faults confess
And let us love each other well
In Christian Holiness.

The climax is vs. 6, its last:

No race nor creed can love exclude
If honored be God's name,
Our brotherhood embraces all
Whose Father is the same.

31.   Nie lass, wenn andre klagen,
Mich eh ich helfe fragen:
Was wird mir denn dafür?
O Gott nach deinem Bilde,
Verleih die reinste Milde,
Die wärmste Menschenliebe mir! [Werkmeister, ibid., p. 57.]

32.   Von Hexerey und Zauberspiel,
Und von dergleichen Sachen hält
Nachbar Martin gar zu viel,
Man möchte kaum sich lachen
Er mahlt drey Kreuzchen an die Wand,
Und denkt, er hat den Geist verbannt. [Ibid., p. 63.]

33.   Nein, keinem hast du es vergönnt,
Den je der Tod von uns getrennt,
Auf Erden sichtbar noch zu seyn
Vernunft und Schrift sagt dazu: Nein! [Ibid., p. 63.]

34. Proposal of Benedikt Peuger mentioned in a report on the historiography of Enlightenment liturgiology by Alexander Schnütgen in
Jahrbuch für Liturgiewissenschaft, XIII (1933), 434–36.

35. *Liturgisches Journal*, III (1803), 16.

36. See chapter 2.

37. Thiel, pp. 29–33.
38. Giessler, pp. 108–16. Reformers in the various Christian churches tailored baptismal rites to every conceivable type of catechumen: infant, sickly infant, illegitimate infant—none of whom would be asked any ritual questions—peasant, noble, old, young, male, and female. See Thiel, pp. 33–35.
39. In Hitz und Kält,
    Im offenen Felt,
    Im schüchternen Wald
    Mein Horn erschallt.
    In Kummer und Plage
    Dem Wild ich nachjage
    Und bleibe dabei
    Diana dir treu. [Giessler, p. 50.]
    The word pietist is used loosely and figuratively here to suggest a more personal than theological state of Christian belief.
40. Richtet Euch zu dem Beten
    Fromme Kirchfahrtherschar,
    Wir haben es vonnöten
    Wir seind nit aus der Gefahr. [Mayer, "Liturgie, Aufklärung," p. 85.]
41. A. Schnütgen reporting on the historiography of Enlightenment liturgiology in *Jahrbuch für Liturgiewissenschaft*, X (1930), 414.
42. Mein Jesus kann addieren
    Und kann multiplizieren
    Selbst dort, wo lauter Nullen sind. [Moser, *Evangelische Kirchenmusik*, p. 221.]
43. In a later chapter we shall see that the rationale for restoring the chant in the nineteenth century rested in part upon the thesis that Gregorian music was built upon the Latin language and would therefore aid in displacing the vernacular fostered by the Enlightenment. The theories about an interdependence between Gregorian music and Latin text are today still being debated by its admirers and detractors. For it seems that the vernacular is to be the usual language of future Catholic rites. Cf. John Rayburn, *Gregorian Chant: A History of the Controversy Concerning its Rhythm* (New York, 1964), p. 66; Francis P. Schmitt, "Leaning Right?" in *Crisis in Church Music* (Washington, 1967), p. 57; *Sacred Music*, Spring 1970.
44. In practice the Proper of the Mass—which constitutes the largest part of the Gregorian repertoire—has been replaced by "appropriate hymns." This means the end of attempts to adapt the Gregorian music to English words. Such adaptation had been proposed by, for example, Jan Kern, *The Adaptation of the Vernacular to Gregorian Chant* (Toledo, Ohio, 1964). None of these efforts have been

very popular. Scarcely any Gregorian chant is sung among English-speaking Catholics today.

See the bibliographical précis "Aufklärungszeit" in each issue of the *Jahrbuch für Liturgiewissenschaft.*

45. Wilhelm Bäumker, *Das katholische deutsche Kirchenlied* (Saint Louis, 1883–1911), IV, 13–15. Bäumker himself is a good example of the reaction described.

46. Thiel, pp. 8–14.

47. Eichsfeld's Catholics later came under the jurisdiction of the archbishop of Regensburg, which helps account for publication in the Cäcilian journal, *Kirchenmusikalisches Jahrbuch* (Regensburg), XVII (1902) and XIX (1904) of Hermann Müller, "Urkundliches zum Eichsfelder Kirchengesange im 19. Jahrhundert."

48. Ibid. (1902), p. 91.

49. Ibid., p. 103.

50. Ibid., p. 102.

51. Ibid., p. 118.

52. Cf. Bäumker, III, 13–18, for several examples of similar events throughout the Germanies.

53. Bäumker, III, 15–60.

54. Müller, XIX (1904), 149–51.

55. Ibid.

56. Some other eighteenth-century suggestions for achieving unity of action: The people should always receive communion at Mass, but only at Mass. Priests who offer private Masses should receive no stipend. Thiel, p. 23. Confessions should be public, with private advice given in the confessional. Thiel, p. 24. Reform of marriage and baptism would be common to all Christians; here are some of the most frequent proposals: Marriage should be treated as a public contract, not a private religious vow. Thiel, p. 5. Baptism should be for adults only and should be administered at the high altar in full view of the congregation; thereafter, all present should ratify the Christian initiation by uniting in a suitable hymn. Thiel, pp. 33–35.

57. Thiel, p. 27. The baptistry should be within the main body of the church so that all could witness the Christian initiation as per the previous footnote.

58. Paul Gottfried, "Catholic Romanticism in Munich, 1826–1834" (Ph.D. diss., Yale University, 1967), p. 52.

59. The other church is the Kapuzinergruft. Mayer, pp. 67–71.

60. Longyear, *Schiller,* p. 126.

61. Ursprung, *Restauration,* pp. 7–9, 61–71.

62. Leupold, pp. 24–29.

63. Josef L. Altholz, *The Churches in the Nineteenth Century* (In-

dianapolis, 1967), p. 19; Justinus Febronius von Hontheim, *De Statu Ecclesiae* (Bullioni [Frankfurt am Main], 1765).

64. Ernst B. Koneker, *The Liturgical Renaissance in the Roman Catholic Church* (Chicago, 1954), pp. 21–27.

65. Piozzi, p. 325.

66. Werkmeister, *Beyträge zur Verbesserung*, pp. 386–87.

67. Ibid.

68. Ibid., p. 399.

69. Ibid., p. xvii.

70. Giessler, pp. 176–80.

71. Werkmeister, *Einleitung zum Gebrauche*, pp. 12–13 and passim. He did make a concession to those who would use religious rites for mass aesthetic education, for he thought that schoolmasters, amateurs, and young women—all of whose talents had been ignored by the church—could build music even in small parishes.

72. Bibliographical report, "Aufklärungszeit," *Jahrbuch für Liturgiewissenschaft*, II (1922), 179.

73. Bockheimer, "Karl Theodor Anton Maria von Dalberg," *Allgemeine deutsche Biographie*, IV, 703–8.

74. See *Jahrbuch für Liturgiewissenschaft*, II (1922), 180; Knipfer, p. 258.

75. Müller, XVIII, 95 and passim.

76. Otto Wetzstein, *Die religiöse Lyrik der Deutschen im 19. Jahrhundert.* (Neustrelitz, 1891), pp. 46–50.

77. The territory of this ecclesiastical state had been "mediatized" to Baden by Napoleon in 1803.

78. Giessler, pp. 180–94.

79. See chapter 6.

80. Vierbach, p. 17.

81. Ibid., pp. 59–62.

82. V. A. Winter, *Liturgie was sie seyn soll oder Theorie der öffentlichen Gottesverehrung* (Munich, 1809), p. 226.

83. Ibid.

84. Ibid., p. 227.

85. The reference is to Galatians, 3:28, quoted on the title page of his *Liturgie.*

86. Winter, pp. 85–86.

87. Mayer, pp. 104–7.

88. Jean Sarrailh, *La crise religieuse en Espagne à la fin du XVIIIe siècle*, The Taylorian Lecture (Oxford, 1951), pp. 18–19.

89. Ibid., p. 10.

90. Ibid., pp. 11–12.

91. Ibid., pp. 13–14.

92. Josef Froberger, "Das Entstehen und der Aufstieg der spanischen Romantik," *Spanische Forschungen der Goerresgesellschaft*, I (Münster, Westphalia, 1930), pp. 280–81.
      A similar Erastian spirit was also moving the French and Spanish Bourbon monarchies to cancel other ultramontane influences like the Jesuits, whose order had been abolished in 1773. In Romance nations, Jansenists were still actively pruning elaborate liturgies.

93. John P. Marschal, "The Thread of Renewal in the American Church," *America*, CXIII, no. 21 (November 1965), 622.

94. The laicism which American Catholic church histories written before the 1960s so deprecate never flourished enough to threaten the hierarchy. The only recognition of it above the parochial level died with England in 1842. European counterparts of his constitutionalism persisted for another decade. See *Jahrbuch für Liturgiewissenschaft*, XIV (1934), 516. For a sympathetic account of later ethnic pluralism in the American Catholic Church, see Andrew M. Greeley, *Critic*, Summer 1976, pp. 13ff., and several books.

95. In the Clements Library, The University of Michigan.

96. R. Adamski, "Unbekannte Volksliturgie in Deutschland," *Der Seelsorger*, VI (1930), 379–83, 427–30.

97. As I have witnessed it in several cities. This custom was probably a concession granted during the Reformation to forestall the attractions of Protestantism. Like concessions were also enjoyed by the Uniate churches taken from Orthodoxy at various times. Both concessions would seem to have their roots in a kind of Slavic "Gallicanism" extending back to the medieval times of Saints Cyril and Methodius.

98. Cf. H. S., Comments on Jewish music, *Cäcilia*, XVIII (1842), 16–21. This journal was published by Schott in Mainz from 1824 to 1845. See also Abraham Idelsohn, *Jewish Music in Its Historical Development* (New York, 1948), pp. 218ff.

99. Abraham Idelsohn, *Jewish Liturgy in Its Historical Development* (New York, 1932), p. 69.

100. Idelsohn, *Jewish Music*, pp. 41, 218ff; Herman Berlinski, "The Organ in the Synagogue," *Music*, II, no. 7 (July 1968), 28–29, and II, no. 11 (November 1968), 34–37.

101. Paul Nettl, *Forgotten Musicians* (New York [1951]), p. 42.

102. Ibid., p. 46.

103. Heinrich Heine, "Der Rabbi von Bacharach," *Heines Werke* (Berlin [n.d.]), V, 40–41.

104. Idelsohn, *Jewish Music*, pp. 246–353; *Jewish Liturgy*, pp. 268–300.

105. Palmer, *Age* II, 572.

106. *Jahrbuch für Liturgiewissenschaft*, VI (1926), 425.

CHAPTER 4

1. Cf. synoptic gospels, e.g., "the Sermon on the Mount," Matthew 5; Paul, Epistle to the Corinthians; Roger Wilkinson, "The Divine Persuasion," *The Center Magazine* (May 1970); George Grant, *Time as History* (Toronto, 1971), passim; Jacques Ellul, *La Technique*, passim; Rosemary Ruether, *The Radical Kingdom* (New York, 1970), passim. Augustine, *Civitas Dei*, is, of course, the foremost example of such a Weltanschauung.

2. Cf. Christopher Dawson, "The Gods of Revolution," *Times Literary Supplement*, 28 July 1973, p. 881.

3. See, for example, Clifford Hill, "Pentecostalist Growth—Result of Racialism?" *Race Today*, July 1972, pp. 187–90.

4. In his *Lettre à M. d'Alembert*.

5. Giessler, pp. 90–92.

6. L. Balet and E. Gerhard, *Die Verbürgerlichung der deutschen Kunst, Literatur und Musik im 18. Jahrhundert* (Leipzig, 1935), pp. 206ff. See also Section One of Loesser.

7. For theological and literary examples from the time, Cf. M. H. Abrams, *Natural Supernaturalism* (New York, 1971), pp. 17–70.

   From visual art, Bernini's *St. Theresa in Ecstasy*, though of an earlier period, is the best-known use of subjective passionate intensity to express the Apocalyptic vision of the ultimate consummation of history. The sexual symbolism is a daring intrusion of the supposed lowly and sensual into the supposedly etheral and spiritual. The Saint is obviously dead to her old consciousness—that is the point of her life, her writings, and of Bernini's explanation of it to the faithful. Counterreformation Catholicism utilized a popular religion of the feelings.

   The vast conversion and confession literature and art continues. One of the most orthodox is Charles Reich's *The Greening of America* (New York, 1970), which is so full of the illusions of western piety that its righteousness exceeds even that of nuns who used to collect pennies to ransom pagan babies.

8. Perhaps this is a return to the worship of an earth mother, the Great White Goddess of Robert Graves's imagination. More likely, it is an attempt by the human psyche and its societies to balance rational objectivity, the supposedly Apollonian or masculine, with subjective passion, the supposed Dionysian or feminine.

9. Oliver, *The Encyclopedists*, passim.

10. Walter Lott, "Zur Geschichte der Passionskomposition von 1650–1800," *Archiv für Musikwissenschaft*, III (1921), 314.

11. Ibid., p. 320. The liturgical formulae of the Moravian Brethren mediated between pietists and rationalists to a certain extent.

12. Kerman, p. 64.

13. The Protestant varieties of pietism may appear unbaroque because of their simplicity, but, like the baroque, they are emotionally charged.

14. Jacques Barzun, *Classic, Romantic, and Modern* (Garden City, N.Y., 1958), p. 213, note to p. 96.

15.   Ich lauf dir nach
       Mit stetem Ach,
       Mit Seufzen und mit Sehnen
       Ich suche dich ganz inniglich
       Mein liebster Schatz mit Tränen.
       Denn dein Geruch erweckt in mir,
       Herr Jesus, ew'ge Liebesgier.
     Mayer, p. 85, quoting M. Pirker, *Das deutsche Liebeslied in Barock und Rokoko* (1922), p. 56.

16. Gay, in *Enlightenment*, I, for example, deliberately minimizes the religious component of the Aufklärung. By so doing he seems to recognize the fact that at least some scholars have perceived something different in its attitude toward religion, especially those beliefs found among Germans.

17. Hildegarde Tepe, "Der Einfluss Klopstocks und seiner Schule auf das katholische Kirchenlied," *Kirchenmusikalisches Jahrbuch*, XX (1907), 146.

18. Longyear, p. 94.

19. *Encyclopaedia Britannica*, XIII, 428.

20. J. G. Herder, "Versuch einer Geschichte der lyrischen Dichtkunst," *Sämtliche Werke*, ed. Bernard Suphan (Berlin, 1878), XXXII, 107.
     According to Gerhard Kaiser, *Klopstock, Religion und Dichtung* (Gütersloh, 1963), Klopstock was attempting a synthesis of pietism and the Enlightenment (p. 63). He believed that singing is the most important part of communal worship—more important than merely spoken or thought prayer because it is more communal. He was not formally a Herrnhuter, but was the poet of what they stood for (p. 190ff).

21. Longyear, p. 88.

22. See Johann Georg Hamann, "Aesthetica in Nuce," *Sämtliche Werke* (Vienna, 1949–57), II, 197.

23. "Reviewing the first part of Herder's masterpiece, *Ideen zur Philosophie der Geschichte der Menschheit*, Kant praised its bold, free imagination, but criticized Herder's attempt to explain unknown prehistory by equally unknown forces. "This," said Kant severely, "is mere metaphysic; it shows what happens when a scientist despairs of finding the truth by scientific means—he turns to poetry. The

task of philosophy, he added a little sententiously, is to trim rather than to cultivate the luxuriant tree of imagination." *Werke*, IV, 179–90. "The review is a touching moment in the history of the late Enlightenment: the representative of a great but aging movement faces the representative of a new dispensation, refusing to believe that change is progress, defending science against fancy, rigor against vagueness, and criticism against a resurgence of mythmaking." Gay, *Enlightenment*, I, 87.

24. See F. B. Artz, review of F. M. Barnard, *Herder's Social and Political Ideas* in *American Historical Review*, LXXI (April 1966), 989. Also see Klemens von Klemperer, Review of George L. Morse, *The Crisis of German Ideology: Intellectual Origins of the Third Reich*, in ibid., LXXI (January 1966), 680ff. The bold logic in "some things some romanticists said sound like some things some Nazis said, therefore, romanticism caused Nazism" has sold many books. However, such a tidy thesis seems ignorant of the fact that in western Europe, the Germans were more or less outsiders in a century when French classicism set the standards. To recognize and dignify Germanic culture is more likely to forestall a later revolt.

25. Knipfer, pp. 241ff.

26. Ibid. Herder's student, Goethe, who was "assuredly non-Christian," also thought that "improving" the old chorales was vandalism. He thought that if the song, by which he meant the words and music together, helped one to share the poet's ecstasy, it had done its work, and there was no need to worry whether it was logical. It was enough to be human. Knipfer, p. 237; Cf. Romain Rolland, "Goethe's Interest in Music."

27. Gillian Lindt Gollin, *Moravians in Two Worlds* (New York, 1967), pp. 7–11.

28. Ibid., p. 15.

29. Charles Winfred Douglas, *Church Music in History and Practice* (New York, 1962), p. 36.

30. Gollin, p. 15.

31. Wetzstein, pp. 170ff; Leupold, pp. 36ff.

32. Lang, *Music in Western Civilization*, p. 470. When Moravian settlements faded into insignificance because of secularizing influences or bankruptcy, the utopian socialists had begun to fulfill the same function. Cf. chapter 8.

33. Bos, "Johann Bernhard Basedow," *Allgemeine deutsche Biographie*, II, 113–24.

34. Ibid.

35. Bäumker, II, 10f.

36. Charles L. Etherington, *Protestant Worship Music: Its History and Practice* (New York, 1962), pp. 160ff.

37. Altholz, p. 26.

38. Erik Routley, *Hymns and Human Life* (London, 1952), pp. 11f.
39. William J. Reynolds, *A Survey of Christian Hymnody* (New York, 1963), pp. 54–55.

   Although the foot-stomping, screaming Methodists and the later antiquarian, high-brow Tractarians hardly understood each other, they were alike. Not necessarily because the Wesleyans forced the Anglican Church to introduce hymnody, nor because Tractarian scholars like John Mason Neale deigned to refine and sublimate the Methodists' ecstatic outpouring by recovering similar hymns from early Christianity, but because both emphasized the lyrical, aesthetic side of religion. See chapter 9.
40. Kenneth Scott Latourette, *A History of Christianity* (New York, 1953), pp. 1019–20.
41. Palmer, II, p. 466.
42. Altholz, p. 26.
43. Herbert Butterfield, "Religion and Modern Individualism," *The Role of Religion in Modern European History*, ed. Sidney A. Burrell (New York, 1964), p. 145.
44. Kant, *Werke*, VI: *Die Religion innerhalb der Grenzen der blossen Vernunft*, pp. 341–53.
45. Cf. James Collins, *The Emergence of Philosophy of Religion* (New Haven, 1967), pp. 410–13.
46. Cf. James A. Pike, *What is this Treasure?* (New York, 1966), by a modern religious leader who passed from orthodoxy to liberalism to Romanticism.
47. Fergusson, pp. 98–142.
48. Ludwig Fraenkel, "Abt. Georg Joseph Vogler," *Allgemeine deutsche Biographie*, XL, 169–78.
49. "Guillaume-André Villoteau," *Biographie universelle*, ed. Joseph François Michaud (Paris, 1853–54), XLIII, 530.
50. William Wordsworth, "Advertisement" to *Lyrical Ballads* (1798), in *Harvard Classics* (New York, 1910), XXXIX, 282.

   Like many such manifestos the famous Preface was first offered with a half-ironical apology for offending the "canons" of poetical style: "Readers of superior judgement may disapprove of the style in which many of these pieces are executed. . . . It will perhaps appear to them that wishing to avoid the prevalent fault of the day, the author had sometimes descended too low, and that many of his expressions are too familiar and not of sufficient dignity." Ibid.
51. Schrade, "Herder's Conception of Church Music," p. 90f.
52. Lang, *Music in Western Civilization*, p. 720.
53. Barzun, *Classic, Romantic, and Modern*, p. 87.
54. Ibid., p. 95.
55. Cf. Von Ogden Vogt, *Art and Religion* (Boston, 1960), p. 70. *"Doxa,"* Greek for "opinion," is the root of "dogma."

56. For a similar view of the practice of the Lutheran cult, cf. Piozzi, pp. 387–92.

57. Walter Buszin, *Luther on Music* (Saint Paul, 1958), pp. 119, 120.

58. Georg Rietschl, *Lehrbuch der Liturgik*, ed. Paul Goraff, 2d ed. (Göttingen, 1951), pp. 57, 499. "Humble handmaiden" was the usual translation of *ancilla liturgiae*.

59. Friedrich Blume, *Evangelische Kirchenmusik*, vol. X of Ernst Buecken, ed., *Handbuch der Musikwissenschaft* (Potsdam, 1931), p. 157.

60. Carl von Winterfeld, *Über Herstellung des Gemeine und Chorgesanges in der evangelischen Kirche* (Leipzig, 1848), p. 19.

61. Moser, *Musik im frühevangelischen Österreich*, p. 99.

62. Moser, *Evangelische Kirchenmusik*, pp. 202–3.

63. Cf. Friedrich Schleiermacher, *Brief Outline on the Study of Theology*, ed. of 1830, tr. Terrence Tice (Richmond, Va., 1966), passim and especially pp. 112f.

64. Schrems, p. 138.

65. John Herman Randall, Jr., "Changing Impact of Darwin," in *The Role of Religion*, ed. Burrell, pp. 122–29.

66. Altholz, p. 54.

67. Friedrich Schleiermacher, *On Religion, Speeches to its Cultured Despisers*, trans. E. Graham Waring (New York, 1955), p. 38.

68. Ibid., p. 69.

69. Koppel S. Pinson, *Modern Germany* (New York, 1962), p. 35.

70. Philip Gleason, "Our New Age of Romanticism," *America*, CXVII (7 October 1967), 372. Schleiermacher, *Brief Outline*, p. 140, passim.

71. Cf. Golo Mann, *The History of Germany since 1789*, trans. Marian Jackson (New York, 1968), pp. 24–34.

72. Moser, *Evangelische Kirchenmusik*, pp. 226–27.

73. Wetzstein, p. 131; Lang, *Music in Western Civilization*, p. 801.

74. Longyear, *Schiller*, p. 24.

75. Gleason, p. 374.

76. R., "Hinblicke auf alte und neue kirchliche Gesänge," *Liturgisches Journal*, VI (1807), 1–55.

77. R——ph, "Kirche und Theater," *Liturgisches Journal*, VI (1807), 375–92. See chapter 6.

78. Wilhelm Ehmann, "Der Thibault-Behaghel Kreis," *Archiv für Musikforschung*, IV (1939), 38.

79. Altholz, p. 109.

80. Arthur Hutchings, *Church Music in the Nineteenth Century* (New York, 1967), p. 30.

81. Gleason, p. 374.

82. Knipfer, p. 266.

83. Moser, *Evangelische Kirchenmusik*, pp. 245–46.

84. Edmond Vermeil, *Jean-Adam Moehler et l'école catholique de Tübingen* (Paris, 1913), pp. 36, 440–41.
85. Schleiermacher, *Brief Outline*, p. 110.
86. Hutchings, p. 30; Blume, p. 159.
87. Schrems, p. 195.
88. Ibid., p. 196.
89. Ibid., p. 197.
90. Ibid., pp. 132ff.
91. Gleason, p. 375.
92. Schrems, p. 126.
93. Herbert Hafter, *Der Freiherr vom Stein in seinem Verhältnis zu Religion und Kirche* (Berlin, 1932).
94. Altholz, p. 109.
95. Johann E. Häuser, *Geschichte des christlichen insbesondere des evangelischen Kirchengesanges und der Kirchenmusik von Entstehung des Christentums an, bis auf unsere Zeit* (Leipzig, 1834), p. iii.
96. Ibid., pp. 60–61.
97. Ibid., p. 243.
98. Ibid., p. 238.
99. Ibid., p. 209.
100. Ibid., pp. 179f.
101. Ibid., pp. 176–78.
102. Ibid., pp. 205, 251ff, *passim*.
103. Ibid., p. 234.
104. Moser, *Evangelische Kirchenmusik*, p. 240.
105. Ludwig Schöberlein, *Über den Ausbau des Gemeindegottesdienstes* (Gotha, 1859), passim, especially pp. 1–12, 215–35.
106. Moser, *Evangelische Kirchenmusik*, p. 235.
107. Josef Gregor, "Die deutsche Romantik aus den Beziehungen von Musik und Dichtung W. H. Wackenroders," *Sammelbände der Internationalen Musikgesellschaft*, X (1908–9), 526–27.
108. Wetzstein, p. 128.
109. Carl von Winterfeld, *Zur Geschichte der heiligen Tonkunst* (Leipzig, 1850–52), II, 109.
110. Edwin Liemohn, *The Chorale, through Four-Hundred Years of Musical Development as a Congregational Hymn* (Philadelphia, 1953), p. 83.
111. Ibid., pp. 102ff.
112. V. Andersen, "Nicolai Frederik Severin Gruntvig," *Dansk Biografisk Leksikon* (Copenhagen, 1936), VIII, 356–57.
113. Latourette, pp. 1145–47.
114. Altholz, pp. 114f. Those who did not submit to the state's agenda were mostly old-style Lutherans, many of whom brought their pietistic-conservative views to the United States and institutionalized

them in the Missouri Synod (ibid., p. 110). The inspirer of confessional, as distinguished from territorial, Lutheranism was Wilhelm Loehe, who founded a Lutheran liturgical movement and worked in practical Christian charities (ibid.).

115. Max Weber, *The Rational and Social Foundations of Music* (Carbondale, Ill., 1958).

116. Cf. Irving Massey, *The Uncreating Word: Romanticism and the Object* (Bloomington, Ind., 1970), p. 66; and Schiller, "Über naive und sentimentalische Dichtung," *Sämtliche Werke*, XII, 161–263.

117. Innocence was not some new fad of the sentimental beginnings of the romantic revival. "From the Old Testament, through the Pelagian heresy of the fifth century, to the moral optimism of Shaftsbury, the problem comes into focus again and again. Along the way there is the pastoral tradition, Theocritus, through Dio Chrysostum, to Sidney, Montaigne, and the cult of the noble savage. The major poem of the seventeenth-century England, *Paradise Lost*, deals with the loss of innocence; the greatest German seventeenth-century novel is entitled *Simplicissimus*; the pursuit of the primitive in every form throughout the eighteenth century is a forlorn hope for the recovery of innocence. But the simultaneous lament about the decline of poetry (there are exceptions such as Young's *Conjectures*, but they are rare) betrays the conviction that civilization is fatal to man's emotional powers. On all sides we hear that the growth of knowledge spells the death of the imagination. Shakespeare could be great only because he was *not* learned." Massey, pp. 68–69.

118. Massey, p. 74.

CHAPTER 5

1. A succinct discussion of such theories from Longinus to Freud is found in Abrams, *The Mirror and the Lamp*, pp. 70–99 and passim. Further remarks on the historical and communal nature of romanticism may be found in Walter Wiora, "Die Musik in Weltbild der deutschen Romantik," in *Beiträge zur Geschichte der Musikanschauung im 19. Jahrhundert*, ed. Walter Salmen (Regensburg, 1965), pp. 11–50.

2. See Sigmund Freud, *Civilization and Its Discontents*, trans. James Strachey (New York, 1962), passim.

3. Abrams, *The Mirror and the Lamp*, p. 145.

4. C. M. Bowra, *Primitive Song* (New York, 1962), p. 35; Reginald Nettel, *A Social History of Traditional Song* (London, 1969).

5. When defining an education that liberates, as opposed to training that limits, Aristotle used the analogy of play. Similar ideas are current today among progressive educational psychologists. In fact the Greek word which is the root of "school" means leisure. Aristotle, *Politics*, Chapters 2–7; Bruno Bettelheim, *The Uses of Enchantment: The Meaning and Importance of Fairy Tales* (New York, 1976); Huizinga, *Homo Ludens*; Guardini, *Spirit*.

6. Barzun, *Of Human Freedom*, p. 75.

7. Guardini, *Spirit*; Dilthey, passim; Bruno Nettl, *Music in Primitive Culture* (Cambridge, Mass., 1956), passim.

8. See Hans T. David, "Cultural Functions of Music," *Journal of the History of Ideas*, XII (June 1951), 423–39.

9. Rev. Norman J. O'Connor, "Father O'Connor's Jazz Anthology," Radio Station WUOM, Ann Arbor, Mich., 23 December 1967.

10. Guardini, *Spirit*, p. 177.

11. Nettl, pp. 10–11. Cf. Wiora, pp. 17–39. Many writers also exalted sixteenth-century polyphony because it seemed a model reconciliation between high and popular art, text and tone, which eighteenth-century reformers seemed to place in opposition. See chapter 6. See also J. Coghlan, *An Essay on the Church Plain Chant* (London, 1782), pp. 1–5; *L'art du plain-chant* (Ville-franche-de-Rouergue, 1765); Schrems, passim.

12. Nettl, p. 148.

13. Jean-Jacques Rousseau, "Plain-chant," *Dictionnaire, Oeuvres*, XII, 85. The work of 1765.

14. Ibid., "Motet," XII, 451.

15. Martin Gerbert, *Scriptores ecclesiastici de musica sacra . . . Ex variis Italiae, Galliae, et Germanicae codicibus manuscriptis collecti et nunc primum publica luce donati (Typis San-Blasianus, 1784)*, facsimile ed. (Rome, 1931), 3 vols.

16. Alexander Schnütgen, "Aufklärungszeit," *Jahrbuch für Liturgiewissenschaft*, XIII (1936), 432–33.

17. Warren Dwight Allen, *Philosophies of Music History* (New York, 1962), pp. 49–50; Charles Burney, *A General History of Music* (New York, 1957), I, 97, 422, 424; Sir John Hawkins, *A General History of the Science and Practice of Music* (New York, 1963), I, 278n; Johann Nikolaus Forkel, *Allgemeine Geschichte der Musik* (Leipzig, 1788), II, i–iii.

18. See F.-J. Fétis, *Histoire générale de la musique depuis les plus anciens jusqu'à nos jours* (Paris, 1869), I, v; Georges Marie Raymond, *Lettre à M. Villoteau* (Paris, 1811), pp. 12, 105–6. Guillaume-André Villoteau (1752–1839) had been by turns an itinerant musician, orientalist, a cleric in minor orders moving from one cathedral choir to another, a choirmaster, and an officer of dragoons. Under Napoleon he was an ethnomusicologist with the expedition

to Egypt. He employed the music he heard there as examples in his almost-forgotten tomes on the *Analogie de la musique avec les arts qui ont pour objet l'imitation du langage.* "Villoteau," *Biographie universelle,* XLIII, 520. See also chapter 8.

19. Alexandre Choron, *Considérations sur la nécessité de rétablir le chant de l'église de Rome dans toutes les églises de l'empire français* (Paris, 1811); Choron, *A Dictionary of Music and a Summary of the History of Music* (London, 1824), p. 299; Hutchings, p. 93.

20. I do not deny that de Maistre and other primarily political writers were important. But whenever anyone outside his own camp heard him coming, ears were closed. Chateaubriand and Lamennais won many sympathizers because they approached such questions obliquely. I am not concerned here with Edmund Burke or the whole galaxy of traditionalist Germans.

21. Giuseppe Mazzini, *Scritti editi ed inediti, Edizione nazionale* (Imola, 1906), XIV, 106.

22. Hector Berlioz, *Les années romantiques* (Paris, 1904), p. 257.

23. Franz Liszt, "Lyon," *Album d'un voyageur,* ler cahier, I (Leipzig, 1840), Vol. II, p. 5. Cf. Léon Guichard, "Liszt, Wagner et les relations entre la musique et la littérature au XIXe siècle," *Report of the Eighth Congress of the International Musicological Society* (New York, 1961), p. 324. See also E. E. Y. Hales, *Pio Nono: A Study in European Politics and Religion in the Nineteenth Century* (New York, 1962).

24. Léon Guichard, *La musique et les lettres au temps du romantisme* (Paris, 1955), pp. 144–48; see also Poisson, p. 349; Claude Carcopino, *Les doctrines sociales de Lamennais* (Paris, 1942), pp. 144ff, 364, 401; Peter Kivy, "The Child Mozart as an Aesthetic Symbol," *Journal of the History of Ideas,* XXVIII (June 1967), 249ff.

25. Félicité de Lamennais, *Esquisse d'une philosophie* (Paris, 1840–46), I, v.

26. Ibid., III, 126f.

27. Ibid., p. 134.

28. Ibid., p. 328.

29. Ibid., pp. 339–40. Cf. also André Pons, *Droit ecclésiastique et la musique sacrée,* IV: *La restauration de la musique sacrée* (St. Maurice, Switzerland, 1961), passim.

30. Lamennais, *Esquisse,* III, 134, 340.

31. Ibid., pp. 136–37.

32. Ibid., p. 142.

33. Ibid., p. 145.

34. Ibid., p. 150.

35. Ibid., p. 339. Cf. F. A. de Chateaubriand, "Musique," *Génie du Christianisme,* in *Œuvres Complètes* (Paris, 1859), II, 301.

36. Hales, *Pio Nono,* p. 115.

37. "I hate the mob, uninitiated in the service of the muses," a classicist aphorism taken from the Roman poet, Horace. Charreire, p. 103.
38. Hans Eckardt, *Die Musikanschauung der französischen Romantik* (Kassel, 1935), p. 42.
39. Alec R. Vidler, *Prophecy and Papacy: A study of Lamennais, the Church, and the Revolution* (New York, 1954), p. 69.
40. Paul Delatte, *Dom Guéranger, Abbé de Solesmes* (Paris, 1909), I.
41. Ernest Sevrin, *Dom Guéranger et Lamennais* (Paris, 1933), p. 190.
42. Ibid., p. 334. In a lengthy review the *Jahrbuch für Liturgiewissenschaft*, XIII (1936), 442–44, stated that "as a whole this book must be believed," and added that many of the local variations which ultras like Guéranger destroyed were actually more in accord with Catholic doctrine than the ultramontane emphasis on devotion to Mary.

     When Guéranger's generation died out at Solesmes, so did the romantic theory that chant, and indeed all music, began in heightened speech. On the controversy which followed see chapter 11 and Rayburn, p. 15ff.
43. Sevrin, p. 204.
44. Eremitic, eastern-style monasticism gave the name *monachos* before Benedict of Nursia wrote his widely followed communitarian *Rule* ca. A.D. 500. Gregorian music has an equivalent of harmonic progression when sung in a church with a long reverberation. The music argues for a while after the singers finish and at length agrees, teleologically—as is proper in a Christian church—on a final consonance.

     Medieval Christians believed that the *opus Dei*, whether in chapel, scriptorium, or field, benefited all mankind. The monk exercised his privilege of participating in this office by processing to the chapel every three hours of his life, opening the treasured *liber* (the work of another's lifetime), and singing *in choro*. When towns, cathedrals, and bishops surpassed the monasteries as centers of culture, the bishops invited distinguished clergy to be canons of their cathedral choirs. A canon's duty was to perform the canonically prescribed *opus Dei*, the office, in the Cathedral by singing the sacred words to their equally sacred music.
45. Alexander Schnütgen, Review of *Der Mönch in der Dichtung des 18. Jahrhunderts (einschliesslich der Romantik)* by A. Ritschl, *Jahrbuch für Liturgiewissenschaft*, IX (1930), 425.

     During the late eighteenth and early nineteenth centuries, monasticism was suppressed and reestablished in nearly all countries where it had survived the Reformation. However, the chronologies are not in step: Joseph II suppressed most of the monasteries in his domains in 1780; Portugal and Spain suppressed them in 1834–35, when they were being reestablished in France; after Italy and Germany were unified, they suppressed many monasteries. Some writers point out that Benedict made every member of his "school for service of the Lord" exist "um des Ganzen willen": [Cf. Arthur O. Lovejoy, "A Symposium on the Meaning of Romanticism for the Historian of Ideas," *Journal of the History of Ideas*, II (1941), 273–75.] Yet Benedict mitigated the absolutism of certain monastic rules preceding his by placing the abbot under the rule. "Um des Ganzen Willen," the abbot's power is not to be thought of as absolute. Cf. Benedictus, *Regula* (London, 1952), pp. 144ff. Moreover, for several centuries, monasticism was one of the few careers open to talent and did preserve the liberating life of the intellect and the arts in Europe. Part of the rationale for dissolving the monasteries two hundred years ago was to transfer such fruits, loyalties, and talents to the state.

Monasticism's friends and enemies speak much about its various denials of the world. Celibacy has few defenders post-Freud, but in the excessively familial feudal era, it made possible the mortmain which assured the continuity of a utopian community of prayer and work. In exchange for the repressive vows of chastity, poverty, and obedience, the community offered the individual many opportunities for sublimation. Benedictines may have been the first offenders against the Teutons' natural rambunctiousness; only the Wordsworthian conservationists approach the cloistered monks as the last defenders of peace and quiet.

46. Olivier Rousseau, *The Progress of the Liturgy* (Westminster, Md., 1951), p. 24.
47. Koenker, *Liturgical Renaissance in R.C. Church*, pp. 10, 205, nn. 6, 7, and 8.
48. O. Rousseau, pp. 172, 48.
49. Koenker, Loc. cit.

Most of the Gallican rites Guéranger and his friends were so zealous against were nothing so non-Roman as the German *Singmesse*, which survived until it became canonical again in 1964. These lost rites seem to have been different sets of the Proper and a different melodic tradition for the same text.

50. Joseph Schmidt-Georg, "Ein handschrifliches neugallikanisches Graduale aus dem Jahre 1852," *Festschrift Karl Gustav Fellerer* (Regensburg, 1962), pp. 477–80.
51. Aloys Kunc, *Le plain-chant romain et le nouveau chant liturgique de Toulouse* (Auch, 1861), p. 15.
52. Ch. Vervoitte, *Considérations sur le chant ecclésiastique, à propos du retour à la liturgie romaine* (Rouen, 1856), passim., especially pp. 407–11.
53. In scientific paleography, the oldest extant manuscript does not necessarily represent the oldest or most reliable tradition of manuscripts. Collation is a subtle prosecution whereby oblique questions lead to

unwilling confessions. It is an art one learns by doing and digging rather than by legislating.

54. Ann Fremantle (ed.), *The Papal Encyclicals* (New York, 1956), pp. 134–52.
55. Altholz, p. 60. Meanwhile the traditionally militant Jesuits worked to spread devotion to the Sacred Heart of Jesus. A burning heart crowned in thorns was the badge which the Vendéean rebels had worn in their crusade against secular Paris during the French Revolution. It symbolized a pietistic devotion to the sufferings of Jesus on the cross.
56. C.-A. Sainte-Beuve, *Nouveaux lundis* (Paris, 1864), II, 3.
57. D'Ortigue, *Balcon*, p. 282.
58. Ibid.
59. On the way he always took the opportunity to beat down the enemies of his friend, Berlioz, whose progressive music he thought stifled by the Conservatoire. Ibid., pp. 377ff.
60. Ibid., p. 404.
61. D'Ortigue, *La Musique à l'Eglise*, p. 33.
62. Joseph L. d'Ortigue, *Dictionnaire liturgique, historique et théorique de plain-chant et de musique à l'église au moyen âge et dans les temps modernes* (Paris, 1853), cols. 1211–13.
63. D'Ortigue, *Balcon*, p. viii.
64. "Culte," chap. 1, "Cloches," *Génie*, pp. 399ff.
65. D'Ortigue, *Dictionnaire*, p. 390, "Cloche."
66. D'Ortigue, *Du théâtre italien et de son influence sur le goût musical français* (Paris, 1840), p. 266.
67. D'Ortigue, *La musique à l'église*, pp. 400–408.
68. (Paris, 1829), p. 48.
69. D'Ortigue, *La musique à l'église*, pp. xii–xiii.
70. P. Couturier, *Décadence et restauration de la musique religieuse* (Paris, 1862), pp. 10–24.
71. D'Ortigue, *La musique à l'église*, p. 72.
72. Ibid., p. 362. D'Ortigue and his friend Hector Berlioz engaged in a lifelong amiable controversy concerning the plain chant. See Hector Berlioz, *A travers chants: Mozart, Weber, and Wagner, and Various Essays on Musical Subjects*, trans. Edwin Evans, Sr. (London [1918]), pp. 68–70.

By the time Berlioz and d'Ortigue died in the 1860s, the chant restoration was beginning to be realized, largely through the essential and well-known efforts of the monks of Solesmes.

Also standing on the shoulders of Choron and that earlier generation was Félix Danjou, who discovered the *Montpellier Graduale*, which proved to be the Rosetta Stone of medieval neumatic notation. Edmond Coussemaker, who published the correct melodic solution to the medieval manuscripts in 1852 (Rayburn, *Gregorian Chant*, p. 10), still held the romantic view of chant: "It is the tune that spreads the song," he said, "in the middle ages there were no museums. Art was experienced by the people in daily life" ("Memorial," *Cäcilian Kalendar*, III [1878], 76–77). To him, musical archaeology was not an attempt to make one age the epigone of another. Coussemaker took up Abbot Martin Gerbert's eighteenth-century work and published manuscripts of and about old music which had been found in the meantime. Edmond de Coussemaker, *Scriptorum de musica medii aevi novam seriam a Gerbertina alteram collegit nuncque primum edidit* (Paris, 1864–76), 4 vols. (Photogravure ed.: Milan: Bolletino bibliografico musicale, 1931).

D'Ortigue's friend Louis Niedermeyer took up Choron's work by founding an Ecole de Musique Religieuse et Classique (see chapter 8). D'Ortigue edited the magazine *Maîtrise* (Paris, 1857–61, monthly) to publicize their aims. Through the distinguished students the school graduated, it did have an effect on what music was heard in French churches. However, the Messes de Musique and compositions by students of theirs like Fauré, Gigout, Méssager, Buesser, and Boellman often broke out of the theological straitjacket which the founders of the school thought they could live within.

73. Augustin Gontier, *Le plain-chant* (Le Mans, 1860), p. 35.
74. German Catholic scholars liked to claim Catholic and Gregorian origins for the Reformation chorales which they thought re-extended the musical priesthood to all believers. Abt Vogler (1749–1814), who was Carl Maria von Weber's teacher and a musical polymath, defended Chant in 1813 with arguments like Choron's and added that he thought the Protestant chorales were merely a fragment of it. (Georg Josef Vogler, *Über Choral- und Kirchengesänge* [Munich, 1813], pp. 29ff.) In 1833, which was the year when Guéranger re-established the Benedictine liturgy at Solesmes, the Protestant, Karl Spitta, published his *Psalter und Harfe*, which was one of the foremost collections of German chorales. The next year, a Catholic writer, Dr. F. T. Friedmann, complained in the Rhineland's general musical magazine, *Cäcilia* (vol. XI [1834], p. 71), that even though the Catholic Church is rich in hymn literature, most music histories speak only of "Protestant chorales." These, he asserted, are mostly versions of Gregorian chant. He urged that Catholics re-assemble authentic versions of the Chant service books for their hymnological value. In the same issue of *Cäcilia*, another article answered the charge that Chant's modes are joyless and therefore unable to express a modern congregation's emotions. (Dr. Deycks,

"Über das Wesen des Kirchenstils," 145–49. *Cäcilia* was published by Schott in Mainz from 1824–44 and not connected to the later Roman Catholic Cecilian Society.)

Beginning around mid-century, the split between musicians and theologians mirrored a growing antipathy between two Europes—especially two Frances—which no longer spoke to each other. Churchmen and their followers gave up trying to reach the century they hated. Art, they said, should insulate the faithful from the world, not communicate with it. Musicians and scholars gained an ever-more-solid respect for Gregorian Chant and the old polyphony, but mostly got on with the business of making modern music and left the theologians talking to themselves.

The eminent German Protestant musicologist, Carl von Winterfeld, warned that a relevant liturgy would come only through new compositions suited to the times. He doubted that in politically troubled France the Church could ever again encompass society as the Mennaisians wished. Germany's enthusiast for classic polyphony and Gregorian Chant also warned that the Roman Church might have to give up its universal language—and the music built on it—in order to reach the masses. The Reformation had given fine music to the people. So today, he said, let the researchers finish their work, but let them not fail to sponsor contemporary music. Winterfeld praised the zeal of those trying to restore "gothic music." This he thought was preferable to the style of the most popular church composer, Lesueur, whose compositions, despite many edifying passages, were written more for an imperial chapel than for "an assembly of Christians of every status, age, and educational level." He claimed that the result of Lesueur's and Choron's work had been that the "people no longer sing in our churches. Rather, all one hears, even in the smallest parishes, is a cheap imitation of the Napoleonic Imperial style." (*Zur Geschichte*, II, 217, 219, 253.)

75. See "The Liturgical Movement," in *The Twentieth Century Encyclopedia of Catholicism* (New York, 1964), CXV, 11ff.

76. Robert Louis Stevenson, *Across the Plains* (New York, 1905), pp. 106–7. See the well known novels by Chateaubriand, *Atala* and *René*.

CHAPTER 6

1. Karl Gustav Fellerer, "Palestrina," *Sacred Music*, XCIV (Autumn 1965), 66–67.

2. See Donald Keene, *Twenty Plays of the No Theatre* (Columbia, 1970), pp. 10ff.

3. Karl Fellerer, *Der Palestrinastil und seine Bedeutung in der vokalen Kirchenmusik des achtzehnten Jahrhunderts* (Augsburg, 1929), passim.

4. A. Schnütgen, Review of *Der Briefwechsel Friedrich und Dorothea Schegel, 1818–1820* by H. Finke, *Jahrbuch für Liturgiewissenschaft*, III (1923), 239.

5. Piozzi, p. 273.

6. Charles Burney, *An Eighteenth-Century Musical Tour in France and Italy*, ed. Percy Scholes (London, 1959), p. 231.

7. Felix Mendelssohn, *Letters*, ed. G. Seldon-Goth (New York, 1945), pp. 89–90, 144.

8. Ibid., p. 145. Perhaps Mendelssohn had a northerner's prejudice against the aria-recitative form, which traditionally employed melismas to set the chapter headings while leaving the rest of the Tenebrae services in psalm-tone recitatives.

9. Ibid., p. 240.

10. Berlioz, *Memoirs*, pp. 154–61.

11. Louis Leclercq [Ludovic Celler], *La Semaine Sainte au Vatican, étude musicale et pittoresque* (Paris, 1867), pp. 43, 134.

12. Cf. Giuseppe Baini, *Über das Leben und die Werke des G. Pierluigi da Palestrina genannt der Fürst der Musik*, trans. Franz Sales Kandler, ed. R. G. Kiesewetter (Leipzig, 1834), 2 vols., passim. The original was in Latin.

13. Louis Leclercq, pp. 151–55.

14. Cf. Burney, pp. 231f.

15. Louis Leclercq, pp. 151–55.

16. Schrade, in Hoelty-Nickel, p. 83.

17. Marie Henri Beyle [Stendhal], *The Red and the Black*, trans. Lowell Bair (New York, 1958), p. 201.

18. Cf. Chateaubriand, "Des cloches," *Génie*, in *Œuvres*, II, 399ff. Also see *Génie*, pp. 301–4, 399–587, and passim.

19. Cf. Hans Müller, "Wilhelm Heinse als Musikschriftsteller," *Vierteljahrschrift für Musikgeschichte*, III (1871), 561–605.

20. Hamann, *Sämtliche Werke*, II, 143–49.

21. Walter Salmen, "Herder und Reichardt," *Herder-Studien*, ed. Walter Wiora (Würzburg, 1960), pp. 284–95.

22. Schrade, in Hoelty-Nickel, p. 86.

23. Herder, *Sämtliche Werke*, XVI, 253–67; cf. also the poem "Die Tonkunst. Eine Rhapsodie," which follows the essay, pp. 268–72.

   In 1786, the year of the Ems Punctuation, some German Catholic bishops proposed to replace operatic music with the "old Italian Masters." [Ursprung, *Restauration*, p. 8.]

24. Moser, *Die evangelische Kirchenmusik*, p. 216.

25. Salmen, pp. 105–6.

26. In *On Religion, Speeches to Its Cultured Despisers*, p. 108.

27. Gregor, "Die deutsche Romantik," pp. 504–29.
28. Heinrich Wackenroder, *Werke und Briefe*, I: *Herzensergiessungen eines kunstliebenden Klosterbruders* (Jena, 1910), 136–37. The translation is taken from Oliver Strunk, *Source Readings in Music History* (New York, 1950), p. 752.
29. Cf. Ursprung, *Restauration*, pp. 7–9.
30. Ibid. For Cecilianism, see chapter 11.
31. Cf. Jürgen Kindermann, "Romantische Aspekte in E. T. A. Hoffmanns Musikanschauung," in *Beiträge*, ed. Salmen, pp. 51–59; Martin Geck, "E. T. A. Hoffmanns Anschauungen über Kirchenmusik," in ibid., pp. 61–71.

   Perhaps, as Prof. Lang says (*Music in Western Civilization*, pp. 795ff.), Hoffman was merely a sober Biedermeyer who abhorred truly popular music, good or not, even Weber's *Freischütz*. Nevertheless, Hoffman's essay is a précis of many similar ones written at that time.
32. Ernest Theodor Hoffmann, "Über alte und neue Kirchenmusik," *Musikalische Schriften* (Leipzig, n.d.), p. 256.
33. Ibid., p. 278.
34. Ibid., p. 250.
35. Ibid., pp. 267ff.
36. Ibid., pp. 270–71.
37. Ibid., pp. 258, 274, and 276.
38. E. T. A. Hoffmann, *Die Elixiere des Teufels* (Munich, 1961), pp. 21, 84–85, 121–25.
39. Gustav Schilling, *Enzyklopaedie der gesamten musikalischen Wissenschaften* (Stuttgart, 1835–38), IV, 93.
40. W. C. Müller, review of *Die Tonkunst in der Kirche* by K. Kocher, *Cäcilia*, II (1825), 144.
41. G. Weber, "Über das Wesen des Kirchenstyls," *Cäcilia*, III (1825), 188.
42. Ibid., p. 187.
43. Ibid.
44. Beethoven, *Letters*, pp. 191, 240.
45. Robert Schumann, *On Music and Musicians*, ed. Konrad Wolff, trans. Paul Rosenfeld (New York, 1964), p. 87.
46. Richard Wagner, *Gesammelte Schriften und Dichtungen* (Leipzig, 1897–98), II, 335.
47. Chateaubriand, *Génie*, pp. 399–585, passim.

   The relationship between art and nature—nurture and nature—had also been a favorite theme of Renaissance aestheticians. See, for example, Shakespeare's *The Winter's Tale*. Renamed nature versus culture, the debate persists. See the Conclusion.
48. Lamy, p. 20.

49. For a catalogue of such opinions, see Evans; Eckardt; Guichard, *La musique et les lettres au temps du romantisme*, p. 76.

50.   . . . ne voyait rien par l'angle étincelant,
    Car son esprit, du monde immense et fourmillant
    Qui pour ses yeux nageait dans l'ombre indéfinie,
    Eteignait la couleur et tirait l'harmonie.
    Victor Hugo, *Oeuvres complètes* (Paris, n.d.), III, 529–38.

51. Guichard, pp. 76–80, 111–13, passim. The authors are speaking of organ and other church music performed in the complete acoustical, visual, and cultural environment of a great French church.

52. Honoré de Balzac, "La Duchesse de Langeais," *Oeuvres complètes illustrées* (Paris, 1901), XVIII, 190.

53. *Cours Familier, Entretien* XXXIX, chapter 10, quoted in Evans, p. 34. But Lamartine limited this impression to the refined listener who needed no words to interpret the emotion of the music. He thought that composers who would reach a whole congregation ought to use words, or at least a program.

54. Ursprung, *Restauration*, pp. 25–29.

55. Ehmann, IV, 38.

56. Ibid., III and IV.

57. Ibid., IV, 54.

58. Cf. Fellerer, "Palestrina," *Sacred Music*, LXXX, 65.

59. Giuseppe Baini, *Über das Leben und die Werke des G. Pierluigi da Palestrina genannt der Fürst der Musik*, trans. Franz Sales Kandler, ed. R. G. Kiesewetter, (Leipzig, 1834).

60. Lang, *Music in Western Civilization*, p. 233.

61. Albert Camus, *L'étranger* (Paris, 1957), p. 175.

62. Stendhal, *The Red and the Black*, p. 498.

63. Gottfried, pp. 4ff.

64. Besides Sailer's circle, at least two other Catholic groups in Germany were trying to reconcile Catholic tradition and humanism. One was the Münster Circle, led by F. L. Stolberg, a poet who favored Basedow's plan for public education by deliberate use of all human faculties with less emphasis on memory work. The Münsterites knew Hamann and declared that poets can reach the truth without calculation, but they avoided giving any credit to the "non-Christian, Rousseau." The other group were the Tübingen theologians led by Johann Adam Möhler, author of *Symbolik*. They flourished in Württemberg and Bavaria in the 1820s and 30s. For both these groups, ultramontane control of state and church seemed less a problem than the "Protestant Jesuits" from the "machine-state, Prussia." Therefore, for them, religion remained a question of adhering to Catholic dogma. Cf. Edmond Vermeil, *Jean-Adam Möhler et l'école catholique de Tubingue* (Paris, 1913), 300ff. Also see by Vermeil's stu-

dent, Pierre Brachin, *Le Cercle de Muenster, 1789–1806, et la pensée religieuse de F. L. Stolberg* (Lyons, 1951), pp. 255–403.

65. Hubert Schiel, *Johann Michael Sailer* (Regensburg, 1952), passim; Philip Funk, *Von der Aufklärung zur Romantik* (Munich, 1925), chap. 4.

66. Some Catholic historians have not known what to make of Sailer. For example, on page 4 of Olivier Rousseau, one reads that Sailer was the German Francis de Sales, but was tainted by rationalism and looked upon the breviary as a means of instruction. Later, on page 59, one reads that Sailer thought the liturgy important in the communal spirit of Christianity and that he proposed "possible and practical reforms." The implication here is that the Enlightenment was impractical. Dom Rousseau later assures us that German romanticism began after the Napoleonic wars in Germany and has nothing important in common with French romanticism!

67. Cooper, pp. 113–14.

68. The king had read Sailer's *Gebetbuch* (1785), *Homilien* (1819), *Sieben Sakramente* (1809), and *Christliche Monat* (1826). A. Schnütgen, review of H. Schiel, *Bischof Sailer und Ludwig I von Bayern, Jahrbuch für Liturgiewissenschaft*, XIII (1936), 440; Pinson, p. 54.

69. Egon Caesar Conte Corti, *Ludwig I. von Bayern* (Munich, 1960), p. 158.

70. Lola Montez was a Spanish dancer who infatuated the king and became his mistress.

   Sailer's absorption into the hierarchy of his country coincided with the end of his ex-student's liberalism. The revolutions of 1830 in France, Belgium, and Poland frightened the king into imposing censorship. The cordial entente between the king and parliament ceased when they refused to vote him more money for public buildings. By 1837 the ultras were in power and ended free thought; in the forties the king's mistress was the real ruler of Bavaria. By forty-eight, Bavarians were glad to be rid of Ludwig.

71. Schiel, pp. 688–90.

   In the vein of Sailer's *Die Weisheit auf der Gasse*, Father, later Cardinal, Diepenbrock wrote a sonnet in 1836 "An die deutsche Sprache oder Rein Deutsch und der Rhindeutsche." His plea was like Sailer's: be enlightened, Catholic Germans, but be free of French hubris. Vigener, pp. 76ff. Diepenbrock was a delegate to the Frankfurt parliament. Though he professed belief in the right of revolution, he "tried to restrain the Catholic population of Berlin from violence" when the Prussian king rejected the German crown. He was made a cardinal in 1850. In 1852 he threatened to resign "and prove Rome operated on money" when the curia was about to indulge an aristocrat's desire for a divorce, which would be out of reach for a commoner. Vigener, p. 92. Sailer's protégé was akin to those Rhineland and south German prelates who led the progressives at Vatican II: Catholic but not curial, intellectual but not scholastic.

72. Schiel, 702.
73. Georg Jakob, "Karl Proske," *Cäcilian Kalendar*, II (1877), 30.
74. See chapter 11.
75. Jakob, 38.
76. Ibid., pp. 30ff.
77. Anton L. Mayer, "Liturgie, Romantik, und Restauration," *Jahrbuch für Liturgiewissenschaft*, X (1930), 77–135.
78. Ibid., where Mayer is pleased to "save" the Restoration by concluding "The more we connect Restoration art with classicism, the farther have we separated it from romanticism" (p. 115). The Roman Church, he says, saved itself by discarding *gemeinschaftlos* (p. 100) and improvisatory (p. 115) romanticism.

When the Austrian Catholic musicologist Tittel relates the Enlightenment's penetration into the cultural life of Bavaria, he does the same. He puts Sailer with the *Aufklärer*, for he thinks that Sailer "tried to restore the classic liturgy" because he preferred "truth to baroque exaggeration." Next he mentions musical restorers, whom he thinks were restoring classicism—ebullients like Wackenroder and Hoffmann. He finds one resemblance only between Enlightenment and romanticism: neither is wholly orthodox; therefore, both are anathema. But the latter is worse. Ernst Tittel, *Österreichische Kirchenmusik: Werden, Wachsen, Wirken* (Vienna, 1961), p. 268.

CHAPTER 7

1. Jungmann, pp. 323ff.
2. Cf. Ruether, *Radical Kingdom*, passim.
3. George Lichtheim, *Short History of Socialism* (New York, 1970), p. 63.
4. Cf. Ruether, passim.
5. Claude-Henri, Comte de Saint-Simon, *Selected Writings*, ed. and trans. F. M. H. Markham (Oxford, 1952), p. xxxi.
6. Claude-Henri, Comte de Saint-Simon, *Nouveau Christianisme: Dialogues entre un conservateur et un novateur,* in *Œuvres* (Paris, 1966), III, 102ff.
7. Jacques Barzun, *Darwin, Marx, Wagner: Critique of a Heritage* (Garden City, 1958), p. 314; Barzun, *Of Human Freedom*, chap. 4.
8. Cf. Greenberg, p. 15, n. 4.

9. Frank E. Manuel, *The Prophets of Paris* (Cambridge, 1962), p. 143. In *Paideia* Werner Jaeger asserts that medieval Christian practice was perhaps the most complete application ever of the musical—i.e., imaginative—education planned for Plato's *Republic*.

10. Manuel, p. 126.

11. Claude-Henri, Comte de Saint-Simon, *Opinions littéraires philosophiques et industrielles* (Paris, 1825), pp. 341–42.

    The Utopians were actually reinvigorating an old theory lost sight of by the doctrinaire capitalists. That is, the creation of wealth is but one aspect of communal life and should therefore be kept subordinate to higher goals and moral judgments. See Lichtheim, *Short History*, p. 8.

12. Donald D. Egbert, "The Idea of 'Avant Garde' in Art and Politics," *American Historical Review*, LXXIII (December 1967), 343.

13. Ibid., p. 347.

14. Sébastien Charléty, *Histoire du saint-simonisme (1825–1864)* (Paris, 1931), p. 169.

15. A. J. L. Busst, "The Image of the Androgyne in the Nineteenth Century," in *Romantic Mythologies*, ed. Ian Fletcher (New York, 1967), p. 25.

16. J. W. von Goethe, *Faust* (Stuttgart and Berlin, n.d.), p. 49.

17. Ibid., p. 65.

18. Busst, pp. 26–27. The androgynous insight which the Saint-Simonians were groping toward recurs throughout historic art and in contemporary psychology. It is especially strong in romantic thought and art. Cf. William Blake, *The Marriage of Heaven and Hell*; Abrams, *Natural Supernaturalism*, pp. 37–46.

19. *Bon* and *bonne* are the masculine and feminine forms for "good." Manuel, *Prophets* (Torchbook ed.), p. 152. Unless the references to this work are indicated by "Torchbook," they are to the Harvard, 1962, edition.

20. Manuel, p. 158.

21. Ibid., p. 309.

22. Ibid., pp. 185–89, 309, 342.

23. Cf. Sigmund Freud, *Civilization and Its Discontents*, passim, especially pp. 55ff; Karl Marx and Friedrich Engels, *The Manifesto of the Communist Party*, trans. Samuel Moore (Peking, 1965), pp. 55ff.

24. Manuel, pp. 186–89.

25. Egbert, p. 347.

26. E. M. Butler, *The Saint-Simonian Religion in Germany* (New York, 1968), passim.

27. Barzun, *Berlioz* (Meridian ed.), p. 101.

28. Egbert, p. 347.

29. Barzun, *Berlioz* (complete ed.), I, 480. Neither Liszt nor Berlioz became a member of the sect.

30. See chapter 8.
31. I have in mind the spectacles written and produced by the late Reverend Daniel A. Lord, S.J. These allegories in a style somewhere between Calderón and Radio City Music Hall sometimes had almost a thousand players on stage.
32. Cf. chapters 1 and 2.
33. René Brancour, *Félicien David* (Paris [1911]), p. 14.
34. Charléty, p. 166.
35. Brancour, p. 19.
36. Charléty, p. 169.
37. Ibid., pp. 171–74.
38. Manuel, *Prophets* (Torchbook ed.), p. 152.
39. Brancour, p. 21.
40. Ibid., p. 21, n. 2.
41. Père Enfantin was probably among the first after Goethe to propose breaching the Isthmus of Suez with a canal. It was, of course, an ex-Saint-Simonian, Ferdinand de Lesseps, who organized the realization of this dream.
42. Brancour, pp. 21ff.
43. Ibid., pp. 24ff.
44. Barzun, *Berlioz* (Meridian ed.), p. 226.
45. Brancour, pp. 44ff. Barzun, *Berlioz*, I, 100–101.
46. E.g., Goethe, *Faust I.*
47. Brancour, pp. 68ff.
48. Ibid., p. 84.
49. Ibid., p. 108.
50. Manuel, p. 306.
51. Ibid., p. 197.
52. Charles Gide, "Introduction," *Selections from the Works of Fourier,* trans. Julia Franklin (London, 1901), pp. 74–75.
53. François Marie Charles Fourier, *Œuvres complètes* (Paris, 1841–45), III, 348ff.
54. I do not consider Comte's and other systems because they were not erected into cults. The immediate European religious forerunners of utopian socialism require a chapter of their own (chapter 4).
    Analogies in nineteenth- and twentieth-century American life require separate books.
55. Critique of E. T. A. Hoffmann's *Undine* in *Allgemeine musikalische Zeitung,* XIX (1817), 201.
56. Dilthey, pp. 197ff.
57. Leo A. Loubère, "The Extreme Left in Lower Languedoc," *American Historical Review,* LXXIII (April 1968), 1040; E. M. Butler, *The Saint-Simonian Religion in Germany,* p. 436.
58. Barzun, *Darwin, Marx, Wagner,* pp. 142–55; Egbert, p. 348; E. J. Hobsbawm, *Primitive Rebels: Studies in Archaic Forms of Social*

Movement in the 19th and 20th Centuries (New York, 1959), pp. 168–69; George Lichtheim, *The Origins of Socialism* (New York, [1970]); Lichtheim, *Short History of Socialism*, p. 44.

CHAPTER 8

---

1. Hugo Leichtentritt, *Music, History, and Ideas* (Cambridge, 1961), p. 215; Arnold Hauser, *The Social History of Art*, III, (New York, 1951); Carl Dahlhaus, "Romantik und Biedermeier, Zur musikgeschichtlichen Charakteristic der Restaurationszeit," *Archiv für Musikwissenschaft*, XXXI (1974), pp. 33ff; Kurt Stephenson, "Musikalisches Biedermeier in Hamburg," *Beiträge zur Hamburgischen Musikgeschichte* (Hamburg, 1956), pp. 7–14.
2. J. H. Plumb, "The Commercialization of Leisure in Eighteenth-Century England," address to the *Anglo-American Historians' Conference*, University of London, 5 July 1972.
3. Cf. Ellul, *La Technique, passim*; Knepler, I, 466ff, 492ff.
4. See Richard Mount-Edgecumbe, The Second Earl of Mount-Edgecumbe, *Musical Reminiscences, Chiefly respecting the Italian Opera in England from 1773 to the present time* (London, 1828), pp. 128ff, 160, 167ff, and passim.
5. According to J. H. Plumb we need histories of precisely such things. "Commercialization of Leisure." Cf. Bernarr Rainbow, *The Land without Music: Musical Education in England 1800–1860 and its Continental Antecedents* (London, [1967]).
6. W. H. Bruford, *Theatre, Drama, and Audience in Goethe's Germany* (London, 1950), p. 354.
7. Lang, *Music in Western Civilization*, p. 726.
8. Ernest Walker, *A History of Music in England* (Oxford, 1952), p. 257.
9. Paul Henry Lang, "Handel—Churchman or Dramatist," in *Festschrift Friedrich Blume* (Basel, 1963), p. 214.
10. Balet and Gerhard, p. 266.
11. Mount-Edgecumbe, pp. 46f.
12. Vol. II, p. 893.
13. Joseph Haydn, *Die Jahreszeiten nach Thomson* (Vienna [n.d.]), pp. 104–54. Eberhard Preussner, *Die bürgerliche Musikkultur; ein Beitrag zur deutschen Musikgeschichte des 18. Jahrhunderts* (Hamburg 1935), p. 75.
14. Combarieu, *Histoire*, II, 527.

    Some observers demurred. Lord Mount-Edgecumbe (p. 128) thought that the vogue of oratorios was a proper extension of the English tradition of employing serious music in church. He did not think that Handel's transplanted arias recalled the frivolous, light-operatic style Edgecumbe thought prevalent in Roman Catholic church music (pp. 178–79).

15. Fiedler, *Love and Death in the American Novel*, p. 23.
16. Lang, *Music in Western Civilization*, p. 967. In the mid-eighteenth century most cities had a musical *collegium* or its equivalent, which provided music for a circle of dues-paying patrician amateurs. By the end of the century the *collegia* were selling subscriptions to their concerts to anyone who wished to pay. In Beethoven's time public concerts with box office tickets were accepted on the continent. The idea of box office tickets probably originated in England with the light musical entertainments in the Vauxhall Gardens, where an admission fee was charged. Loesser, pp. 174, 181, 205, 237, 91–94, 107, 119.
17. Wilfred Mellers, *Music and Society* (New York, 1950), pp. 137ff.
18. Elie Siegmeister, *Music and Society* (New York, [1930s?]), p. 51.
19. Wackenroder, *Werke und Briefe*, I, 141–42. The translation has been taken from Strunk, p. 759.
20. From his "Rossini's 'William Tell,' " Strunk, p. 825.
21. Eckardt, pp. 60f.
22. See the complaints, for example, in *Cäcilia*, XXIII (1844), 114–20.
23. Wagner, *Gesammelte Schriften und Dichtungen*, I, 186–93.
24. Barzun, *Berlioz* (Meridian), pp. 54f.
25. Guichard, p. 76.
26. See the first four sections of Loesser.
27. Eckardt, p. 51.
28. Horstig, "Fantasien über den Einfluss der Tonkunst auf die Veredlung des Menschen," *Cäcilia* 1824, pp. 59–66; see *Allgemeine musikalische Zeitung*, November 1801, cols. 80–87. For a Marxist analysis, see Knepler, I, 485ff.
29. François-Joseph Fétis, *La musique mise à la portée de tout le monde; exposé succinct de tout ce qui est nécessaire pour juger de cet art, et pour parler sans l'avoir étudié*, 2d ed. (Paris, 1834); Friedrich Nietzsche, *The Birth of Tragedy* and *The Case of Wagner*, trans. Walter Kaufmann (New York, 1967); August Kahlert, *Cäcilia*, 1834, pp. 235–44; Barzun, *Classic, Romantic, and Modern*, p. xxi.
30. Felix Mendelssohn, *Letters*, pp. 81f; Joseph d'Ortigue, *Du théâtre italien*, 225–245.
31. Mendelssohn, *Letters*, p. 354.
32. Ibid., pp. 81–83 (June 1830).
33. See, for example, D. F. Weber, "Über die Ausbildung und Veredlung des musikalischen Gehörs," *Allgemeine musikalische Zeitung*, April, 1801, p. 503; G. W. Fink in Gustav Schilling, *Enzyclopaedie*, IV, 93–4.
34. D. F. Weber, ibid.

35. G. Goyau, "Les Origines populaires du Concordat," *Revue des deux mondes*, XV (1903), 919.
36. Eckardt, pp. 20f.
37. J.-J. Rousseau, "Plain-chant," *Dictionnaire de Musique, Œuvres*, XIII, (Paris, 1824), 85 (Reproduces the edition of 1765).
38. Eckardt, p. 31. See also Guichard, pp. 165–68.
39. Ehmann, 21ff.
40. Hector Berlioz, *Evenings with the Orchestra*, trans. Jacques Barzun (New York, 1956), p. 234.
41. D'Ortigue, *La musique à l'église*, p. 120.
42. Cf. Alexis de Tocqueville, *Democracy in America* (New York, 1961), II, 128ff.
43. Jacobs, "Postscript," *Choral Music*, pp. 387f.
44. Strunk, p. 868.
45. Jacobs, "Postscript," pp. 387f.
46. See chapter 2.
47. Balet and Gerhard, pp. 70–71.
48. Alexandre Choron, *Manuel complet de musique vocale et instrumentale, ou encyclopédie musicale*, III: *Instrumentation, union de la musique avec la parole* (Paris, 1836–39), pp. 105–12.
49. Cf. René Le Forestier, *La Franc-Maçonnerie templière et occultiste aux XVIIe et XIXe siècles* (Paris, 1970); Heinrich Dietel, *Beiträge zur Frühgeschichte des Männergesangs* (Würzburg, 1938), p. 74.
50. Ibid.
51. Ibid., pp. 43ff.
52. Ibid., p. 199; Rainbow, *Land without Music*, p. 72ff.
53. Schilling, *Enzyclopädie*, V, 97–101.
54. Otto Elben, *Der volkstümliche deutsche Männergesang* (Tübingen, 1887), pp. 73ff.
55. Friedrich Schmidt, *Das Musikleben der bürgerlichen Gesellschaft Leipzigs im Vormärz* (Leipzig, 1912), pp. 1–13, 204–8.
56. Balet and Gerhard, p. 37.
57. Gunter Hempel, "Das Ende der Leipziger Ratsmusik im 19. Jahrhundert," *Archiv für Musikwissenschaft*, XV (1958), 187–97.
58. M. G. Fr. in H., "Das grosse Musik- und Sängerfest in Mainz am 8 und 9 August, 1835," *Cäcilia* [Mainz], XVII, 287–96.
59. De Tocqueville, *loc. cit.*, and vol. II, *passim*.
60. M. G. Fr. in H. in *Caecilia*, XVII.
61. Jacobs, "Postscript," p. 391.
62. Eberhard Schmidt, "Zur gottesdienstlichen Musik in einer mitteldeutschen Kleinstadt im 18. und 19. Jahrhundert," *Jahrbuch für Liturgik und Hymnologik*, VI (1961), 144–62.
63. Peter Gay, *Weimar Culture* (New York [1968]). Seems to identify a romantic impulse with a bad impulse. The question is what one *does* with this impulse.

64. Mount-Edgecumbe, pp. 179ff.
65. Erik Routley, *Hymns Today and Tomorrow* (Nashville, 1964), p. 131.
66. Millar Patrick, *Four Centuries of Scottish Psalmody* (New York, 1949), pp. 152–200.
67. Hutchings, pp. 76f.
68. Percy A. Scholes, *The Mirror of Music, 1844–1944* (London, 1947), I, 3, 23.
69. Theodore M. Finney, "The Oratorio and Cantata Market: Britain, Germany, America," in Jacobs, pp. 217–30; Rainbow, *Land without Music*, p. 104. Several English cities installed monumental organs in public halls so that "the millions" could hear organ music. The organs grew with a town's pride in having the largest—and loudest. Scholes, *Mirror*, III, 587.
70. Berlioz, *Evenings with the Orchestra*, pp. 229–236.
71. Rainbow, *Land without Music*, pp. 111ff.
72. William L. Crosten, *French Grand Opera: An Art and a Business* (New York, 1948), p. 49.
73. Schuré, "Critiques," *Revue des Deux Fondes*, 1884, p. 790, quoted in Elisabeth Bernard, "Jules Pasdeloup et les Concerts Populaires," *Revue de Musicologie*, LVII (1971), 178.
74. Reynolds, pp. 85, 89.
75. John B. Wilson, "An Analogue of Transcendentalism," *Journal of the History of Ideas*, XXVII (September 1966), 461.
76. Henry Wilder Foote, *Three Centuries of American Hymnody* (London, 1941), pp. 180f.
77. Basil Willey, *The Eighteenth-Century Background* (New York, 1940), p. 183.
78. Louis F. Benson, *The English Hymn: Its Development and Use in Worship* (New York, 1915); reprint, (Richmond, Va., 1962), pp. 177 and 470.
79. Edward Deming Andrews, *The Gift to Be Simple: Songs, Dances and Rituals of the American Shakers* (New York, 1962), pp. 8, 157, passim.
80. L. W. Ellinwood, *The History of American Church Music* (New York, 1953), p. 74.
81. Margaret Johnson Wright, "Music of the Sacred Harp," *American Guild of Organists Quarterly*, XI (April 1966), 47ff.
    Night-time, clear-channel radio stations were probably the second; on them one still hears, though in diminishing numbers, authentic revival preachers, advertisements for shape-note hymnals, and homey moral advice. Shape-note hymnals helped to mediate hymns from the Old Country into American folklore, where they influenced popular music—witness the country 'n western moralism or pop-gospel hits such as "Bridge over Troubled Water."

82. Richard Franko Goldman, "After Handel—in Britain and America," in Jacobs, pp. 183–200.

83. Benson, p. 378. Some congregations found it consistently Protestant to let the talents God had elected do the singing. Although the liturgical churches continued to limit their official ministry to a priesthood or its heirs, the leftward, nonliturgical churches and sects in America now have "ministers of music." Sophisticates, including nontheists, are often surprised to see small-town Baptists or Methodist churches mount the Mozart or Brahms Requiem or some other large musical enterprise.

84. Etherington, *Protestant Worship Music*, p. 170.

85. Ibid.

86. Emile Capouya, Review of *The Life of the Mind in America*, by Perry Miller, *Commonweal*, LXXXIII (17 December 1965), 351–52.

87. Cf. Noel Q. King, *The Religions of Africa* (New York, 1920); Bernard Katz, *The Social Implications of Early Black Music in the United States* (New York, 1969); Henry Pleasants, *Serious Music and All that Jazz* (New York [1967]).

88. Cf. Henry Pleasants, *Serious Music and All That Jazz*. The "African" churches, which were founded during the Reconstruction to keep certain denominations white, also emphasize the musical side of their Christianity. In these churches elaborate hierarchies of ministers, chanted (and therefore formal) ritual, and solo musicians mix gracefully—as they did at Dr. Martin Luther King, Jr.'s funeral —with lay participation in the ministry, informal testimony, and community singing.

89. Henry A. Kmen, *Music in New Orleans: The Formative Years, 1789–1841* (Baton Rouge, 1966), p. 3.

90. Ibid., pp. 226–27.

91. Ibid., p. 236.

92. Ibid., p. 4.

93. Ibid., p. 46.

94. Ibid., pp. 201–2.

95. Ibid., p. 205.

96. Ibid.

97. Ibid.

98. Luke, 1:68–79. See also *Liber Usualis*, pp. 1921ff.

99. These are usually supposed to have begun only after the Confederate soldiers pawned their regimental bands' instruments, making them cheap enough for ex-slaves. Kmen discards this theory (p. 266).

100. On All Souls Day a catafalque covered with the usual funeral pall, but containing no corpse, was usually erected in Catholic churches

and the entire funeral Mass and absolution, short of the actual burial rite, performed. During the rest of the year, families so inclined might request such a Requiem Mass with catafalque on the various monthly and yearly commemorations of their deceased.

101. Kmen, p. 207.
102. Ibid., p. 150.
103. Walter Rundell, Jr., review of *Music in New Orleans: The Formative Years, 1789–1841*, by Henry A. Kmen, *American Historical Review*, LXXIII (October 1967), 221–22.
104. Kmen, passim.
105. Manuel Garcia [*fils*], *Ecole de Garcia, traité complet de l'art du chant* (Paris, 1878), pp. 100ff.
106. John Kouwenhoven, *Made in America: The Arts in Modern Civilization* (Garden City, N.Y., 1948), pp. 1–117.
107. Kmen, p. 200.
108. Wolfgang Sauer, "Nationalist Socialism: Totalitarianism or Fascism?" *American Historical Review*, LXXIII (December 1967), 224.
109. By aiming to improve the quality of everyone's life, while learning from the people, popular aesthetic education worked to overcome those caste divisions exploited by the Nazis and their ilk. Romantic exaltation of the artist amounted to idealizing a career of talent and freedom to pursue one's coherent vision. Art is neither blue-collar nor white-collar; imagination knows no class lines, but "rational" civil-service and university entrance examinations help to create and maintain them.

It was the Jews' misfortune to have become de facto part of Germany's ruling class out of proportion to their numbers. Thus they became double victims of left-over medieval prejudices against "deicides" combined with modern resentment against the new university caste.

CHAPTER 9

1. Jane Austen, *Pride and Prejudice* (New York: Books, Inc., n.d.), p. 99.
2. Sir Kenneth Clark, *The Gothic Revival: An essay in the History of Taste* (New York, 1962), p. 357; Bernarr Rainbow, *The Choral Revival in the Anglican Church (1839–1872)* (London, 1970) 86, 240–46. For a strongly-argued contrary opinion see Donald Greene, "The Via Media in an Age of Revolution; Anglicanism in the 18th Century," *The Varied Pattern: Studies in the 18th Century*, ed.

Peter Hughes and David Williams (Toronto, 1971), pp. 297–320. Nevertheless, prevalent attitudes toward the poetic and musical sides of religion were quite narrow.

3. Edmund Fellowes, *English Cathedral Music* (London, 1928), pp. 192ff.
4. Horton Davies, *Worship and Theology in England*, IV: *From Newman to Martineau, 1850–1900* (Princeton, 1962), p. 74.
5. Lang, *Music in Western Civilization*, pp. 683f.
6. Brinton, *The Political Ideas of the English Romanticists, passim.*
7. Cf. Edmund Burke, "Reflections on the Revolution in France," *Works* (Boston, 1881), III, 274ff.
8. M. H. Abrams, *The Mirror and the Lamp*, p. 105.
9. John Herman Randall, Jr., *The Career of Philosophy*, II: *From the German Enlightenment to the Age of Darwin* (New York, 1965), p. 506.
10. Ibid.
11. Abrams, *The Mirror and the Lamp*, p. 225.
12. Preface to *Lyrical Ballads* (1800), *Harvard Classics*, XXXIX, 294ff.
13. Randall, p. 506.
14. Basil Willey, *Nineteenth Century Studies* (New York, 1949), p. 268.
15. Ibid.
16. Hoxie N. Fairchild, "Romanticism and the Religious Revival in England," *Journal of the History of Ideas*, II (1941), 337. He is speaking of romanticism in general, but his words are applicable to Coleridge.
17. [Samuel Taylor] Coleridge, *Prose and Poetry* (New York, 1965), p. 94. Written in 1791, before he knew Wordsworth.
18. S. T. Coleridge, *Biographia Literaria* (Oxford, 1907), II, 9–11, 12, 56.
19. Benson, p. 438.
20. Ibid., p. 451.
21. See Henry Bett, "The Evangelical Religion and Literature," *Studies in Literature* (Port Washington, N.Y., 1968), pp. 9–28; Davies, *1690*, 196.
22. L. E. Elliott-Binns, *The Early Evangelicals: A Religious and Social Study* (Greenwich, Conn., 1953), p. 81.
23. R. W. Church, *The Oxford Movement: Twelve Years, 1833–1845* (London, 1922), pp. 11, 13.
24. Robert Murrell Stevenson, *Patterns of Protestant Church Music* (Durham, 1953), p. 134. The Portuguese "Chapel" was a large church, which the Catholics of London entered through the embassy diplomatically immune to the laws against Recusants.
25. That is, Gregorian chant.
26. Norman Demuth, ed., *An Anthology of Music Criticism* (London, 1947), p. 219.
27. William Fleming, *Arts and Ideas*, p. 669. Among the Italianizers,

as Newman and his circle were called, neomedieval architecture, rites, and music were thought a confession of irrelevance. Davies, *1850*, p. 6.
28. Cf. Davies, *1850*, p. 28.
29. John Ruskin, *The Stones of Venice* (Boston, 1887), III, II, sec. 39, p. 63.
30. Hauser, I, 201.
31. Cf. Irwin Panofsky, *Gothic Architecture and Scholasticism* (Latrobe, Pa., 1951), p. 64.
32. Cf. A. Hauser, I, 233–44.
33. Clark, *The Gothic Revival*, p. 131.
34. Davies, *1690*, p. 279.
35. Edmund Sheridan Purcell, *The Life and Letters of Ambrose Phillipps de Lisle* (London, 1900), I, 223.
36. Augustus Welby Pugin, *Contrasts, or A Parallel between the Noble edifices of the Middle Ages and the Corresponding Buildings of the Present Day: Showing the Present Decay of Taste* (London, 1845), passim.
37. Cf. Davies, *1850*, p. 35, n. 51.
38. Douglas, *Church Music in History*, p. 214.
39. Not to be confused with Ambrose Philips (ca. 1675–1749).
40. Cf. Francis J. Guentner, "A Nineteenth-Century Chant Revival," *Sacred Music* XCII (1965), 31–32.
41. Ibid., p. 30.
42. *Dublin Review*, XXII (March, 1847), 147, quoted in Guentner, p. 35.
43. Rev. Henry Formby, *The Plain Chant, The Image and Symbol of the Humanity of our Divine Redeemer and the Blessed Mary* (London, 1848), p. 10.
44. In *The Brothers Karamazov*.
45. Randall, p. 508.
46. Lionel Trilling, *Matthew Arnold* (New York, 1955), p. 47.
47. Ibid., p. 51.
48. Edward Alexander, *Matthew Arnold and John Stuart Mill* (London, 1965), passim.
49. A concise history of the background and progress of the Broad Church idea is found in Trilling, *Matthew Arnold*, pp. 45ff. and passim.
50. Trilling, p. 10.
51. Ibid., p. 13.
52. Ibid, p. 33.
53. Davies, *1690*, p. 286.
54. Trilling, pp. 55–56.
55. Matthew Arnold, *St. Paul and Protestantism* (New York, 1924), p. 348.

56. Ibid., p. 178.
57. Davies, *1690*, pp. 383ff.
58. Ibid., p. 295.
59. Ibid., p. 297.
60. Altholz, p. 140.
61. Cf. Alan H. Hamilton, "The Social Gospel," in Burrell, p. 101.
62. Cf. Altholz, p. 140.
63. Cf. Egbert, pp. 349ff.
64. Cf. the writings of Paul Goodman for a similar nostalgia.
65. F. D. Maurice, *Social Morality* (London, 1872), pp. 6ff.
66. Ibid., pp. 397–414.
67. Cf. Davies, *1850*, pp. 74ff, 98.
68. Latourette, pp. 1149–52.
69. Also true east of the Rhine; see Wetzstein, pp. 182–98.
70. Patrick, pp. 139, 141.
71. J.-J. Rousseau, "Lettre à M. Perdriau," *Ecrits sur la musique*, p. 251.
72. Reynolds, *A Survey of Christian Hymnody*, p. 54.
73. Hermann Müller, p. 108.
74. Daniel Robert, *Les églises reformées en France (1800–1830)* (Paris, 1961), p. 231.
75. William D. Maxwell, *A History of Worship in the Church of Scotland* (London, 1955), p. 166.
76. Patrick, p. 213.
77. Ibid., p. 260.
78. Davies, *1850*, pp. 164f.
79. Richard Garnett, "Edward Irving (1792–1834)," *Dictionary of National Biography*, XXIX, 52–56.
80. William Hazlitt, "Rev. Mr. Irving," *The Spirit of the Age*, in *Complete Works*, ed. P. P. Howe (London, 1932), XI, 38–46; Thomas Carlyle, "Edward Irving," *Reminiscences* (London, 1887), II, 1–120.
81. Davies, *1850*, p. 155.
82. *Encyclopaedia Britannica*, V, 42–43.
83. Altholz, p. 119.
84. *Encyclopaedia Britannica*, XIV, 705.
85. Davies, *1850*, p. 168.
86. George Bernard Shaw, *Major Barbara* (Baltimore, 1967), pp. 93f.

CHAPTER 10

1. Stendhal [Marie-Henri Beyle], *Vie de Rossini* (Paris, 1922), I, 53–64; Francis Toye, *Rossini: A Study in Tragi-Comedy* (New York, 1947), p. xii.

2. Such is the opinion of, for example, René Wellek, in *Romanticism Reconsidered*, ed. Northrop Frye (New York, 1972), p. 132.
3. Altholz, p. 71.
4. Cf. Francesco Pitocco, "Ricerche sul sansimonismo in Italia. Lambruschini: la sua formazione culturale e il sansimonismo nella sua idea di riforma religiosa," *Studi e Materiali di Storia delle Religioni*, XXXIX (1968); 343. Stendhal [Marie-Henri Beyle], *The Charterhouse of Parma*, trans. C. K. Scott Moncrieff (Garden City, N.Y., 1933).
5. Christopher Hibbert, *Garibaldi and His Enemies* (Boston, 1966), pp. 6ff.
6. Giuseppe Garibaldi, *Memoirs*, ed. Alexandre Dumas, trans. R. S. Garnett (London, 1931), p. 39.
7. Hales, *Pio Nono*, pp. 110ff; Guido de Ruggiero, *The History of European Liberalism*, trans., R. G. Collingwood (Boston, 1964), pp. 314ff. Hales seems to think that Mazzini was an evil man because he came from a Jansenist household and inserted Condorcet's *Tableau du progrès de l'esprit* in his prayerbook in place of the Ordinary of the Mass. Since Ruggiero is enamored of nineteenth-century, laissez-faire liberalism, he flirts with saying Mazzini was wrong because "unsuccessful."
8. Hales, *Pio Nono*, p. 110.
   Thomas Carlyle's and Europe's opinion of Mazzini was expressed ["Mazzini," *Encyclopaedia Britannica*, XV, p. 130] in a letter to *The Times*: "I have had the honor to know Mr. Mazzini for a series of years, and, whatever I may think of his practical insight and skill in worldly affairs, I can with great freedom testify that he, if I have ever seen one such, is a man of genius and virtue, one of those rare men, numerable unfortunately but as units in this world, who are worthy to be called martyr souls; who in silence, piously in their daily life, practice what is meant by that." Sir Charles Gavan Duffy, *Conversations with Carlyle* (New York, 1892), pp. 109–11.
9. Raffaello Monterosso, *La Musica nel Risorgimento* (Milan, 1948), pp. 10–11.
10. Giuseppe Mazzini, *Philosophy of Music*, in *The Life and Writings of Joseph Mazzini*, trans. Arthur Livingstone (London, 1891), IV.
11. Ibid., pp. 4, 7–9.
12. *Mousiké* in the *paideia* was, of course, a combination of the arts. [See Anderson, *Ethos and Education in Greek Music*, passim; Nietzsche, *Birth*, passim; Jaeger, *Paideia*.]
13. Mazzini, *Philosophy of Music*, pp. 20–21.
14. Ibid., pp. 29ff.; Jean-Pierre Barricelli, "Romantic Writers and Music: The Case of Mazzini," *Studies in Romanticism*, XIV (1975), 97.
15. Mazzini, *Philosophy of Music*, pp. 42–48.

16. Ibid., p. 46.
17. Ibid., p. 48.
18.　Si risorga, e sempre duri
　　　Libertá in sui splendor! [Monterosso, p. 34.]
　　　Italy stood in the same relationship to Austria and Napoleonic France as Finland to the USSR and Germany in World War II. Napoleon's defeat seemed a disaster. In December 1973 the 1799 Roman Republic was represented in an excellent exhibition. Cf. *Roma Giacobina, Catalogo*, ed., Maria Elisa Monti Tittoni and Lucia Palladini Cavazzi.
19. Monterroso, p. 35. Many such phrases used the verb *sorgere* (to arise), cognate of *risorgimento* (resurgence).
20. Ibid., p. 36.
21. Fleming, pp. 622, 629.
22. Ruggiero, p. 310.
23. Monterosso, p. 294; R. J. B. Bosworth, "Verdi and the Risorgimento," *Italian Quarterly*, XIV (1970), 3–27.
24. Monterosso, pp. 378–79. One thing which totalitarian states have learned from romanticism is to stifle it by censoring everything, even "unpolitical" styles of art.
25. Cf. Elsa Bienenfield, "Verdi and Schiller," *Musical Quarterly*, XVII (1931), 204–8.
26. William Albert Herrmann, *Religion in the Operas of Giuseppe Verdi* (Ann Arbor, 1964), pp. 49–61.
27. Ibid., pp. 9–10; George Martin, *Verdi: His Music, Life and Times* (New York, 1963), pp. 8–22, 287.
28. Albert Maecklenburg, "Verdi and Manzoni," *Musical Quarterly*, XVII (1931), pp. 209–17.
29. Bosworth, pp. 6–12; Herrmann, pp. 64ff.
30. Herrmann, pp. 108–9.
31. Ibid., p. 66.
32. Frits Noske, "Ritual Scenes in Verdi's Operas," *Music and Letters* LV (1973), 416ff; Walter H. Rubsamen, "Music and Politics in the Risorgimento," *Italian Quarterly*, V (1961), 101.
33. A. C. Keys, "Schiller and Italian Opera," *Music and Letters*, XLI (1960), 223–37; Barricelli, 108, 111.
34. Keys, p. 229; Noske, p. 415; Rubsamen, passim; see also chap. I and Appendix 1 of the present work; Janus Liebner, "Der Einfluss Schillers auf Verdi," *International Musicological Society*, Congress Report, 1972, pp. 222–25.
35. Act III, sc. ii.
36. Act IV, sc. ii.
37. Herrmann, p. 135.
38. Monterosso, p. 295.
39. Herrmann, pp. 28ff.
40. Ibid., p. 100.

41. Alfred Einstein, *Music in the Romantic Era* (New York, 1957), p. 110.
42. Herrmann, p. 7.
43. Ibid., p. 258.
44. *Inni* usually have more lyrical texts and florid music than do hymns. Though the words are cognate, a hymn always reminds one of a northern, protestant chorale, where music is subordinate to the text. An *inno* seems to turn music loose—to the despair of musical puritans. Yet the florid Italian variety is true to the ancient meaning of hymn, which was a song to the fertility god Hymen, then a song of the marriage bed, finally the lyric to any passionate or religious encounter.
45. Monterosso, p. 53.
46. Ibid., pp. 124–26.
47. Paul Nettl, *National Anthems* (New York [1967]), p. 32.
48. P. M. Pasinetti, "Notes on the Poetic Images of the Patria," *Italian Quarterly*, XVII, XVIII (1961), 65, 69; Charles Speroni, "Popular Songs and Hymns of the 'Risorgimento,' " *Italian Quarterly*, XVII, XVIII (1961), 73f.
49. Monterosso, p. 62.
50. Heinrich Heine, "Italien. I, Reise von München nach Genua," *Reisebilder* XIX and XXVII, in *Werke*, VII–VIII, 43ff, 56ff.
51. Monterosso, pp. 180ff, 42, 84.
52. Pasinetti, pp. 65, 69; Speroni, pp. 73f.
53. To the island of Gaeta in the Kingdom of Sicily.
54. Hales, *Pio Nono*, p. 130.
55. Ferdinand de Lesseps, *Ma mission à Rome* (Paris, 1849), p. 3.
56. Monterosso, p. 117.
57. Ibid., p. 41.
58. A duet from this opera, "Amour sacré de la patrie," was welcomed like a new *Marseillaise* [ibid.]. When it had been sung by Adolphe Nourrit at Brussels in 1830, it became the signal for the revolution there.
59. Ruggiero, pp. 298–324.
60. Professors like Hobsbawn and de Ruggiero are sometimes as utopian as any of the romantics. Like the liberals of the nineteenth century, they believe in John Stuart Mill's utopia where the fittest idea really does survive. As if modern biologists still believed it! Of course, Mill's own idea of utility was romantic enough to transcend the debater's and businessman's calculus—as we know from his Wordsworthian rather than Malthusian argument in favor of population control. Cf. John Stuart Mill, *Principles of Political Economy* (London, 1862), vol. 2, bk. IV, chap. 6, p. 325.

The professors seem to talk as though there will come a time when most people will do research and reason to conclusions. The romantics knew that emotional attraction is what one must condition first, last, and always, if one wishes to move a group of people. For example, Hobsbawm, in a chapter on "Ritual in Social Movements," misses the point. *Primitive Rebels*, pp. 150–74. After a twelve-page disquisition discounting the relevance of the ritual side of economic and political organizations since the Middle Ages, he characterizes those of the century pre-1848 as "ritualized to the point of resembling an Italian opera rather than a revolutionary body" (p. 162). Yet, "the secret revolutionary brotherhood was by far the most important form of organization for changing society" (ibid.)!

I would argue that in the Middle Ages the guilds' rituals taught the dignity of labor. A parody of ecclesiastical or courtly ritual made the guildsman feel that his vocation was as worthy as a cleric's or courtier's. When the Protestant reformers made the reading of God's Word a possibility and a necessity, they did the same thing. They dignified a revolution.

The story of the survival of a conscious desire to master the non-rational is told best in H. Stuart Hughes, *Consciousness and Society* (New York, 1958). But even Hughes is quite unhistorical when he balks at recognizing the crucial importance of the romantic mentality for following generations.

61. Monterosso, p. 57.

CHAPTER 11

1. Cf. Eric Hoffer, *The True Believer: Thoughts on the Nature of Mass Movements* (New York, 1951), p. 58; Barzun, *Of Human Freedom*, chap. 4.
2. Crane Brinton, *The Anatomy of Revolution* (New York, 1952), p. 230. For organized religion's original but decreasing pliability during the Revolutionary Era, see part 1, and Palmer, *Age*, II, 353ff.
3. Karl Gustav Fellerer, *The History of Catholic Church Music*, trans. Francis A. Brunner (Baltimore, 1961), p. 173.
4. Cf. Carner, "The Mass," *Choral Music*, pp. 231ff.
5. Barzun, *Classic, Romantic, and Modern*, p. 109.
6. Eckardt, pp. 40–41.
7. Hector Berlioz, "The Puritans of Church Music," *Evenings with The Orchestra*, trans., Barzun, pp. 190–91. The words "Da robur" (give us strength) were usually boomed out *fortissimo*, to the despair of some theologians.
8. Berlioz is punning on "monody," which is music consisting of a single melodic line, as in Gregorian chant.
9. Johan Huizinga, *The Waning of the Middle Ages* (Garden City, N.Y., 1954), p. 156.

10. Clément, p. 336.
11. Ibid., pp. i–xiii.
12. Ibid., pp. 89–104.
13. Ibid., p. 343.
14. Ibid., p. 441.
15. Cf. Louis Lambillotte, *Esthétique, théorie et pratique du chant grégorien, restauré d'après la doctrine des anciens et les sources primitives* (Paris, 1855).
16. N. Cloet, *Examen du mémoire sur les chants liturgiques du R. P. Lambillotte ou Réponse au R. P. Dufour.* (Paris, 1857), p. 108.
17. D'Ortigue, *La musique à l'église*, p. 325.
18. Combarieu thought that they did not even tell the truth. He thought they deceived the public by making promises which they would not keep, proclaimed discoveries which did not exist, and avoided essential questions. Jules Combarieu, "Le Charlatanisme dans l'archéologie musicale au XIXe siècle et le problème de l'origine des neumes," *Rivista musicale italiana*, II (1895), 2–4.
19. Cf. chapter 5.
20. Rayburn, p. 26.
21. T. A. Burge, "The Vatican Edition of the *Kyriale* and its Critics," *Irish Ecclesiastical Record*, XIX (1906), reprinted in *Cäcilia*, LXXXVI (1959), 334.
22. Ibid.
23. Pons, IV, pp. 79ff.
24. Rayburn, p. 8.
25. Pons, IV, p. 87.
26. Pius X, *The Motu Proprio of Pope Pius X on Sacred Music*, in *The White List of the Society of St. Gregory of America* (New York, 1939), pp. 7ff.
27. Pons, IV, 33.
28. Ibid., pp. 31–46.
29. Cf. Ibid., passim.
30. See chapter 3.
31. Despite these attempts to drive out all but the most ultramontane styles and despite the defection of the Old Catholics and other cismontanes following the declaration of papal infallibility at the First Vatican Council, vernacular rites survived the nineteenth century in Germany by being called an accompaniment to a Low Mass, rather than a *Singmesse*, which had to be in Latin. The Sacred Congregation of Rites legitimized the existing practice in 1943 [Cf. Koenker, p. 150; Jungmann, I, p. 155].
32. Cf. chapter 6.
33. *Cäcilian Kalendar*, IX (1883), 44–52.
34. Anton Walter, "F. X. Witt. Miniaturbild seines Lebens und Wirkens," *Kirchenmusikalisches Jahrbuch*, V (1890), 33.

35. A. Walter, p. 48; see chapter 6, this volume; Karl Gustav Fellerer, "Grundlagen und Anfänge der kirchenmusikalischen Organisation Franz Xaver Witts," *Kirchenmusikalisches Jahrbuch*, LV (1971), 41ff.
36. Fellerer, "Grundlagen," pp. 59ff.
37. Paul Henry Lang, "Patrimonium Musicae Sacrae," p. 126; see chapter 6.
38. *Cäcilian Kalendar*, I (1876), 32ff.
39. Ibid., pp. 64–85.
40. Moser, *Evangelische Kirchenmusik*, p. 217.
41. Hutchings, pp. 77–94.
42. Wetzstein, p. 70.
43. Guido M. Dreves, *Ein Wort zur Gesangbuch-Frage* (Freiburg, 1885), p. 89.
44. A. Walter in *Kirchenmusikalisches Jahrbuch*, I (1886), 89–91.
45. Ibid., II, 10–13.
46. Cf. Bäumker, III, IV, passim.
47. Rembert Weakland, "Music and Liturgy in Evolution," in *Crisis in Church Music*, 10.

    This generation's "folk" Mass fulfills the same psychological function as last century's Marian hymn. This Catholic pietism touches the Protestant revival tradition, where hymns are also sung as popular songs, more or less uncritically and indiscriminately. The Reformed, Lutheran, Episcopalian, and even the Baptist rites, are a via media where hymns have always been an integral part of a quasi-liturgical scheme and more easily drift into art music. Erik Routley, *The Music of Christian Hymnody* (London, 1957), p. 151.

48. Knipfer, pp. 210–21.
49. Cf. Ibid., pp. 283ff.
50. Cf. Bäumker, II, 10.
51. Koenker, p. 34; Giessler, pp. 206–14.
52. Cf. Einstein, p. 100.
53. Erwin Doernberg, *The Life and Symphonies of Anton Bruckner* (London, 1960), p. 30.
54. Cf. Hutchings, pp. 90ff.
55. Sitwell, p. 26.
56. Richard Wagner, *Prose Works*, trans. William Ashton Ellis (London, 1897), VI, 211–24; the original is in Wagner, *Gesammelte Schriften*, X, pp. 213ff.
57. Ibid., pp. 250–62. The idea that there must be but one allegory-maker reminds one of Plato's similar thoughts in the *Republic* on the need for an "official" music to teach morality. Plato, too, had been disappointed in a romanticism—the epistemological populism of Socrates, who had thought that absolute truth was accessible to the plainest slaves and the most exalted mystics, though not to those

successful bourgeois, the Sophists. Cf. Plato, *Meno* and also *Euthyphro, Crito.*
58. Wagner, *Gessammelte Schriften*, III, 25.
59. Elliot Zuckerman, *The First Hundred Years of Wagner's Tristan* (New York, 1964), p. 29.
60. Cf. Barzun, *Darwin, Marx, and Wagner*, pp. 292–93.
61. Lang, *Music in Western Civilization*, p. 696.
62. Dent, "Italian Opera," p. 500. "Wagner and Brahms once accepted by the leaders of musical thought, it was hardly possible to avoid accepting as a general principle of musical criticism the supposition that whatever was German was good, and whatever was Italian was bad. To that they added the subsidiary principles that as a general rule, sacred music was superior to secular, and instrumental music to vocal, exception being made only for polyphonic choral writing, solo singing of a strictly declamatory type and, of course, German Lieder.

"These principles once established, it was only natural that eighteenth century Italian opera should be regarded as the concentrated expression of all that was most evil in the art of music."
63. Liszt to his cousin Eduard Liszt, Lamara-Bache *Letters*, I, 295. Estergom is usually written "Gran" in western languages.
64. Cf. *Revue musicale*, XIV (May 1928), 190ff.
65. Mellers, *Man and His Music*, p. 46.
66. Combarieu, *Histoire*, III, 157–58.
67. Tittel, pp. 278, 280.
68. Ibid., p. 272.
69. Sitwell, p. 256.
70. Liszt, *Letters*, II, 192.
71. From a Letter to Kappellmeister Joseph Boehm in Vienna, 22 June 1879, *Letters*, II, 354.
72. Combarieu, *Histoire*, III, pp. 153–54.
73. Bence Szabolsci, *The Twilight of Ferenc Liszt*, trans. András Deák (Budapest, 1959), p. 36.
74. Sitwell, p. 229.
75. Szabolsci, pp. 9ff.
76. Liszt, *Letters*, II, 457. In 1884.
77. Kenneth Clark, *The Gothic Revival*, pp. 218, 221.
78. Cf. Lang, "Patrimonium," p. 120. "Obedience to the liturgical spirit is for the artist much more than paying heed to merely legal commands, yet for some time the best musical minds have been prevented by the latter from fulfilling the former. The legislators on liturgical music have failed to consider that while music as a vehicle for religious expression is innate in man, that emotion beyond words takes refuge in music, as a phenomenon music exists for its own sake. . . . The religious is only one of many factors. . . . The litur-

gists like the curia itself were determined to be impregnable, as a result they failed to establish communication with the musicians. . . . The hostility to music, strongly present in the writings of some of the Church Fathers (whence it found its way into Calvinism and the denominations inspired by it) created a supposed dichotomy between musical effort undertaken with and that undertaken without a predominant religious spirit" [ibid.].

Indeed it was not until the Second Vatican Council that the Roman Church took seriously the core of romantic propaganda. Previous documents spoke of music not as integral, but as assisting. The recent *Constitution on the Liturgy* decreed that music is an integral part of the Liturgy. *Documents of Vatican II*, ed. Walter M. Abbott, (New York, 1966), 17.

CHAPTER 12

1. Norman O. Brown, *Love's Body* (New York [1966]), *passim*; Maisie Ward, *Young Mr. Newman* (New York, 1948), p. 239; F. X. Shea, S.J., "Religion and the Romantic Movement," *Studies in Romanticism*, IX (1970), 285–321.
2. Lytton Strachey, *Eminent Victorians* (Garden City, N.Y. [n.d.]), pp. 16ff.
3. Louis Bouyer, *Newman: His Life and Spirituality*, trans. J. Lewis May (New York, 1958), pp. 6f.
4. Ibid., p. 6.
5. M. Ward, pp. 5, 11. The family were musical enough for his sister to dare to criticize Handel, whose music was at that time the idol of the English public. She found him dull.

   Quite in his childhood his mother wrote to him after a concert, "We were fascinated by the Dutchman [as Newman had christened Beethoven to annoy his music master] and thought of you and your musical party frequently. John Henry Newman, *Letters and Correspondence*, ed. Anne Mozley (London, 1919), I, 16.

   In his autobiographical novel, *Loss and Gain* (London, 1919), p. 96, Newman had the hero's father say, "I never knew a boy who so placed his likings and dislikings on fancies."
6. M. Ward, p. 41.
7. Geoffrey Faber, *Oxford Apostles: A Character Study of the Oxford Movement* (New York, 1934), p. 74.
8. Cardinal John Henry Newman, *Apologia Pro Vita Sua* (Garden City, N.Y., 1956), p. 125.
9. Bouyer, p. 14.

10. Ibid., pp. 14–16.
11. Newman, *Letters and Correspondence*, I, 16.
12. Bouyer, p. 17.
13. M. Ward, pp. 94–97.
14. Bouyer, p. 14. Louis Bouyer is an orthodox Catholic and an avowed admirer of Newman.
15. Faber, p. 45.
16. M. Ward, p. 46.
17. Newman, *Letters and Correspondence*, I, p. 46.
18. M. Ward, pp. 44, 73.
19. Cf. Ibid., pp. 78ff.
20. See Newman, *Essays Critical and Historical* (London, 1919), I, 387–422; *Historical Sketches* (London, 1908), I, 98; *Difficulties of Anglicans* (London, 1908), I, pp. 90–91. See also Ronald Knox, *Enthusiasm* (New York, 1961), pp. 422–548.
21. Cf. H. Francis Davis, "Was Newman a Disciple of Coleridge?" *Dublin Review*, October, 1945, pp. 165–73.
22. Wilfrid Ward, *The Life of John Henry Cardinal Newman* (London, 1921), II, 354–55.
23. Cf. Church, p. 71.
24. Cf. Werner Stark, "The Social Philosopher," in *John Henry Newman Centenary Essays*, ed. Henry Tristram (London, 1945), pp. 155–77.
25. Newman, "Who's to Blame," in *Discussions and Arguments on Various Subjects* (London, 1924), p. 315.
26. Davies, *1690*, pp. 270–80.
27. Bernard Christopher O'Halloran, *Richard Hurrell Froude: His Influence on John Henry Newman and the Oxford Movement* (Ph.D. diss., Columbia University, 1965), passim.
28. Henry Tristram, "With Newman at Prayer," in *J. H. N. Centenary Essays*, p. 113.
29. Cf. W. G. Roe, *The Reception of Lamennais' Religious Ideas in England in the Nineteenth Century.* (London, 1966), pp. 94–114.
30. Bouyer, p. 247; F. X. Shea, S.J. "Religion and the Romantic Movement," in *Studies in Romanticism*, IX (1970), 285–96.
31. Newman, *Apologia* (Image ed.) p. 287. In the introduction to Bouyer, H. Francis Davis quoted that same sentence and recognized that it is the linchpin of Newman's life.
    Cf. Jacques Barzun, *Science, the Glorious Entertainment* (New York [1964]).
32. Yngve Brilioth, *Three Lectures on Evangelicalism and the Oxford Movement* (London, 1934), p. 29.
33. M. Ward, p. 104.
34. Ibid., p. 108.
35. Davies, *1690*, pp. 271ff.

36. M. Ward, p. 108.
37. Herbert Clegg, "Evangelicals and Tractarians," *Historical Magazine of the Protestant Episcopal Church*, XXXV (1966), 146.
38. M. Ward, p. 162.
39. April 1, 1840, quoted in M. Ward, p. 363.
40. R. D. Middleton, "The Vicar of St. Mary's," in *J. H. N. Centenary Essays*, pp. 127–38.
41. M. Ward, p. 320.
42. Ibid., p. 32.
43. Matthew Arnold, *Discourses in America* (London, 1889), pp. 139–40.
44. M. Ward, p. 321.
45. Ibid., p. 271.
46. Faber, p. 343.
47. *Tracts for the Times* (London, 1834–43), nos. 80, 87.
48. Brilioth, pp. 31f.
49. Elliott-Binns, p. 373.
50. John Smith Simon, *John Wesley, the Master Builder* (London, [1927]), pp. 89ff.
51. Faber, p. 226.
52. Ibid.
53. Ibid., p. 342.
54. M. Ward, p. 146.
55. Ibid.
56. Cf. Faber, pp. 140ff.
57. M. Ward, p. 408.
58. Bouyer, p. 121.
59. See below.
60. In that same year, the Benedictines returned to Solesmes; Karl Spitta published his *Psalter und Harfe*, a collection of German chorales; Liszt was at work on his *Fragment über Kirchenmusik*, Lamennais on his *Paroles d'un croyant* in the style of Chateaubriand; shape-note hymnals were bringing regular singing even to America's backwoods; and scholars in Berlin and Regensburg were preparing new editions of Palestrina.
61. George M. Trevelyan, *British History in the Nineteenth Century and After (1782–1919)* (London, 1937), p. 238.
62. Altholz, p. 95.
63. Cf. Froude on Keble in M. Ward, p. 148.
64. John Keble, *The Christian Year: Lyra Innocentium and Other Poems* (London, 1914), pp. 555f.
65. Cf. Abrams, *The Mirror and the Lamp*, pp. 144ff.
66. John Keble, *Lectures on Poetry*, trans. E. K. Francis (Oxford, 1938), I, 42–47. The lectures were delivered in Latin with the poetic examples translated into Theocritan Greek.

67. Faber, p. 92.
68. Georgina Battiscombe, *John Keble: A Study in Limitations* (London, 1963), pp. 107, 237, 318.
69. Faber, pp. 92ff.
70. Ibid., p. 93.
71. Davies, *1690*, pp. 249f.
72. Faber, p. 85. For example, there is little propaganda for specific rituals in the *Tracts for the Times.*
73. Faber, p. 363.
74. M. Ward, pp. 78ff.
75. Faber, p. 282.
76. William James, *The Varieties of Religious Experience* (New York, 1958), p. 349.
77. Faber, p. 287.
78. Ibid., p. 293.
79. *Apologia* (Image), pp. 163–65.
80. Ibid., p. 145.
81. John Henry Newman, "John Keble" [a review of *Lyra Innocentium*] (1846), *Essays Critical and Historical*, II, 433ff. Such remarks on the dying tradition of liturgical churches are heard today from religious conservatives, to be sure. But one finds that the sophisticated nonbeliever is likely to share Newman's aesthetic, if not his theological, appreciation of a dear, retired ancestor.
82. W. James, p. 350. The Protestant "meek lover of the good," alone with his God, visits the sick, etc., for their own sakes, contrasted with the elaborate "business" that goes on in Catholic devotion. . . . An essentially worldly-minded Catholic woman can become a visitor of the sick on purely coquettish principles, with her confessor and director. . . . She is a professional "devote." [James, *Varieties*, p. 350, footnote 5].
83. *Apologia, passim.*
84. J. Lewis May, "Quis Desiderio," in *J. H. N. Centenary Essays*, pp. 94ff.
85. Strachey, pp. 16ff.
86. Cf. Faber, p. xii.
87. Davies, *1850*, p. 300.
88. Cf. F. V. Reade, "The Sentimental Myth," *J. H. N. Centenary Essays*, pp. 139–54.
89. Newman, *The Idea of a University* (London, 1925), pp. 184f.
90. Cf. M. Ward, p. 356.
91. Newman, *Fifteen Sermons Preached before the University of Oxford* (London, 1918), pp. 345–47. The italics are mine.
92. Maria Edgeworth (1767–1849), an Irish Jane Austen.
93. *Loss and Gain*, p. 23. The speaker is the character Charles Reding, who stands for the spirit which ultimately possessed Newman.

94. Newman, *An Essay in Aid of a Grammar of Assent* (London, 1924), p. 359; Cf. W. James, pp. 72–3, 327.

95. Newman, *An Essay in Aid of a Grammar of Assent*, p. 351.

96. "Christianity has thrown gleams of light on 'man' and his literature; but as it has not converted him, but only choice specimens of him, so it has not changed the characters of his mind or of his history.

    "If literature is to be made a study of human nature, you cannot have a Christian literature. . . . Give up the study of man, as such, if so it must be; but say you do so. Man is a being of genius, passion, intellect, conscience, power. He exercises these various gifts in various ways, in great deeds, in great thoughts, in heroic acts, in hateful crimes. He founds states, he fights battles, he builds cities, he ploughs the forest, he subdues the elements, he rules his kind. He creates vast ideas, and influences many generations. He takes a thousand shapes and undergoes a thousand fortunes. . . . He pours out his fervid soul in poetry; he sways to and fro, he soars, he dives, in his restless speculations; his lips drop eloquence; he touches the canvas, and it glows with beauty, he sweeps the strings and they thrill with an ecstatic meaning. He looks back into himself, and he reads his own thoughts, and notes them down; he looks out into the universe, and tells over and celebrates the elements and principles of which it is the product. Such is man: put him aside, keep him before you; but whatever you do, do not take him for what he is not." *The Idea of a University*, pp. 229–30. Man is changeable. Christianity is not, though it "develops."

97. Newman, *Apologia* (Image), p. 163; Cf. W. Ward, *Life of J.H.N.*, pp. 191–92.

98. Charles Dickens, *Hard Times* (New York, 1966), p. 17.

99. Davies, *1850*, p. 310.

100. Ibid., p. 303.

101. Newman, *Sermons Preached on Various Occasions* (London, 1927), pp. 75–90.

102. May, *J.H.N. Centenary Essays*, p. 97.

103. For Newman, as for Dante, Vergil is a half-Christian prophet between the pagan sibyl and Christ.

104. Newman, *Historical Sketches*, II, 407–8.

105. May, *J.H.N. Centenary Essays*, p. 97.

106. Newman, "The Second Spring," in *Sermons Preached on Various Occasions*, pp. 163–82.

107. Aristotle, *The Poetics* (London, 1953), especially chap. 7.

108. Geoffrey Tillotson, "Newman's Essay on Poetry," in *J.H.N. Centenary Essays*, pp. 178–200.

109. Ibid., p. 184.

110. Newman, "Poetry with Reference to Aristotle's Poetics," *Essays Critical and Historical*, I, 1–9.

111. Ibid., p. 7.
112. Newman, *Loss and Gain*, pp. 18–21.
113. Newman, "Poetry," *passim*.
114. Dickens, *Hard Times*, p. 27.
115. The force of Marx's writings comes from his portrayal of the debasing of the lower classes from poetry to machinery; likewise the mature Mill.
116. Friedrich Nietzsche, *Jenseits von Gut und Böse zur Genealogie der Moral* (Stuttgart, 1953), pp. 21–22.
117. Altholz, p. 95.
118. Church, p. 47.
119. Newman, *Apologia* (Image), p. 287.
120. *Ibid.*, p. 145, speaking of the events of 1828–30.
121. Newman, *Idea of a University*, p. 223.
122. Nietzsche, *Jenseits von Gut und Böse*, sec. 14, p. 21.
123. Evelyn Underhill, "The Spiritual Significance of the Oxford Movement," *Hibbert Journal*, XXXI (1932–33), 405.
124. Cf. *Tracts for the Times*, I.
125. Newman, *Loss and Gain*, pp. 327–29.
126. Newman, *Apologia*, p. 369.
127. Saint Cecilia may have been a legend, either in total or as a musician. The scriptural or passion plays which Philip staged in his church, the Oratory, were popularly called "oratorios."
128. Tristram, in *J.H.N. Centenary Essays*, 119.
129. Newman, *Sermons Preached on Various Occasions*, p. 242.
130. "Spernere mundum, spernere nullum, spernere seipsum, spernere sperni." Tristram, *J.H.N. Centenary Essays*, p. 120. He joined the Oratory, whose church is a flamboyant baroque edifice with a reputation for music on Brompton Road in the middle of London's temples to Victorian commerce, empire, exploration, and science.
131. Bouyer, p. 353, quoting Newman's journal for 15 December 1859.
132. John Henry Newman, *Meditations and Devotions* (London, 1912), II, no. 12, pp. 470–71.
133. Newman, *Difficulties of Anglicans*, pp. 70–115.
134. Cf. Davies, *1850*, pp. 32ff.
135. Newman, speaking through Charles Reding, in *Loss and Gain*, p. 285.
136. Newman, *Apologia* (Image ed.), pp. 286–87.
137. Bouyer, p. 364.
138. Ibid., p. 386.
139. David Gwilym James, *The Romantic Comedy* (London, 1948), p. 266.
140. Although Tractarianism often devolved into ritualism, its net result was probably fuller participation among those who came to the Anglican rites. The fact that fewer and fewer people came was prob-

ably not because of the aesthetic reforms, but because of scientism and interest in things nonreligious. Davies, *1850*, p. 209. By adding hymn singing, the Tractarians did away with the parish clerk who had been the people's proxy. The culminating project of the Oxford movement for mass expression was *Hymns Ancient and Modern*, whose texts were published in 1860 with the tunes following a few years later. The editors announced that they sought to dispose of the notion that because most people are uncritical, they do not need to be given good art. (Though the book officially established congregational singing in the Anglican Church, it had the side effect of ending the folk tradition of metrical psalms.) Careful ritual and vivid sermons did accomplish the romantic dream of retaining a bit of the sublime for at least some of the brethren. The Anglican High Mass replaced the doctrinal exposition as the culminating service in that church, which has tried to integrate the Roman evocation of the Most High with a nonauthoritarian church. Davies, *1850*, p. 130.

Some of the Tractarians were fined and imprisoned for tampering with the religion of the state (ibid., pp. 114ff). Many of the second generation Tractarian priests earned public—even liberal—sympathy because of their well-known and respected work in some of the foulest slums of London (ibid., p. 115).

On the other hand, Tractarian ritualism drove the Methodists, who had been the original lyricists in the Anglican Church, to the left in order to avoid any taint of Romanism. Methodists probably still had more singing than any other Christian body (ibid., p. 253). The African Methodists in the Southern United States seemed to have successfully combined a high-church zeal for formal meetings with charismatic individual expression. The African Methodist Episcopal church was noted for chanting its services.

CONCLUSION

1. The word *idea* originally meant "things seen." *Eideia* is the neuter plural past participle of the Greek verb "to see." Perhaps the emergence of this metaphor is properly dated with the beginnings of writing and complex urban civilizations. In any case, as McLuhan and Walter Ong, among others, are fond of pointing out, the rational tradition is fundamentally spatial and visual (Cf. Shea, "Religion and the Romantic Movement," pp. 285ff).

2. In Book I of *The Republic* Plato called music the most potent of the arts. He did not say that it is the highest art; rather, he implied that the music we hear is a *phenomenon*, which speaks to our physi-

cal nature. True music, Plato thought, is like pure mathematics, an *idea* knowable only by the soul. The music the ears perceive is a sensual and potentially dangerous activity if left unguided. Because the appeal of music is so immediate and indeterminate, it ought not to exist for its own sake but only as the servant of a conscious verbal message.

Taking a romantic viewpoint, Arthur Schopenhauer turned Plato's argument around. Schopenhauer agreed that all representation acquired greater meaning and intensity through music. However, "far from being a mere aid to poetry, music is certainly an independent art; in fact it is the most powerful of all the arts, and therefore attains its ends entirely from its own resources." (Arthur Schopenhauer, *The World as Will and Representation*, translated by E. F. J. Payne, [New York, 1966], II, chap. 39, "On the Metaphysics of Music," p. 448). "Music reveals, beyond the manifestations of the senses, the inner will that arouses them. The forms initially abstracted by perception are a little like an external rind or bark detached from things, and therefore remain abstractions and nothing but abstractions, whereas music gives off the inner germ or force from which all reality develops—in other words the heart or essence of that which makes us what we are. Concepts are *universalis post rem*, while music gives us *universalia ante rem* and in addition a reality which is *universalia in re*" (Barricelli, 113).

Cf. also Karl Gustav Fellerer, "Kreation und Rezeption der Musik," *International Review of the Aesthetics and Sociology of Music* VI (1975), 213; Sue Evelyn Coffman, "Music as Idea and Image in English Romantic Poetry" (Ann Arbor: University Microfilms, 1976).

3. The experienced world, while it is always an object of sense, cannot be confined to what can be perceived by the neural flow. A Lockean bolting together of sense data is as inadequate for an artistic as for a religious mind. Upon this common insight, the traditional religious impulse and the romantic plea for the repoeticizing of life allied.

4. The composite term Judeo-Christian is used advisedly because many of the romantics asserted that they were reemphasizing the Hebraic as against the Hellenic component of western civilization. "In the spirit of Hebrew poetry" they sometimes eschewed the Latin and Greek mottoes favored by the philosophes to head their books with Hebrew inscriptions. Both components are, broadly speaking, derived from the "romantic" side of the ancient world, the Hellenistic, with its rather unclassical diversity and intensity. The fact is that the Hebraic and Hellenistic components were probably more important in shaping the various western syntheses than the fifth-century Athenian classicism customarily emphasized by formal educa-

tion and secular humanism, which have primarily textual and visual emphases that present the ancient world as more strictly classical than it really was.

See also William Barrett, *Irrational Man* (Garden City, N.Y., 1958), and two lecture series on the Canadian Broadcasting Corporation: George Grant, "Time as History," *The Massey Lectures, 1974,* and George Steiner, "Nostalgia for the Absolute," *The Massey Lectures, 1975.*

According to Steiner, Marx and Freud took over the idea of original sin from religion. They also employed other versions of primal fall from perfection. Prometheus, who stole fire, caused alienation from the natural rhythms of light and dark, heat and cold, killing and eating. And Oedipus, whose moving on two, rather than four, feet and supposed sexual guilt implied a repression of natural tendencies. From these taboos followed kinship, law, language, definition, and the whole net of civilization with its concomitant discontents. Definition was the key to the prohibitions and repressions necessary for placid community life.

One might think that a movement which was rather sympathetic to religious tradition and practice would have been welcomed by the churches, especially the Roman Catholic. Just the contrary occurred. Although there was much romantic religious activity, the churches—especially the Roman Catholic—were far less ready to cope with romantic than with Enlightenment interpretations of religion. Theologians produced volumes of apologetics attempting to refute the philosophes. Romanticism, however, was usually ignored or dismissed. (See, for example, the series of articles on eighteenth- and nineteenth-century liturgical reform in the *Jahrbuch für Liturgiewissenschaft* published in the 1920s, which summarizes the ecclesiastical thinking on Christian ritual during the Age of Democratic Revolution.) Meanwhile, romantic ways of conceiving the humanities became normal in secular circles. Today ecclesiastical scholars are attempting to learn a more complete appreciation of human experience from secular culture, unaware that some ideas which seem new were borrowed from the poetical traditions and ritual practices of Judaism and Christianity.

5. See Appendix 1.
6. Wiora, "Die Musik im Weltbild . . ." p. 12. Harry C. Payne, in "The Reconstruction of Ritual Drama: 1860–1920," (paper delivered before the Duquesne History Forum, Pittsburgh, 23 October 1976), describes how the Cambridge School of classical archaeologists perceived that the ritual sources of drama remain part of its essence. Their theories were well-suited to an intellectual and artistic climate already concerned with apparently lost or hidden ritual patterns.

7. Barzun, *Classic, Romantic, and Modern*, p. 188.
8. Hughes, *Consciousness and Society*, p. 13.

APPENDIX 1

1. Clifford Geertz, "Religion as Cultural System," in *Anthropological Approaches to the Study of Religion*. Association of Social Anthropologists, Monograph no. 3 (London, 1968).
2. Claude Lévi-Strauss, *Structural Anthropology*, trans. Claire Jacobson and Brooks Grundfest Schoepf (New York, 1963), p. 210.
3. Ibid., p. 211.
4. Ibid., p. 230.

APPENDIX 2

1. Rogers, pp. 23–29.

SELECTED BIBLIOGRAPHY

BOOKS AND ARTICLES

Abrams, M. H. *The Mirror and the Lamp: Romantic Theory and the Critical Tradition.* New York: Norton, 1958.

——. *Natural Supernaturalism.* New York: Norton, 1971.

Adorno, Theodor W. *Introduction to the Sociology of Music.* Translated by E. B. Ashton. New York: Seabury, 1976.

Ahlstrom, Sydney E. *A Religious History of the American People.* New Haven: Yale University Press, 1962.

Ahrens, Liselotte. *Lamennais und Deutschland.* Münster (Westphalia): Helios, 1930.

Allen, Warren Dwight. *Philosophies of Music History.* New York: Dover, 1962.

Altholz, Josef L. *The Churches in the Nineteenth Century.* Indianapolis: Bobbs-Merrill, 1967.

Andrews, Edward Deming. *The Gift to be Simple: Songs, Dances and Rituals of the American Shakers.* New York: Dover, 1962.

Aulard, A. *Christianity and the French Revolution.* Translated by Lady Frazer. Boston: Brown, Co., 1927.

——. *La culte de la raison et la culte de l'Etre suprême.* Paris: F. Alcan, 1892.

Balet, L., and Gerhard, E. *Die Verbürgerlichung der deutschen Kunst, Literatur und Musik im 18. Jh.* Leipzig: J. Ginsberg, 1935.

Barnard, F. M. *Herder's Social and Political Ideas.* Oxford: Clarendon Press, 1965.

Barricelli, Jean-Pierre. "Romantic Writers and Music: The Case of Mazzini." *Studies in Romanticism*, XIV (1975), 95–117.

Barzun, Jacques. *Berlioz and the Romantic Century*, 2 vols. 2d edition. New York: Columbia, 1969.

———. *Classic, Romantic, and Modern*. Garden City, N.Y.: Anchor Books, 1958.

———. *Darwin, Marx, Wagner: Critique of a Heritage*. Garden City, N.Y.: Anchor Books, 1958.

———. *The Energies of Art*. New York: Vintage Books, 1962.

———. *Of Human Freedom*. Philadelphia: Lippincott, 1964.

———. *Science the Glorious Entertainment*. New York: Harper and Row [1964].

Beethoven, Ludwig van. *Letters, Journals, and Conversations*. Translated and edited by Michael Hamburger. New York: Anchor Books, 1960.

Benson, Louis F. *The English Hymn: Its Development and Use in Worship*. New York: Doran, 1915.

Berger, Morroe. Trans. and ed. *Madame de Staël on Politics and National Character*. Garden City, N.Y.: Doubleday, 1964.

Berlinski, Herman. "The Organ in the Synagogue," *Music*, II (July and November, 1968), 28–29, 34–37.

Berlioz, Hector. *Les années romantiques*. Edited by Tiersot. Paris: Calmann-Lévy, 1904.

———. *Evenings with the Orchestra*. Translated by Jacques Barzun. New York: Alfred A. Knopf, 1956. Reprinted Chicago: Phoenix Books, 1973.

———. *Memoirs, 1803–1865*. Translated by E. Newman Holmes. New York: Tudor, 1935.

———. *Les musiciens et la musique*. Paris: Calmann-Lévy, 1903.

———. *A travers chants: Mozart, Weber, and Wagner, and Various Essays on Musical Subjects*. Translated by Edwin Evans, Sr. London: William Reeves, [n.d.].

Bernard, Élisabeth. "Jules Pasdeloup et les Concerts Populaires." *Revue de musicologie*, LVII (1971), no. 2, 150–78.

Bettelheim, Bruno. *The Uses of Enchantment: The Meaning and Importance of Fairy Tales*. New York: Knopf, 1976.

Bienenfield, Elsa. "Verdi and Schiller." *The Musical Quarterly*, XVII (1931), 204–8.

Billeter, Bernhard. "Die Musik in Hegels Ästhetik." *Die Musikforschung*, XXVI (1973), 295–310.

Bloom, Harold. "First and Last Romantics." *Studies in Romanticism*, IX (1970), 225–32.

Blume, Friedrich, *Evangelische Kirchenmusik*. Vol. X. of *Handbuch der Musikwissenschaft*. Edited by Ernst Bücken. Potsdam: Akademische Verlagsgesellschaft Athenaion, 1931.

Bosworth, R. J. B. "Verdi and the Risorgimento." *Italian Quarterly*, XIV (1970), pp. 3–27.

Bouyer, Louis. *Newman: His Life and Spirituality*. Translated by J. Lewis May. New York: P. J. Kennedy and Sons, 1958.

Brancour, René. *Félicien David*. Paris: Renouard, 1911.

Brinton, Crane. *The Anatomy of Revolution*. New York: Vintage Books, 1952.

————. *The Political Ideas of the English Romanticists*. Ann Arbor: University of Michigan Press, 1966.

Broudy, Harry S. *Enlightened Cherishing: An Essay on Aesthetic Education*. Urbana: University of Illinois Press, 1972.

Bruford, W. H. *Culture and Society in Classical Weimar, 1775–1806*. London: Cambridge University Press, 1962.

————. *Theatre, Drama, and Audience in Goethe's Germany*. London: Routledge and Kegan Paul, 1950.

Brunot, Ferdinand. "Le culte catholique en français sous la Révolution." *Annales Historiques de la Révolution Française*, II (1925), 208–27, 325–44.

Brunschwig, Henri. *Enlightenment and Romanticism in Eighteenth-Century Prussia*. Translated by Frank Jellinek. Chicago: University of Chicago Press, 1974.

Burney, Charles. *Dr. Burney's Musical Tours in Europe*. Vol. 1: *An Eighteenth-Century Musical Tour in France and Italy*. Vol. II: *An Eighteenth-Century Musical Tour in Central Europe and the Netherlands*. London: Oxford University Press, 1959–60.

————. *A General History of Music: From the Earliest Ages to the Present Period (1789)*. 2 vols. New York: Dover, 1957.

Buschkoetter, Wilhelm. "Jean François LeSueur." *Sammelbände der Internationalen Musikgesellschaft*, XIV (1912), 58–154.

Butler, E. M. *The Saint-Simonian Religion in Germany: A Study of the Young German Movement*. New York: Fertig, 1968.

Carcopino, Claude. *Les doctrines sociales de Lamennais*. Paris: Presses Universitaires de France, 1942.

Carlson, Marvin. *The Theatre of the French Revolution*. Ithaca, N.Y.: Cornell University Press, 1966.

Carlyle, Thomas. "Edward Irving." Pp. 1–120 in *Reminiscences*, vol. II, edited by Charles Eliot Norton. London: Macmillan, 1887.

Cartwright, Michael T. "Diderot critique d'art et le probleme de l'expression." *Diderot Studies*, XIII (1969), 13–267.

Charléty, Sébastien. *Histoire du saint-simonisme (1825–1864)*. Paris: Paul Hartmann, 1931.

Chateaubriand, F. A. de. *Oeuvres complètes*. Paris: Furne, 1859.

Choral Music: A Symposium. Edited by Arthur Jacobs. Baltimore: Penguin, 1963.

Choron, Alexandre-Etienne. *Considérations sur la nécessité de rétablir le chant de l'église de Rome dans toutes les églises de l'empire français.* Paris: Courcier, 1811.

Clark, Sir Kenneth. *The Gothic Revival: An essay in the History of Taste.* New York: Holt, Rinehart and Winston, 1962.

———. *The Romantic Rebellion.* New York: Harper and Row, 1973.

Coffman, Sue Evelyn. "Music as Idea and Image in English Romantic Poetry." Ph.D. dissertation, North Texas State University, 1976. Ann Arbor, Mi.: University Microfilms, 1976.

Coleman, Francis X. J. *The Aesthetic Thought of the French Enlightenment.* Pittsburgh: University of Pittsburgh Press, 1971.

Collins, James. *The Emergence of Philosophy of Religion.* New Haven: Yale University Press, 1967.

Cooper, Martin. *Beethoven: The Last Decade.* London: Oxford University Press, 1970.

Crisis in Church Music. Washington: The Liturgical Conference, 1967.

Crosten, William Loran. *French Grand Opera: An Art and a Business.* New York: King's Crown Press, 1948.

Dahlhaus, Carl. "Romantik und Bierdermeier." *Archiv für Musikwissenschaft,* XXXI (1974), 22–42.

David, Hans T. "Cultural Functions of Music." *Journal of the History of Ideas,* XII (June 1951), 423–39.

Davies, Horton. *Worship and Theology in England.* Vol. III: *From Watts and Wesley to Maurice, 1690–1850.* Vol. IV: *From Newman to Martineau, 1850–1900.* Princeton: Princeton University Press, 1961–62.

Davison, Archibald T. *Church Music, Illusion, and Reality.* Cambridge: Harvard University Press, 1960.

Diderot, Denis. *Oeuvres complètes.* 20 vols. Paris: Garnier Frères, 1876.

Dietel, Heinrich. *Beiträge zur Frühgeschichte des Männergesangs.* Würzburg: Richard Mayr, 1938.

Dilthey, Wilhelm. *Von deutscher Dichtung und Musik.* Berlin: B. G. Teubner, 1933.

D'Ortigue, Joseph. *Le balcon de l'opéra.* Paris: E. Renduel, 1833.

———. *Dictionnaire liturgique, historique et théorique de plain-chant et de musique d'église au moyen âge et dans les temps modernes.* Paris: Ateliers Catholiques, 1853.

———. *Du théâtre italien et de son influence sur le goût musical français.* Paris: Au dépot central des meilleures productions de la presse, 1840.

———. *De la Guerre des dilettanti ou la Révolution opérée par M. Rossini dans l' opéra.* Paris: Librairie de l'Avocat, 1829.

———. *La musique à l'église.* Paris: Didier, 1861.

Douglas, Charles W. *Church Music in History and Practice.* New York: Scribner, 1962.

Dowd, David L. "Art as Propaganda in the French Revolution: A Study of Jacques-Louis David." Ph.D. dissertation, University of California, 1946.

Duckles, Vincent. "Johann Nicolaus Forkel: The Beginning of Music Historiography." *Eighteenth-Century Studies*, I (Spring 1968), 277–90.

Dufrane, Louis. *Gossec: Sa vie et ses œuvres*. Paris: Fischbacher, 1927.

Eckardt, Hans. *Die Musikanschauung der französischen Romantik*. Kassel: Bärenreiter, 1935.

Egbert, Donald D. "The Idea of 'Avant Garde' in Art and Politics." *American Historical Review*, LXXIII (December 1967), 339–66.

Ellinwood, L. W. *The History of American Church Music*. New York: Morehouse-Gorham, 1953.

Elliott-Binns, L. E. *The Early Evangelicals: A Religious and Social Study*. Greenwich, Conn.: Seabury Press, 1953.

Etherington, Charles L. *Protestant Worship Music: Its History and Practice*. New York: Holt, Rinehart and Winston, 1962.

Evans, Raymond Leslie. *Les romantiques français et la musique*. Paris: Honoré Champion, 1934.

Faber, Geoffrey. *Oxford Apostles: A Character Study of the Oxford Movement*. New York: Scribner, 1934.

Fairchild, Hoxie N. "Romanticism and the Religious Revival in England." *Journal of the History of Ideas*, II (1941), 337.

Fellerer, Karl Gustav. *Beiträge zur Choralbegleitung und Choralverarbeitung in der Orgelmusik des ausgehenden 18. und beginnenden 19. Jahrhunderts*. Strassburg: Heitz, 1932.

———. "Grundlagen und Anfänge der Kirchenmusikalisches Organisation Franz Xaver Witts." *Kirchenmusikalisches Jahrbuch*, LV (1971), 33–60.

———. *The History of Catholic Church Music*. Translated by Francis A. Brunner. Baltimore: Helicon, 1961.

———. "Kreation und Rezeption der Musik." *International Review of the Aesthetics and Sociology of Music*, VI (1975), 201–27.

———. *Der Palestrinastil und seine Bedeutung in der vokalen Kirchenmusik des achtzehnten Jahrhunderts*. Augsburg: Filser, 1929.

———. *Soziologie der Kirchenmusik*. Cologne: Westdeutscher Verlag, 1963.

———, ed. *Geschichte der katholischen Kirchenmusik*. Vol. II. Kassel: Bärenreiter, 1976.

Fellowes, Edmund. *English Cathedral Music*. London: Methuen, 1948.

Fergusson, Francis. *The Idea of a Theater*. Princeton: Princeton University Press, 1968.

Festschrift Friedrich Blume. Edited by A. A. Abert. Basel: Bärenreiter, 1963.

Festschrift Karl Gustav Fellerer. Edited by Heinrich Hüschen. Regensburg: Gustav Bosse, 1962.

Fiedler, Leslie A. *Love and Death in the American Novel.* New York: Delta, 1966.

Flaherty, M. G. "Opera and Incipient Romantic Aesthetics in Germany." Pp. 205–17 in *Studies in Eighteenth-Century Culture,* vol. III: *Racism in the Eighteenth Century.* Proceedings, American Society for Eighteenth-Century Studies. Cleveland: Case Western Reserve, 1973.

Foote, Henry Wilder. *Three Centuries of American Hymnody.* London: Oxford University Press, 1941.

Foster, Donald H. "The Oratorio in Paris in the Eighteenth-Century." *Acta Musicologica,* XLVII (1975), 67.

Fourier, François Marie Charles. *Oeuvres complètes.* 6 vols. Paris: Aux Bureaux de la Phalange, 1841–45.

Froberger, Josef. "Das Entstehen und der Aufstieg der spanischen Romantik." Pp. 276–99 in *Spanische Forschungen der Görresgesellschaft.* Reihe I. Münster (Westphalia), 1930.

Fubini, Enrico. "Per una storiografia sociologica della musica," *Nuova rivista musicale italiana,* X (1976), 41–48.

Funk, Philip. *Von der Aufklärung zur Romantik.* Munich: Pustet, 1925.

Funt, David. "Diderot and the esthetics of the Enlightenment." *Diderot Studies,* XI (1968).

Gay, Peter. *The Enlightenment: An Interpretation.* Vol. I: *The Rise of Modern Paganism.* Vol. II: *The Science of Freedom.* New York: Knopf, 1967 and 1969.

Geertz, Clifford. "Religion as Cultural System." In *Anthropological Approaches to the Study of Religion.* Association of Social Anthropologists, Monograph no. 3. London: Tavistock, 1968.

Gerold, Théodore. *Les pères de l'église et la musique.* Paris: Felix Alcan, 1931.

Giessler, Rupert. *Die geistliche Lieddichtung der Katholiken im Zeitalter der Aufklärung.* Vol. X of *Schriften zur deutschen Literatur für die Görresgesellschaft,* edited by Günther Müller. Augsburg: Benno Filser, 1928.

Gill, Frederick C. *The Romantic Movement and Methodism.* London: The Epworth Press, 1954.

Goethe, J. W. von. *Sämtliche Werke. Jubiläums-Ausgabe.* Stuttgart and Berlin, 1902–7.

Gollin, Gillian Lindt. *Moravians in Two Worlds.* New York: Columbia University Press, 1967.

Gottfried, Paul. "Catholic Romanticism in Munich, 1826–1834." Ph.D. dissertation. Yale University, 1967.

Graham, Ilse. *Schiller's Drama: Talent and Integrity.* New York: Barnes and Noble, 1971.

Greene, Donald. "The Via Media in an Age of Revolution: Anglicanism in the 18th Century." Pp. 297–320 in *The Varied Pattern: Studies in the 18th Century*, edited by Peter Hughes and David Williams. Toronto: Hakkert, 1971.

Greenberg, Clement. *Art and Culture*. Boston: Beacon Press, 1965.

Guardini, Romano. *The Spirit of the Liturgy*. New York: Sheed and Ward, 1935.

Guichard, Léon. "Liszt, Wagner et les relations entre la musique et la littérature au XIXe siècle." Pp. 323–32 in *Report of the Eighth Congress, 1961. International Musicological Society*. New York: Bärenreiter Kassel, 1961.

———. *La musique et les lettres au temps du romantisme*. Paris: Presses Universitaires de France, 1955.

Hamann, Johan Georg. *Sämtliche Werke*. 6 vols. Vienna: Herder, 1949–57.

Hampson, Norman. *A Cultural History of the Enlightenment*. New York: Pantheon, 1968.

Hanslick, Eduard. *Music Criticism, 1846–1899*. Translated and edited by Henry Pleasants. Baltimore: Penguin, 1950.

Hawkins, Sir John. *A General History of the Science and Practice of Music*. 2 vols. New York: Dover, 1963.

Heine, Heinrich. *Heines Werke*. 9 vols. Berlin: Bong [n.d.].

Herder, Johann Gottfried. *Sämtliche Werke*. 33 vols. Edited by Bernhard Suphan. Berlin: Weidmann, 1877–1913.

Herman, Martin. "The Sacred Music of J.-F. LeSueur." Dissertation. University of Michigan, 1964.

Herrmann, William Albert. *Religion in the Operas of Giuseppe Verdi*. Ann Arbor: University Microfilms, 1964.

Hobsbawm, E. J. *Primitive Rebels: Studies in Archaic Forms of Social Movement in the Nineteenth and Twentieth Centuries*. New York: W. W. Norton, 1959.

Hoffer, Eric. *The True Believer: Thoughts on the Nature of Mass Movements*. New York: Harper and Row, 1951.

Hoffmann, Ernst Theodor. *Musikalische Schriften*. Leipzig: Endes Verlag [n.d.].

———. *Selected Letters of E.T.A. Hoffmann*. Translated by Johanna Sahlin. Chicago: University of Chicago Press, 1977.

Holtman, Robert B. *Napoleonic Propaganda*. Baton Rouge: Louisiana State University Press, 1950.

Hughes, H. Stuart. *Consciousness and Society*. New York: Vintage Books, 1958.

Huizinga, Johan. *Homo Ludens*. Boston: Beacon, 1966.

Huot-Pleuroux, Paul. *Histoire de la musique religieuse*. Paris: Presses Universitaires de France, 1957.

Hutchings, Arthur. *Church Music in the Nineteenth Century*. New York: Oxford University Press, 1967.

Idelsohn, Abraham. *Jewish Liturgy in Its Historical Development*. New York: Holt, 1932.

———. *Jewish Music in Its Historical Development*. New York: Holt, 1948.

Im Geiste Herders. Edited by Erich Keyser. Kitzingen am Main, 1953.

James, David Gwilym. *The Romantic Comedy*. London: Oxford University Press, 1959.

James, William. *The Varieties of Religious Experience*. New York: Mentor, 1958.

John Henry Newman: Centenary Essays. Edited by Henry Tristram, London: Burnes, Oates and Washbourne, 1945.

Jordahn, Ottfried. "Georg Friedrich Seiler—Der Liturgiker der deutschen Aufklärung." *Jahrbuch für Liturgik und Hymnologie*, XIV (1969), 1–62.

Josephs, Herbert. *Diderot's Dialogue of Language and Gesture: Le neveu de Rameau*. Columbus: Ohio State University Press, 1969.

Julian, John. *A Dictionary of Hymnology*. 2 vols. New York: Dover, 1957.

Kaiser, Gerhard. *Klopstock, Religion und Dichtung*. Gütersloh: Gerd Mohn, 1963.

Katz, Bernard. *The Social Implications of Early Black Music in the United States*. New York: Arno Press, 1969.

Keble, John. *Lectures on Poetry*. 2 vols. Translated by Edward Kershaw Francis. Oxford: Clarendon Press, 1912.

Kerman, Joseph. *Opera as Drama*. New York: Vintage Books, 1956.

Keys, A. C. "Schiller and Italian Opera." *Music and Letters*, XLI (1960), 223–37.

Kier, Herfrid. *Raphael Georg Kiesewetter (1773–1850): Wegbereiter des musikalischen Historismus*. Studien zur Musikgeschichte des 19. Jahrhunderts, XIII. Regensburg: Bosse, 1968.

Kivy, Peter. "The Child Mozart as an Aesthetic Symbol." *Journal of the History of Ideas*, XXVIII (June 1967), 249–58.

Kmen, Henry A. *Music in New Orleans: The Formative Years*. Baton Rouge: Louisiana State University Press, 1966.

Knepler, Georg. *Musikgeschichte des 19. Jahrhunderts*. 2 vols. Berlin: Henschelverlag, 1961.

Knief, Tibor. "Die Erforschung mittelalterlicher Musik in der Romantik und ihr geistesgeschichtlicher Hintergrund." *Acta Musicologica*, XXXVI (August-September, 1964), 123–36.

Knox, Ronald. *Enthusiasm*. New York: Galaxy Books, 1961.

Koenker, Ernst B. *The Liturgical Renaissance in the Roman Catholic Church*. Chicago: University of Chicago Press, 1954.

Kouwenhoven, John. *Made in America: The Arts in Modern Civilization.* Garden City, N.Y.: Doubleday, 1948.

Kristeller, Paul O. "Modern Systems of the Arts: A Study in the History of Aesthetics." *Journal of the History of Ideas,* XIII (1952), 17–46.

Lamennais, Félicité de. *Oeuvres complètes.* 12 vols. Paris: Cailleux, 1836–37.

Landormy, Paul. *La musique française de la Marseillaise à la mort de Berlioz.* Paris: Gallimard, 1944.

Lang, Paul Henry. "Aggiornamento in Sacred Music." *Sacred Music* XCII, 11–14.

———. "Diderot as Musician." *Diderot Studies,* XI (1968), 95–107.

———. "The Enlightenment and Music." *Eighteenth-Century Studies,* September 1967, pp. 93–108.

———. *Music in Western Civilization.* New York: Norton, 1941.

———. "The Patrimonium Musicae Sacrae and the task of Sacred Music Today." *Sacred Music,* XCII (Winter 1966–67).

LeForestier, René. *La Franc-maçonnerie Templière et Occultiste aux XVIIIe et XIXe siècles.* Paris: Aubier-Montaigne, 1970.

Leichtentritt, Hugo. *Music, History, and Ideas.* Cambridge: Harvard University Press, 1961.

Leith, James A. *The Idea of Art as Propaganda in France, 1750–1799.* Toronto: University of Toronto Press, 1965.

———. "Music as an Ideological Weapon in the French Revolution," *The Canadian Historical Association, Annual Report, 1966.* Ottawa, 1967, pp. 126–140.

Lenotre, Gosselin. *Le mysticisme révolutionnaire, Robespierre et la "Mère de Dieu."* Paris: Perrin, 1926.

Leupold, Ulrich. *Die liturgischen Gesänge der evangelischen Kirche im Zeitalter der Aufklärung und der Romantik.* Würzburg: Triltsch, 1933.

Lévi-Strauss, Claude. *Structural Anthropology.* Translated by Claire Jacobson and Brooke Grundfest Schoepf. New York: Basic Books, 1963.

Lewis, Gwynne. *Life in Revolutionary France.* New York: Batsford, 1972.

Lichtheim, George. *The Origins of Socialism.* New York: Praeger, 1970.

———. *A Short History of Socialism.* New York: Praeger, 1970.

Liebner, János. "Der Einfluss Schillers auf Verdi." *Kongress-Bericht* of the *Internationale Gesellschaft für Musikwissenschaft,* 1972, pp. 222–25.

Liemohn, Edwin. *The Chorale, Through Four-hundred Years of Musical Development as a Congregational Hymn.* Papers of the Hymn Society, XXV. Philadelphia: Muhlenberg Press, 1953.

Liszt, Franz. *Gesammelte Schriften.* 2 vols. Translated by L. Kamman. Leipzig: Breitkopf und Härtel, 1881.

————. *Letters.* 2 vols. Edited by La Mara. Translated by Constance Bache. London: H. Grevel, 1894.

Liszt, Franz, and Wagner, Richard. *Correspondence.* Translated by Frances Hueffer. 2 Vols. New York: Scribner and Wolford, 1889.

Locke, Arthur. *Music and the Romantic Movement in France.* London: K. Paul, Trench, Truber, 1920.

Loesser, Arthur. *Men, Women, and Pianos.* New York: Simon and Schuster, 1954.

Longyear, Rey Morgan. *Nineteenth-Century Romanticism in Music.* Englewood Cliffs, N.J.: Prentice-Hall, 1969.

————. *Schiller and Music.* Chapel Hill: University of North Carolina Press, 1966.

Lovejoy, Arthur O. "The Meaning of Romanticism for the Historian of Ideas." *Journal of the History of Ideas,* II (1941), 251–78.

Maecklenburg, Albert. "Verdi and Manzoni." *The Musical Quarterly,* XVII (1931), 209–17.

Manuel, Frank E. *The Prophets of Paris.* Cambridge: Harvard University Press, 1962.

Marks, Paul F. "The Application of Aesthetics of Music in the Philosophy of the *Sturm und Drang*: Gerstenberg, Hamann, and Herder." Pp. 219–38 in *Studies in Eighteenth-Century Culture,* vol. III: *Racism in the Eighteenth Century.* Proceedings, The American Society for Eighteenth-Century Studies. Cleveland; Case Western Reserve, 1973.

Martin, George. *Verdi: His Music, Life, and Times.* New York: Dodd, Mead, 1963.

Maxwell, William D. *A History of Worship in the Church of Scotland.* London: Oxford University Press, 1955.

Mayer, Anton L. "Liturgie, Aufklärung und Klassizismus." *Jahrbuch für Liturgiewissenschaft,* IX (1929), 67–128.

————. "Liturgie, Romantik und Restauration." *Jahrbuch für Liturgiewissenschaft,* X (1930), 77–141.

Mazzini, Giuseppe. *Philosophy of Music.* Vol. IV of *The Life and Writings of Joseph Mazzini.* Translated by Arthur Livingstone. London: Smith, Elder, 1891.

Mellers, Wilfred. *Music and Society.* New York: Roy, 1950.

Mintz, Donald. "Mendelssohn and Romanticism." *Studies in Romanticism,* III (Summer 1964), 216–224.

Mongredien, Jean. "La musique du sacre de Napoléon ler," *Revue de Musicologie,* no. 2 (1967), 137–74.

Monterosso, Raffaello. *La Musica nel Risorgimento.* Milan: Vallardi, 1948.

Morelli, Giovanni. "Eloges rendus à un singulier mélange de philosophie, d'orgueil, de chimie, d'opéra." *Rivista Italiana di Musicologica,* IX (1974), 175–228.

Moser, Hans Joachim. *Die evangelische Kirchenmusik in Deutschland.* Berlin: Merseburger, 1954.

Napoléon-Bonaparte. Two long-playing records. Booklet. Paris: Guilde internationale du disque, [n.d.].

Nettel, Reginald. *Music in Five Towns 1840–1914.* London: Oxford University Press, 1944.

———. *A Social History of Traditional Song.* London: Adams and Dart, 1969.

Nettl, Paul. *Forgotten Musicians.* New York: Philosophical Library, 1951.

———. *National Anthems.* Translated by Alexander Gode. 2d enl. ed. New York: Ungar, [1967].

Newman, John Henry, Cardinal. *Apologia Pro Vita Sua.* Garden City, N.Y.: Image, 1956.

———. *An Essay in Aid of a Grammar of Assent.* London: Longmans, Green, 1924.

———. *Loss and Gain: The Story of a Convert.* London: Longmans, Green, 1919.

Nietzsche, Friedrich. *The Birth of Tragedy* and *The Case of Wagner.* Translated by Walter Kaufmann. New York: Vintage Books, 1967.

Noske, Frits. "Ritual Scenes in Verdi's Operas." *Music and Letters,* LIV (1973), 415–39.

Nowak, Adolf. "Hegels Musikästhetik." *Die Musikforschung,* XXIII (1970), 463–64.

Oliver, A. Richard. *The Encyclopedists as Critics of Music.* New York: Columbia, 1947.

Only Then Regale My Eyes. (Color television tape, one hour.) The Detroit Institute of Arts; Wayne State University; Réunion des Musées Nationaux, Paris; and the Corporation for Public Broadcasting. Detroit, 1975.

Ossian. (Catalogue of the exhibition at the Grand Palais.) Paris: Editions des musées nationaux, 1974.

Palmer, Robert R. *The Age of the Democratic Revolution.* 2 vols. Princeton, N.J.: Princeton University Press, 1964.

———. *Catholics and Unbelievers in the Eighteenth Century.* Princeton, N.J.: Princeton University Press, 1939.

Parker, Harold T. *The Cult of Antiquity and the French Revolutionaries.* New York: Octagon Books, 1965.

Pasinetti, P. M. "Notes on the Poetic Image of the *Patria.*" *Italian Quarterly,* XVII–XVIII (1961), 58–72.

Patrick, Millar. *Four Centuries of Scottish Psalmody.* New York: Oxford University Press, 1949.

Paul, Charles B. "Music and Ideology: Rameau, Rousseau, and 1789." *Journal of the History of Ideas,* XXXII (1971), 395–410.

Payne, Harry C. "The Reconstruction of Ritual Drama: 1860–1920." Paper delivered before the Duquesne History Forum, Pittsburgh, 23 October, 1976.

Peckham, Morse. "On Romanticism: Introduction." *Studies in Romanticism,* IX (1970), 217–24.

————. *Romanticism: The Culture of the Nineteenth Century.* New York: Braziller, 1965.

————. *The Triumph of Romanticism.* Columbia: University of South Carolina Press, 1970.

Peers, E. A. *A History of the Romantic Movement in Spain.* 2 vols. London: Cambridge University Press, 1940.

Pierre, Constant. *Les hymnes et chansons de la Révolution.* Paris: Imprimerie Nationale, 1904.

————. *Musique des fêtes et cérémonies de la Révolution française.* Paris: Imprimerie Nationale, 1899.

Piersig, Johannes, ed. *Beiträge zu einer Rechtssoziologie der Kirchenmusik.* Studien zur Musikgeschichte des 19. Jahrhunderts, XXXIV. Regensburg: Bosse, 1972.

Piozzi, Hester Lynch. *Observations and Reflections Made in the Course of a Journey through France, Italy, and Germany.* Ann Arbor: University of Michigan Press, 1967.

Pitocco, Francesco. "Ricerche sul sansimonismo in Italia. Lambruschini: la sua formazione culturale e il sansimonismo nella sua idea di riforma religiosa." *Studi e materiali di storia delle religioni,* XXXIX (1968), 321–66; XL (1969), 283–329.

Plumb, J. H. "The Commercialization of Leisure in Eighteenth-Century England." Address to the Anglo-American Conference of Historians, Fifth semi-annual meeting, London, 5 July 1972.

Poisson, Jacques. *Le romantisme social de Lamennais, 1833–1854.* Paris: J. Vrin, 1931.

Pons, André. *Droit ecclésiastique et la musique sacrée.* Vol. IV: La restauration de la musique sacrée. St. Maurice, Switzerland: Editions Saint-Augustin, 1961.

Preussner, Eberhard. *Die bürgerliche Musikkultur: Ein Beitrag zur deutschen Musikgeschichte des 18. Jh.* Hamburg: Hanseatischer Verlag, 1935.

Prod'homme, J. G. "La musique et les musiciens en 1848." *Sammelbände der internationalen Musikgesellschaft,* XIV (1913), 155–82.

Pugin, Augustus Welby. *Contrasts, or a Parallel between the Noble Edifices of the Middle Ages and the Corresponding Buildings of the Present Day: Showing the Present Decay of Taste.* London: C. Dolman, 1845.

Rainbow, Bernarr. *The Choral Revival in the Anglican Church (1839–1872).* London: Barrie and Jenkins, 1970.

————. *The Land without Music: Musical Education in England 1800–1860 and its Continental Antecedents.* London: Novello, 1967.

Randall, John Herman, Jr. *The Career of Philosophy.* Vol. II: *From the German Enlightenment to the Age of Darwin.* New York: Columbia University Press, 1965.

Rayburn, John. *Gregorian Chant, A History of the Controversy Concerning Its Rhythm.* New York: (privately published), 1964.

Die Religion in Geschichte und Gegenwart. 6 vols. Tübingen: Mohr, 1957–62.

La Révolution Française. (Six long-playing records, booklet.) Paris: Guilde internationale du disque, [n.d.].

Reynolds, William J. *A Survey of Christian Hymnody.* New York: Holt, Rinehart and Winston, 1963.

Ringer, Alexander L. "J.-J. Barthélemy and Musical Utopia in Revolutionary France." *Journal of the History of Ideas*, XXII (July–September, 1961), 355–68.

Robert, Daniel. *Les églises réformées en France (1800–1830).* Paris: Presses Universitaires de France, 1961.

Robiquet, Jean. *Daily Life in the French Revolution.* Translated by James Kirkup. London: Weidenfeld and Nicolson, 1964.

Roe, W. G. *The Reception of Lamennais' Religious Ideas in England in the Nineteenth Century.* London: Oxford University Press, 1966.

Rogers, Cornwell Burnham. *The Spirit of Revolution in 1789: A Study of Public Opinion as Revealed in Political Songs and Other Popular Literature at the Beginning of the French Revolution.* Princeton: Princeton University Press, 1949.

The Role of Religion in Modern European History. Edited by Sidney A. Burrell. New York: Macmillan, 1964.

Rolland, Romain. "Goethe's Interest in Music." *Musical Quarterly*, XVII (1931), 157–94.

———. *The People's Theater.* Translated by Barrett H. Clark. New York: Holt, 1918.

Roma giacobina. Edited by Maria Elisa Monti Tittoni and Lucia Palladini Cavazzi. (Catalogue of the exhibition at the Palazzo Braschi). Rome, 1973.

Romantic Mythologies. Edited by Ian Fletcher. New York: Barnes and Noble, 1967.

Rosenblum, Robert. *Transformations in Late Eighteenth Century Art.* Princeton, N.J.: Princeton University Press, 1974.

Rousseau, Jean-Jacques. *Ecrits sur la Musique.* Paris: Lefevre, 1939.

———. *Politics and the Arts: Letter to M. d'Alembert on the Theater.* Translated and edited by Allan Bloom. Glencoe, Ill.: Free Press, 1960.

Rousseau, Olivier. *The Progress of the Liturgy.* Translated by the Benedictines of Westminster Priory. Westminster, Md.: Newman Press, 1951.

Routley, Erik. *Hymns and Human Life.* London: John Murray, 1952.

———. *Hymns Today and Tomorrow.* Nashville: Abingdon Press, 1964.

———. *The Music of Christian Hymnody.* London: Independent Press, 1957.

Rubsamen, Walter H. "Music and Politics in the 'Risorgimento.' " *Italian Quarterly*, V (1961), 100–120.

Rudé, George. *The Crowd in History, 1730–1848*. New York: Wiley, 1964.

Saint-Simon, Claude-Henri, Comte de. *Oeuvres*. Paris: Editions Anthropos, 1966.

Salmen, Walter. "Herder und Reichardt." Pp. 284–95 in *Herder-Studien*, edited by Walter Wiora. Würzburg: Holzner, 1960.

———. *Johann Friedrich Reichardt: Komponist, Schriftsteller, Kapellmeister und Verwaltungsbeamter der Goethezeit*. Freiburg im Breisgau: Atlantis, 1963.

———, ed. *Beiträge zur Geschichte der Musikanschauung im 19. Jahrhundert*. Studien zur Musikgeschichte des 19. Jahrhunderts, I. Regensburg: Bosse, 1965.

Saloman, Ora Frishberg. "La Cépède's *La Poétique de la musique* and LeSueur." *Acta Musicologica*, XLVII (1975), 144.

———. "The Orchestra in LeSueur's Musical Aesthetics." *Musical Quarterly*, LX (1974), 616–24.

Sambeth, Heinrich Maria. *Die gregorianische Melodien in den Werken Franz Liszts mit besonderer Berücksichtigung seiner Kirchenmusik-Reform-Pläne*. Deutsche Gesellschaft für Musikwissenschaft. 1. Kongress, Leipzig, 1925. Bericht. Leipzig: Breitkopf und Härtel, 1926.

Sarrailh, Jean. *La crise religieuse en Espagne à la fin du XVIIIe siècle*. Oxford: At the Clarendon Press, 1951.

Schiel, Hubert. *Johann Michael Sailer: Leben und Briefe*. 2 vols. Regensburg: Pustet, 1948 and 1952.

Schiller, Friedrich. *On the Aesthetic Education of Man in a Series of Letters*. Translated by Reginald Snell. New York: Frederick Ungar, 1965.

Schleiermacher, Friedrich. *On Religion: Speeches to Its Cultured Despisers*. Translated by E. Graham Waring. New York: Ungar, 1955.

Schmidt, Eberhard. "Zur gottesdienstlichen Musik in einer mitteldeutschen Kleinstadt im 18. und 19. Jahrhundert," *Jahrbuch für Liturgik und Hymnologik*, VI (1961), 144–62.

Schmidt, Friedrich. *Das Musikleben der bürgerlichen Gesellschaft Leipzigs im Vormärz*. Leipzig: Beyer, 1912.

Schmitz, Arnold. "Zum verständnis des Gloria in Beethoven's Missa Solemnis." Pp. 320ff. in *Festschrift Friedrich Blume*, edited by A. Abert. Basel, 1963.

Scholes, Percy A. *The Mirror of Music, 1844–1944*. 2 vols. London: Novello, 1947.

Schopenhauer, Arthur. *Schriften über Musik, im Rahmen seiner Aesthetik*. Edited by Karl Slabenow. Regensburg: G. Bosse, [1922].

———. *The World as Idea and Representation*. 2 vols. Translated by E. F. J. Payne. New York: Dover, 1966.

Schrade, Leo. "Herder's Conception of Church Music." In *The Musical Heritage of the Church*, edited by T. Hoelty-Nickel. Valparaiso, Ind., 1946.

————. *Tragedy in the Art of Music.* Cambridge: Harvard University Press, 1964.

Schrems, Theobald. *Die Geschichte des gregorianischen Gesanges in den protestantischen Gottesdiensten.* Freiburg: St. Paulusdruckerei, 1930.

Schumann, Robert. *On Music and Musicians.* Edited by Konrad Wolff. Translated by Paul Rosenfeld. New York: McGraw-Hill, 1964.

Selby, Robin C. *The Principle of Reserve in the Writings of John Henry Cardinal Newman.* London: Oxford University Press, 1975.

Sevrin, Ernest. *Dom Guéranger et Lamennais.* Paris: Librairie Philosophique, 1933.

Shea, F. X., S.J. "Religion and the Romantic Movement." *Studies in Romanticism*, IX (1970), 285–96.

Siegmeister, Elie. *Music and Society.* New York: Critics Group Press, [1930s].

Simon, John Smith. *John Wesley, the Master Builder.* London: Epworth, 1927.

Sitwell, Sacheverell. *Liszt.* Boston and New York: Houghton Mifflin, 1934.

Soboul, Albert, "Sentiment religieux et cultes populaires pendant la Révolution: Saintes patriotes et martyrs de la liberté." *Annales historiques de la Révolution française*, XXIX (July–September 1957), 193–213.

Speroni, Charles. "Popular Songs and Hymns of the 'Risorgimento.'" *Italian Quarterly*, V (1961), 73–120.

Staël-Holstein, Anne Louise Germaine (Necker), baronne de. *De la littérature considérée dans ses rapports avec les institutions sociales.* 1800. Geneva: Droz, 1959.

————. *De l'Allemagne.* 1810. Paris: Hachette, 1958.

————. *De l'influence des passions sur le bonheur des individus et des nations.* Paris: Maradan, 1818.

————. *Madame de Staël on Politics, Literature, and National Character.* Translated and edited by Monroe Berger. Garden City, N.Y.: Doubleday, 1968.

Starobinski, Jean. *The Invention of Liberty.* Geneva: Skira, 1964.

————. *1789: Les emblèmes de la raison.* Paris: Flammarion, 1973.

Steiner, George. *Nostalgia for the Absolute.* The CBC Massey Lectures for 1975. [Montreal, 1975].

Stemfeld, Frederick W. *Goethe and Music: A List of Parodies and Goethe's Relationship to Music.* New York: New York Public Library, 1954.

Stendhal [Marie-Henri Beyle]. *Vie de Rossini.* 2 vols. Paris: Champion, 1922.

Stevenson, Robert Murrell. *Patterns of Protestant Church Music*. Durham: Duke University Press, 1953.

Stoeffler, F. Ernest. *German Pietism during the Eighteenth Century*. Studies in the History of Religions, XXIV. Leiden: Brill, 1973.

————. *The Rise of Evangelical Pietism*. Studies in the History of Religions, IX. Leiden: Brill, 1965.

Sullivan, J. W. N. *Beethoven, His Spiritual Development*. New York: Vintage Books, [*ca*. 1960].

Thiel, Burchard, O. F. M. *Die Liturgik der Aufklärungszeit. Ihre Grundlagen und die Ziele ihrer Vertreter*. Breslau: Nischkowsky, 1926.

Thrupp, Sylvia L. (ed.). *Millennial Dreams in Action: Studies in Revolutionary Religious Movements*. New York: Schocken, 1970.

Tiersot, Julien. *Les fêtes et les chants de la Révolution Française*. Paris: Hachette, 1908.

Trahard, Pierre. *La sensibilité révolutionnaire (1789–1794)*. Paris: Bolvin, 1936.

Trilling, Lionel. *Matthew Arnold*. New York: Meridian Books, 1955.

Truscott, Harold. "Form in Romantic Music." *Studies in Romanticism*, I (1961), 29–39.

Turner, Frederick Jackson. *Mozart, The Man and His Works*. New York: Barnes and Noble, 1966.

Tuveson, Ernest Lee. *Redeemer Nation: The Idea of America's Millennial Role*. Chicago: University of Chicago Press, 1974.

Ursprung, Otto. *Restauration und Palestrina-Renaissance in der katholischen Kirchenmusik*. Augsburg: Benno-Filser, 1924.

Vidler, Alec R. *Prophecy and Papacy: A Study of Lamennais, the Church, and the Revolution*. New York: Scribners, 1954.

Vierbach, Albert. *Die liturgischen Anschauungen des V. A. Winter*. Munich: Koesel und Pustet, 1929.

Viva V.E.R.D.I.: La musica del Risorgimento in chiave satirica. A Musical and Theatrical Performance. Directed by Michael Aspinall. Rome, 1974.

Vogt, Von Ogden. *Art and Religion*. Boston: Beacon, 1960.

Voltaire [François Marie Arouet]. *Oeuvres complètes*. 52 vols. Edited by Moland. Paris: Barmier, 1877.

Wackenroder, Wilhelm Heinrich. *Werke und Briefe*. 2 vols. Jena: Eugen Diederichs, 1910.

Wagner, Richard. *Gesammelte Schriften und Dichtungen*. 10 vols. Leipzig: Fritzsch, 1897–98.

Ward, Maisie. *Young Mr. Newman*. New York: Sheed and Ward, 1948.

Wearmouth, Robert F. *Methodism and the Working-Class Movements of England, 1800–1850*. London: Epworth, 1947.

Weber, Max. *Prose Works*. Translated by William Ashton Ellis. London: Kegan Paul, Trench, Truebner, 1897.

————. *The Rational and Social Foundations of Music.* Translated and edited by Don Martindale, Johannes Riedel, and Gertrude Neuwirth. Carbondale: Southern Illinois University Press, 1958.

Wellek, René. "Romanticism Reconsidered." Pp. 107–33 in *Romanticism Reconsidered*, edited by Northrop Frye. New York: Columbia University Press, 1972.

Wessell, Leonard P., Jr. "Schiller and the Genesis of German Romanticism." *Studies in Romanticism*, X (1971), 176–98.

Wilson, Arthur M. *Diderot.* New York: Oxford University Press, 1972.

Wilson, John B. "An Analogue of Transcendentalism." *Journal of the History of Ideas*, XXVII (September 1966), 461.

Wiora, Walter, ed. *Die Ausbreitung des Historismus über die Musik.* Studien zur Musikgeschichte des 19. Jahrhunderts, XIV. Regensburg: Bosse, 1969.

————. "Die Musik im Weltbild der deutschen Romantik." In *Beiträge zur Geschichte der Musikanschauung im 19. Jahrhundert.* Edited by Walter Salmen. Studien zur Musikgeschichte des 19. Jahrhunderts, I. Regensburg: Bosse, 1965.

————, ed. *Herder-Studien.* Würzburg: Holzner, 1960.

Wright, Margaret Johnson. "Music of the Sacred Harp." *American Guild of Organists Quarterly*, XI (1966), 47–51.

PERIODICALS

Acta Musicologica.
American Musicological Society Journal.
Die allgemeine musikalische Zeitung. Leipzig, 1798–1848; 1863–65; 1866–82.
The American Historical Review.
Annales historiques de la Révolution Française.
Archiv für Musikforschung.
Archiv für Musikwissenschaft.
Archiv für Religionswissenschaft. 1898–1942.
Cäcilia [Mainz]. 1824–45.
Cäcilian Kalender. 1876–85.
Church History.
Current Musicology.
Diderot Studies.
Eighteenth-Century Studies.
The Historical Magazine of the Protestant Episcopal Church.
The Hymn.
International Review of the Aesthetics and Sociology of Music.

Italian Quarterly.
Jahrbuch der Musikbibliothek Peters.
Jahrbuch für Liturgiewissenschaft. 1921–31.
Jahrbuch für Liturgik und Hymnologie.
Journal des débats politiques et littéraires. 1852.
The Journal of Ecclesiastical History.
The Journal of Modern History.
The Journal of the History of Ideas.
Kirchenmusikalisches Jahrbuch.
Liturgisches Journal [Halle]. 1802–7.
Maîtrise. 1857–61. [I have been unable to locate the volumes listed through 1866.]
Monatshefte für Musikgeschichte. 1869–1905.
Music.
Music and Letters.
The Musical Quarterly.
Die Musikforschung.
Neues Beethoven-Jahrbuch.
Neue Zeitschrift für Musik.
Nuova rivista musicale italiana.
Revue de musicologie.
Revue de musique ancienne et modern. 1856.
Revue de la musique religieuse, populaire et classique.
Revue musicale.
Rivista italiana di musicologica.
Rivista musicale italiana.
Rivista di storia e letteratura religiosa.
Sacred Music.
Sammelbände der internationalen Musikgesellschaft.
Seilers liturgisches Magazin. (Erlangen.) 1784–86.
Studien zur Musikwissenschaft.
Studies in Eighteenth-Century Culture
Studies in Romanticism.
Vierteljahrschrift für Musikwissenschaft. 1884–94.
Worship (Formerly *Orate Fratres*).
Zeitschrift für Religions- und Geistesgeschichte.

INDEX